SIGN GALLERY

FROM THE EDITORS OF **SIGNS OF THE TIMES** MAGAZINE

ST PUBLICATIONS
CINCINNATI, OHIO

ISBN: 0-944094-23-6

Published by:
ST Publications, Inc.
Book Division
407 Gilbert Avenue
Cincinnati, Ohio 45202
Tel. 513-421-205
Fax 513-421-6110

Distributed to the book and art trade in the U.S. and Canada by:
Watson-Guptill Publications
1515 Broadway
New York, NY 10036
Tel. 908-363-4511
Fax 908-363-0338

Distributed to the rest of the world by:
Hearst Books International
1350 Avenue of the Americas
New York, NY 10003
Tel. 212-261-6770
Fax 212-261-6795

Book design by Carole Winters
Art production by Jazmine Atienza

Printed in Hong Kong

10 9 8 7 6 5 4 3 2 1

INTRODUCTION

Designs are changing faster every year in the sign industry and other graphic arts fields. The rapid pace of change is fueled by technological advancement in both the computer programs designers use as well as the materials for the signs themselves. Many things are possible that weren't even five years ago.

Designers must keep current with the technology and the trends, and this book offers the leading edge of both. Many of the signs included maximize the technological advantages of computer-aided design and the versatility of vinyl.

However, the demand for custom, one-of-a-kind signs, continues to be strong as well. Many of the signs included in this collection are of this highly artful and decorative category. Several display the century-old techniques of carving, painting, sandblasting and finishing with goldleaf. These often have the best designs, a reflection of the time and talent spent on each project.

We hope you find some designs that give you good ideas.

The Editors
SIGNS OF THE TIMES

CONTENTS

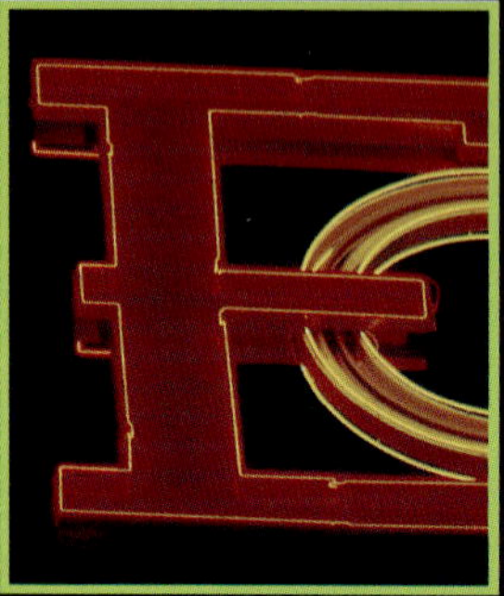
E

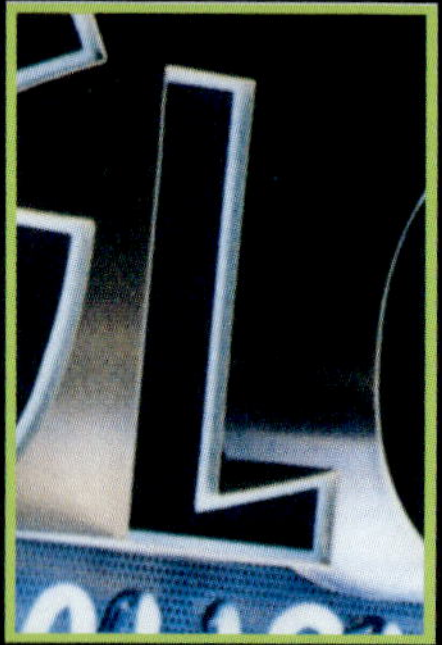
L

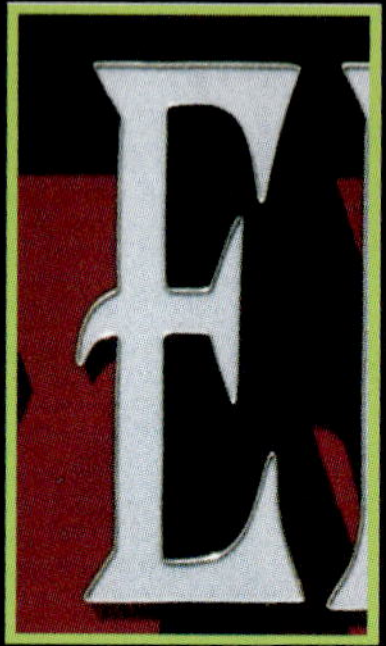
E

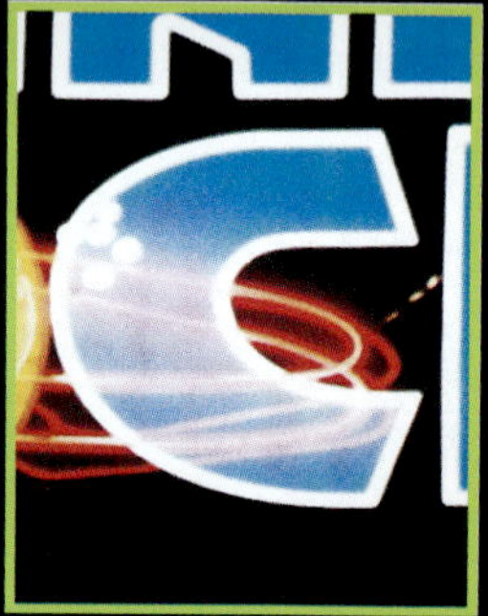
C

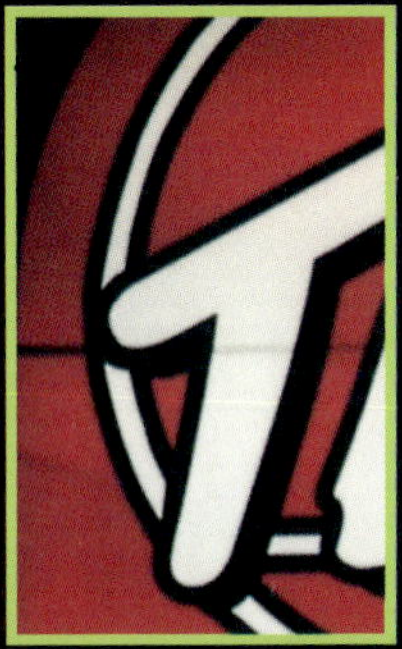

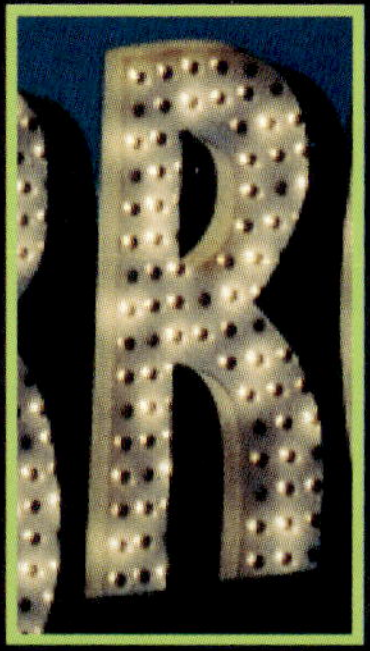

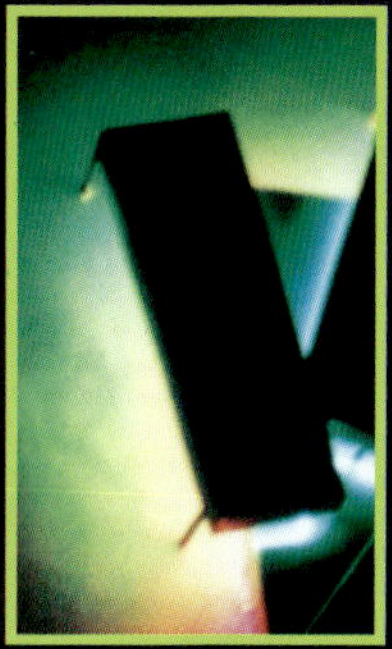

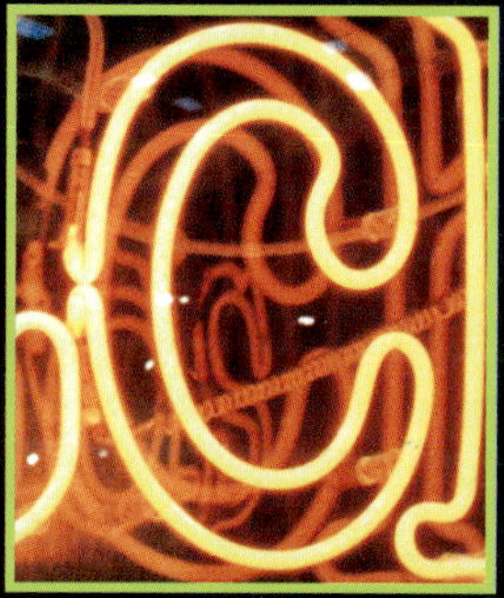

Technological innovations have affected the design and installation of electric signs in the past few years. Most notably, large-format digital imaging has made near-photographic realism economically possible. Any digital image, including existing company logos, can now be output onto vinyl for internally lit signs by electrostatic printers, inkjet printers and by thermal transfer. The question of the moment, especially for outdoor installation, is, “What is the durability?” Given the quality of the media/ink combination and the lamination, the answer ranges anywhere from six months to five years. Another technological advancement involving vinyl is the development of eradicable vinyl, a flexible-face material suitable for backlit awnings. The process, known as eradication, is now widely used. And in the area of neon signage and graphics, an expansion in the use of neon as accent or architectural lighting has meant more business for neon designers and fabricators everywhere. Retailers, architects and designers are taking greater advantage of the penetrating light of neon.

DESIGNERS

Hatch Design Group
3198 "D" Airport Loop Dr.
Costa Mesa, CA 92626
(209) 931-0860

Charles F. Barnard
Ad-Art Electric Sign Corp.
3133 N. Ad-Art Rd.
Stockton, CA 95215
(209) 931-0860

FABRICATOR

Ad-Art Electric Sign Corp.

This 45 x 26-ft. freestanding, dimensional juke-box sign is fabricated around the entrance to a restaurant on the famed Universal City Walk (adjacent to Universal Studios). The sign primarily features metal construction with the facing border formed from Lexan®/polycarbonate rolls. It is back-illuminated with banks of electronically actuated, multi-colored lamps to produce ever-changing rainbow lighting variations.

The center — between Lexan rolls — is surfaced with polished aluminum channel and faced with ripple-patterned amber plastic, internally illuminated with strips of "bud" lighting programmed to provide a "rising bubbles" effect. The recessed top panel has a simulated stack of records and player behind a clear Lexan window. Just below the window is the selection panel, which is routed and polished clear aluminum backed with multi-colored, backlit plastic segments.

Projecting over the entrance is a canopy that has rolled vertical edges with plastic-faced, internally illuminated channel letters and the logo ("star") and "Restaurant." The ceiling is illuminated with a grid of 11w scintillating clear lamps. All the metal surfaces are painted with accents of polished stainless steel and polished clear aluminum.

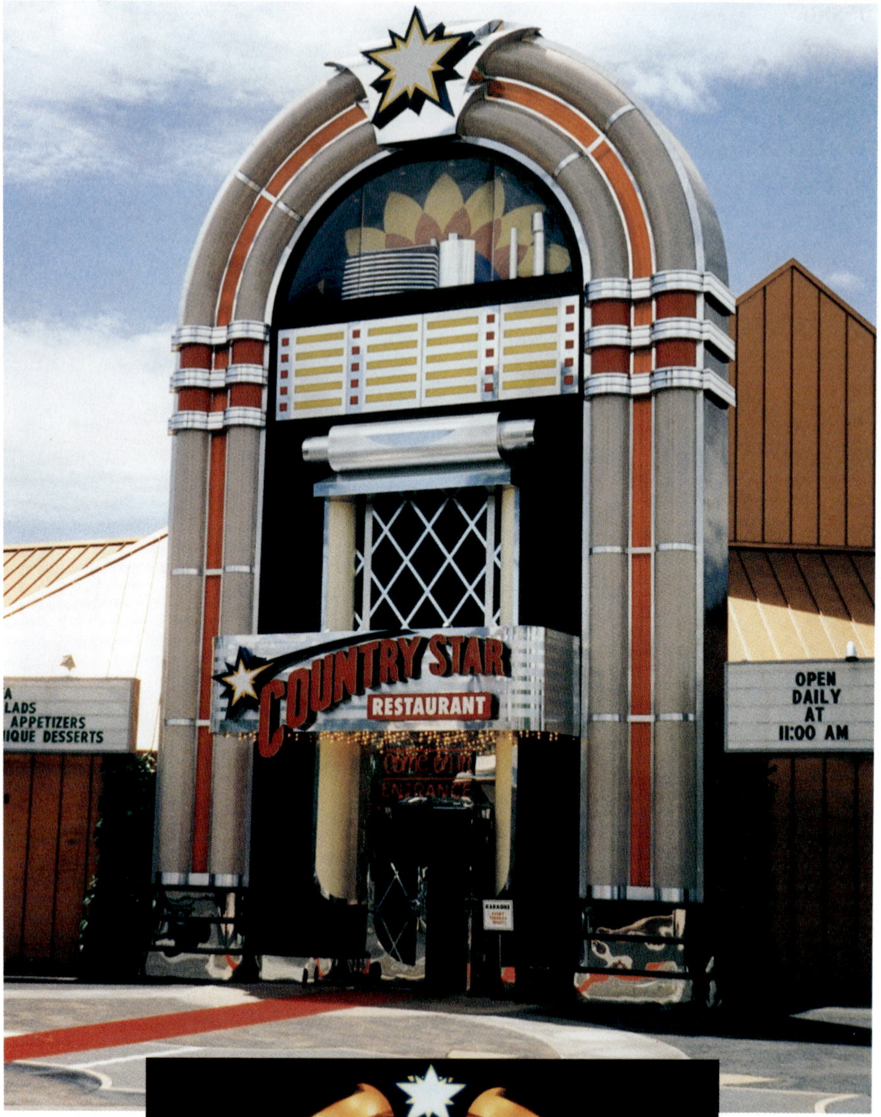

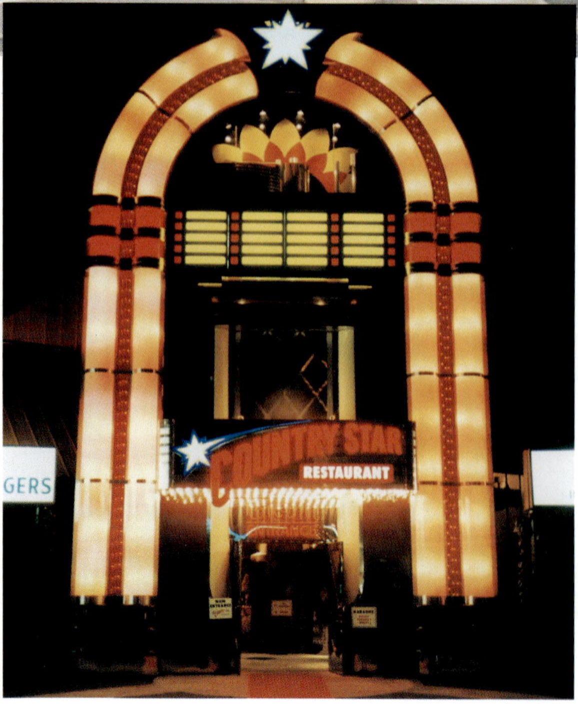

DESIGNERS

Harmon O. Nelson
Cindy Weber
2323 Broadway, Studio 201
San Diego, CA 92102
(619) 239-2312

FABRICATOR

California Neon
4530 Mission Gorge Pl.
San Diego, CA 92120
(619) 283-2191

This sign replaced one that hung over the intersection of University Ave. and 30th St. on a cable system from 1925-1965.

The aluminum enclosure is fabricated in the same shape to replicate the original sign. The 32-in.-high white pan channel letters have 4500K white outline neon with clear Lexan® faces to protect the neon from vandalism.

A decorative stainless-steel shroud constructed in compound curvilinear shapes serves as the transition from the enclosure to the center support. Artisan-quality aluminum-cast collars featuring a Carrotwood-leaf pattern with a brilliant gold powder coat soften the transitions to the base.

An octagonal base is faced with decorative tile from Mexico in an art-deco pattern and colors referencing the historic storefronts. Speakers are incorporated into the enclosure to provide ambient street music and a PA system for special events.

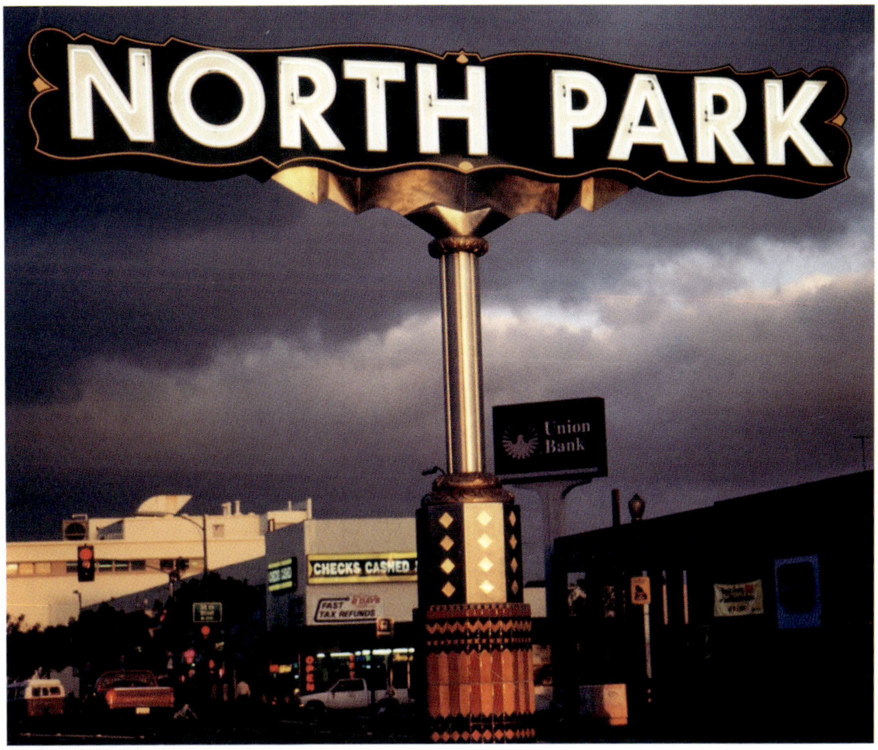

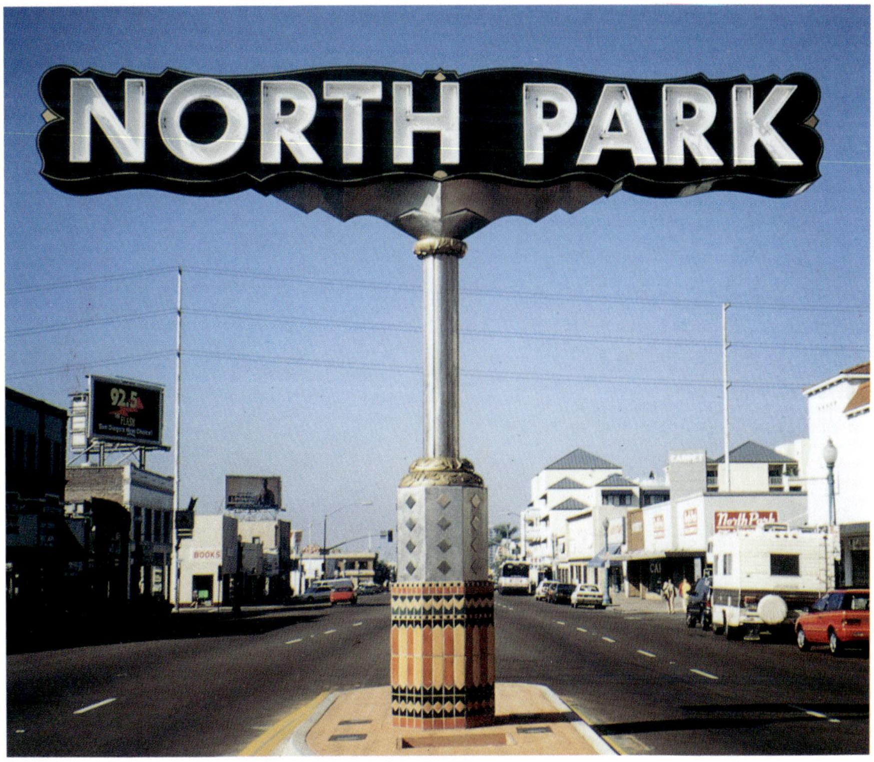

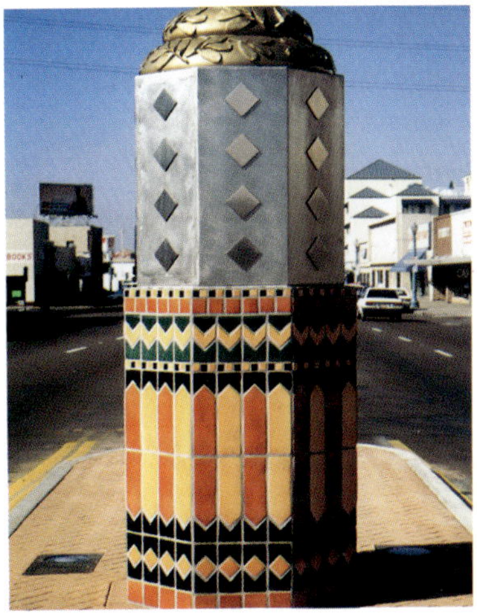

ORIGINAL LOGO / FREESTANDING OR GROUND

ELECTRIC

DESIGNERS

Kevin Hoffman
Doug Nanney
Signco Neon
1705 Austin Rd.
Troy, MI 48083
(810) 528-3100

FABRICATOR

Signco Neon

The 12 x 8-ft. sign has an aluminum frame and cabinet. The channel letters have acrylic faces, and the car is fabricated from polycarbonate. Both are lit with neon.

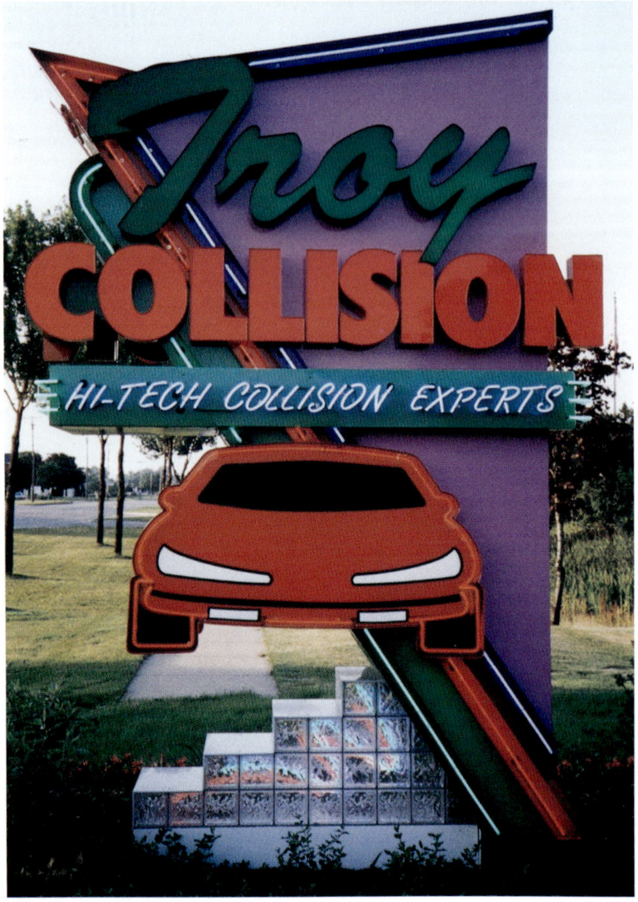

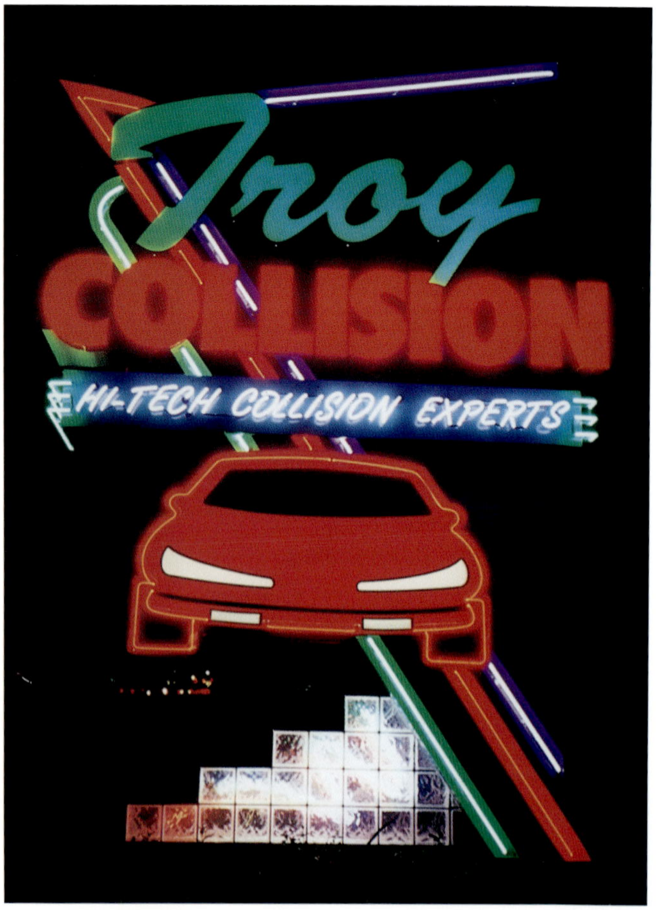

DESIGNER

Nicholas Assoc. Design Consultants Inc.
213 W. Institute, Ste. 704
Chicago, IL 60610
(312) 951-1185

FABRICATOR

Grate Signs, Inc.
4044 W. McDonough St.
Joliet, IL 60431
(815) 729-9700

This 8 x 12-ft. double-faced sign is internally illuminated and has an overall height of 20 ft. The aluminum pylon cover has a stucco finish and hand-painted copy. The Lexan® signface is molded, and the "tiles" and corner designs are fabricated from translucent pressure-sensitive vinyl, applied second-surface.

The faces are airbrushed to create the parchment look, and the remaining copy and graphics are flat sprayed second-surface. The ornate metal work is routed from ¼-in. aluminum plate with single-tube pink neon outlines. Double-tube pink neon — one row on each side — outlines the main body of the sign cabinet.

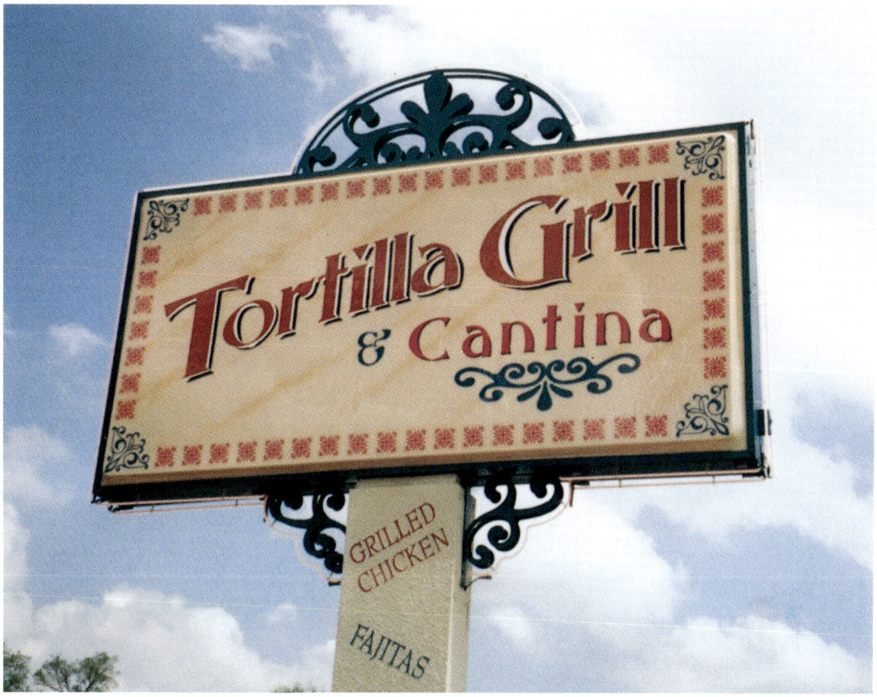

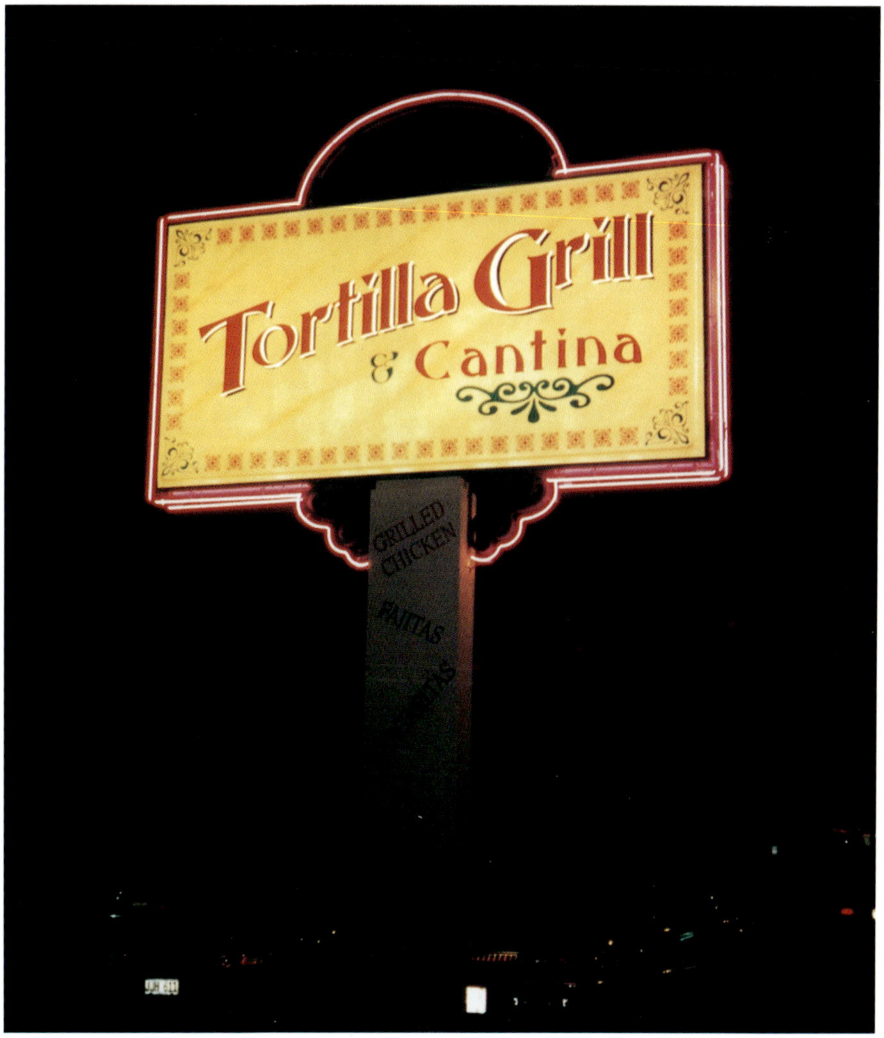

ELECTRIC

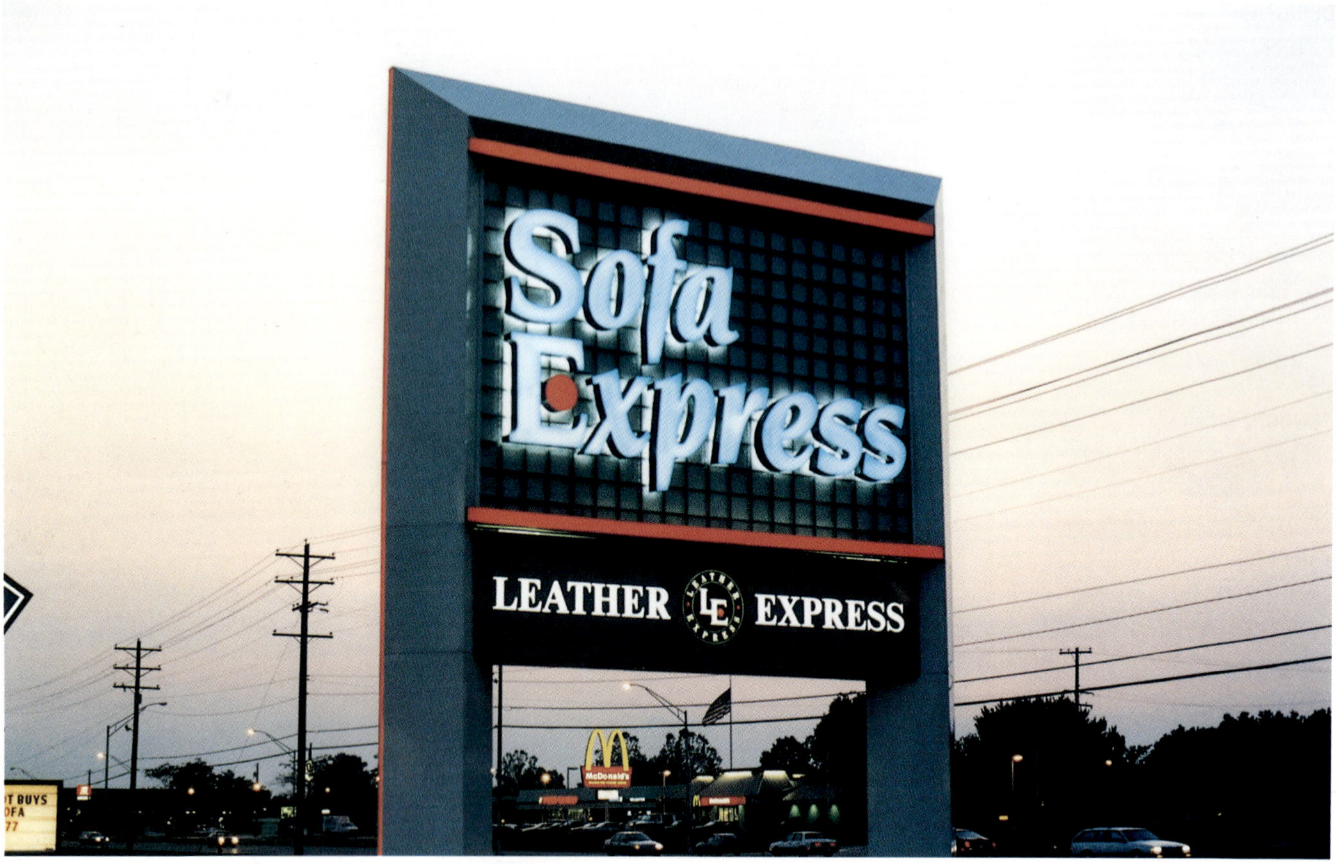

DESIGNER

Steve Quinn
Intergrate, Inc.
32 Warren St.
Columbus, OH 43215
(614) 421-0004

FABRICATOR

Branham Sign Co., Inc.
821 Alton Ave.
Columbus, OH 43219
(614) 258-8803

This 25 x 18 x 4-ft. sign utilizes double 20-in. poles, an aluminum face wrap, and a glass block interior that is halogen lit. The exterior letters are clear black with 6500 white neon. Neon against the glass block gives a halo effect with red neon outlines.

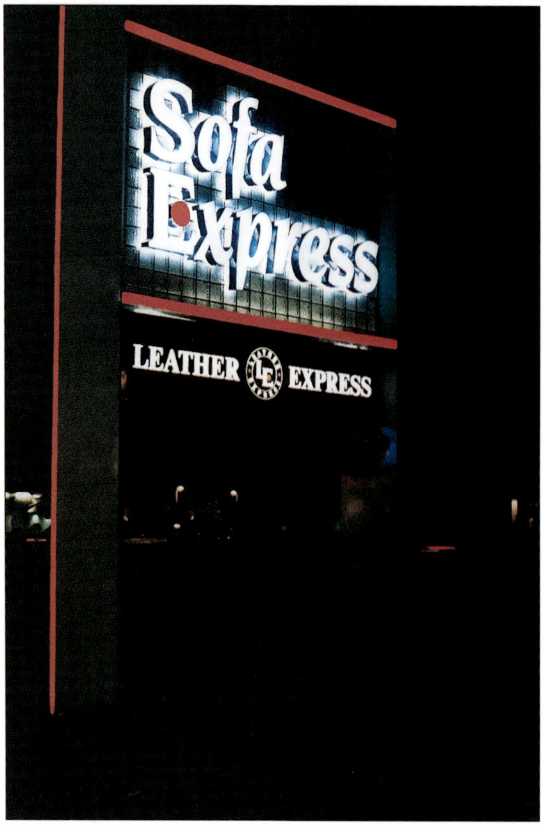

DESIGNERS

David Gamez
Advanced Signing, Inc.
4202 Dividend
San Antonio, TX 78219
(201) 337-4310

William Gottsman
16 Clewes Rd.
Millis, MA 02054
(518) 376-2344

FABRICATOR

Advanced Signing, Inc.

This sign is 100 ft. tall with a 16 x 15½-ft. identifying area. The identifying cabinet is 80 in. x 29 ft., exposed 15mm aluminum in construction with a rotator top.

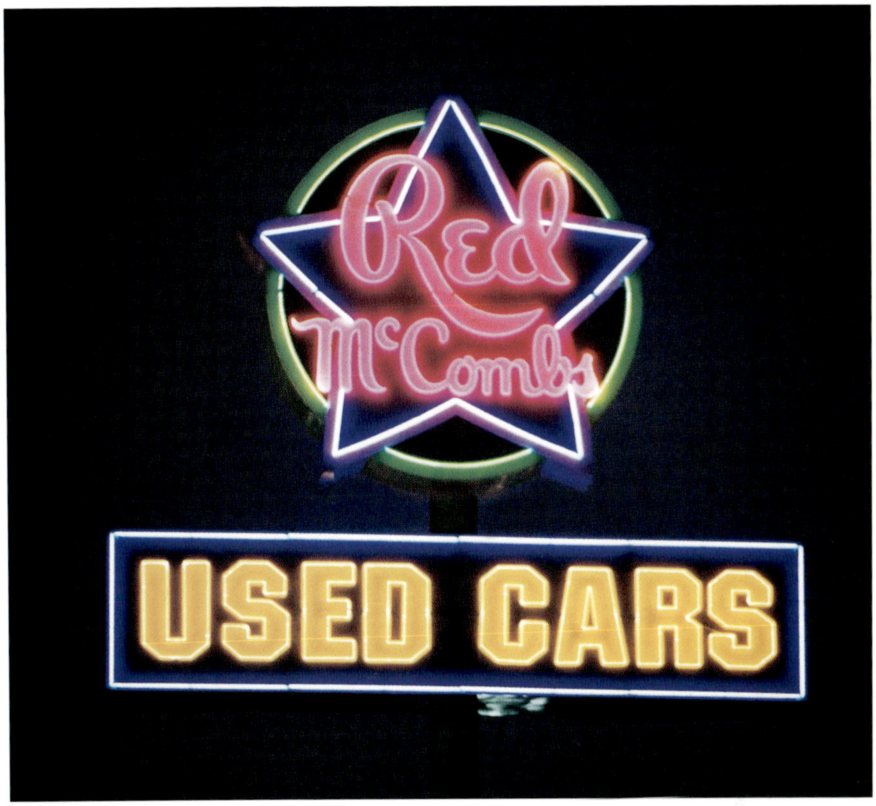

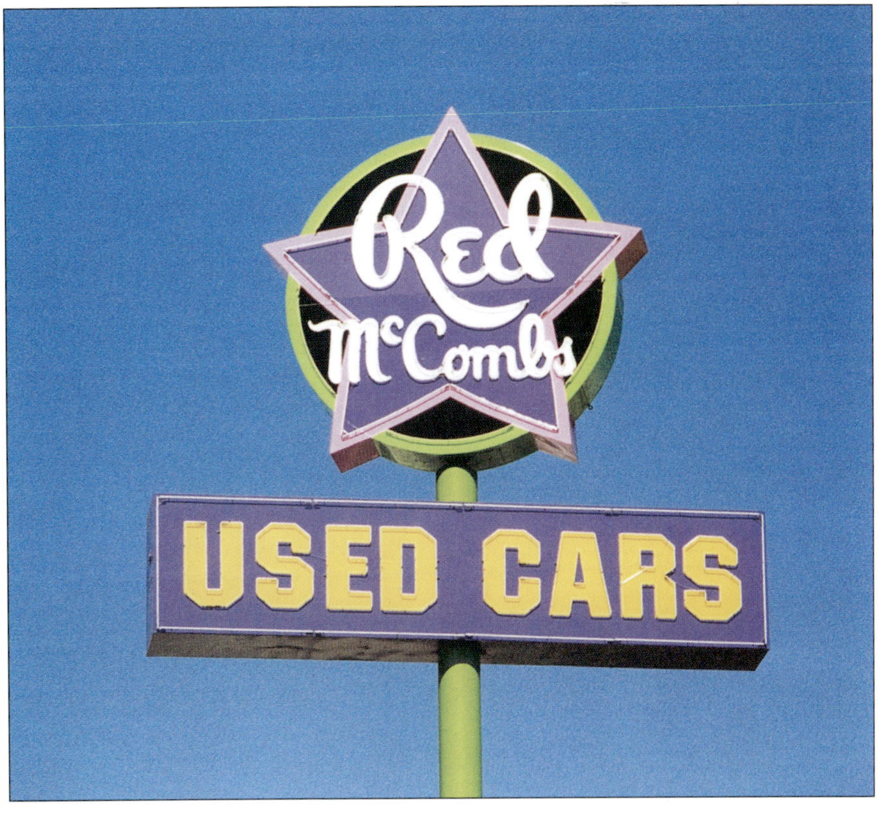

ORIGINAL LOGO / MOUNTED OR PROJECTING
ELECTRIC

DESIGNER

Ray Bailey Architects, Inc.
4100 S. Shepard St.
Houston, TX 77098
(713) 524-2155

FABRICATORS

SmithCraft
2602 W. Encanto Blvd.
Phoenix, AZ 85009
(602) 278-5508

Southern Display, Inc.
1801 Milby St.
Houston, TX 77003
(713) 223-4977

The sign's structure is fabricated from aluminum. The center section of the logo is flat, expanded metal with neon around the border.

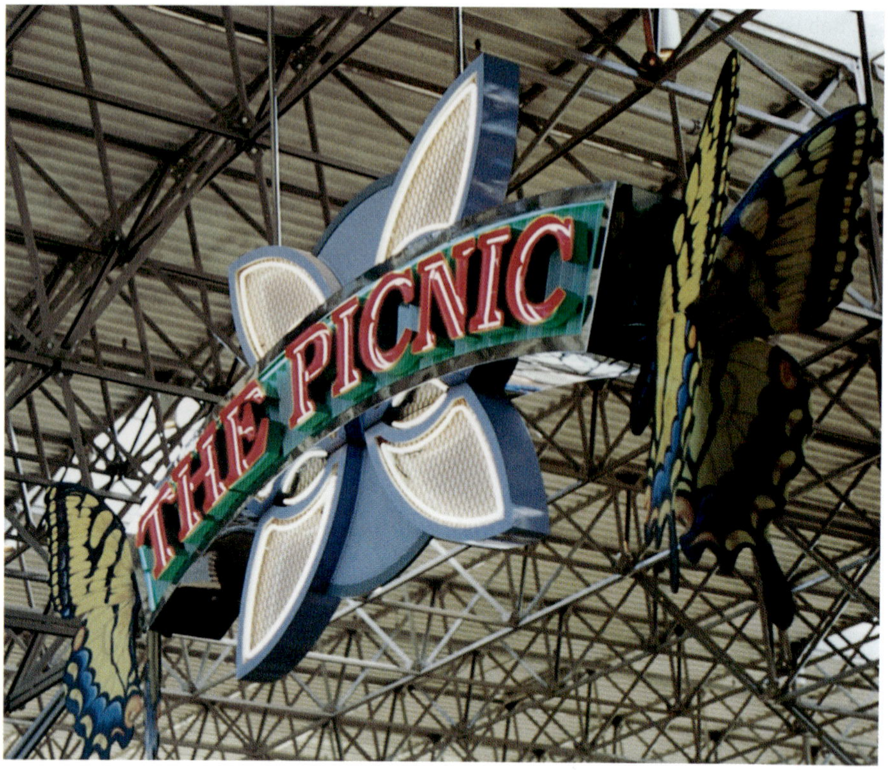

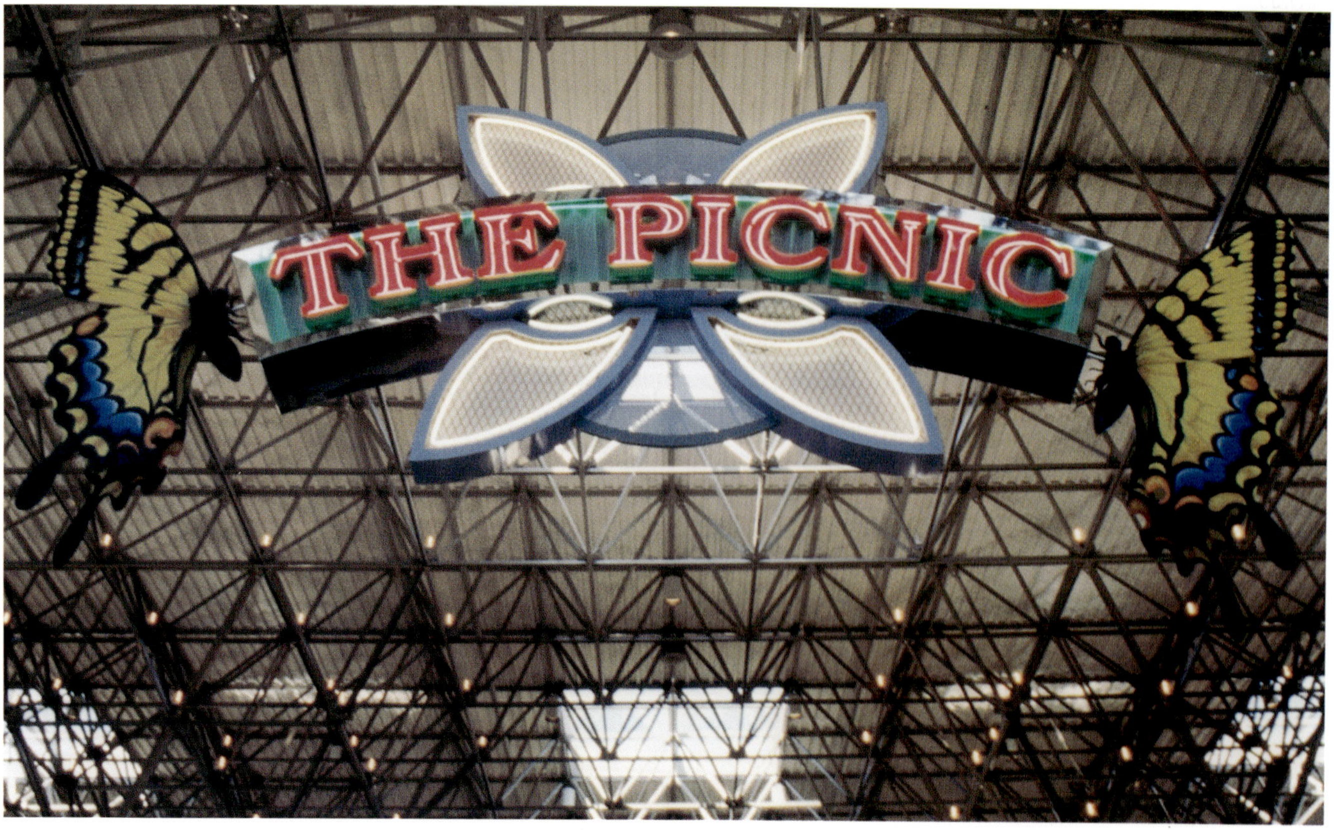

DESIGNERS

Olio (Charlie White III)
Bob Bangum
9½ Wavecrest
Venice, CA 90291
(310) 452-1912

John Myklebust
Design + Architecture
Minnetonka, MN 35343
(612) 931-8026

Richard Orne
The Jerde Partnership
913 Ocean Front Walk
Venice, CA 90291
(310) 399-1987

FABRICATOR

URB 3D Design
2640 Huron St.
Los Angeles, CA 90065
(213) 222-4269

The 3 x 5-ft. two-sided coffee cups hang between the glass storefront of the Classics and the Coffee Cafe on the mezzanine of Universal's City Walk. The cups are framed in plywood and covered with unbleached muslin. The logo on the side is a wood-cut print. There is a low wattage G-40 lamp in each cup so they glow at night.

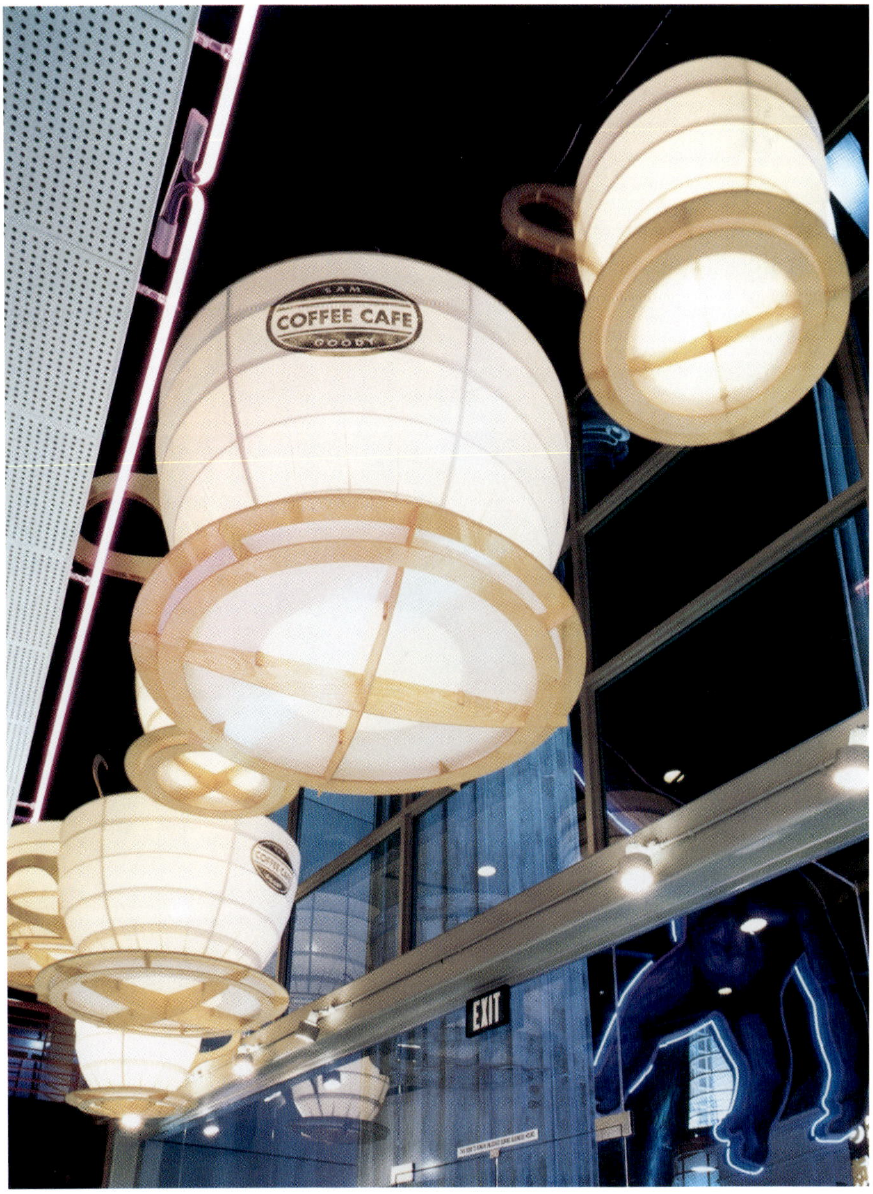

DESIGNER

Judd Brown Designs, Inc.
647 Jefferson Blvd.
Warwick, RI 02886

FABRICATOR

ARTeffects, Inc.
27 Britton Dr.
Bloomfield, CT 06002
(203) 242-0031

This sign incorporates a 4 ft. 9 in. x 10 ft. 4 in. Sunbrella® woven acrylic awning with the 3D logo suspended over the awning. The orb and "Civic" are attached to the existing facade for greater stability.

The letters are fabricated from 4-in., brushed, stainless-steel with a 20-gauge steel face and 3-in. 22-gauge returns with blue neon on the front edges of "Civic." In addition, ¾ in. galvanized tube is used to fabricate the longitude and latitude grid which is sprayed to appear as distressed rusted metal. The semi-sphere is cast acrylic, which is sprayed amber.

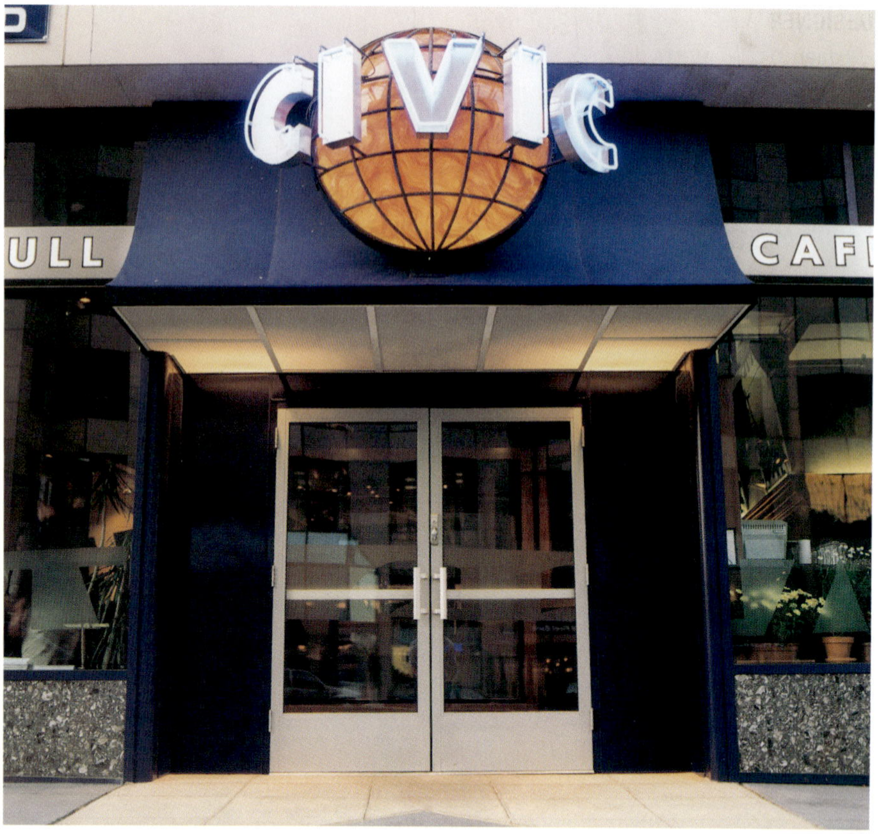

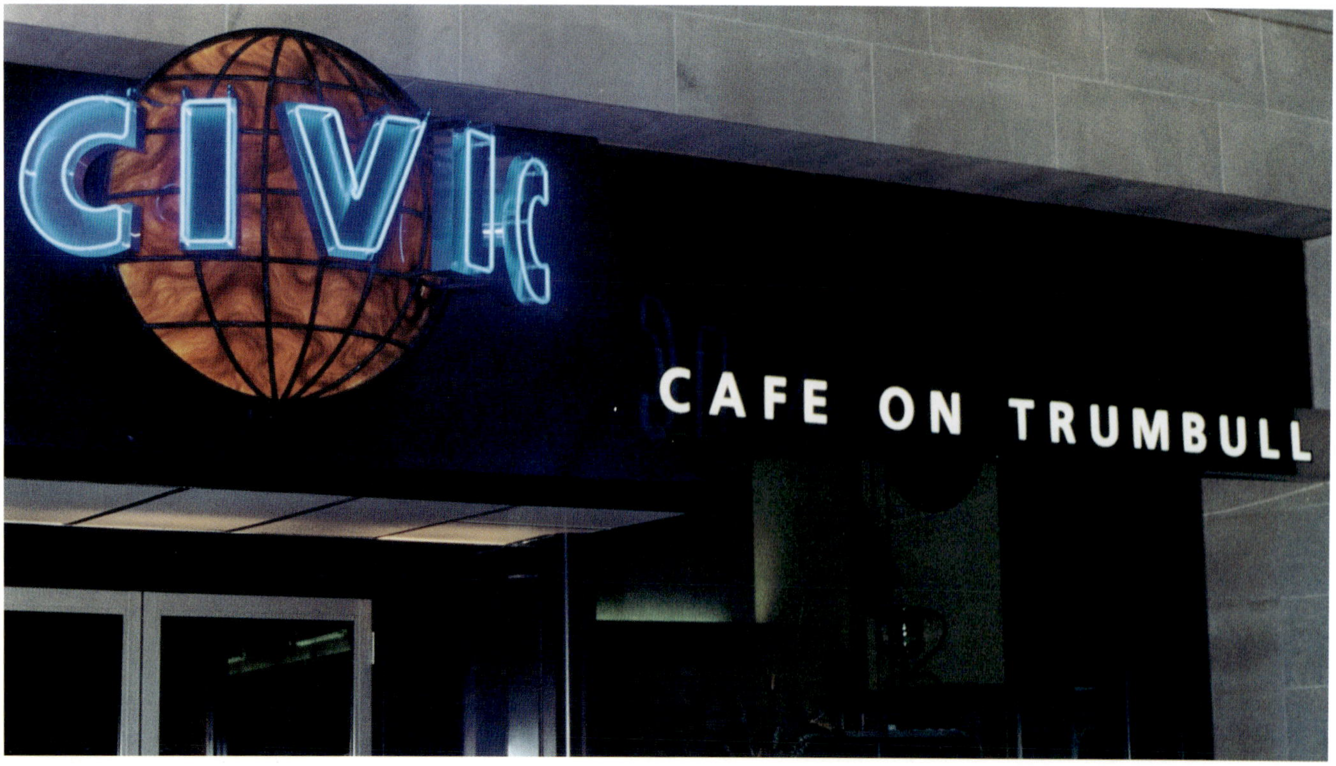

DESIGNER

Juan Luis Longoria
Tapia 1252 Pte.
Monterrey, Mexico 64800
8357 96 52

FABRICATOR

Anuncios Alvarado
Garza Sada #6405
Monterrey, Mexico 64890
8357 33 50

"Iman" translates to "magnet" in English. The back of the 8-ft. irregular pentagon comprises a welded structure covered with stainless-steel sections internally illuminated with fuscia-neon halo light.

The acrylic 3 ft. 4-in. letters have a 4-in.-deep channel and are internally illuminated with green neon halo light. The screw heads are fabricated from acrylic circles with 2-in.-deep channels.

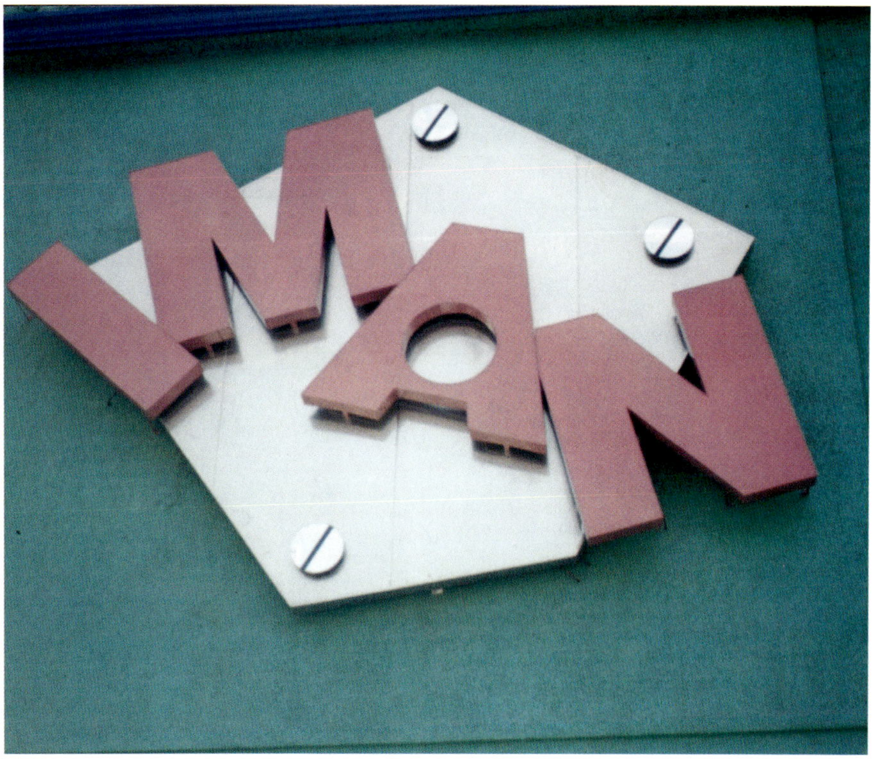

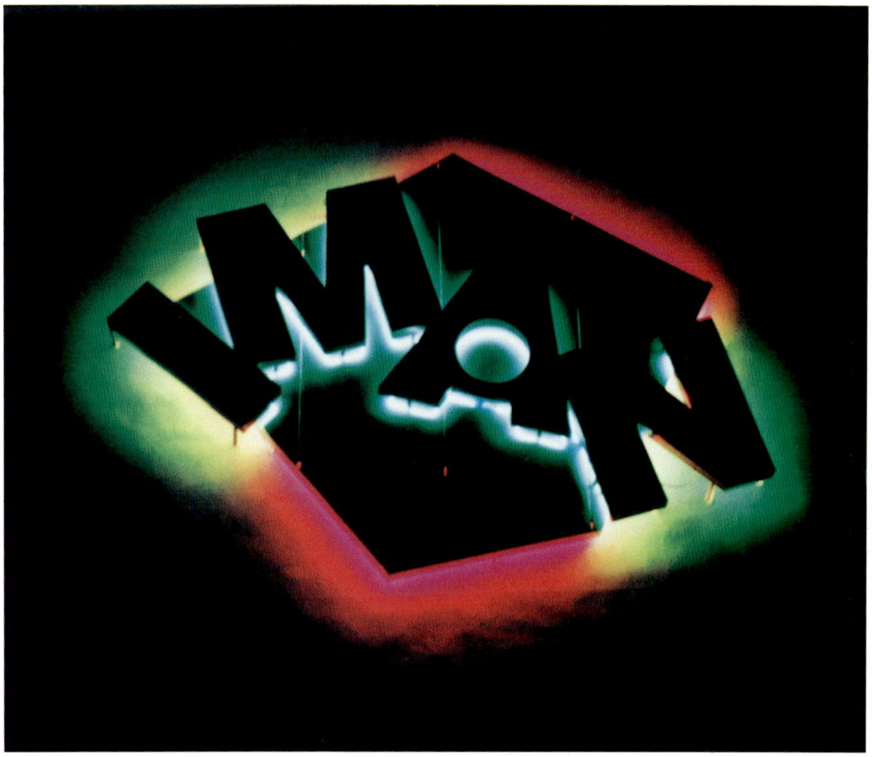

ELECTRIC

DESIGNER

William F. Johnson
ARTeffects, Inc.
27 Britton Dr.
Bloomfield, CT 06002
(203) 242-0031

FABRICATOR

ARTeffects, Inc.

The 24-ft.-long sign bends in the middle following the contour of the outside corner of the supporting wall. The "Food Court" copy is 14 in. high; "The Deli" copy is 3 ft. 9 in. high, and "Bingo" measures 20 in. high. All three of these images light through the face as well as halo a tinted color out of the back.

"The Deli" copy and several of the "confetti" squares have frosted clear lenses which slightly diffuse the light. The exposed argon tubing behind the remaining squares is opaque and lights in halo fashion. The sign is inside a casino; therefore it is always lit.

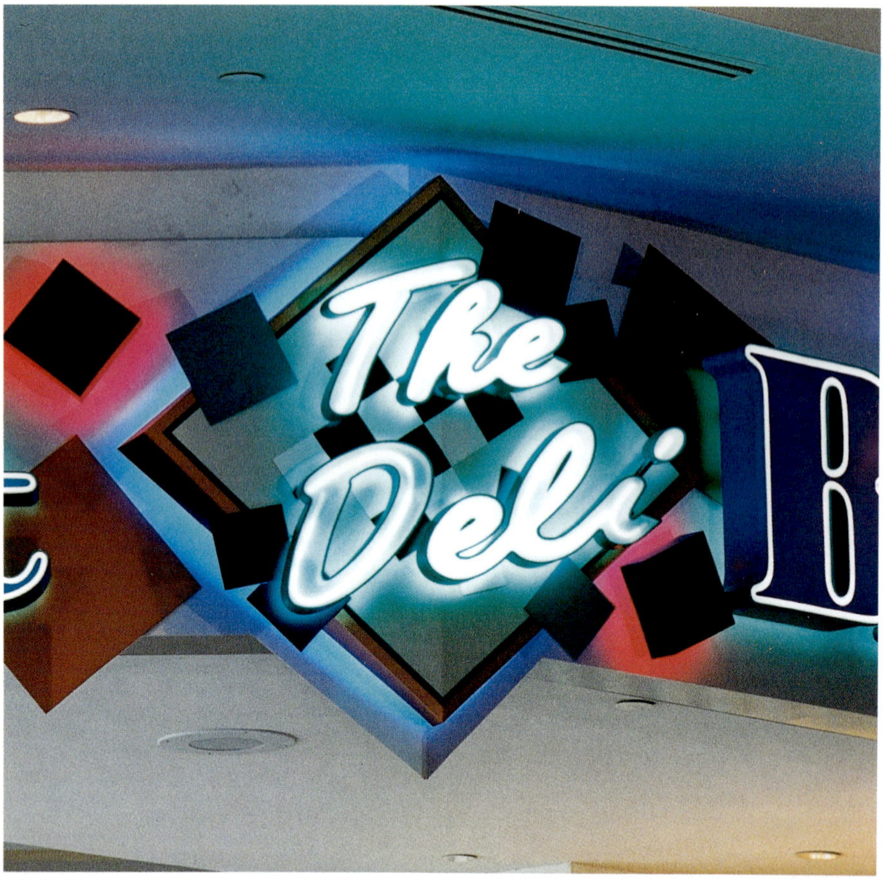

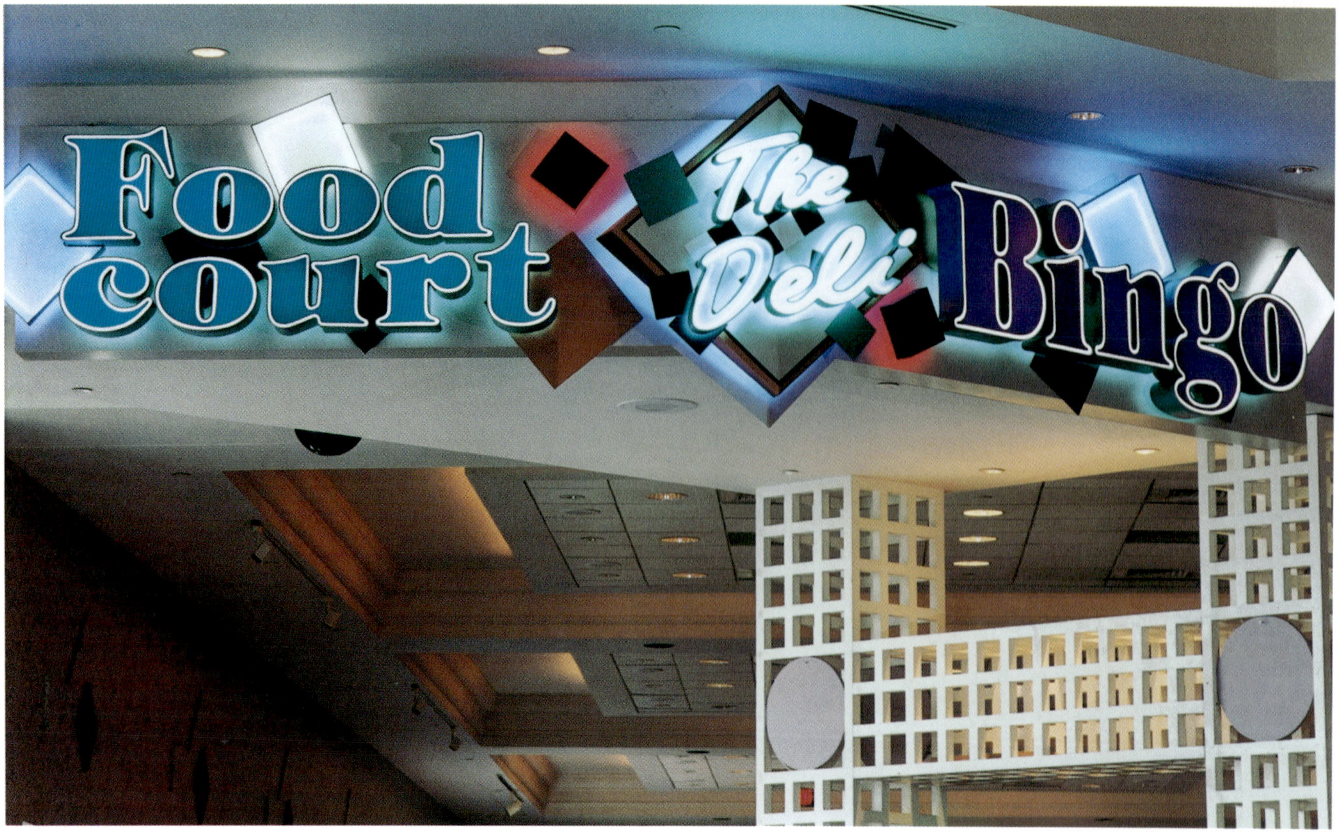

DESIGNERS

Olio (Charlie White III)
9½ Wavecrest Ave.
Venice, CA 90291
(310) 452-1912

John Myklebust
Design + Architecture
10400 Yellow Circle Dr.
Minnetonka, MN 55343
(612) 931-8026

FABRICATOR

Superior Electric Advertising
1700 W. Anaheim St.
Long Beach, CA 90813
(800) 995-9099

King Kong is fabricated of sheet aluminum on a structural steel frame. The two-sided blade sign is 37-ft. tall, outlined in neon. The image is painted. The sign is attached to the building at six points to a 24-in.-round structural column, inside the building. The "Sam Goody" illuminated signs are on an exposed raceway, with neon chases. The letters are open-face channels with neon outline and theatrical lights in the center of the channel letters.

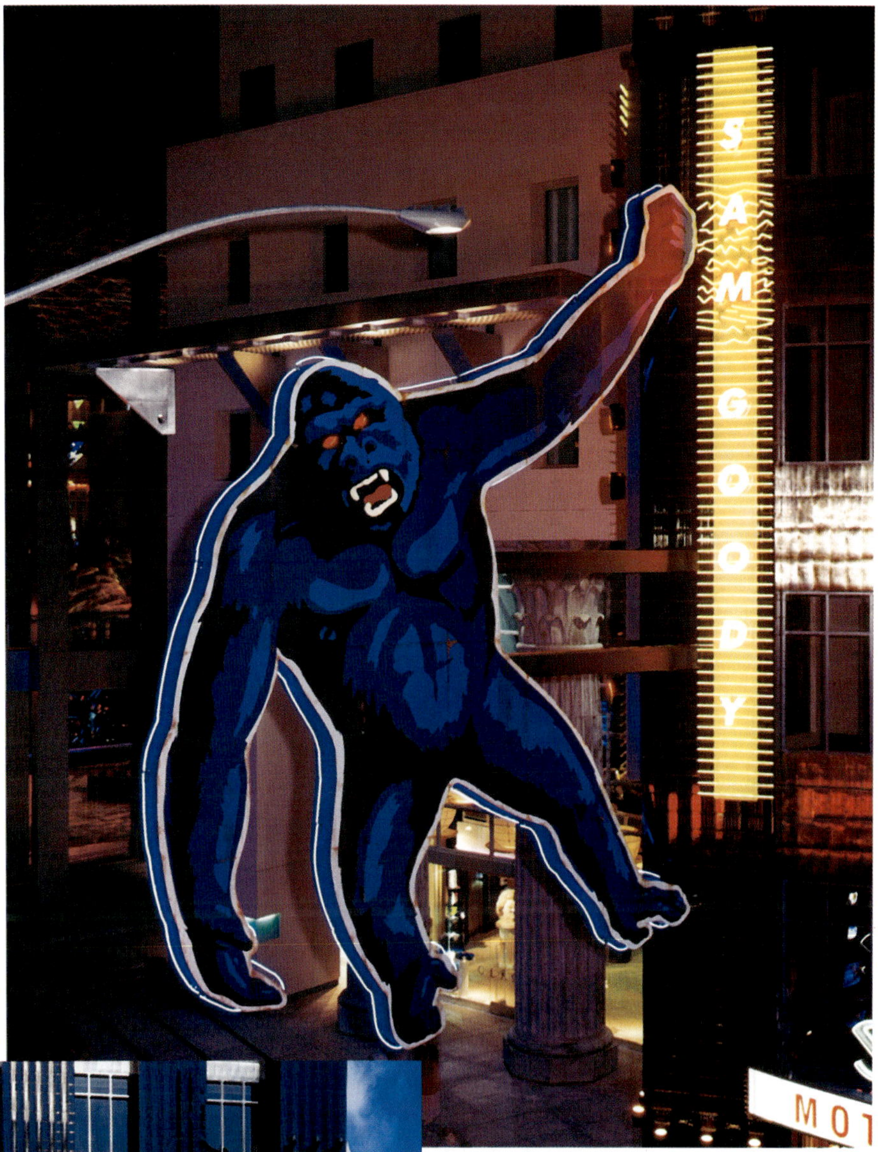

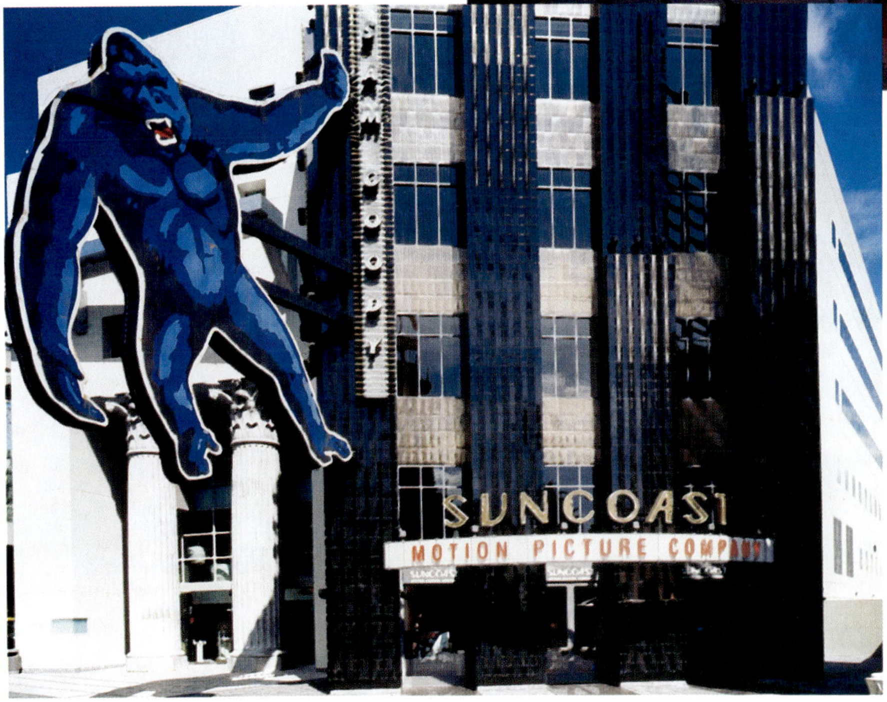

ELECTRIC

DESIGNERS

Jennifer Meyers
Connie Post Designs
5839 Davis Creek Rd.
Barboursville, WV 25504
(719) 633-7763

Les Walker
Gordon Sign Co.
2930 W. 9th Ave.
Denver, CO 80204
(303) 629-6121

FABRICATOR

Gordon Sign Co.

This project entails a main-ID sign plus secondary building signs and more than 100 ft. of two-color neon striping borders on the building. The skeleton-neon "Sofa" letters measure 36 in. In addition, the "Mart" copy is 31-in. pan channel letters with 7-in. pan channel letters below. The radius white polycarbonate ends are used with applied translucent vinyl and cornice on the top and bottom of the sheetmetal sign. A heavy sand finish is also used on the sign. Internal T-12 lighting is used for end illumination.

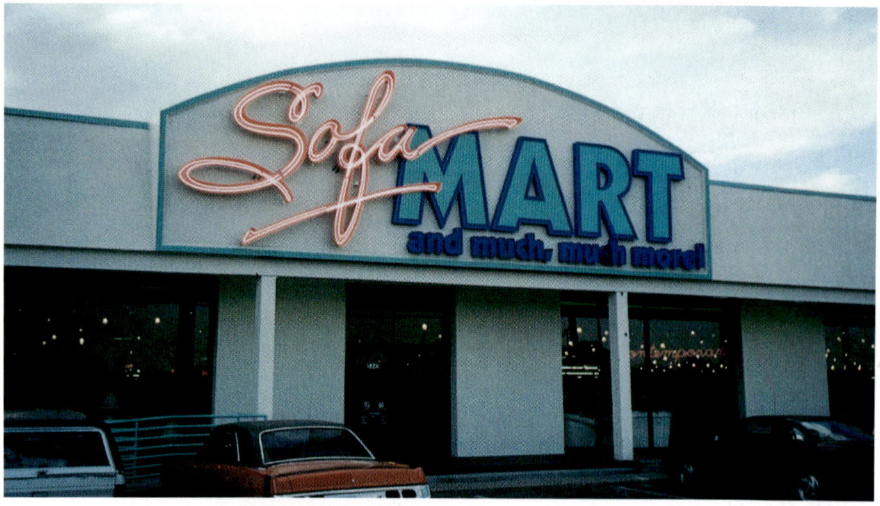

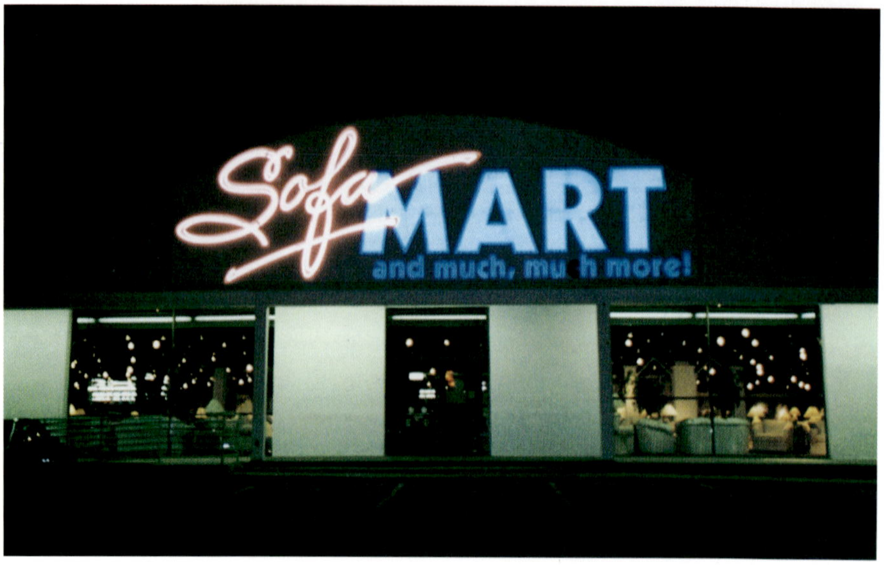

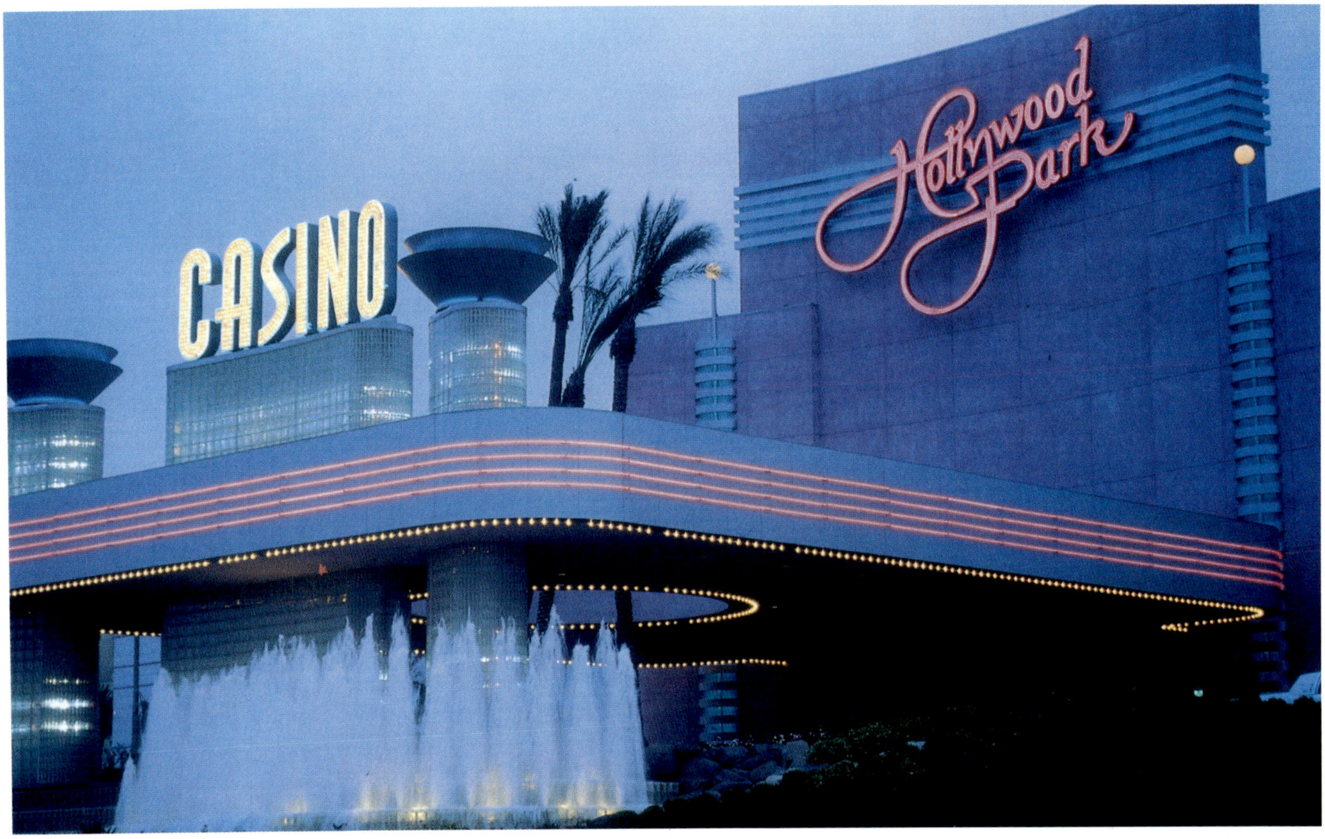

DESIGNER

Alan Lamb
426 N. 44th St.
Phoenix, AZ 85008
(602) 968-3107

FABRICATOR

Local Neon Co., Inc.
12536 Chadron Ave.
Hawthorne, CA 90250
(800) 338-3387

The "Hollywood Park" open-face channel logo measures 25 ft. x 46 ft. 10 in. with exposed neon illumination. The background bars are 12-in. reverse channel illuminated. The "Casino" aluminum channel letters are 10 x 26 ft., also with exposed neon for a border. A total of 8,000 ft. of neon tubing was used.

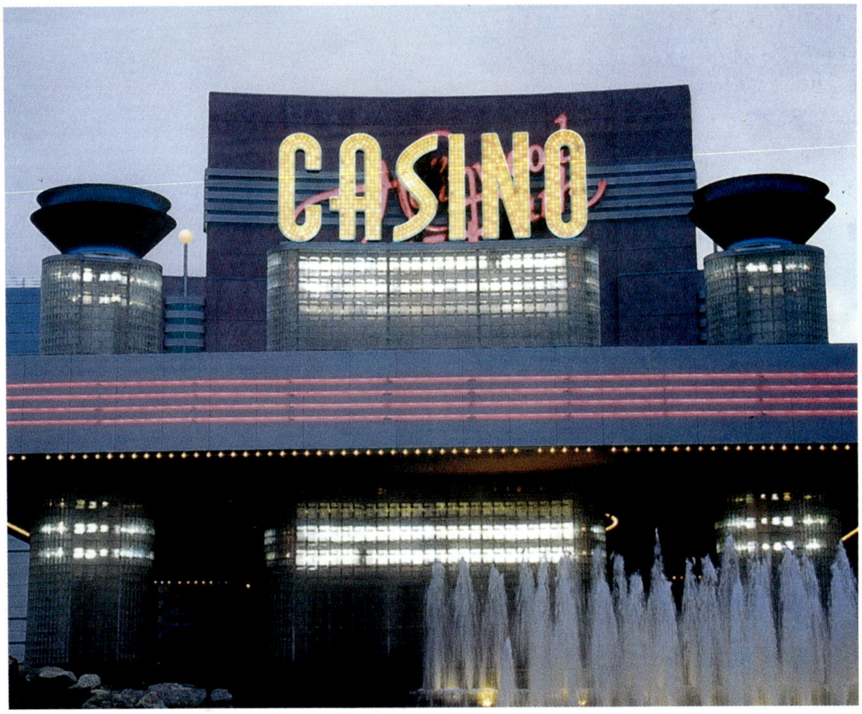

ORIGINAL LOGO / MOUNTED OR PROJECTING

ELECTRIC

DESIGNER

Alan Lamb
Lamb Architects
426 N. 44th St.
Phoenix, AZ 85008
(602) 968-3107

FABRICATOR

Local Neon Co., Inc.
12536 Chadron Ave.
Hawthorne, CA 90250
(800) 338-3387

This 12 x 6-ft. original logo was created to reflect the historical origin for this war game club concept. The acrylic face and reverse halo channel letters are complemented with a concealed line of ruby red neon along the inside perimeter of the temple. The columns and other details are made of Sign Foam® and aluminum.

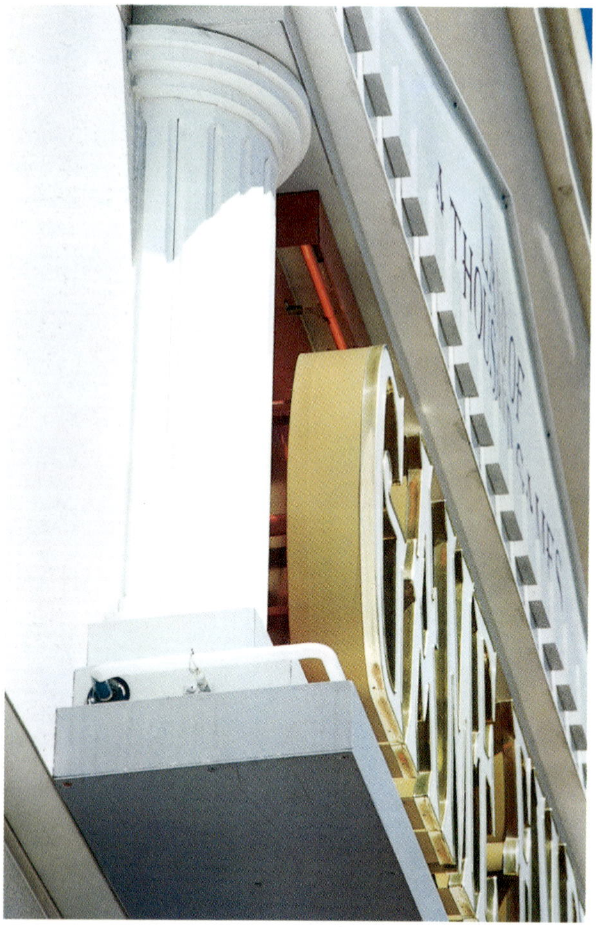

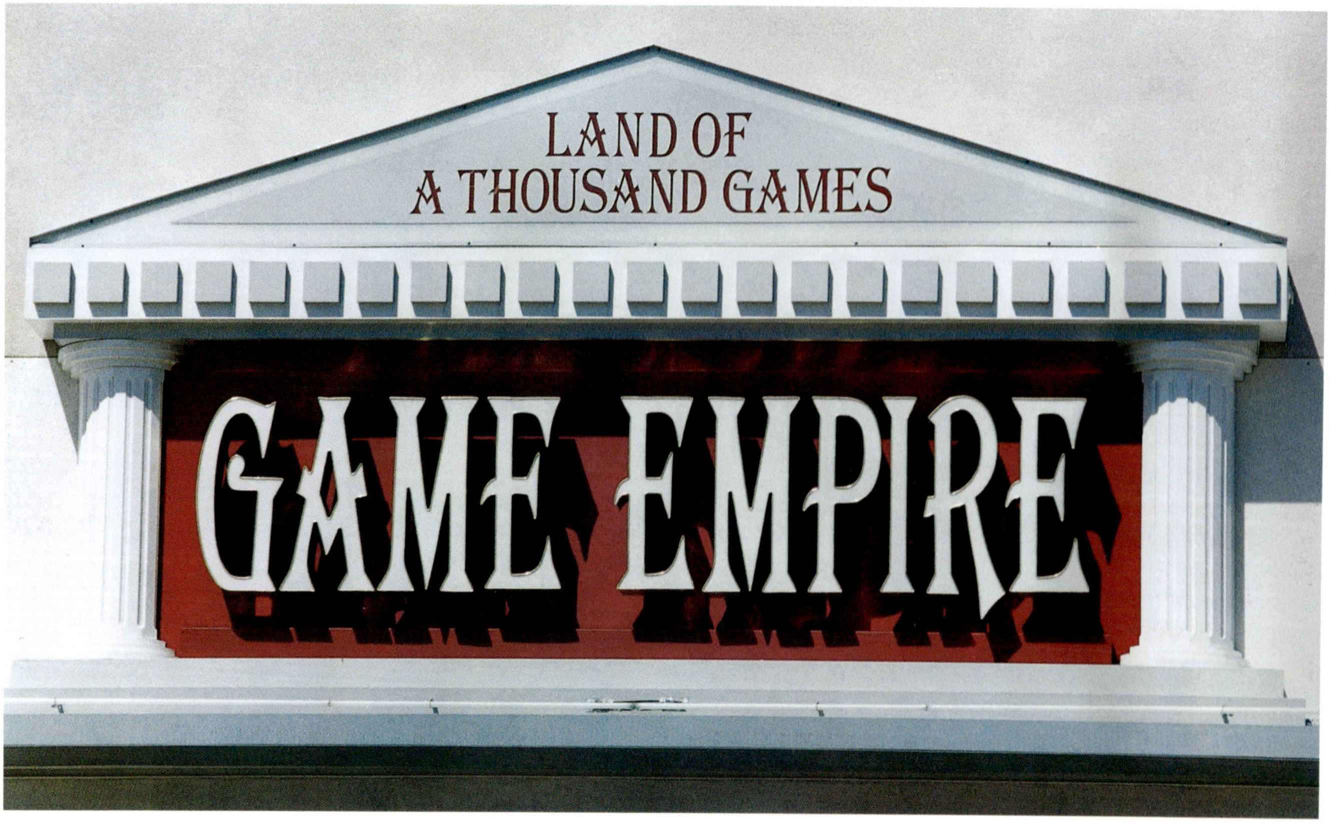

DESIGNER

David Goodwin
Image Works, Inc.
11046 Leadbetter Rd.
Ashland, VA 23005
(804) 798-5533

FABRICATOR

Image Works, Inc.

This 35 x 25-ft. display is constructed of aluminum, acrylic, internal fluorescent tubes and exposed teal neon. The acrylic and fluorescent lighting are designed to produce clarity, while the neon is incorporated to add punch and embellish the nautical theme.

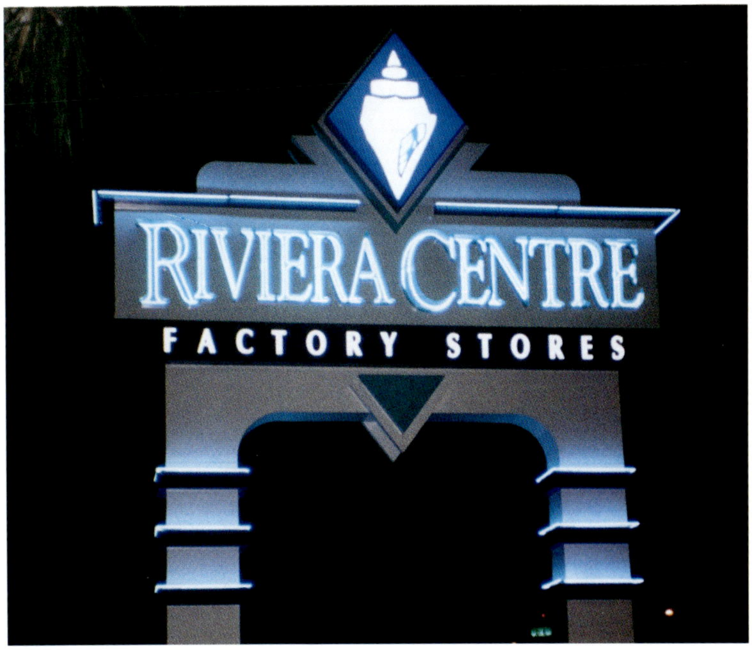

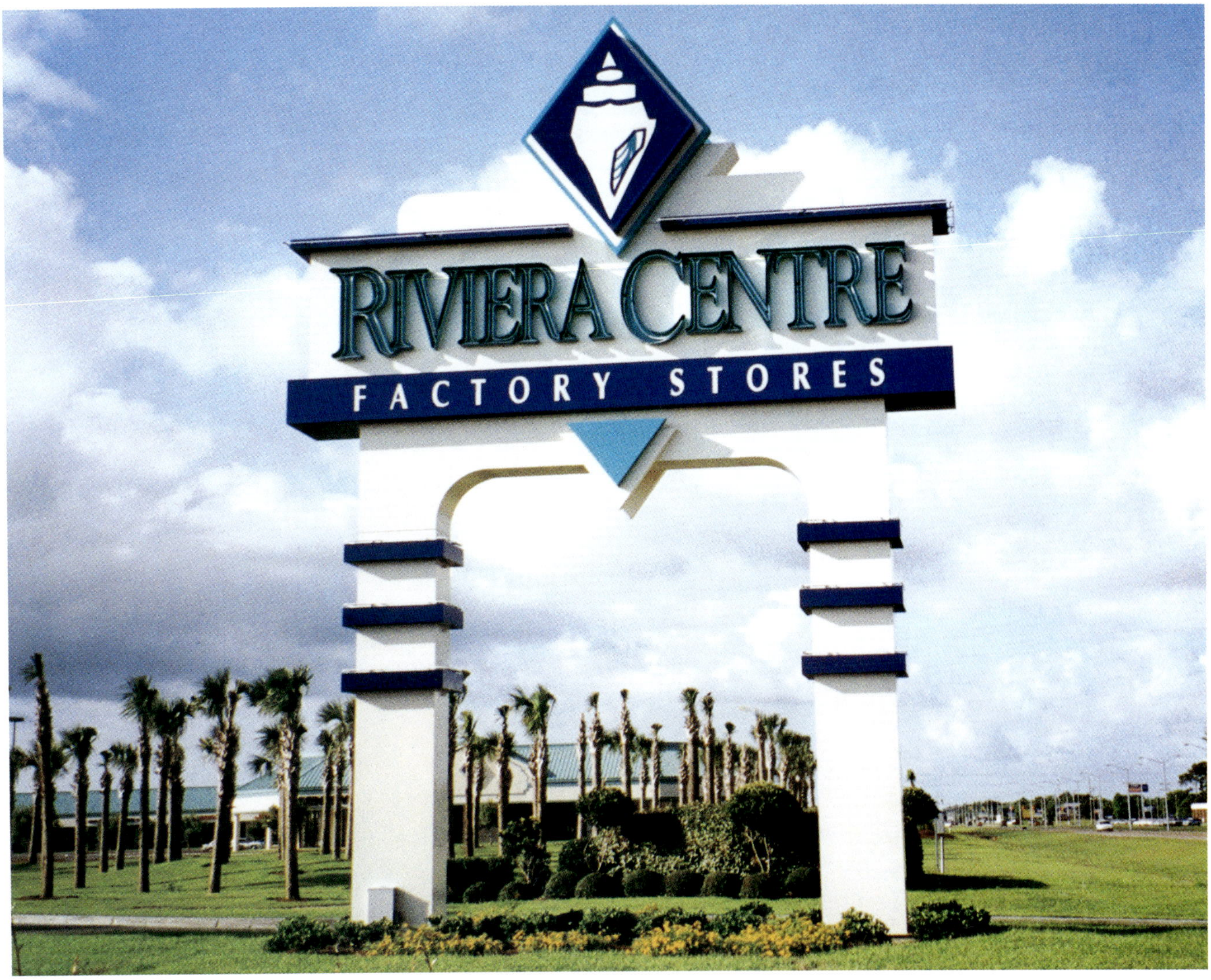

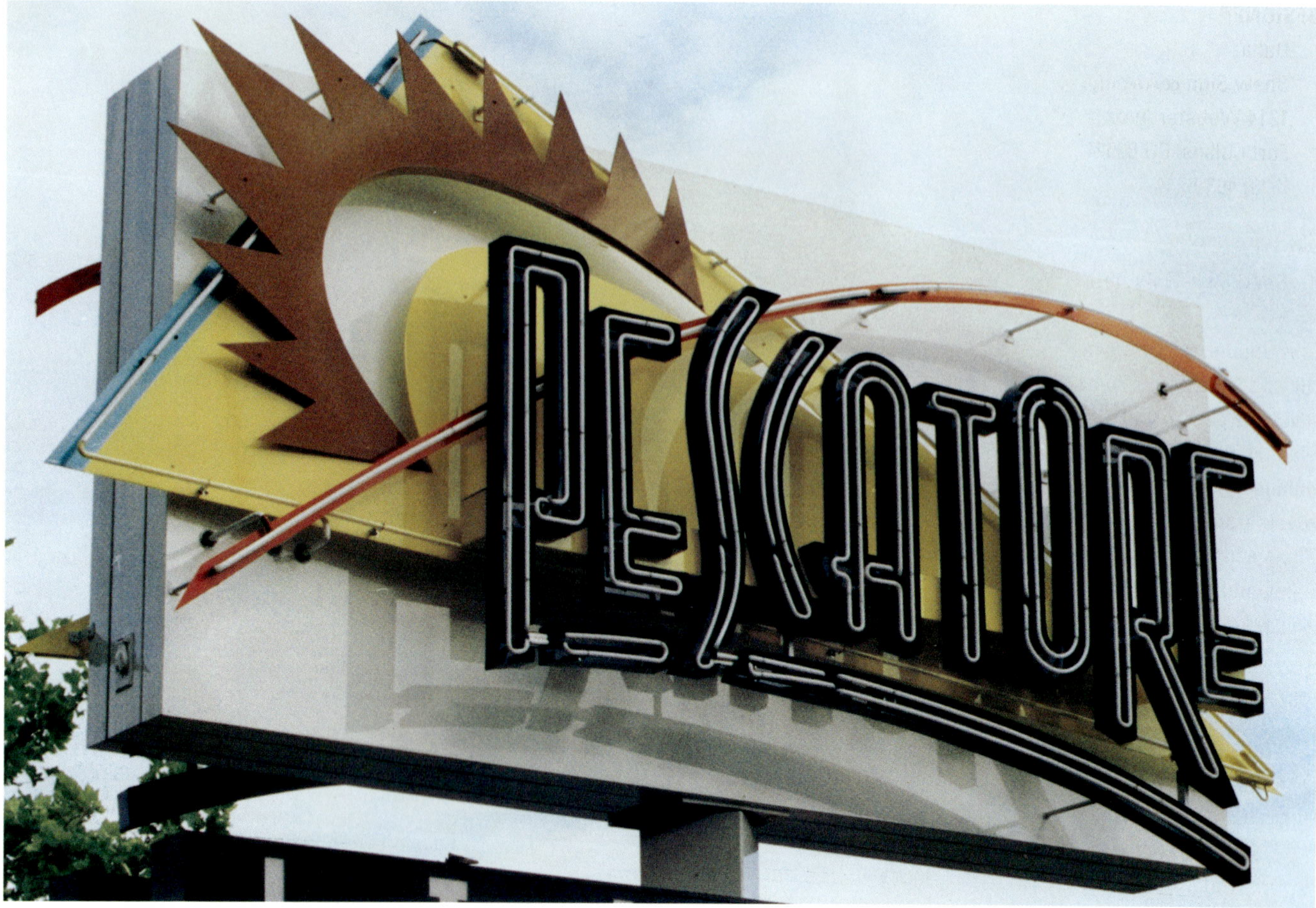

DESIGNER

Val Paul Taylor Design
1735 Westlake Ave. N.
Seattle, WA 98109

FABRICATOR

National Sign Corp.
1255 Westlake Ave. N.
Seattle, WA 98109
(206) 282-0700

This sign includes a 6 x 10-ft., double-face cabinet accompanied by two secondary 1 x 10-ft. cabinets underneath. The pole cover, cabinet, letters, triangle (rolled) and word boxes are all fabricated from aluminum. The exposed neon tubing is blue, yellow-gold, orange and turquoise, with open pan-channel letters on "Pescatore." All graphic elements are pegged off the wall.

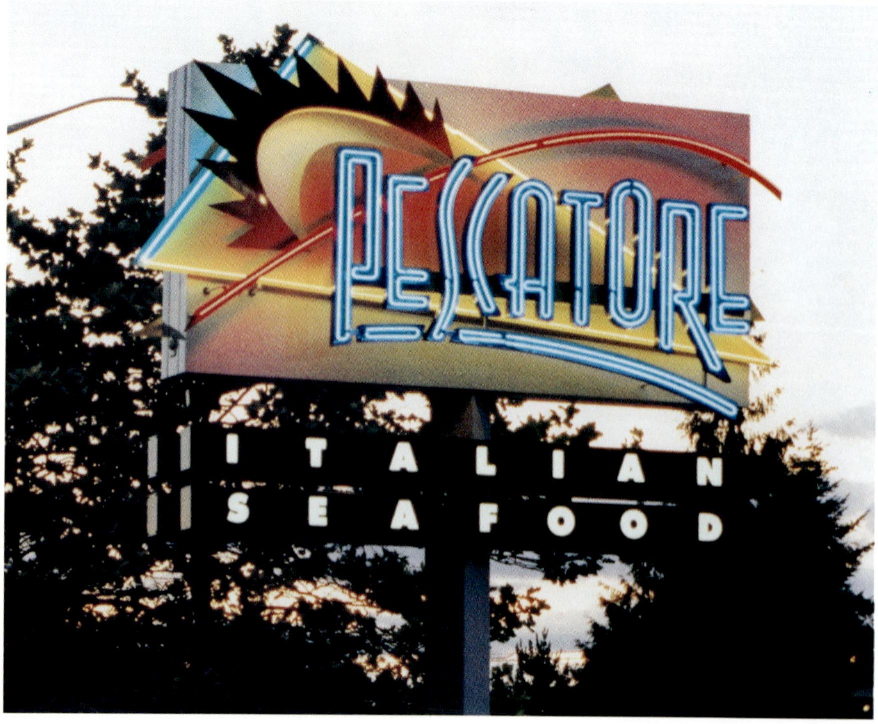

DESIGNER

Dallas Griffin
Shaw Sign & Awning, Inc.
1314 Webster Ave.
Fort Collins, CO 80524
(970) 493-6244

FABRICATOR

Shaw Sign & Awning, Inc.

This double-face monument sign is 9 ft. tall and 12 ft. wide. The fabricated aluminum is painted using pearl-white enamel with a clear-coat finish on the cabinet. "Palmer" features clear-coated, reverse-channel, polished brass letters. The push-through "Flowers" has a 1-in. relief, and the push-through logo has a 2-in. relief.

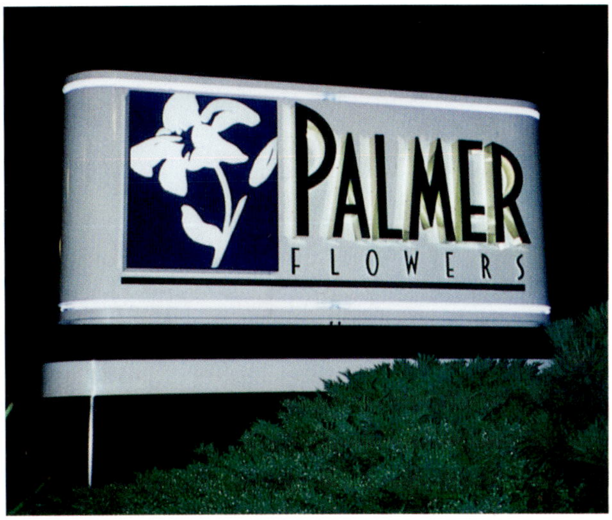

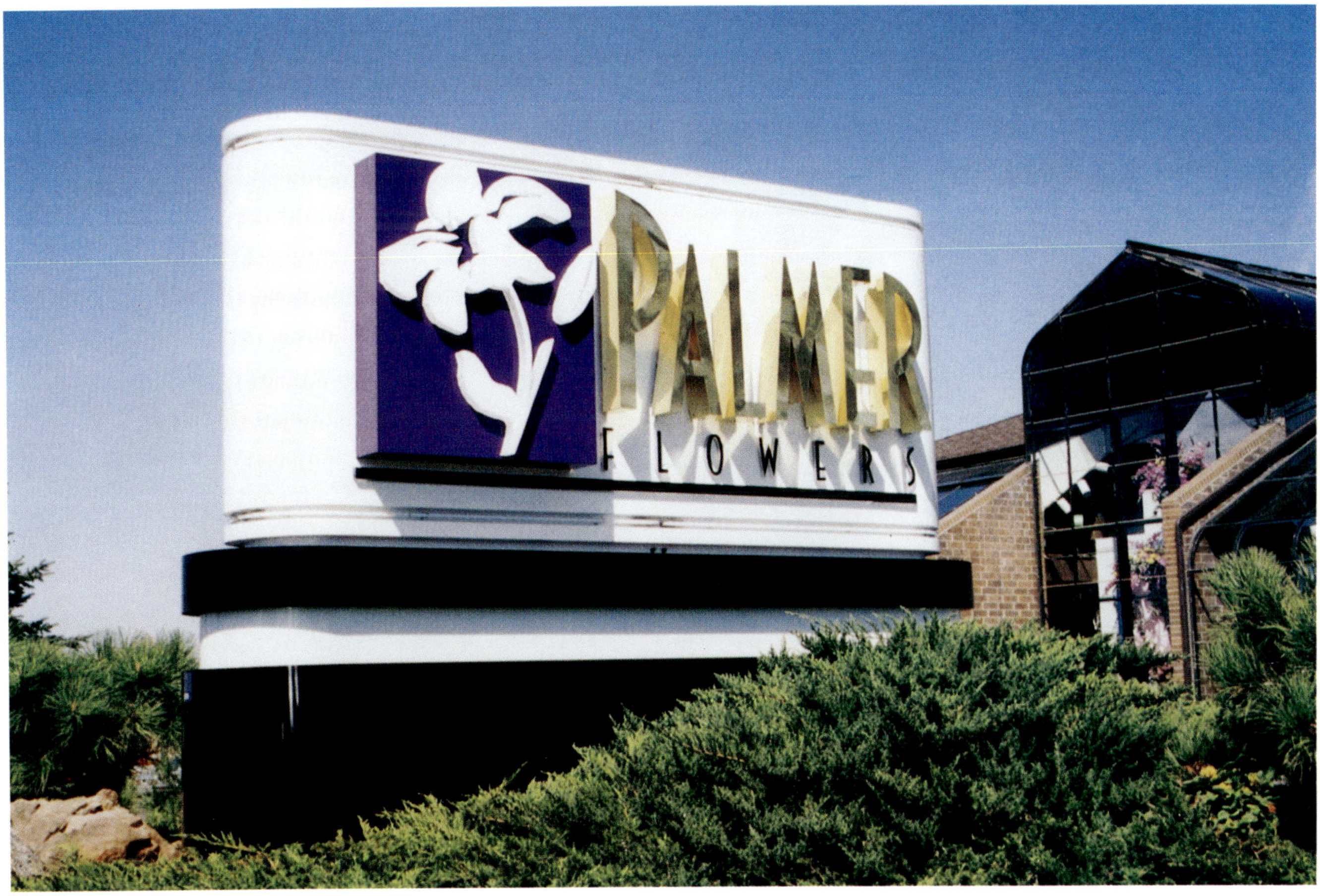

ELECTRIC

DESIGNER

Pierre Beaudoin
Claude Neon Ltd.
(Div. of the Jim Pattison Sign Group)
1855 Hymus Blvd.
Dorval, QC, Canada H9P 1J8
(514) 856-7756

FABRICATOR

Claude Neon Ltd.

This 4 x 6-ft. sign identifies a high school. The 20-in.-thick "book" is fabricated from aluminum. The copy is cut out and filled with backlit plastic.

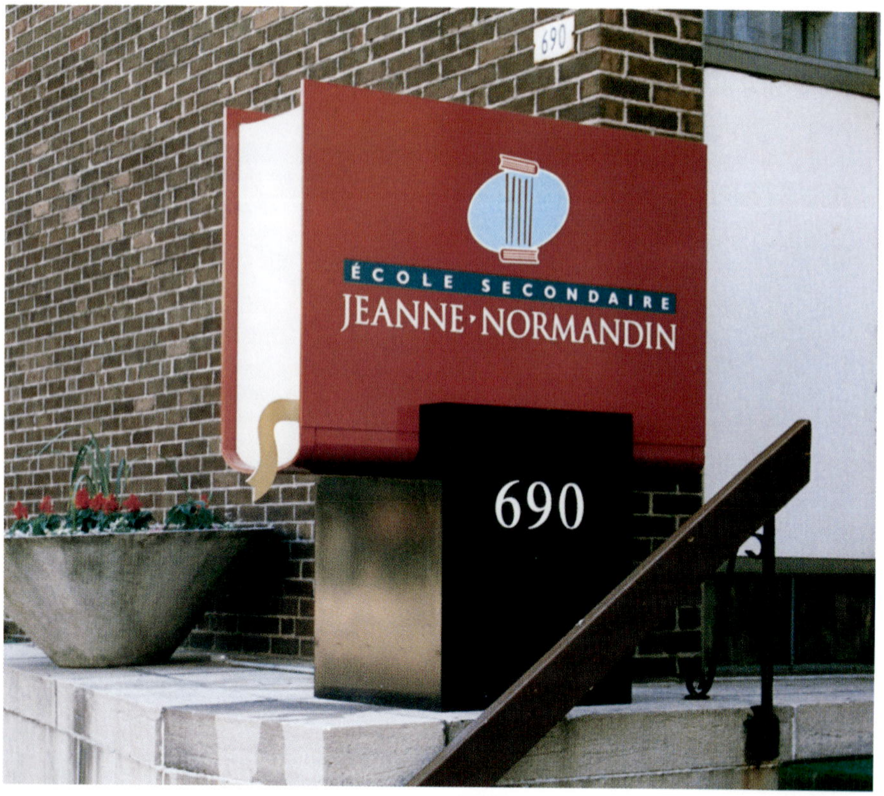

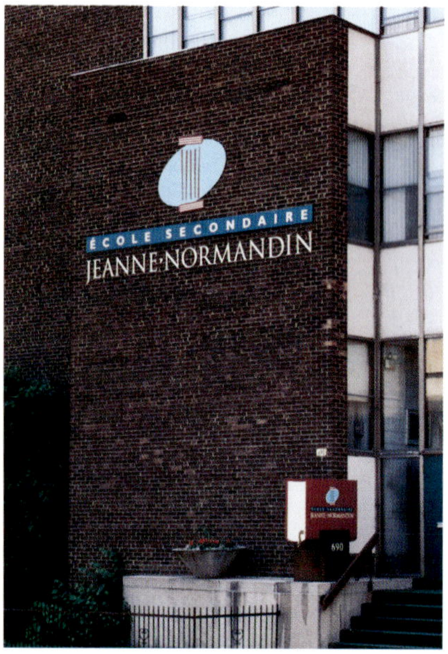

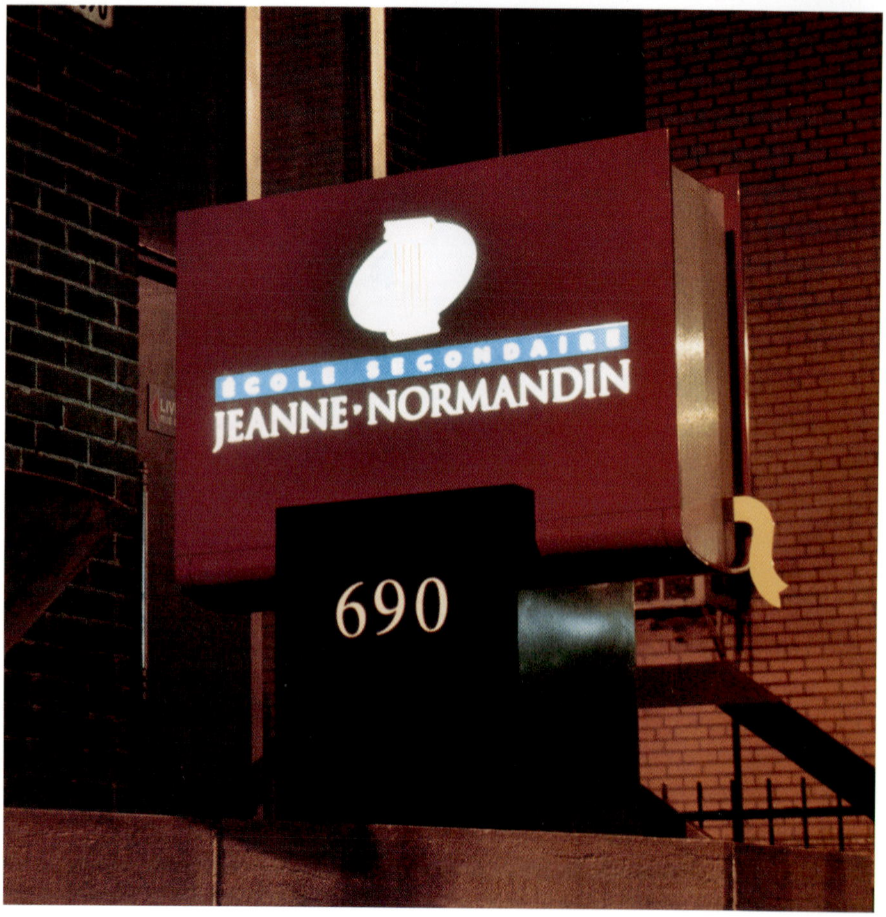

DESIGNERS

Joseph R. Trapani
Ryan-Markland Signs, Inc.
4444 N.E. 8th Ave.
Ft. Lauderdale, FL 33334
(305) 491-3650

S.C.G. & Assoc.
2450 Hollywood Blvd.
Hollywood, FL 33020
(305) 925-7607

FABRICATOR

Ryan-Markland Signs, Inc.

This 7 x 8-ft. sign identifies a nightclub in Nassau, The Bahamas. The 10-in.-deep sign stands 19 ft. above grade. Fabricated from aluminum, the sign features pan-embossed polycarbonate faces. "The Zoo" is open channel letters with purple neon inside; purple neon also surrounds both sides of the sign. A 48-in. aluminum skirt covers the pole and has an imitation stucco finish.

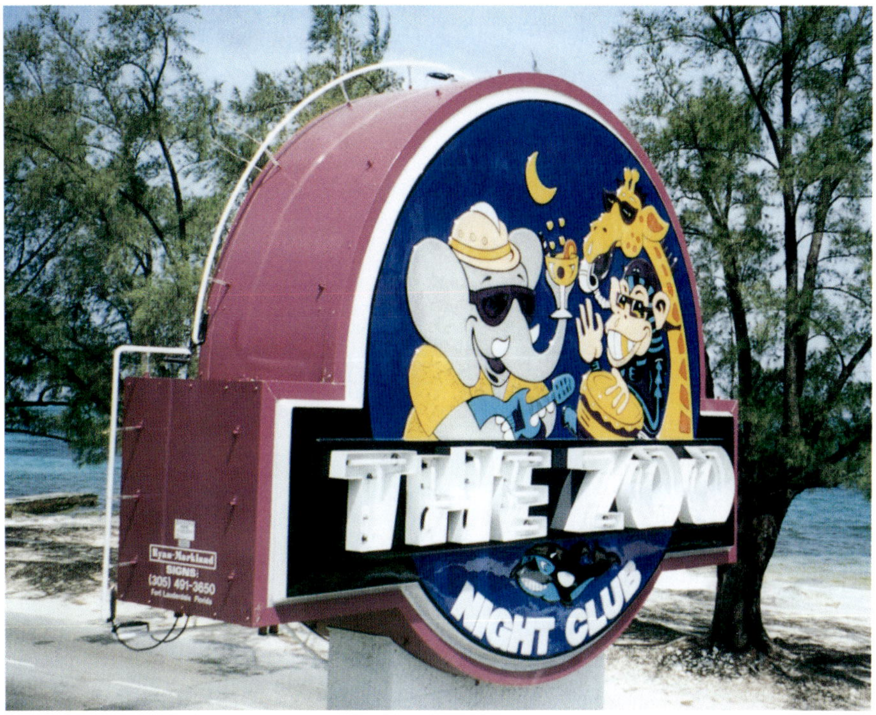

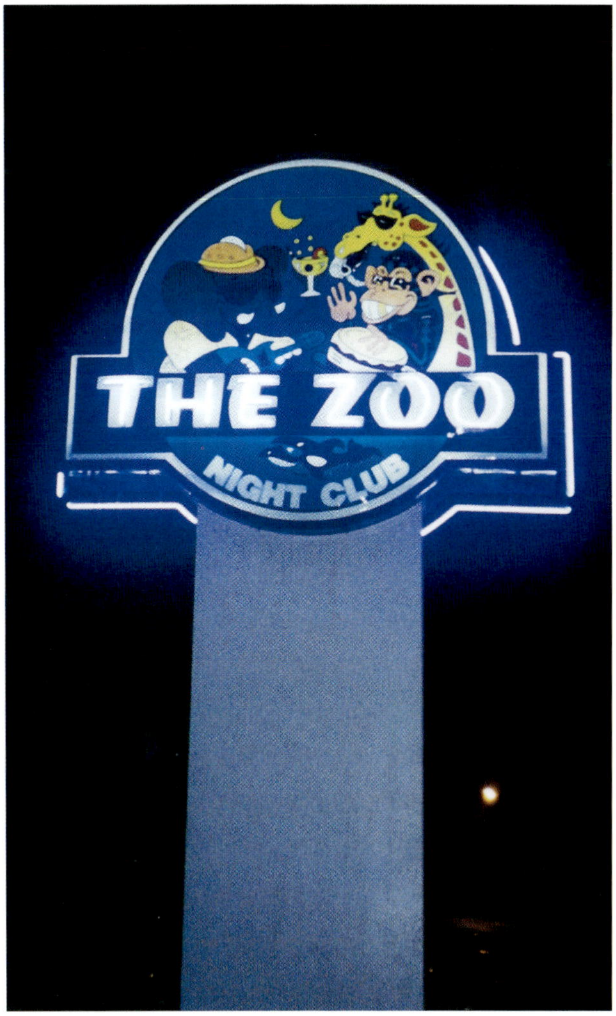

EXISTING LOGO / FREESTANDING OR GROUND

ELECTRIC

DESIGNER

Ron Hull
Gordon Sign Co.
2930 W. 9th Ave.
Denver, CO 80204
(303) 629-6121

FABRICATOR

Gordon Sign Co.

The top portion of the "Volant" sign is a fabricated metal face and cabinet. It features a textured finish and is painted. The "Volant" copy and logo are dimensional 5-in. deep pan channel letters with Plexiglas® faces. The top is illuminated with neon.

The bottom portion features a 3M ScotchPrint® pictorial on a white flexible face. A fabricated metal cabinet has bleed retainers. The interior is illuminated with T-12 lamps.

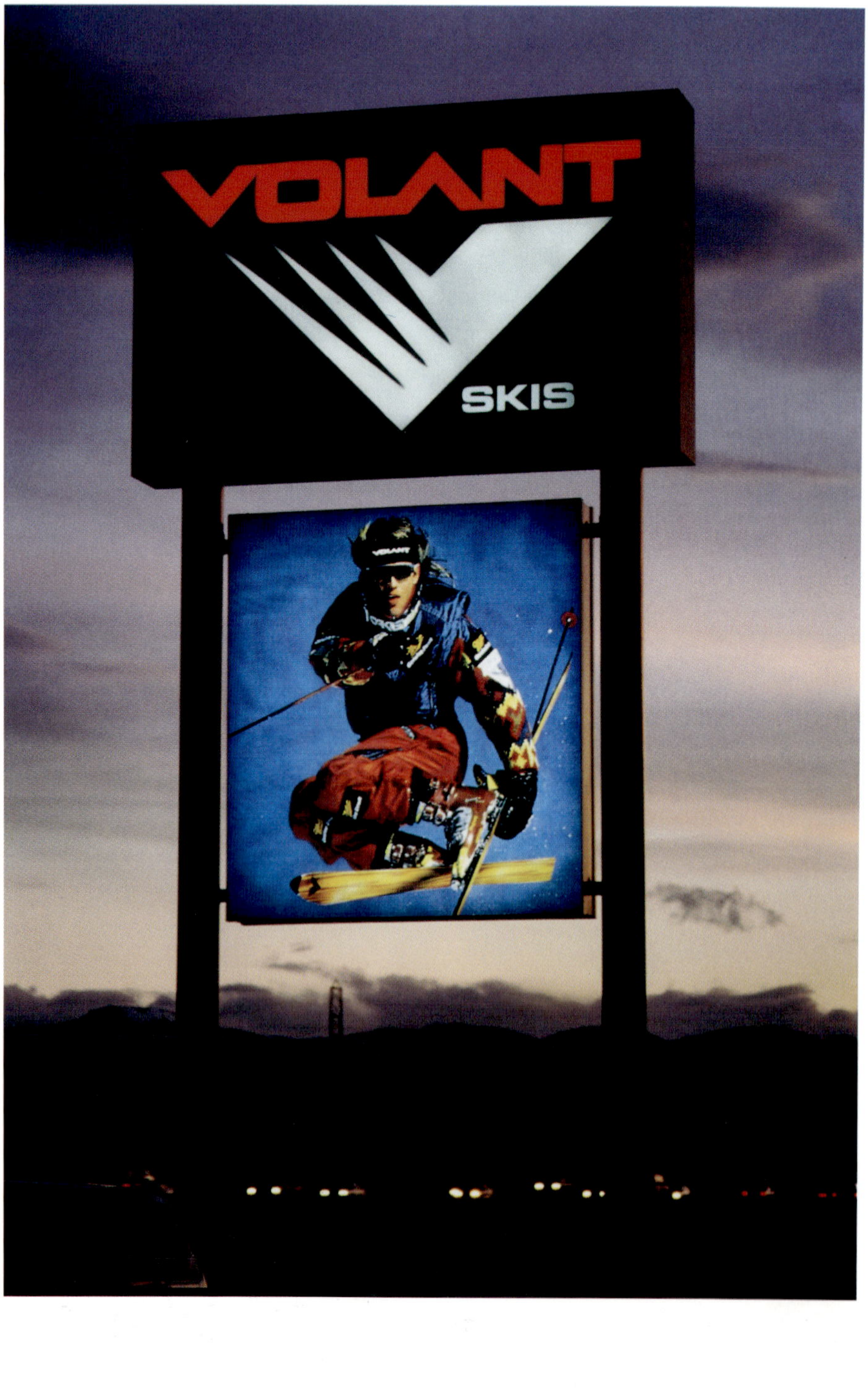

DESIGNER

Dawna Stromsoe Design
11734 Bellagio Rd.
Los Angeles, CA 90049
(310) 471-8917

FABRICATOR

Ad-Art Electric Sign Corp.
3133 N. Ad-Art Rd.
Stockton, CA 95215
(209) 931-0860

This single-face, freestanding, curved-face sign runs 76 x 132 ft. over the entrance display. Mounted on six poles, each 42 ft. in overall height, the 4-ft. channel metal letters are outlined with double-tube white neon and are mounted to an expanded metal mesh background. The 6 x 132-ft. fabricated metal frame is illuminated with one tube of blue and one of purple neon. The "Cineplex-Odeon" letters are open channel construction, illuminated with pink neon, and mounted to a horizontal bar raceway. Poles are striped with bright gold balls on top.

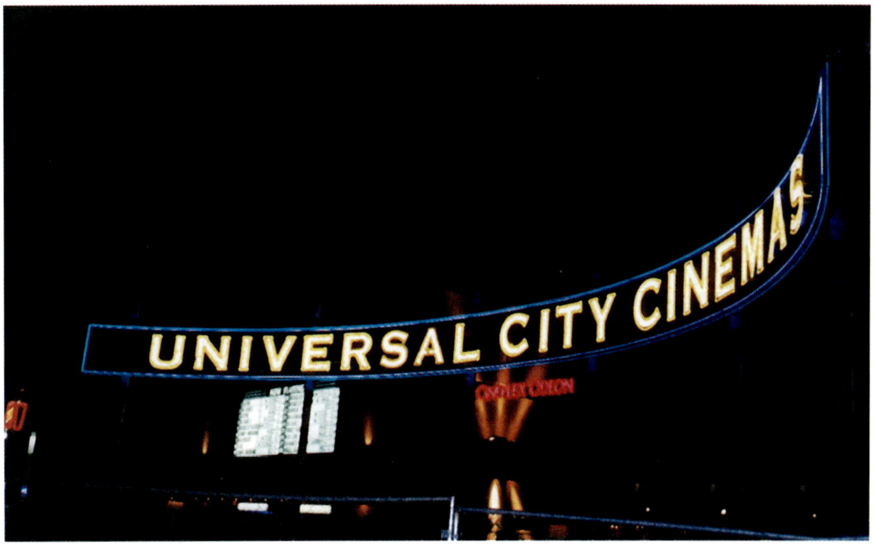

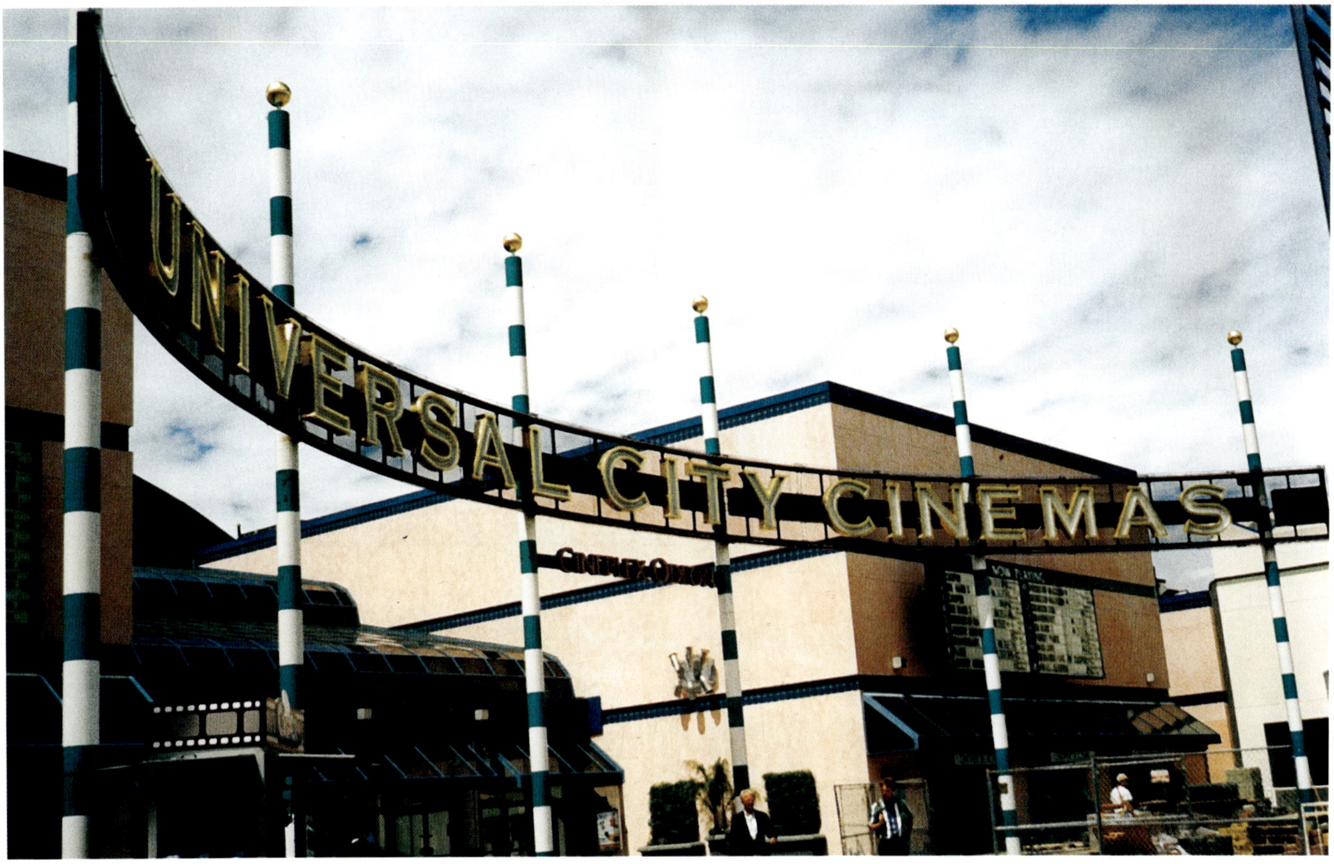

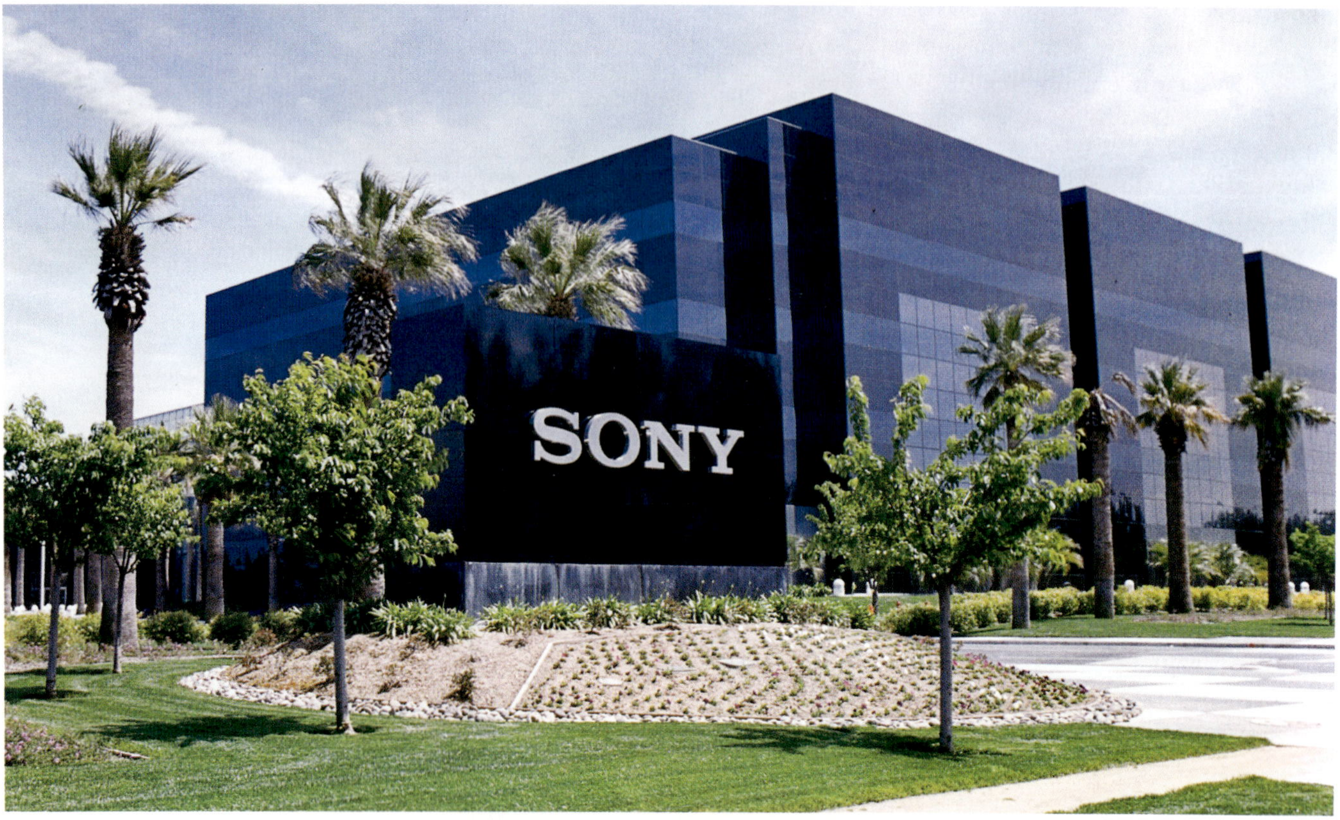

DESIGNER

Spectorgroup
3111 New Hyde Park Rd.
Northills, NY 11040
(516) 365-4240

FABRICATOR

Arrow Sign Co.
1051 46th Ave.
Oakland, CA 94601
(510) 533-7693

This entry monument for "Sony" is comprised of aluminum panels with exposed, ½-in. aluminum seams, and stainless-steel letters with white halo illumination.

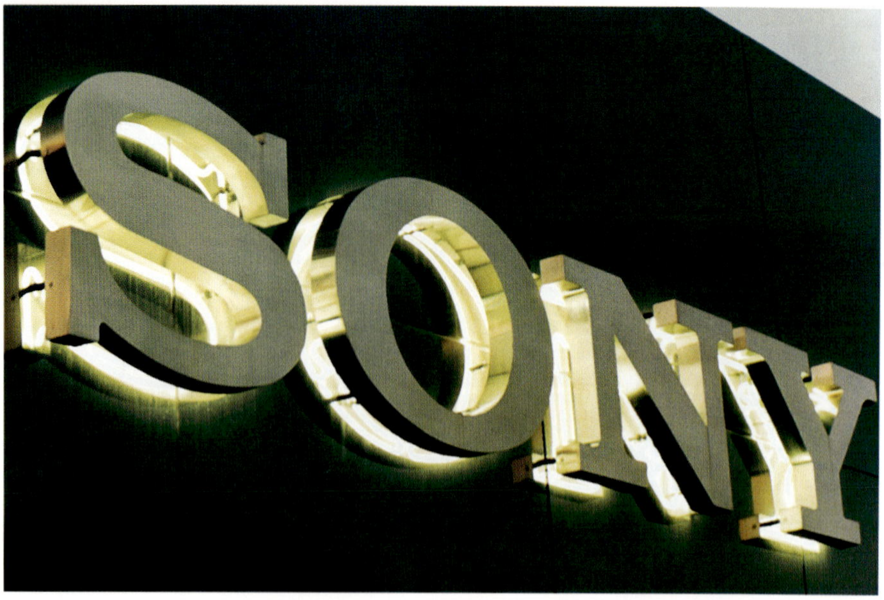

DESIGNER

Val Paul Taylor Design
1735 Westlake Ave. N.
Seattle, WA 98109

FABRICATOR

National Sign Corp.
1255 Westlake Ave. N.
Seattle, WA 98109
(206) 282-0700

This 6 x 10-ft., single-face neon wall sign utilizes fabricated aluminum for the open pan-channel letters, triangle, frame and the word plates. Rolled aluminum is used to create the triangle and the "Italian Seafood" name plates; the copy is routed out. Blue, orange, yellow-gold, white and turquoise neon are exposed, with additional neon behind the routed copy.

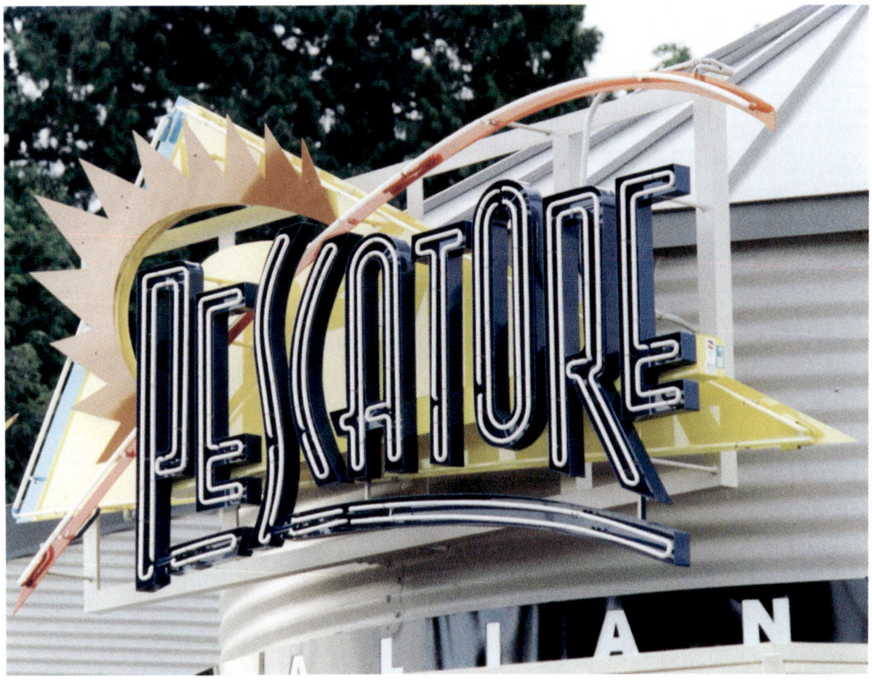

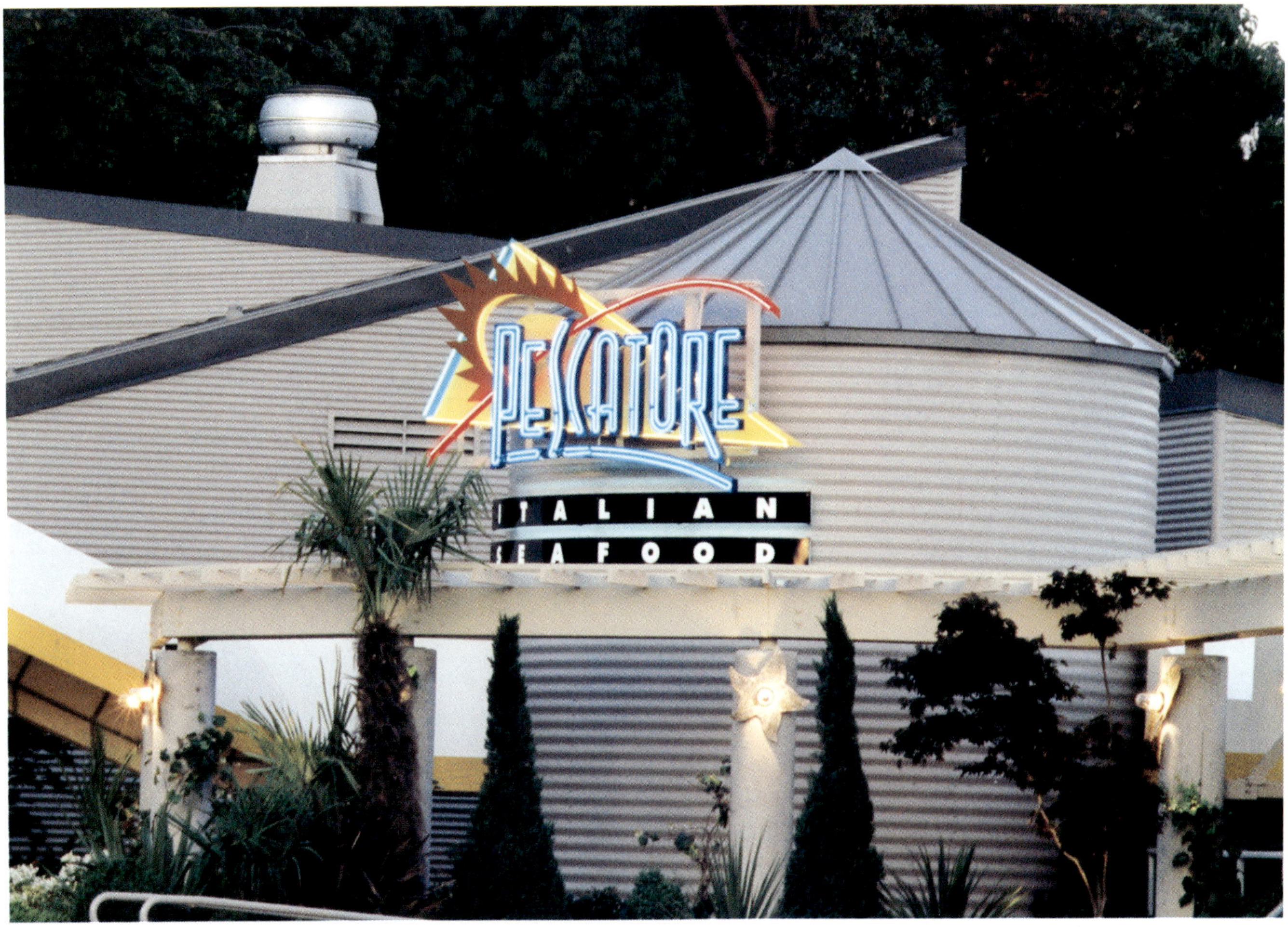

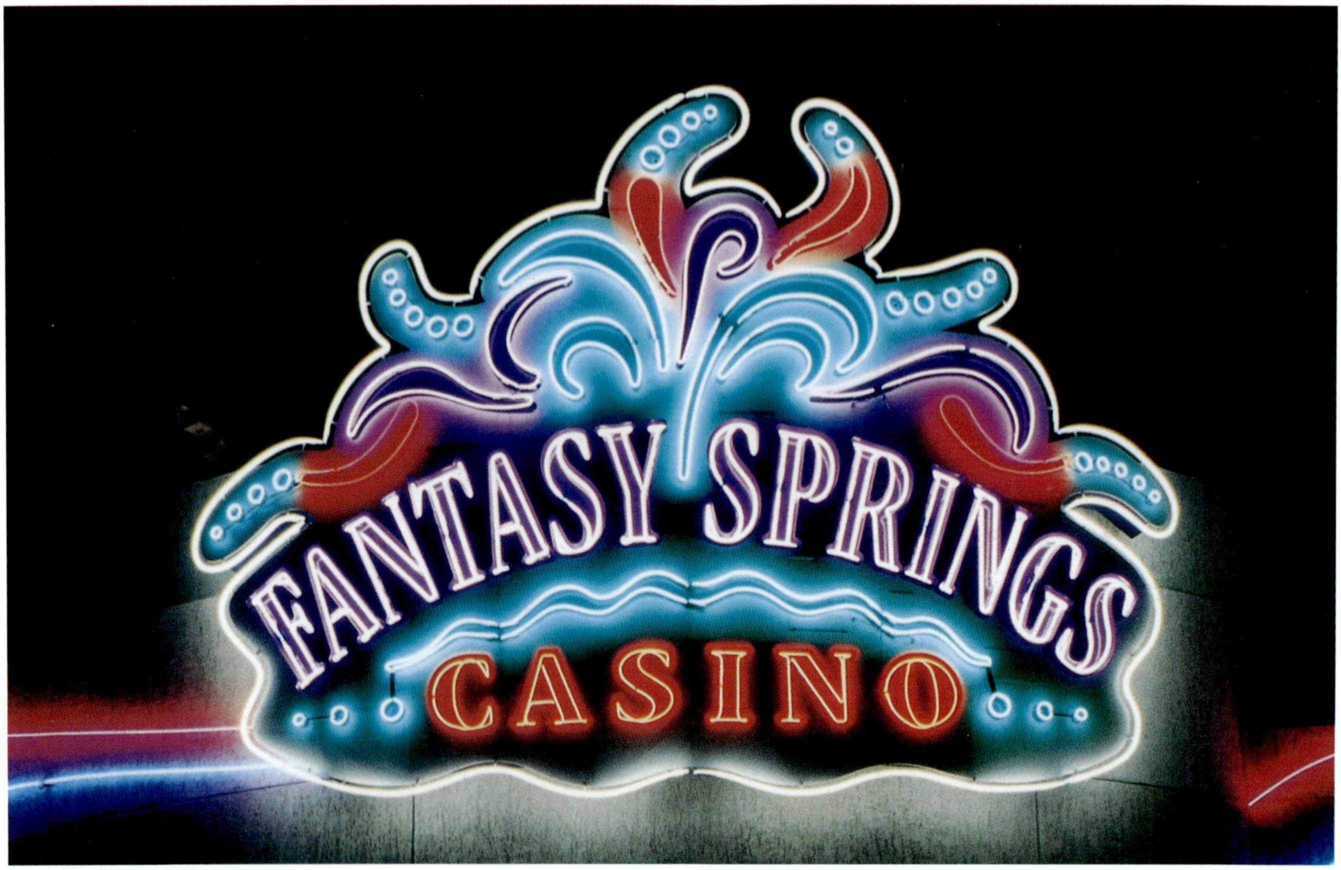

DESIGNER

Mark Mahan
13346 1st Ave. N.E.
Seattle, WA 98125
(206) 361-6600

FABRICATOR

Federal Sign
4602 North Ave.
Oceanside, CA 92056
(619) 941-0715

This single-face, curved, exterior wall sign uses sheetmetal construction with vinyl graphics. The exposed neon is animated to flash upward and outward.

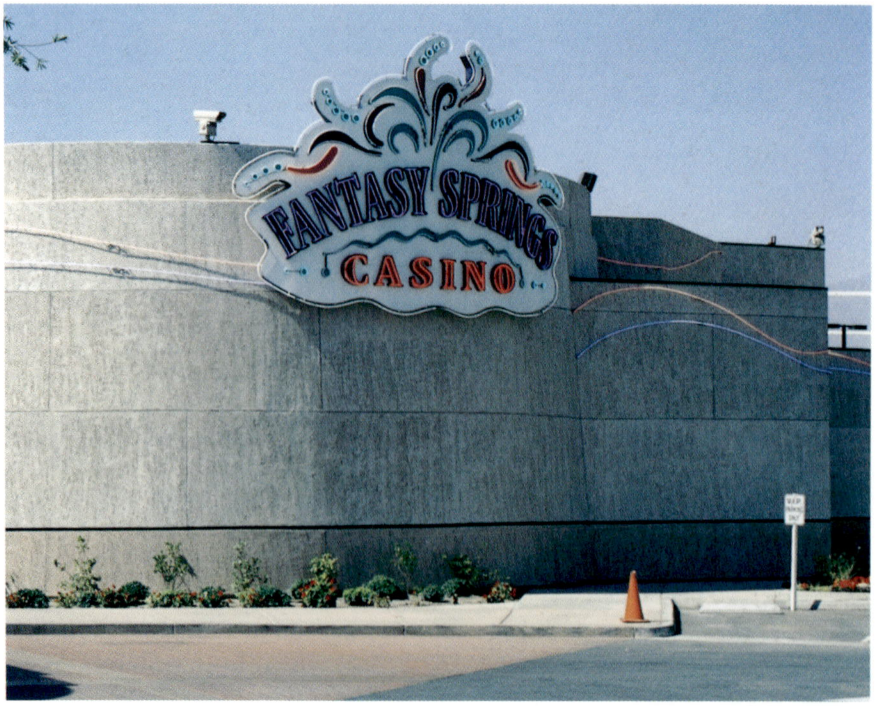

DESIGNERS

Lawrin Rosen
ARTeffects, Inc.
27 Britton Dr.
Bloomfield, CT 06002
(203) 242-0031

Rick Lopez
Peppercorns Grill
357 Main St.
Hartford, CT 06011
(203) 547-1714

FABRICATOR

ARTeffects, Inc.

This 4 x 4-ft. 8-in., double-face projecting sign has a face of 1-in.-thick Sign Foam® material sprayed with Zolatone #40-64 gray stone to mimic granite. The circle's white, exposed, 15mm argon creates a halo effect. The bottles have acrylic faces with frosted, surface-applied vinyl installed over multi-colored neon tubing. "Peppercorns" is white exposed neon; "Grill" is blue exposed neon, and the steel attachment arm is through-bolted to the brick facade.

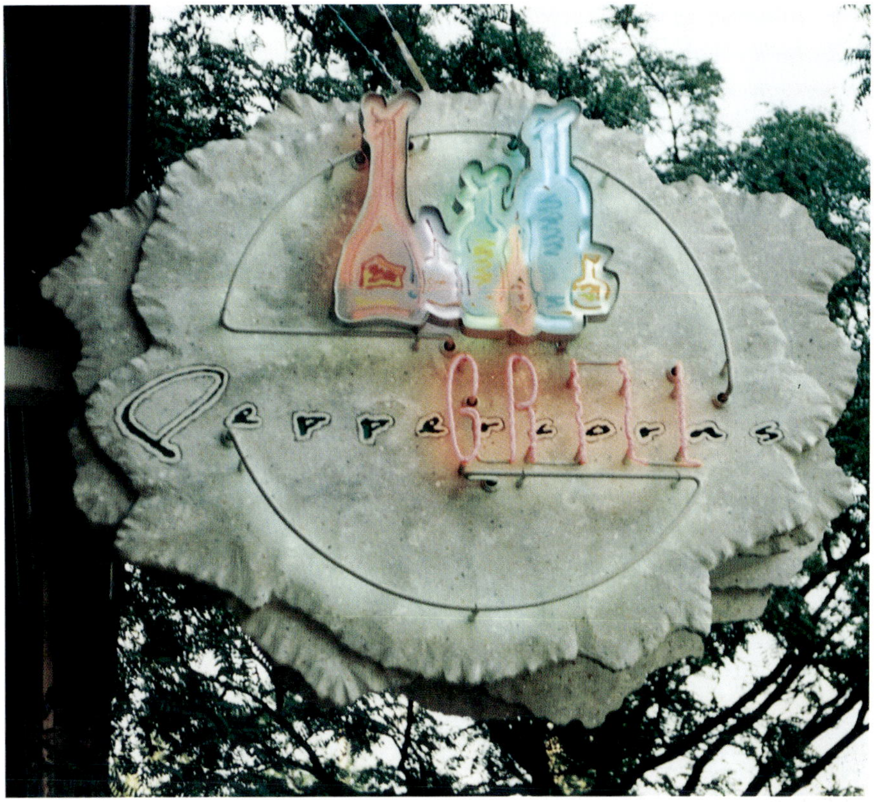

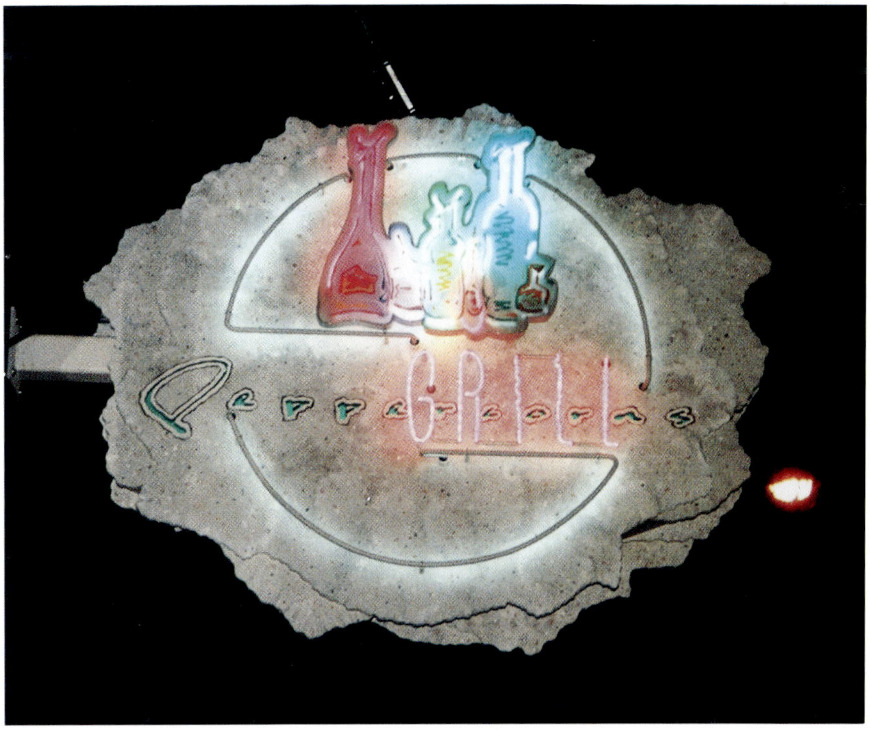

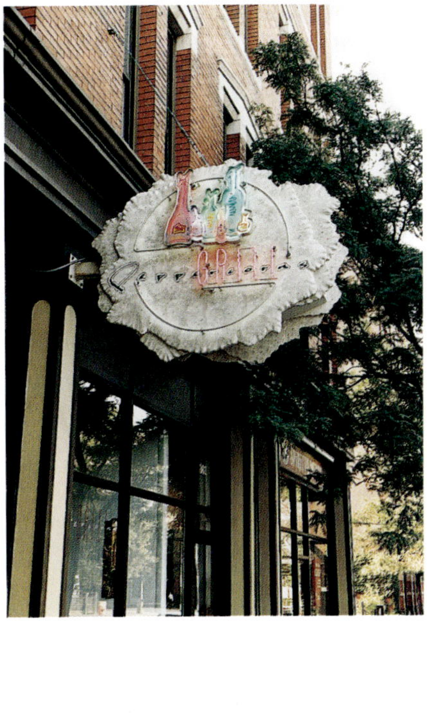

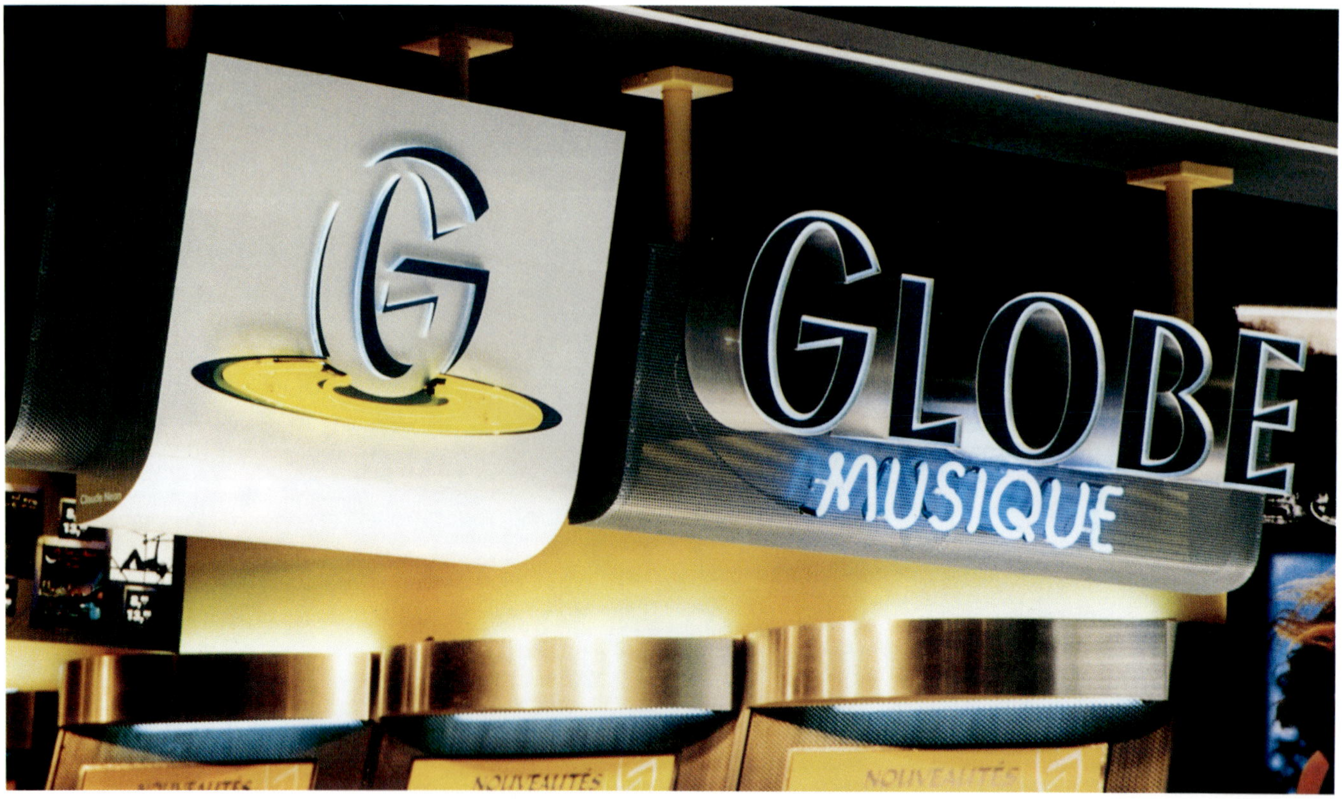

DESIGNER
Diane Fafard
Claude Neon Ltd.
(Div. of the Jim Pattison Sign Group)
1855 Hymus Blvd.
Dorval, QC, Canada H9P 1J8
(514) 856-7756

FABRICATOR
Claude Neon Ltd.

This suspended sign is in a shopping-mall interior. The "Globe" channel letters and "Musique" neon tubing are affixed to a structure covered in perforated aluminum. The "G" logo is cut from clear ½-in. plastic and cemented to a plastic shell covered in vinyl that has a brushed-aluminum finish. The edge and blue face of the "G," as well as the blue contour on the "CD" are backlit. A gold neon tube highlights the "CD."

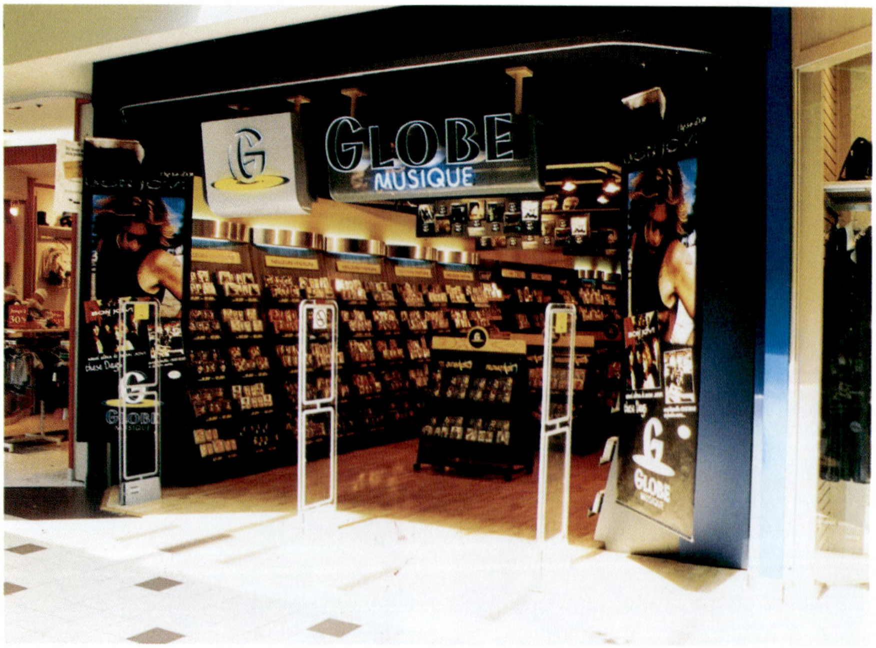

DESIGNERS

Larry Westdal (logo)
1310 65th St.
Emeryville, CA 94607

Eric Flynn
Bud J. Lawson
Sign Designs, Inc.
204 Campus Way
Modesto, CA 95352
(209) 524-4484

FABRICATOR

Sign Designs, Inc.

This curved aluminum sign is 20 ft. long, 3 ft. tall and 42 in. deep. The letters are push-through, with fluorescent illumination and directional flood lamps underneath.

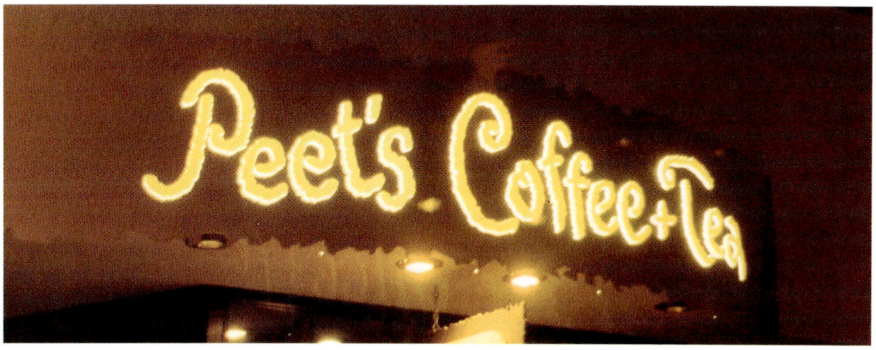

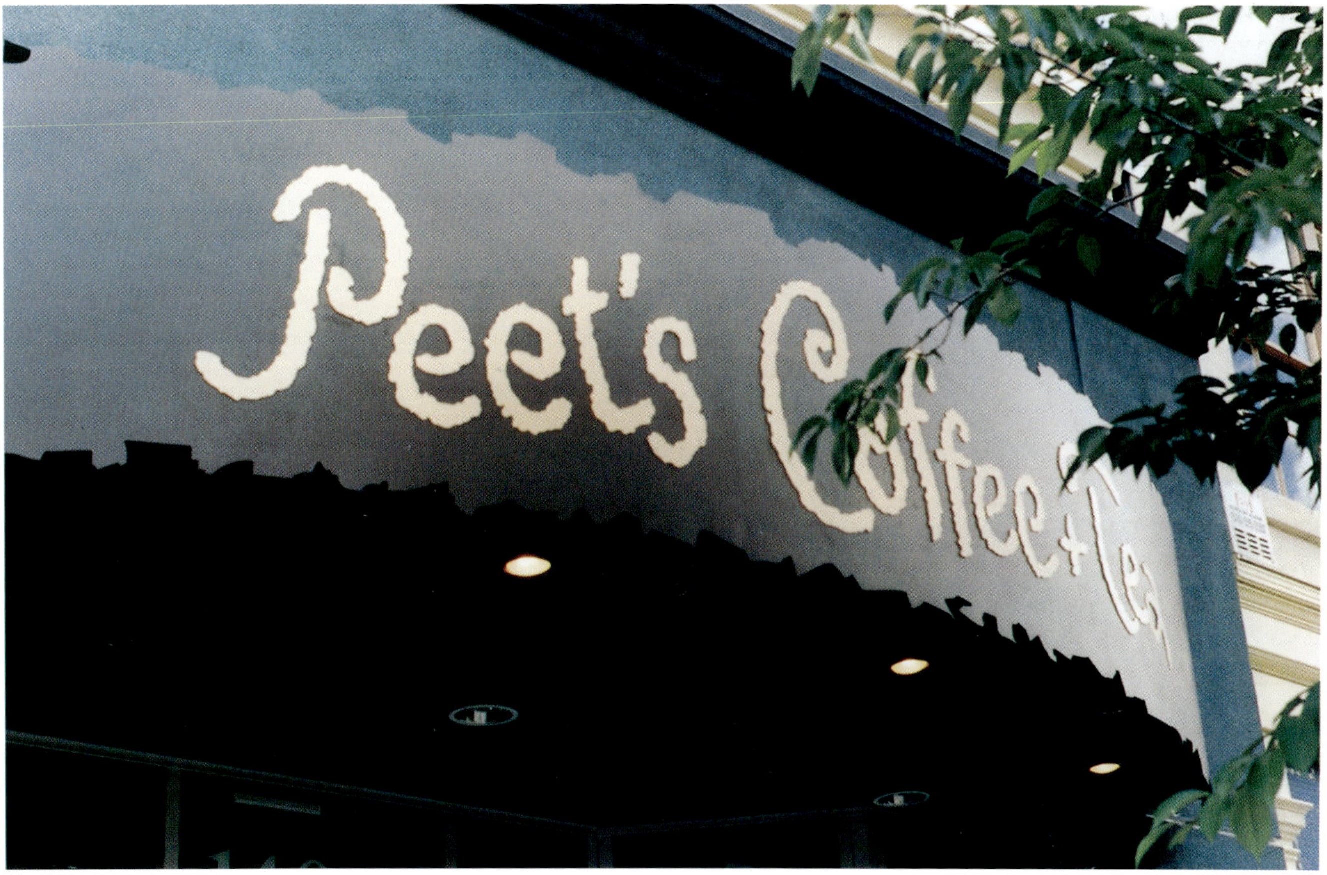

EXISTING LOGO / MOUNTED OR PROJECTING

ELECTRIC

DESIGNER

Kurt Schaeffler
Absolute Signs & Serv.
1311 Commerce Ln.
Jupiter, FL 33458
(407) 744-8030

FABRICATORS

Absolute Signs & Serv.

JTS Signcrafters
815 W. Indiantown Rd.
Jupiter, FL 33458
(407) 743-8976

Made for a rock and roll nightclub, this 6 x 15-ft., single-faced sign is internally illuminated. It has a Lexan®-embossed face with 36-in. Lexan half hemisphere. There are 15mm clear red neon rings around the hemisphere connected to two transformers that are in line with sound control circuitry, which interacts with the music in the club.

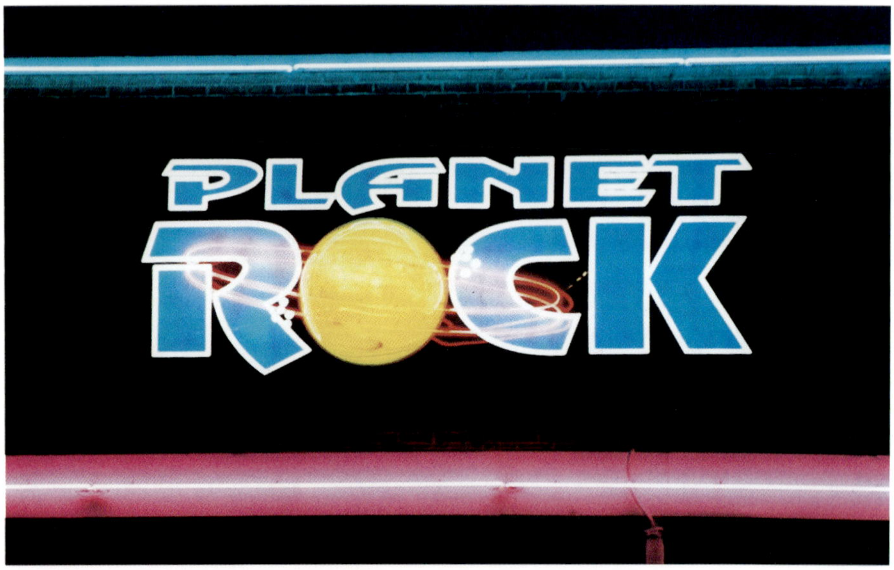

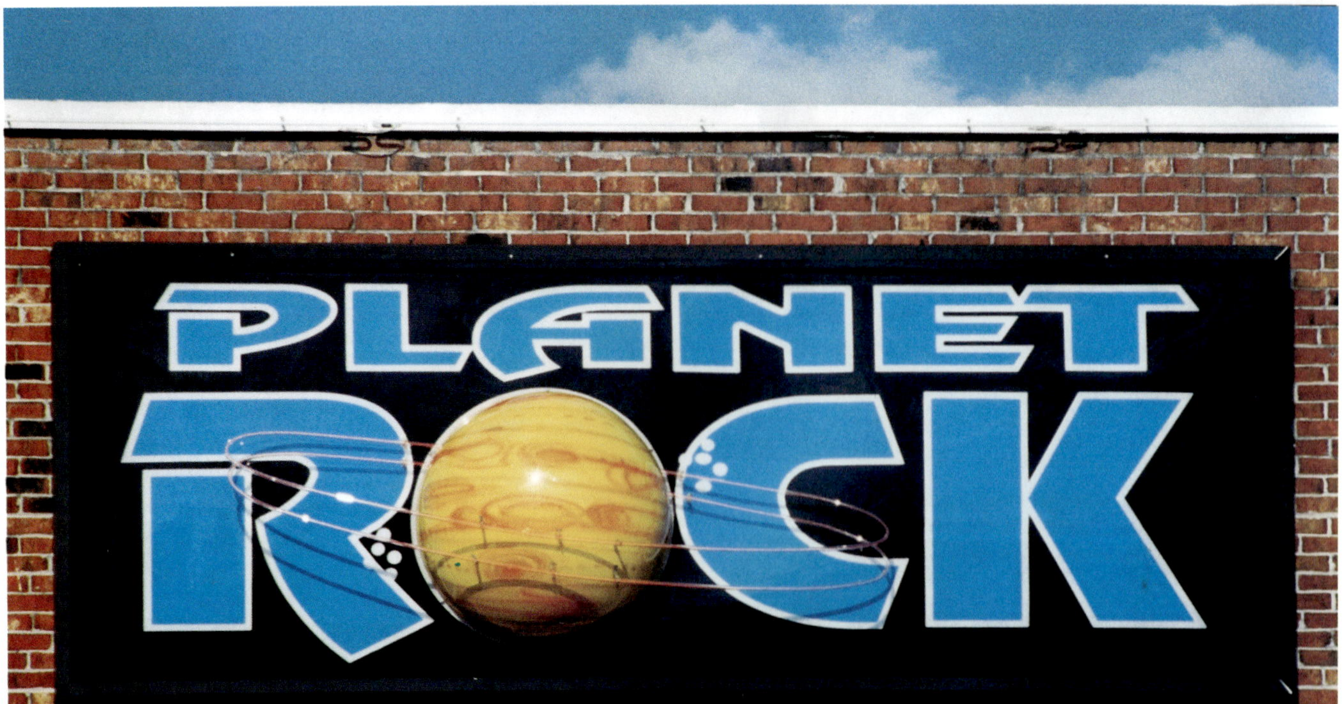

DESIGNER

Ultraneon Sign Co.
5458 Complex St. #401
San Diego, CA 92123
(619) 569-6716

FABRICATOR

Ultraneon Sign Co.

This 12 x 6-ft. aluminum sign has a curved base which projects 18 in. from the wall of the building. The combination of reverse channel letters and exposed neon over a patina finished copper strip adds a sparkling effect to the brushed aluminum background shapes.

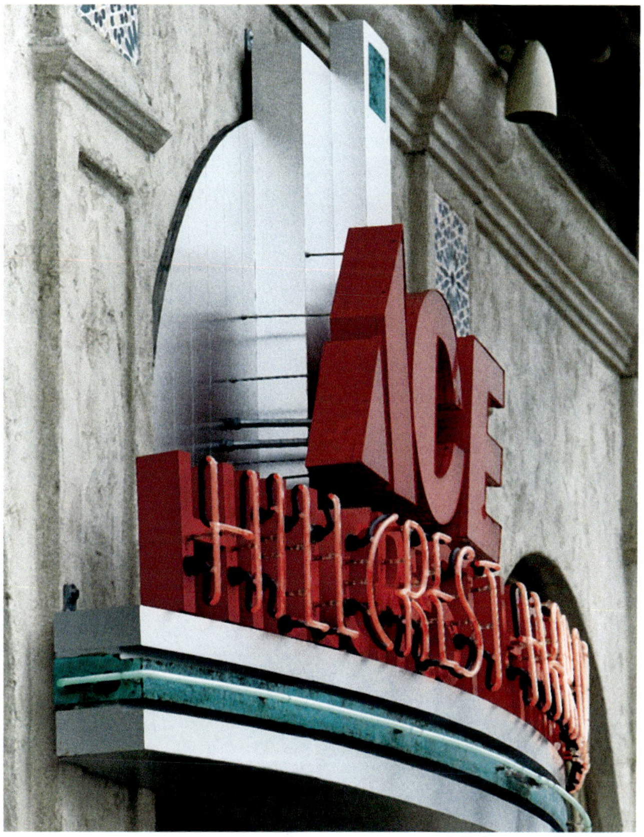

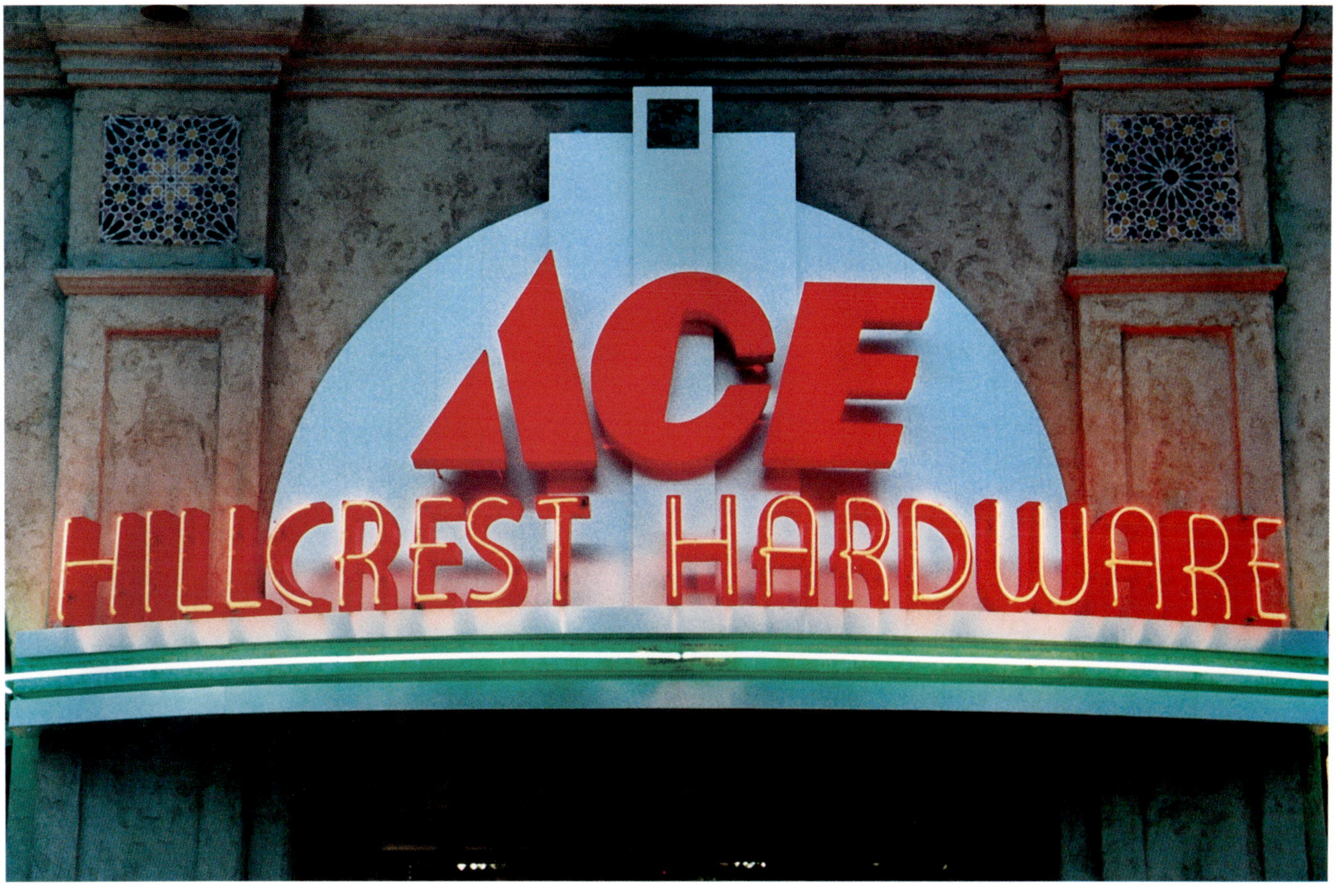

SIGN SYSTEMS

ELECTRIC

DESIGNERS

Sussman/Prejza & Co., Inc.
3960 Ince Blvd.
Culver City, CA 90230
(310) 836-3939

Arrow Sign Co. (construction design)

FABRICATORS

Arrow Sign Co.
1051 46th Ave.
Oakland, CA 94601
(510) 533-7693

Romark Iron Works
3250 Hollis
Oakland, CA 94608
(510) 658-0588

This system identifies tenants of the East Baybridge Center. The 180-ft.-tall main tower is a steel structure. The letter "E" is aluminum plate with exposed neon; the letter "O" is rolled rectangular tubing with an exposed neon outline. The tenant copy is self-contained letters on rolled plate aluminum. The Home Depot sign has a flexible-face bleed with a face retainer. The vertical sign is aluminum plate with vinyl copy. The projecting arm is for a future tenant. The smaller tower sign has the same construction as the larger tower, without the illumination.

The pergola (walkway) signs are extruded aluminum frames with aluminum faces. The copy is routed out and backed with white Plexiglas® acrylic. The internal illumination is white neon. The cabinets are 4 in. deep.

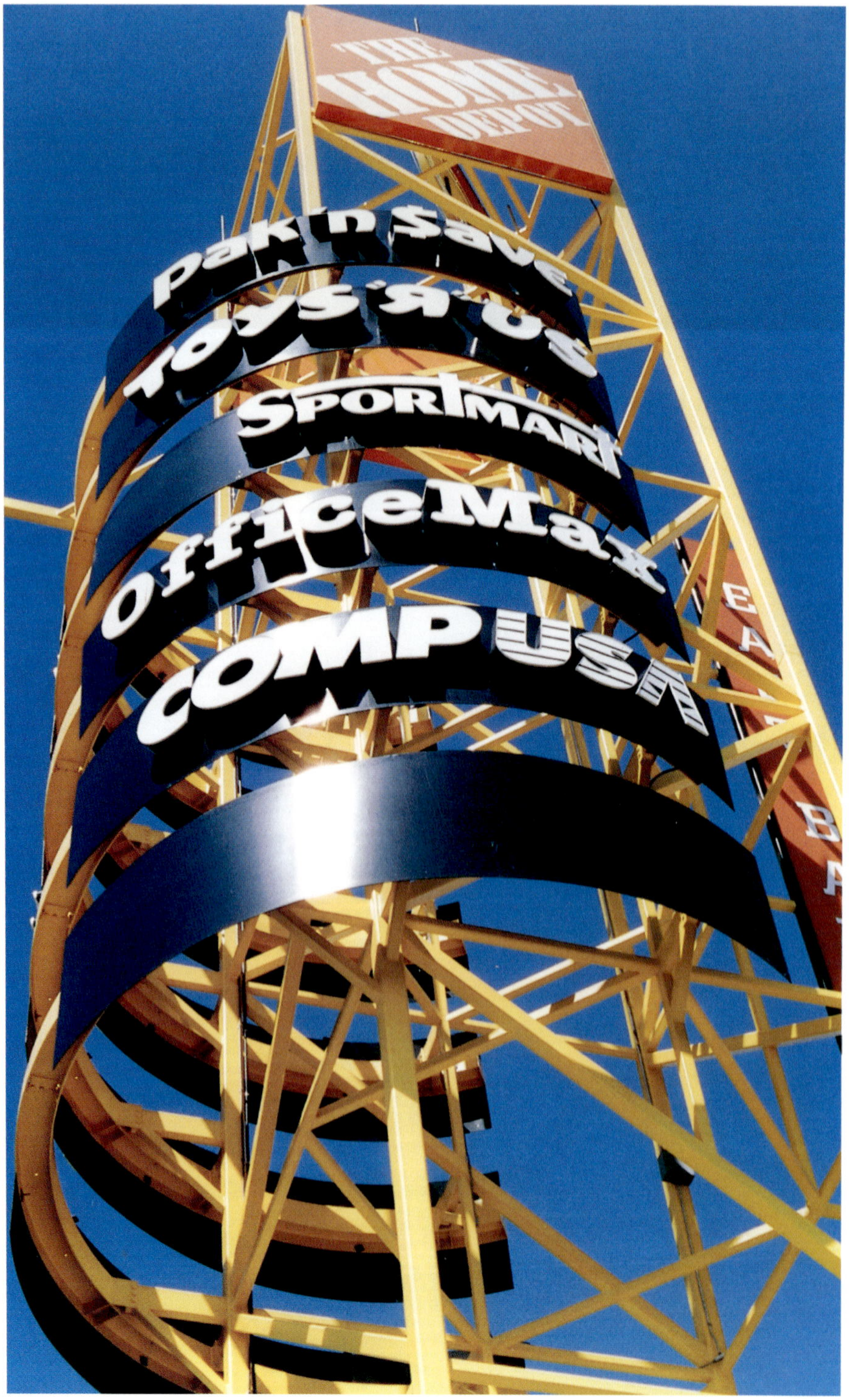

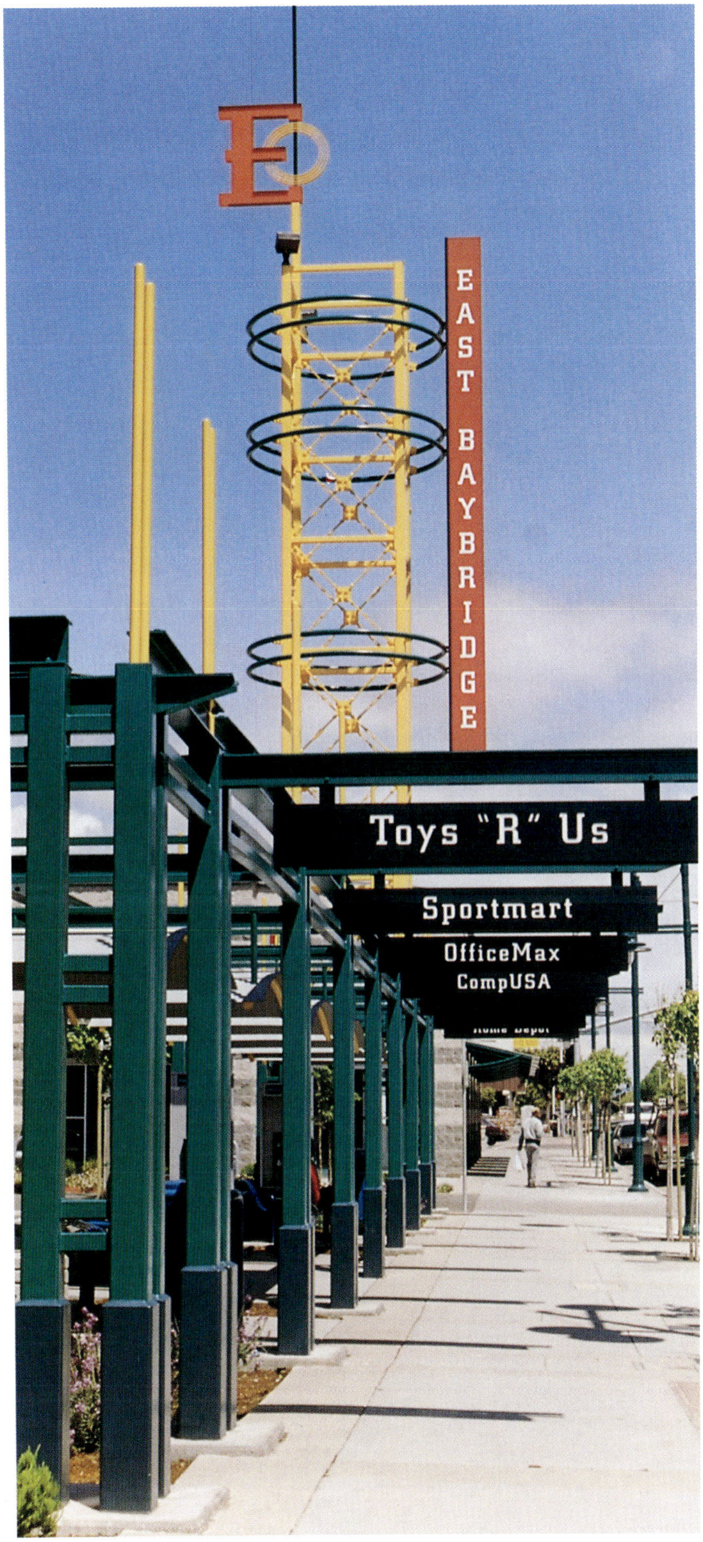
EAST BAYBRIDGE
Toys "R" Us
Sportmart
OfficeMax
CompUSA

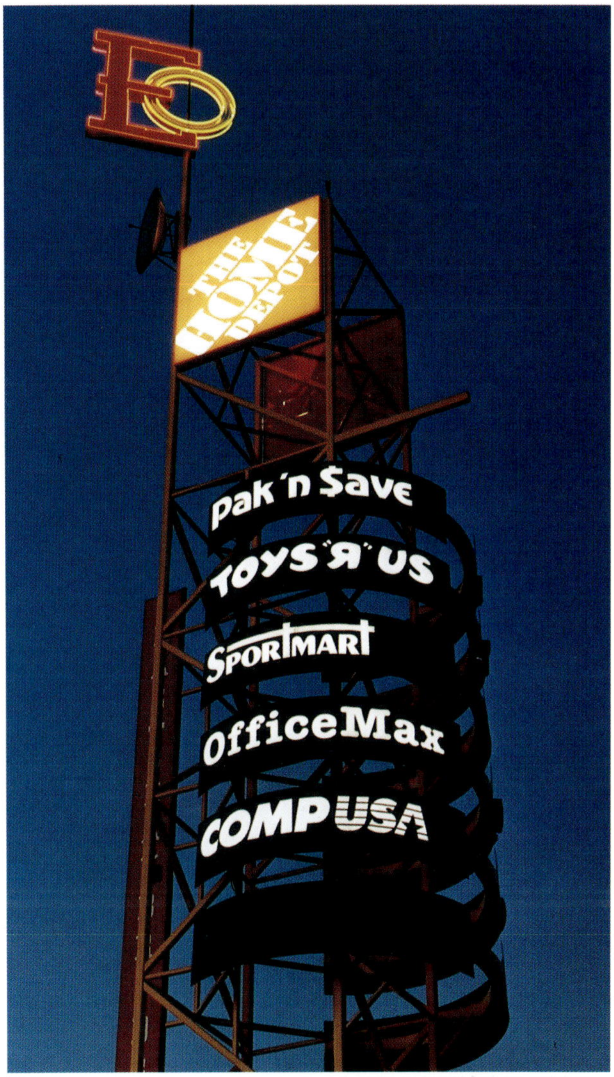
THE HOME DEPOT
Pak 'n Save
TOYS "R" US
SPORTMART
OfficeMax
COMPUSA

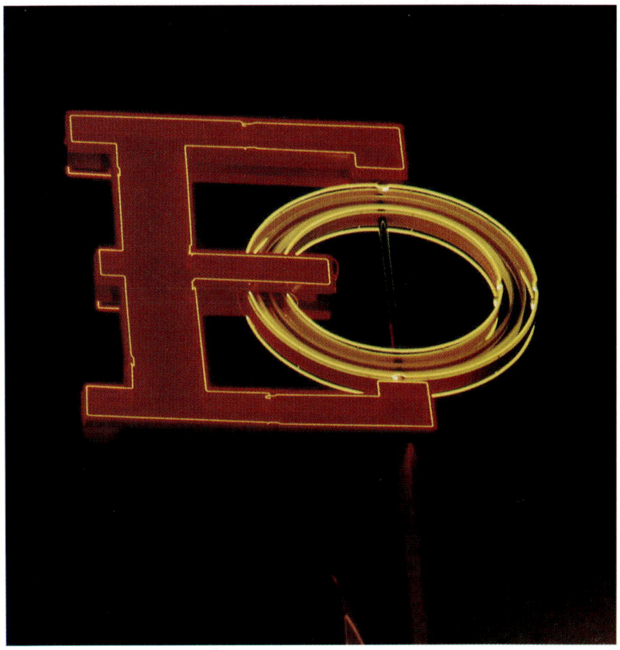

ELECTRIC

DESIGNER

Bob Lee
United Studios Sign Group
2120 North County Rd. #427
Longwood, FL 32750
(407) 831-3484

FABRICATOR

United Studios Sign Group

The Waterways is an apartment community located next to a large body of water. The 10 x 10-ft. original-logo main ID sign features push-through, edge-lit acrylic with polished aluminum copy. It includes a double-sided waterfall element backed with deep-purple neon illumination. Blue coloring was added to the water for a richer aesthetic effect. Secondary illuminated directional signs, non-illuminated signs and regulatory signs (all approximately 3 x 4 ft.) mimic these color and typestyle choices, along with logo placement when appropriate. All of the signs are made from welded aluminum with concealed fasteners. The complete sign, waterfalls and the pumping and chlorination systems were designed and installed by United Studios.

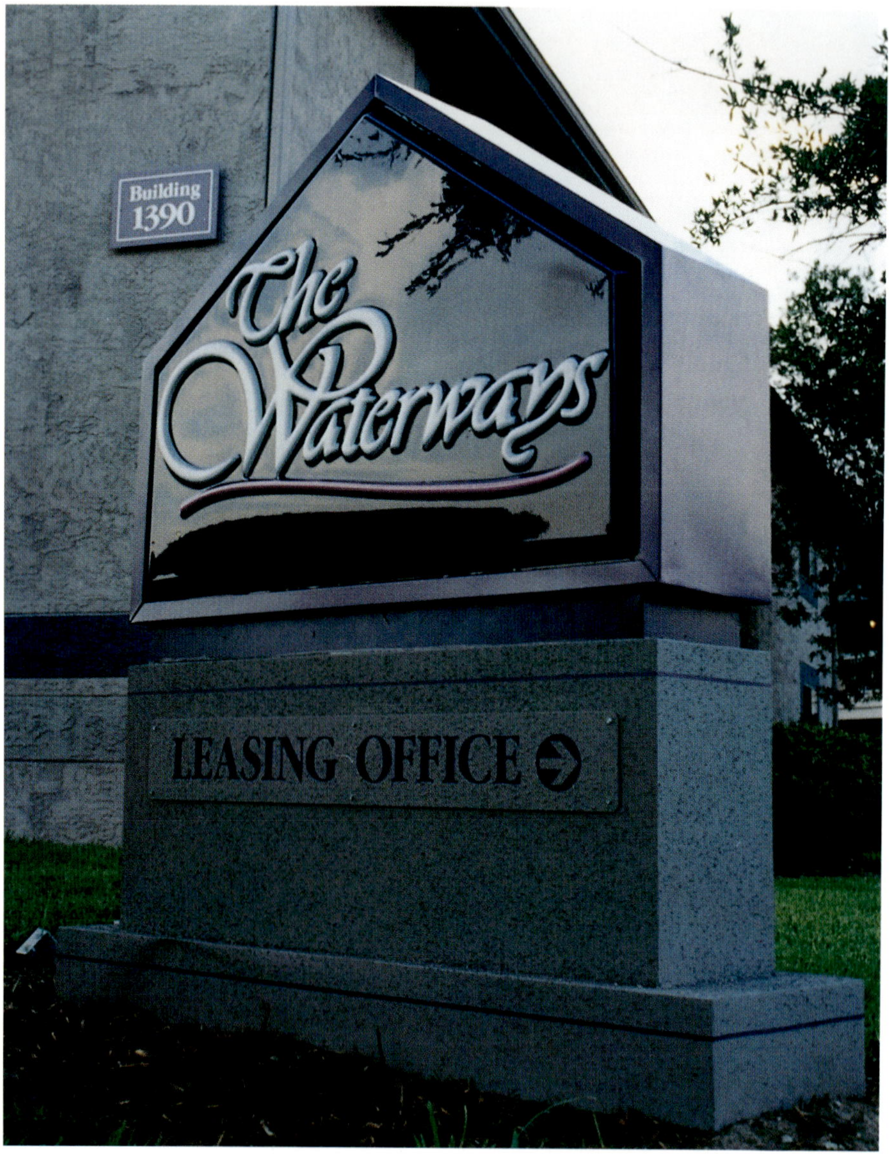

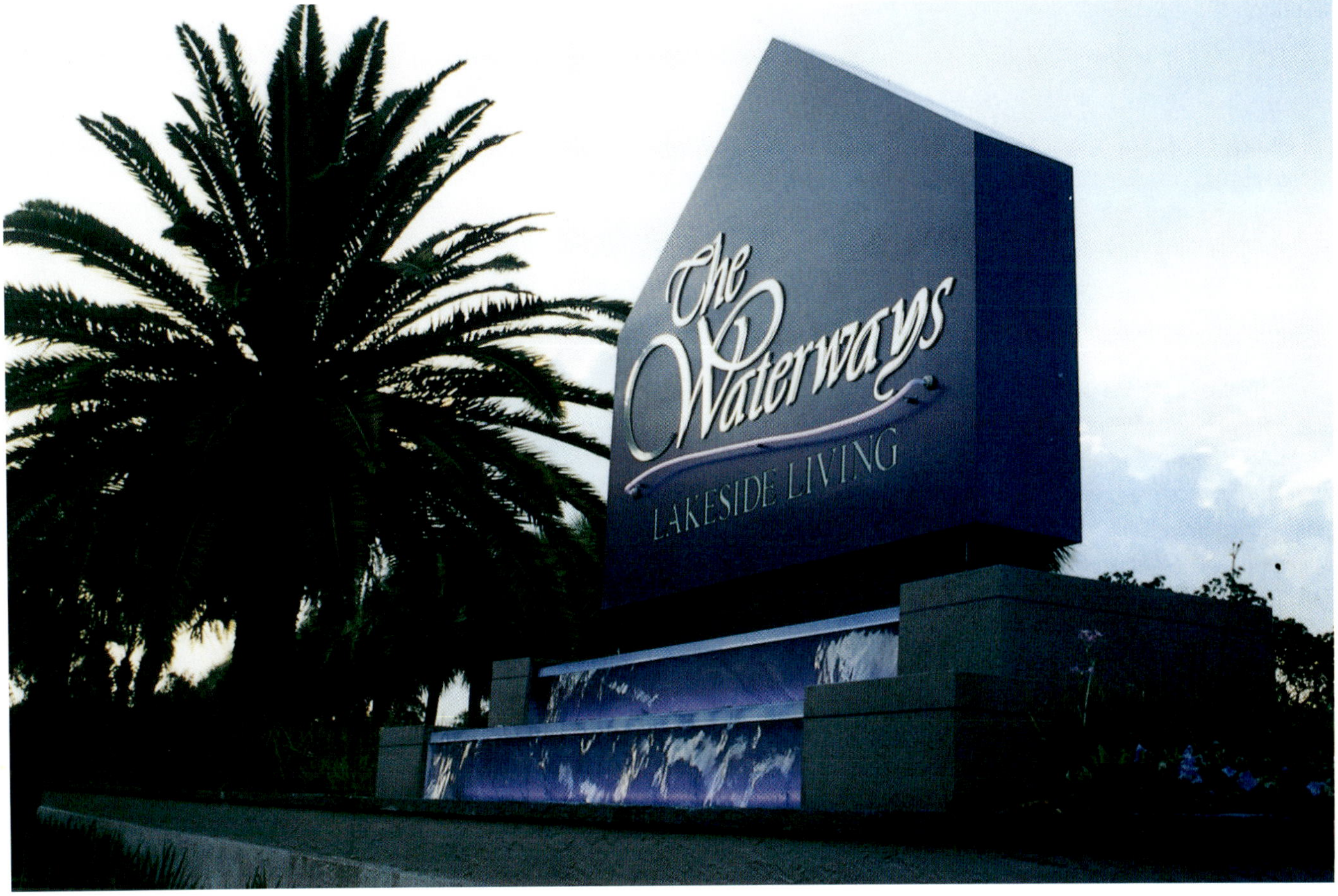
The Waterways
LAKESIDE LIVING

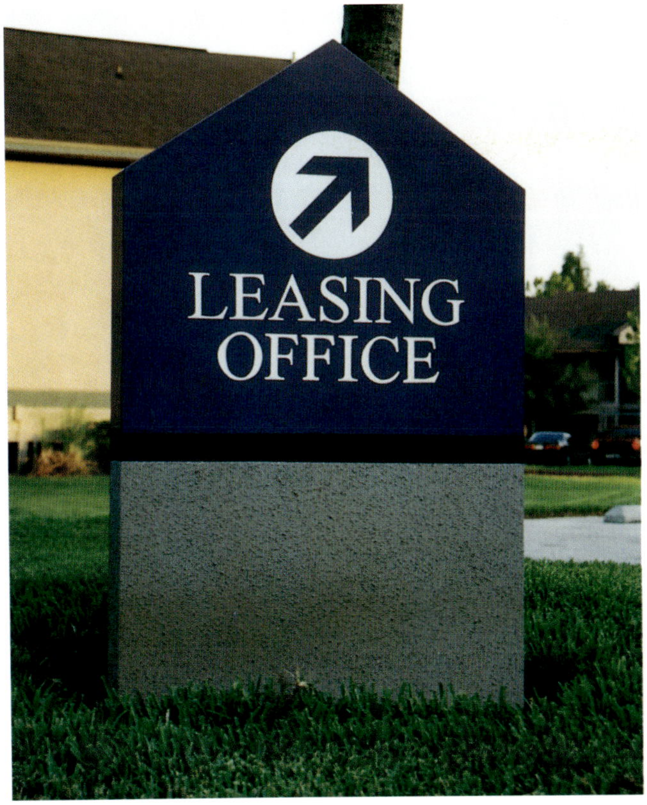
LEASING
OFFICE

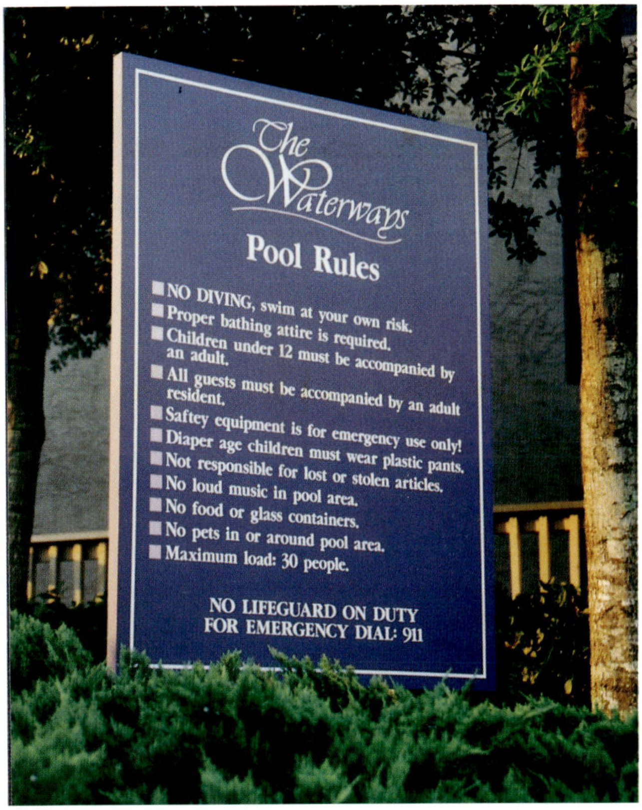
The Waterways
Pool Rules
NO DIVING, swim at your own risk.
Proper bathing attire is required.
Children under 12 must be accompanied by an adult.
All guests must be accompanied by an adult resident.
Saftey equipment is for emergency use only!
Diaper age children must wear plastic pants.
Not responsible for lost or stolen articles.
No loud music in pool area.
No food or glass containers.
No pets in or around pool area.
Maximum load: 30 people.
NO LIFEGUARD ON DUTY
FOR EMERGENCY DIAL: 911

SIGN SYSTEMS ELECTRIC

DESIGNERS

Charlie Stroud
Rick Cardinio
Arrow Sign Co.
1051 46th Ave.
Oakland, CA 94601
(510) 533-7693

FABRICATOR

Arrow Sign Co.

Arrow produced this system for a satellite wagering service. The National Orange wall sign is exposed neon on an aluminum cabinet with routed-out copy and internal neon illumination. The ceiling-mounted sign has pushed-through copy lit with emerald-green neon. The Executive Club sign has a prefinished aluminum cove, a polished copper finish, Avonite® letters and a logo that's inlaid with copper details. Its emerald-green neon is exposed. The teletheatre waves feature ½-in. fiber-optic lighting with a ¾-in. bullnose overlay on two separate illuminators. Sports Bar and Concessions have exposed neon and flat, cut-out acrylic.

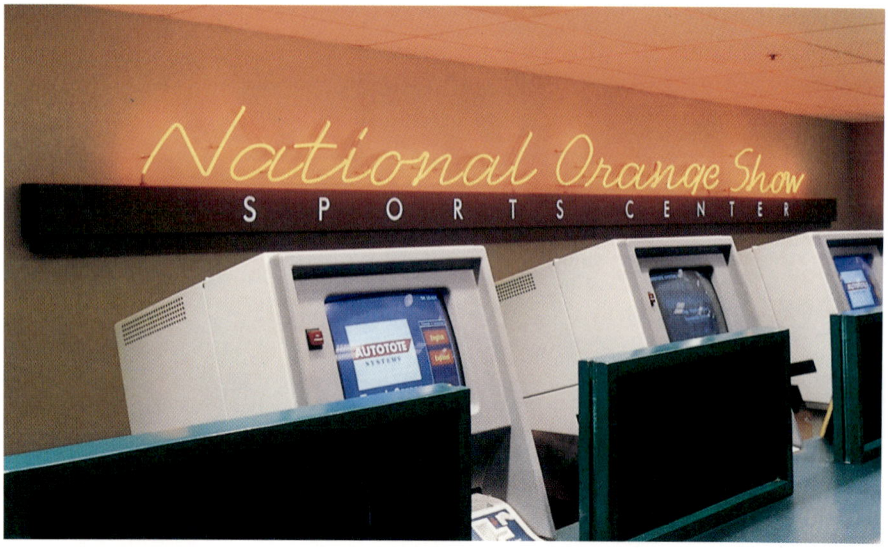

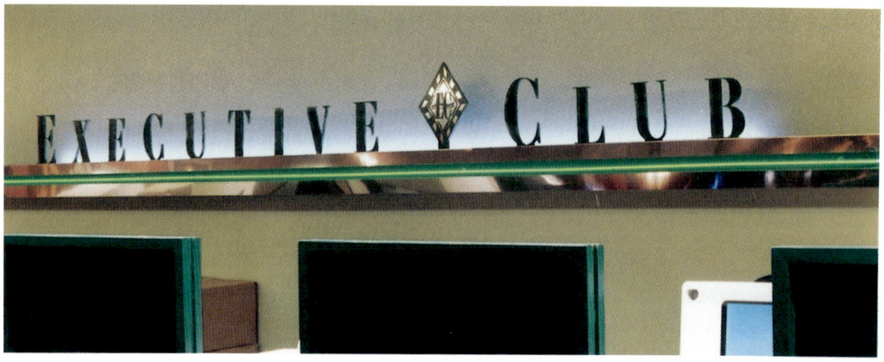

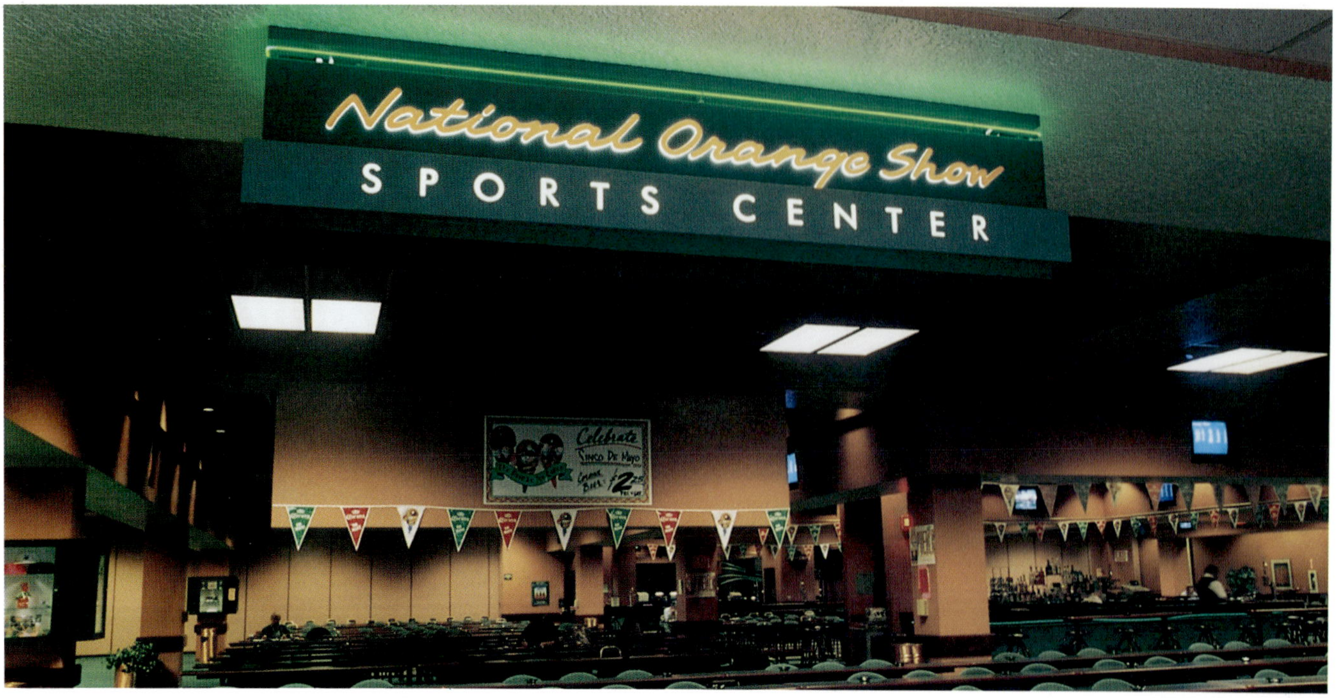

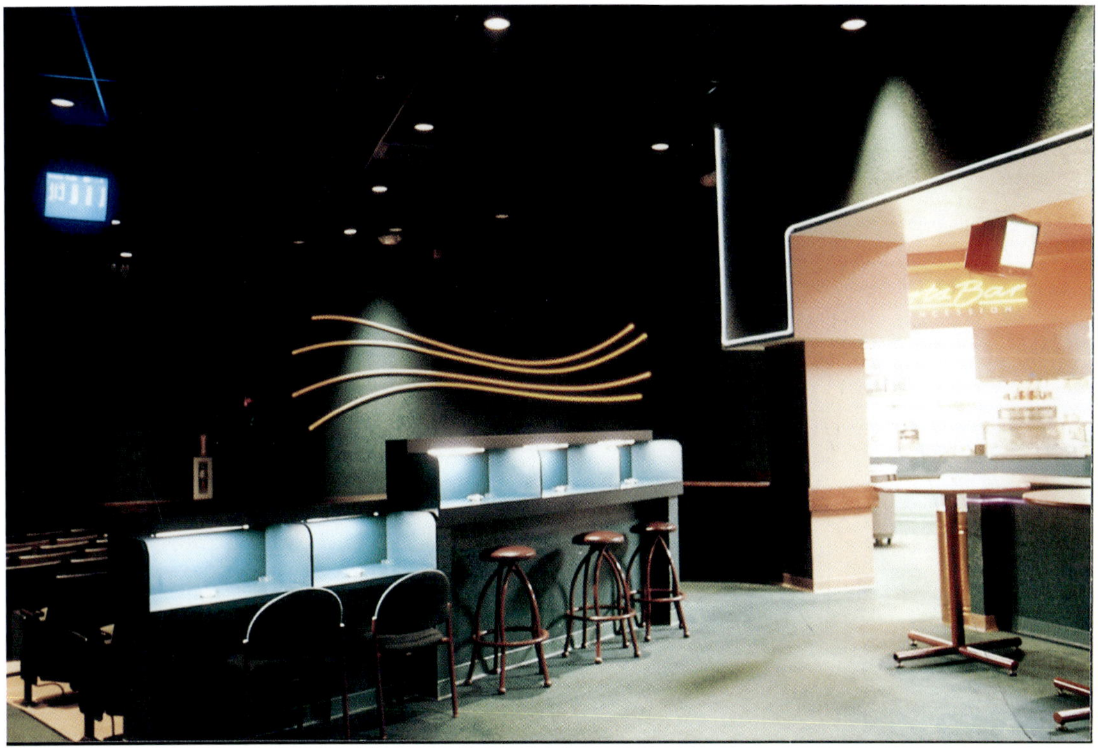

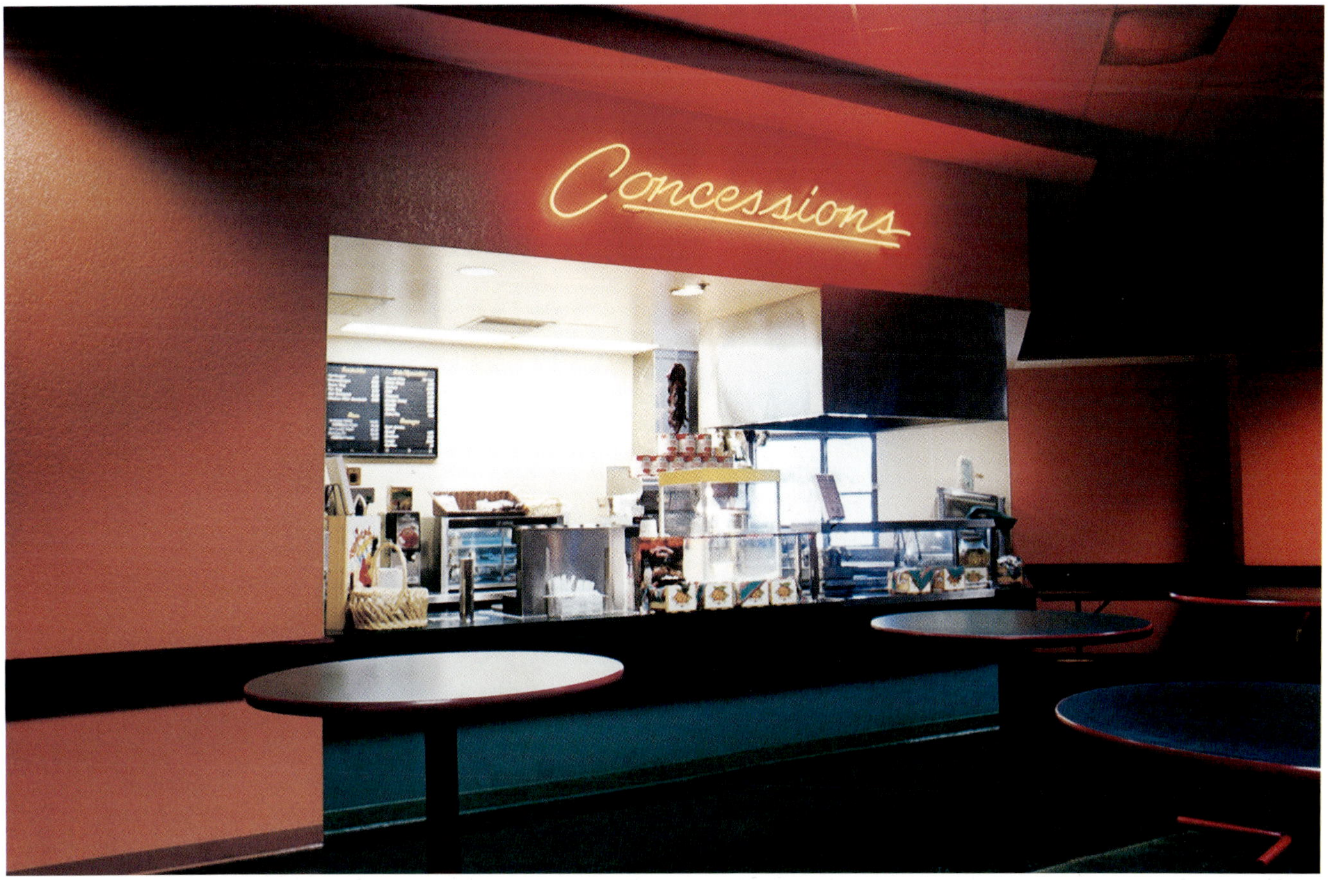
Concessions

DESIGNER

Mark Mahan
13346 1st. Ave. N.E.
Seattle, WA 98125
(206) 361-6600

FABRICATORS

Federal Sign
4602 North Ave.
Oceanside, CA 92056
(619) 941-0715

NBBJ Architects
111 S. Jackson St.
Seattle, WA 98104
(206) 223-5025

The storefront sign for this beauty-aid store has ¼-in.-thick waterjet-cut aluminum letters that are powder-coated black. They're mounted to the glass with VHB® tape. The grass pattern on the ¼-in. Solex glass® is etched second-surface. The light diffuser is a formed, Lexan polycarbonate light shell. Fluorescent "U" lamps provide the illumination. The in-store Aromatics and Skincare glass signs are ¼-in., waterjet-cut glass adhered to Solex glass with VHB tape. The Natural Colors and Custom Fragrance letters are fabricated like the storefront sign, and are pegged off the fixture crown molding.

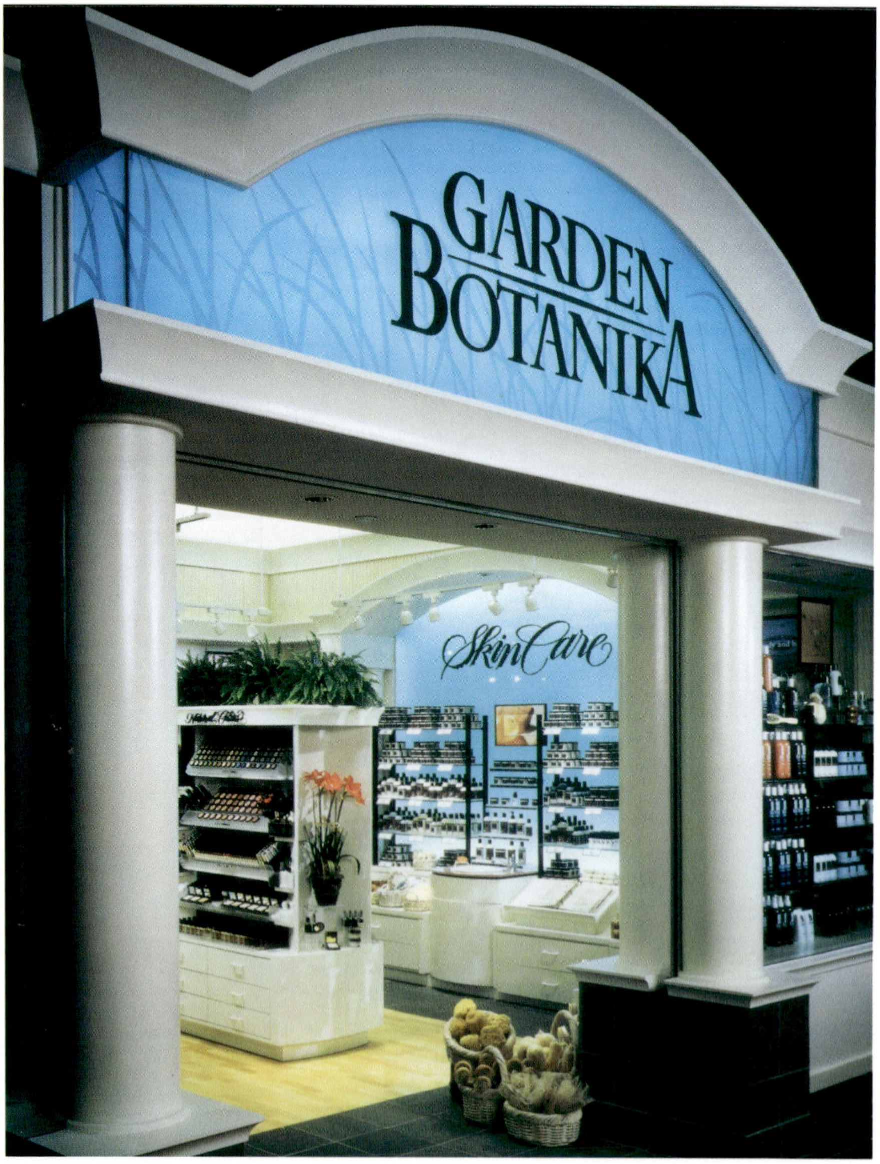

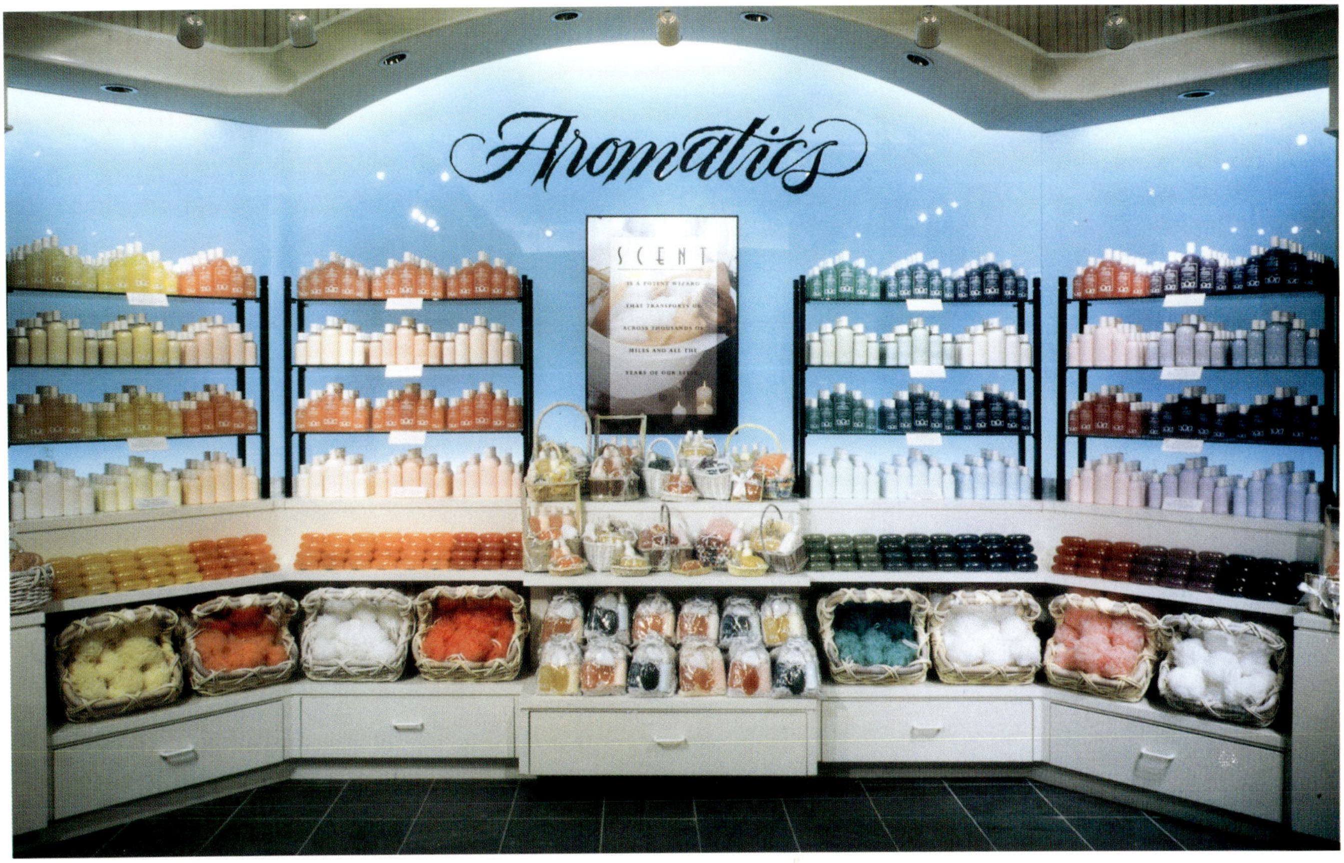
Aromatics
SCENT
IS A POTENT WIZARD
MILES AND ALL THE

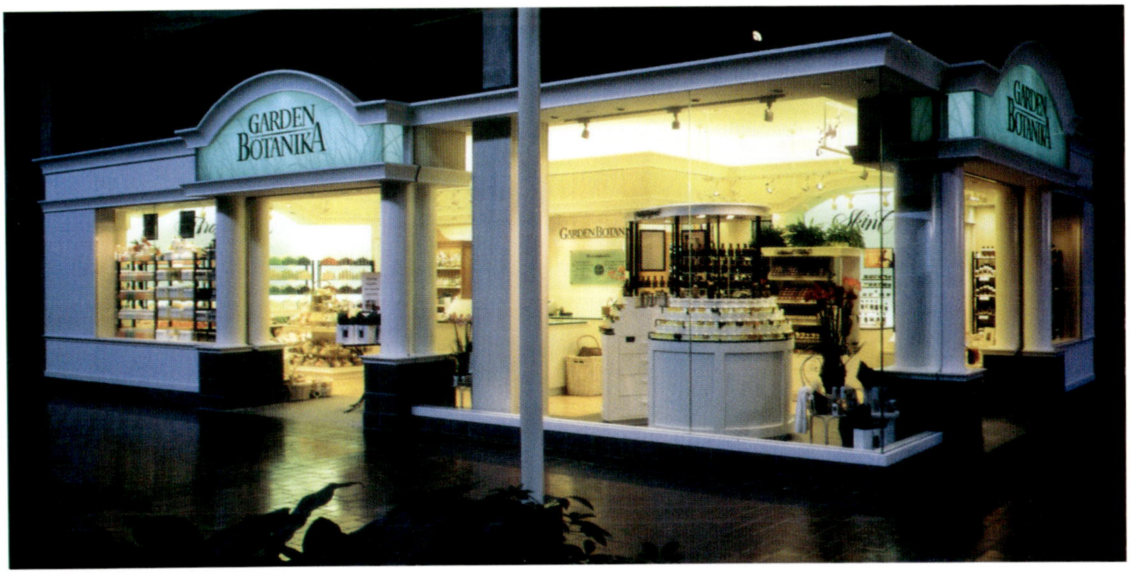
GARDEN BOTANIKA
GARDEN BOTANIKA

SIGN SYSTEMS

ELECTRIC

DESIGNER

Kiku Obata & Co.
5585 Pershing Ave.
St. Louis, MO 63112
(314) 361-3110

FABRICATOR

Gardner Signs, Inc.
8101 S.W. Frontage Rd.
Ft. Collins, CO 80525
(970) 225-1000

The materials used in this project are steel and aluminum. The "Coors Field" letters surrounding the clock are 78-in. tall. Both face and halo illuminate through a perforated, brushed aluminum face. The signage package ties into a theme of purple and brushed aluminum, along with dark green, which is used throughout the stadium's construction. There are two secondary "Coors Field" identification signs, each 54-in. tall. Twelve entry signs, with 15-in. tall letters mounted to a steel bar, above and below, to tie into the "truss" theme throughout the stadium. There are 51 concession display signs, each with reverse pan channel letters, attached to a mesh background in a manner that makes them changeable as necessary. And 41 ad-panel backgrounds each accommodate a 5 x 8-ft. ad graphic.

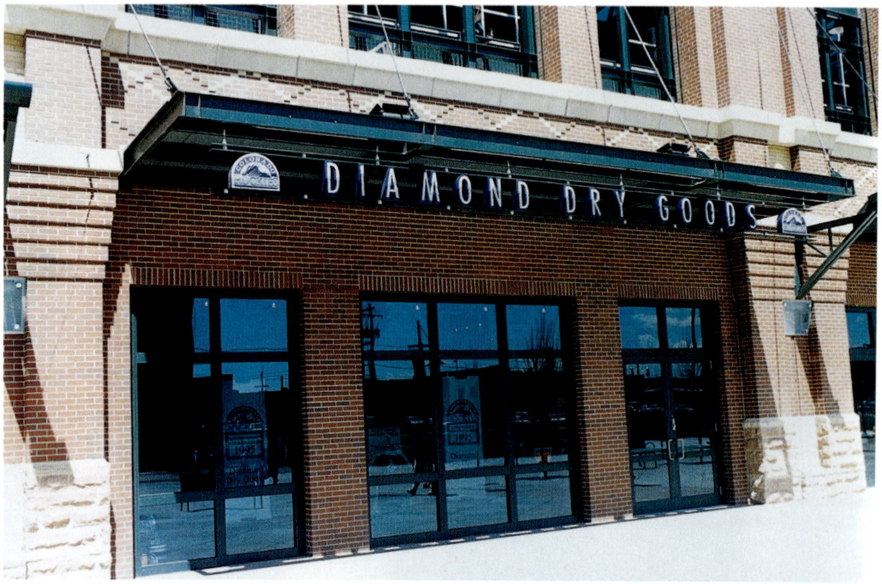

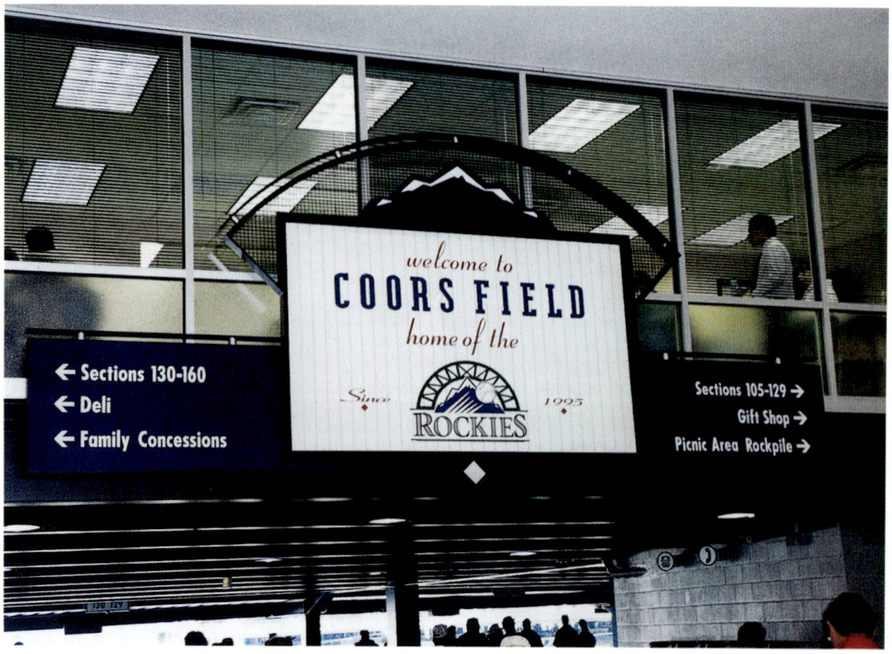

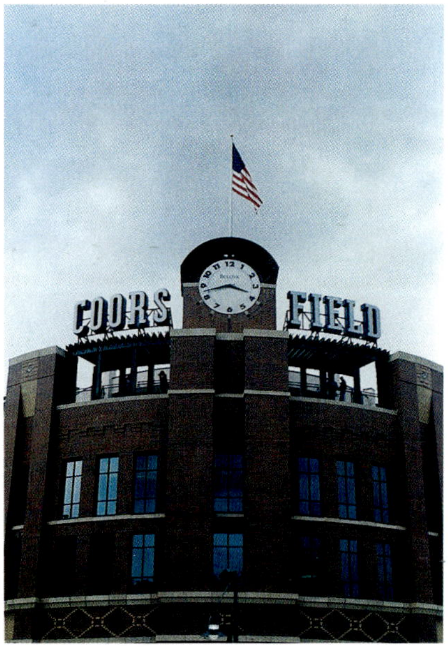

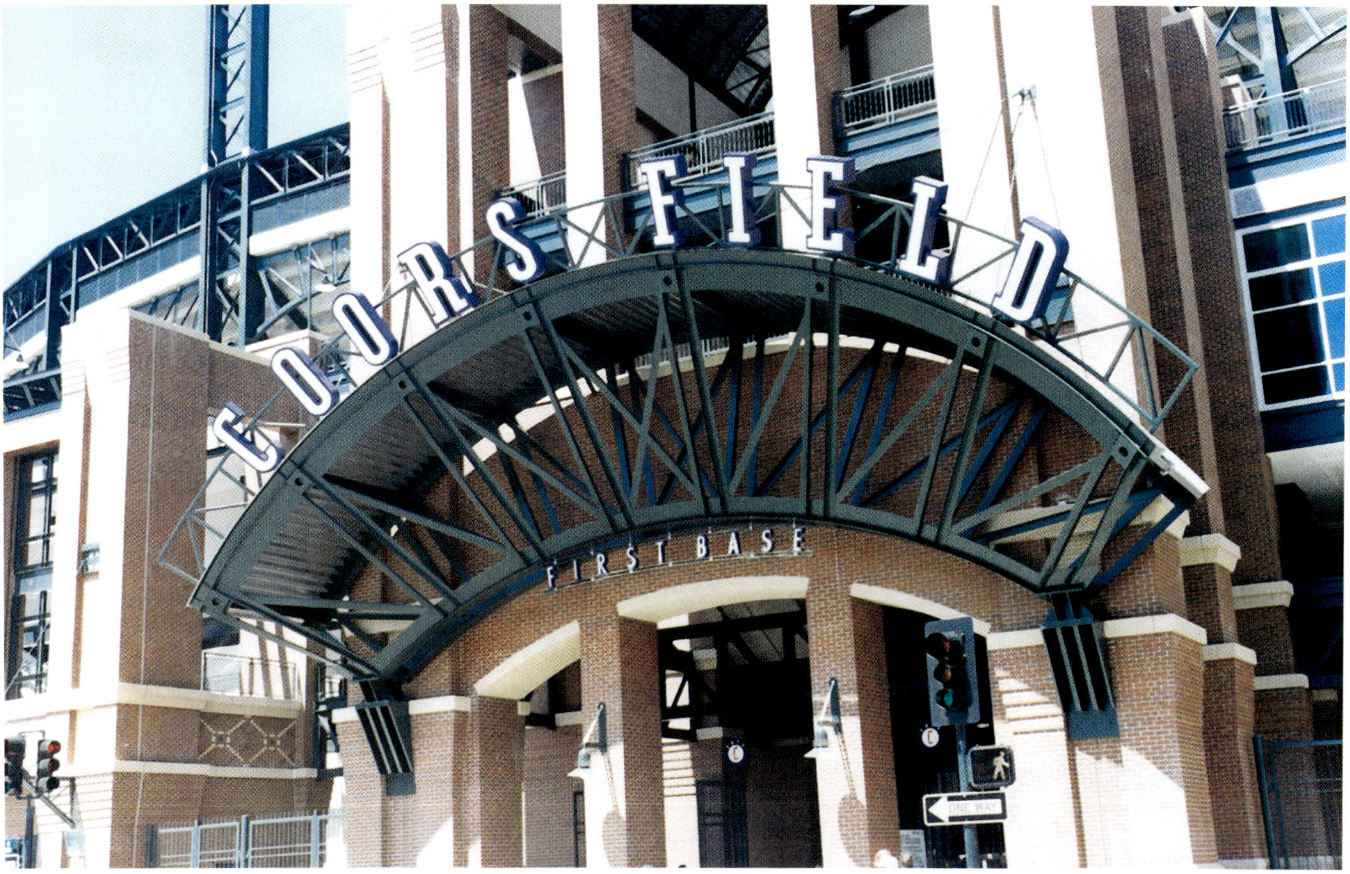
COORS FIELD
FIRST BASE
ONE WAY

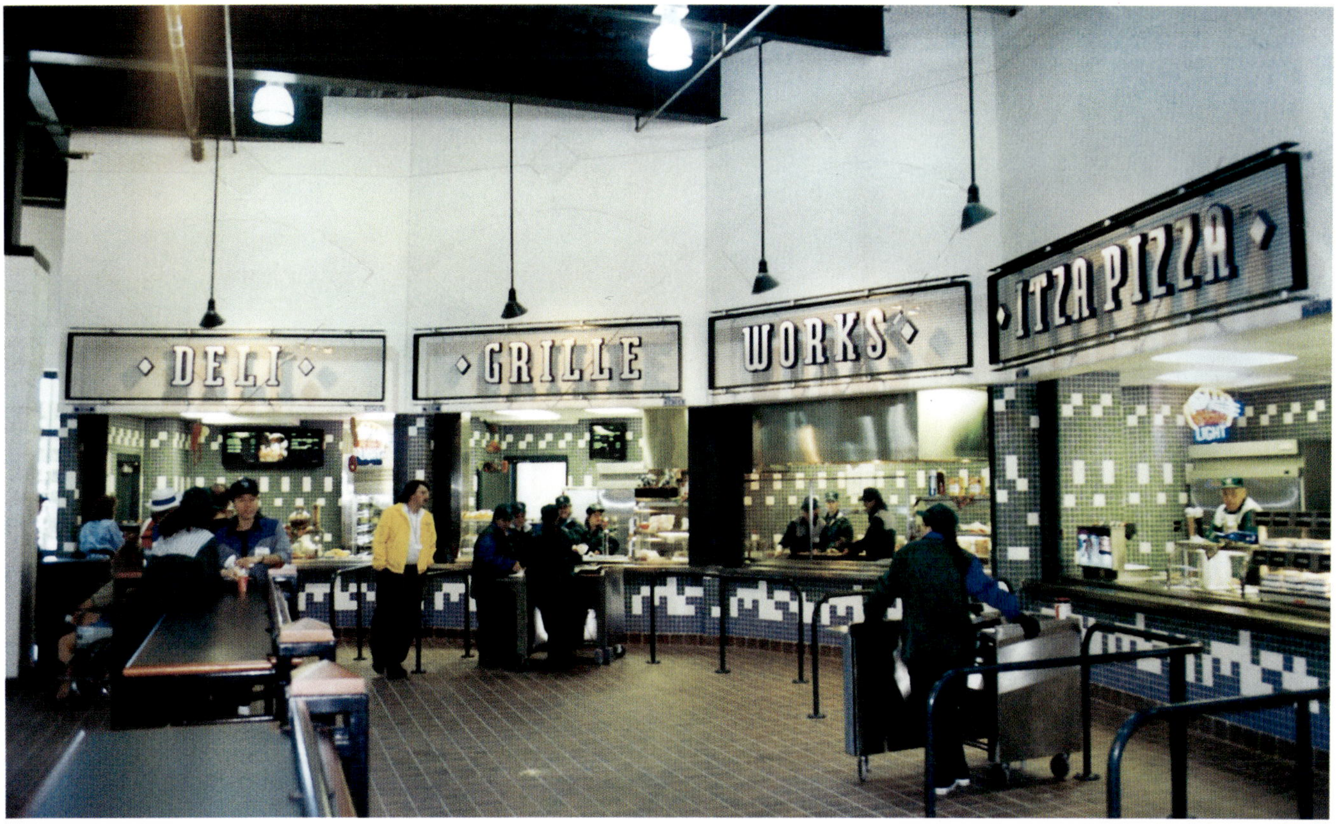
DELI
GRILLE
WORKS
ITZA PIZZA

DESIGNER

David Goodwin
Image Works, Inc.
11046 Leadbetter Rd.
Ashland, VA 23005
(804) 798-5533

FABRICATOR

Image Works, Inc.

Designed for a multi-use theater and entertainment complex, this display consists of two 55-ft.-tall, 27-ft.-wide structures. These structures, joined at the base, form a "V" shape. Graduated blues, Day-glo® red and yellow, and clear coat are used on the display's frame.

"Broadway" bows toward the viewer and is illuminated with scintillating bulbs. Further contributing to the sign's kinetic effect, multi-colored, exposed neon animates outward. The sign's 12 x 15-ft., full-color, electronic message center is also fully animated.

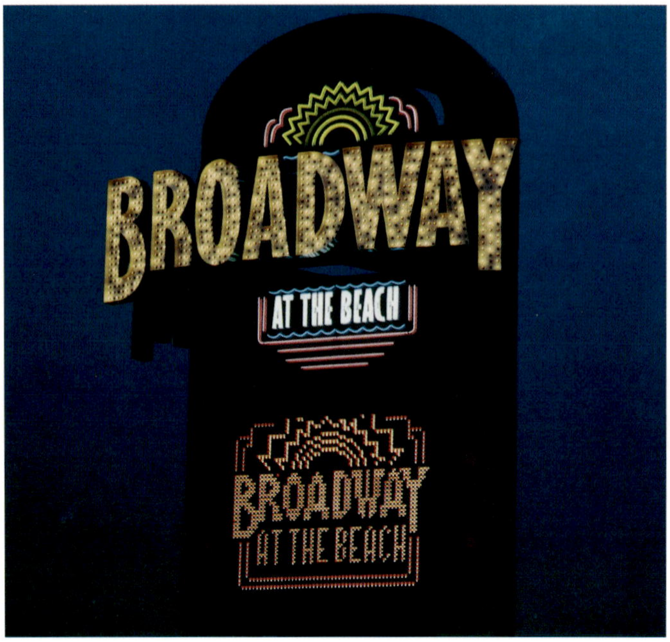

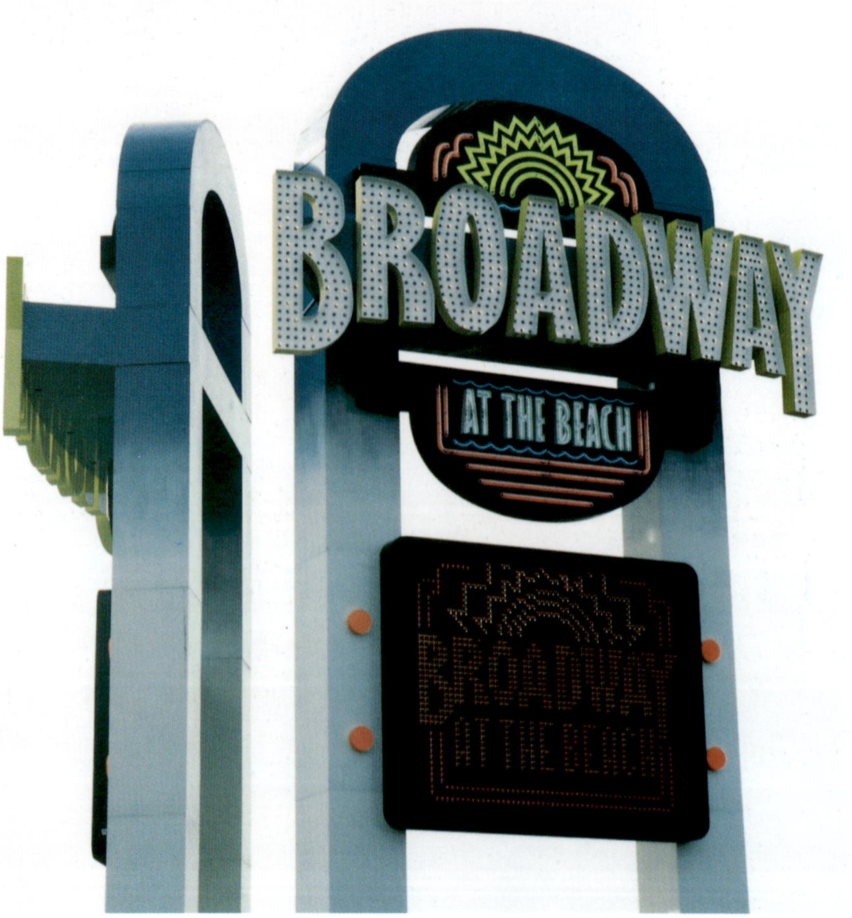

DESIGNER

Display Solutions, Inc.
6301 Best Friend Rd.
Norcross, GA 30071
(404) 662-5400

FABRICATOR

Display Solutions, Inc.
6301 Best Friend Rd.
Norcross, GA 30071
(404) 662-5400

Above this sign's 48 x 96-lamp True-color® lens message center is a painted, backlit, soft-face ID. Below the message center are painted Tri-Vision® advertising panels. The whole display stands 60 ft. 6 in. tall and is 37 ft. wide.

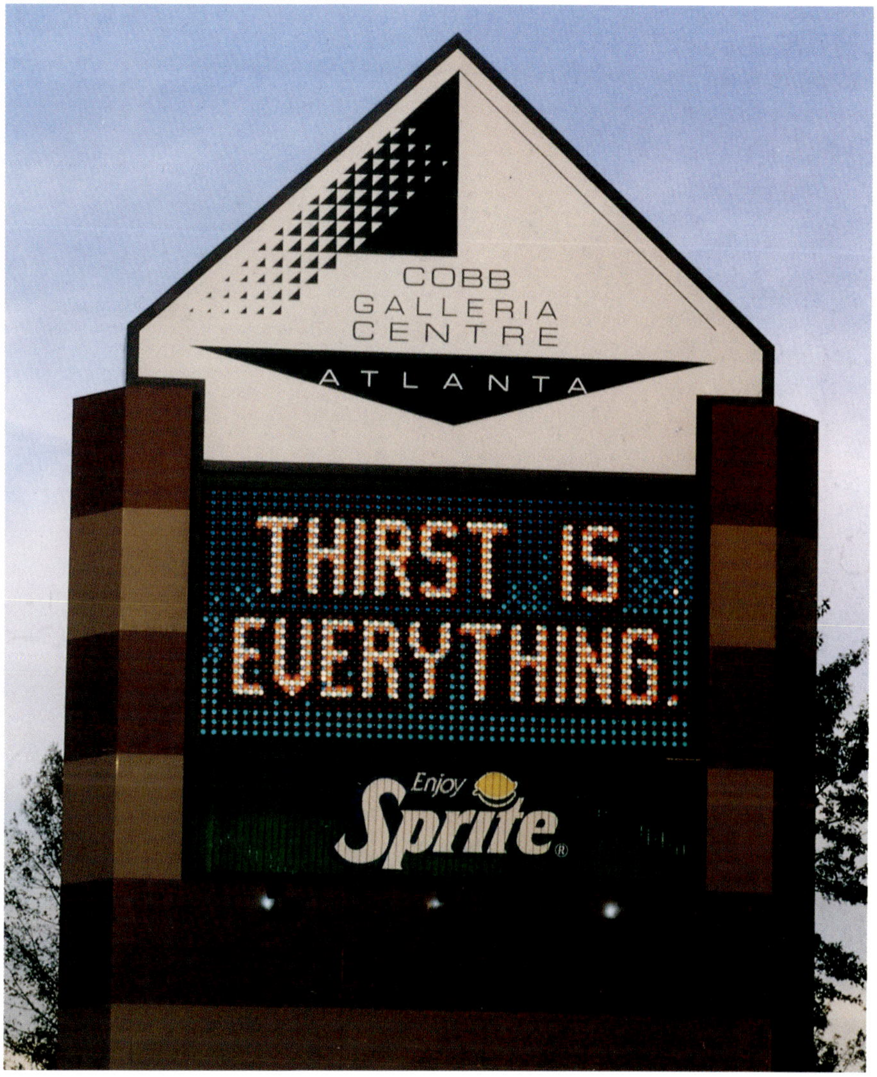

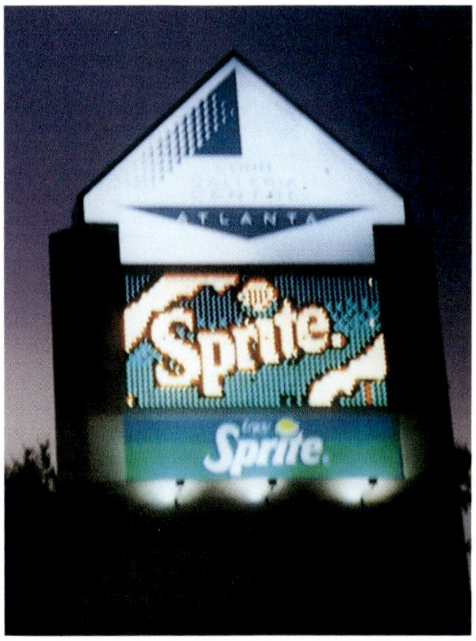

DIGITAL DISPLAY ELECTRIC

DESIGNER

Ray Hanson
ADSystems
12601 New Brittany Blvd.
Fort Myers, FL 33907
(800) 226-7440

FABRICATOR

United Studios Sign Group
2120 N. County Rd. 427
Longwood, FL 32750
(407) 831-3484

To accentuate the French curves of The Florida Aquarium building, Tampa, FL, this sign features a 28-ft., shrouded, deco-designed pole cover — a cover fabricated from aluminum with a masonry-texture finish. Vibrant colors on the masonry mimic those on the ocean floor. The electronic message center is a full-color display.

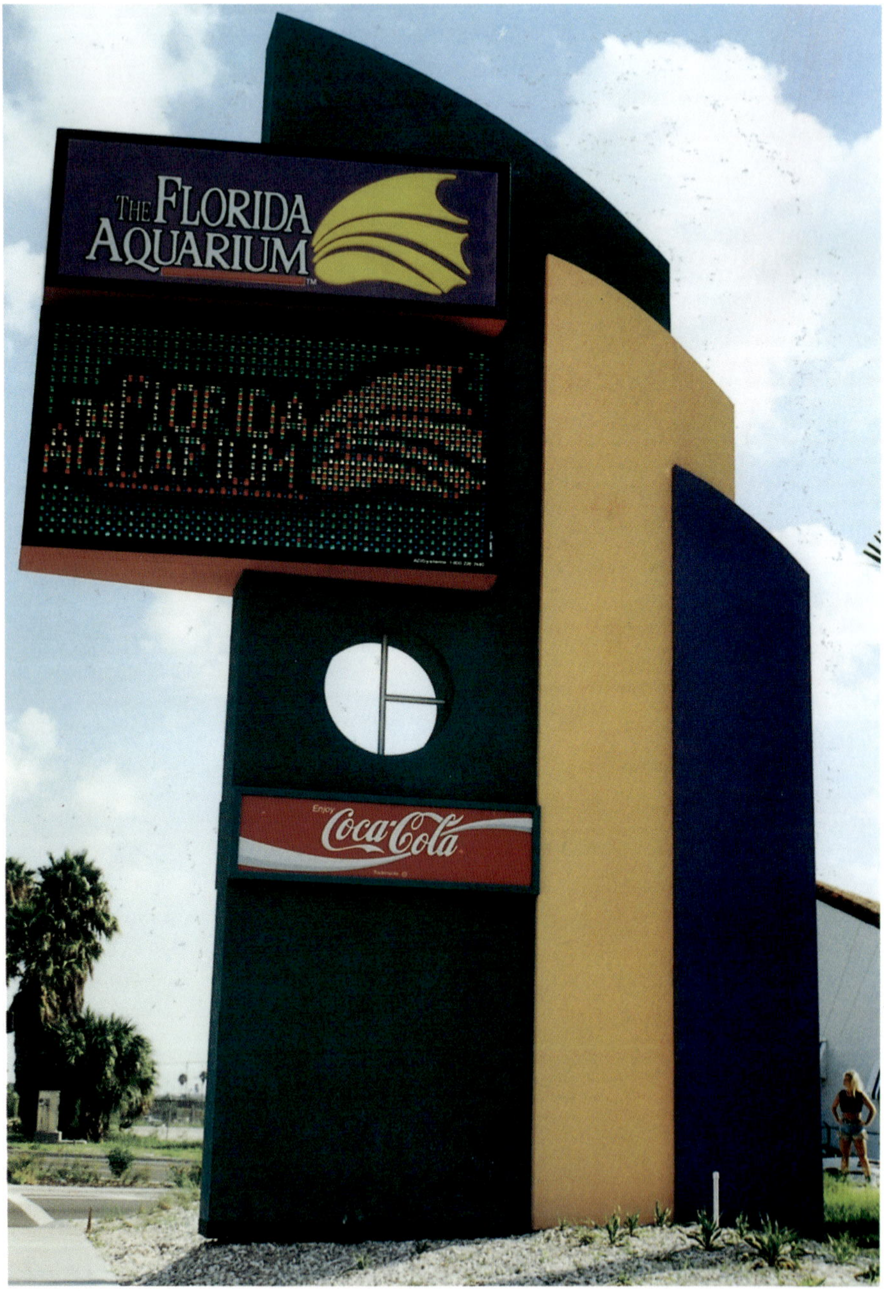

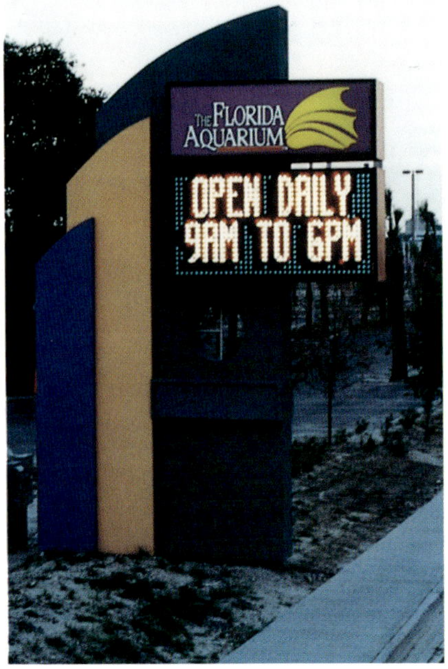

DESIGNER

Chance Martinson
S&S Sign Co.
13190 Stone Ave. N.
Seattle, WA 98133
(206) 365-0422

FABRICATOR

S&S Sign Co.

Bonney Lake Village's double-faced, shopping center sign stands 28-ft. tall and is 14 ft. 6 in. wide. It incorporates skeletal neon copy and graphics, as well as a Daktronics® electronic message center (SunSpot Series).

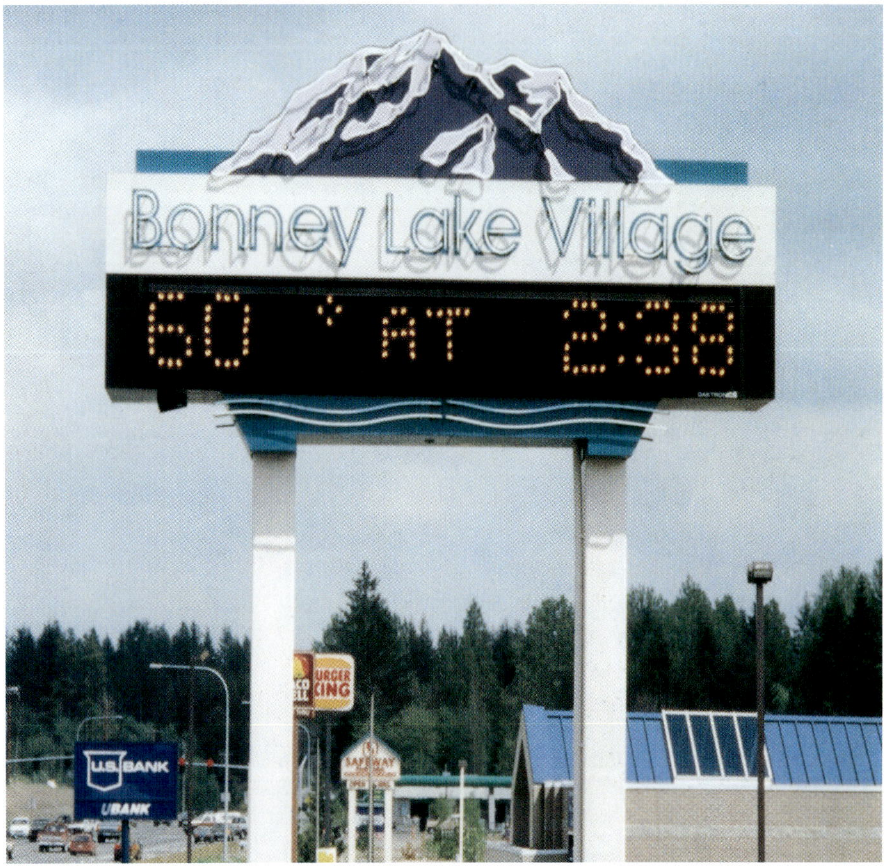

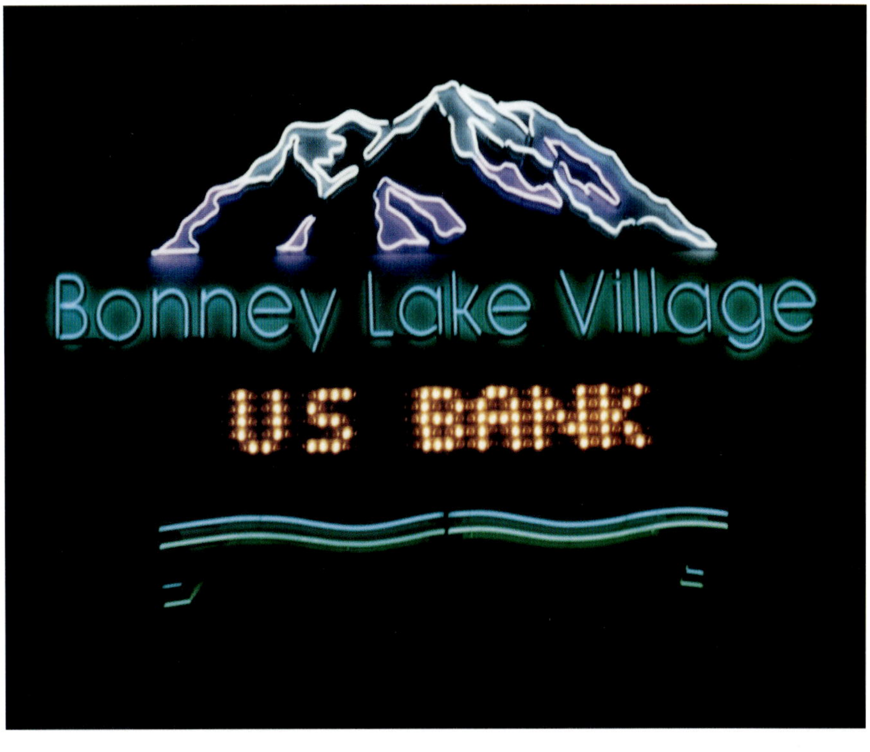

DIGITAL DISPLAY ELECTRIC

DESIGNER

Charles F. Barnard
Ad-Art Electric Sign Corp.
3133 N. Ad-Art Rd.
Stockton, CA 95215
(209) 931-0860

FABRICATOR

Ad-Art Electric Sign Corp.

Measuring 31 ft. high and 28 ft. wide, this single-faced, freestanding arch includes fabricated metal construction, painted metal surfaces and polished, clear, aluminum trim.

The upper signwork — including "Country Star," "Restaurant" and the logo star — is plastic-faced, interior illuminated and of channel construction. All other stars use channel metal construction, are painted, illuminated with multi-colored neon outlines and single-strobe lamps. These lamps light randomly, simulating the "bursting" and "popping" of fireworks. Support stems for these stars are made of polished clear aluminum, illuminated with rows of 11w clear lamps that appear to "travel" outward.

Running through the center of the arch is polished gold aluminum, recess-covered with ripple-patterned amber Plexiglas® acrylic. This reveal is illuminated by rows of "bud" lamps, programmed to travel upward. The 8 x 10-ft., full-color, low-wattage, single-face, electronic message display is remotely programmable.

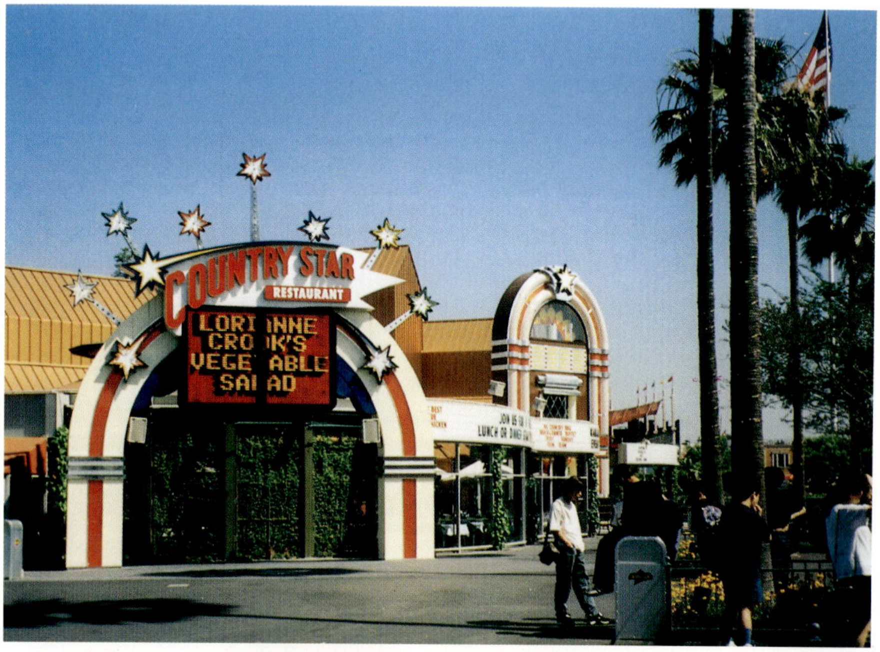

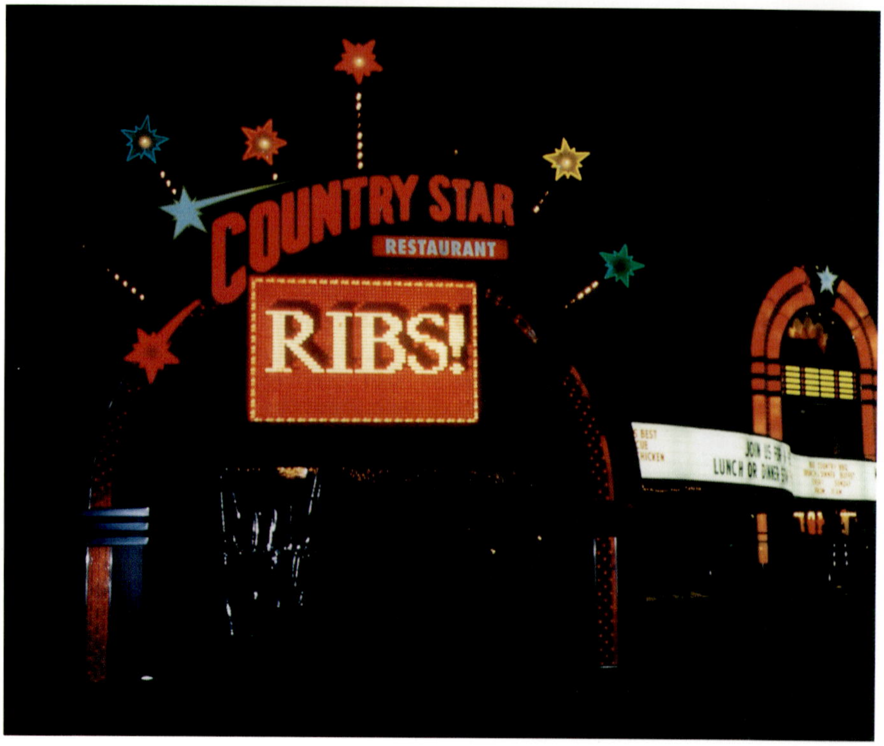

BACKLIT AWNINGS

DESIGNER

Mazzio's Corp.
4441 S. 72 E. Ave.
Tulsa, OK 74145
(918) 663-8880

FABRICATOR

Oklahoma Sign Co., Inc.
2720 E. King Place
Tulsa, OK 74110
(918) 835-5581

Mazzio's pizza restaurant is wrapped continuously on three sides by this 5-ft.-wide, 135-ft.-long backlit awning. The awning's black, red and white color patterns are produced with eradicated fabric and translucent vinyl, and are protected with sprayed clear coating. A simple staple-stitch retention system is used for the frame itself.

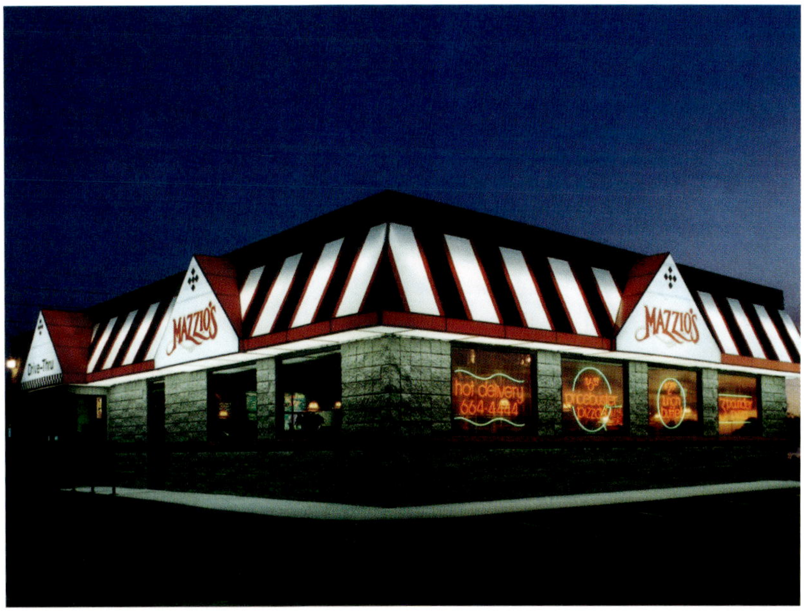

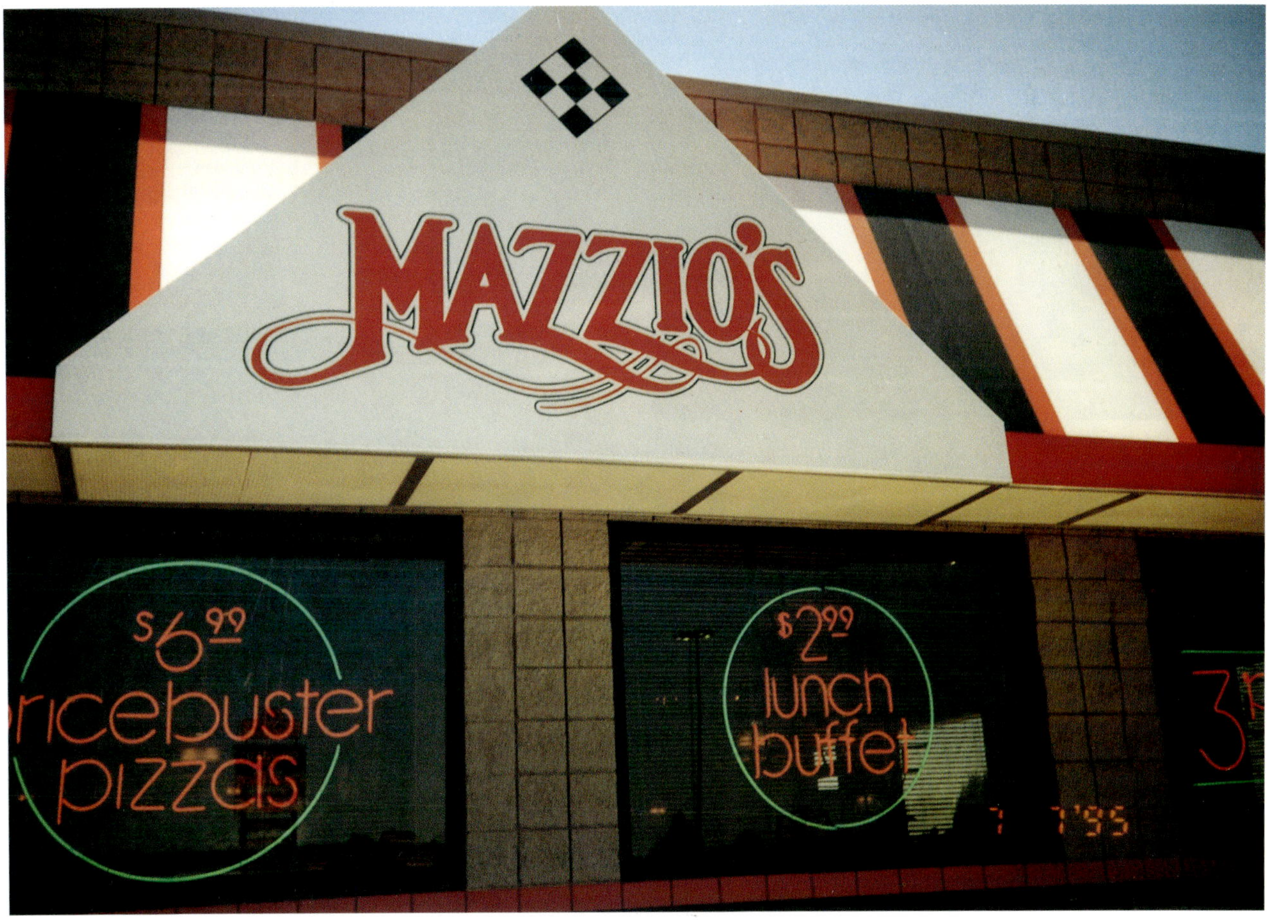

BACKLIT AWNINGS

ELECTRIC

DESIGNER

Anthony Eoff
Awnings & Such/Accent Signs
9000 Daffodil
Houston,TX 77063
(713) 780-1151

FABRICATOR

Awnings & Such/Accent Signs

Designed for a floral shop, this backlit awning incorporates translucent vinyl copy. The main ID section of the canopy is bordered with white chase lights.

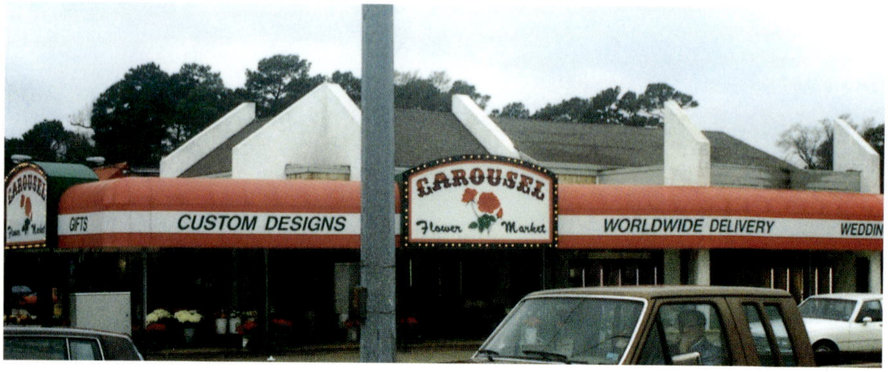

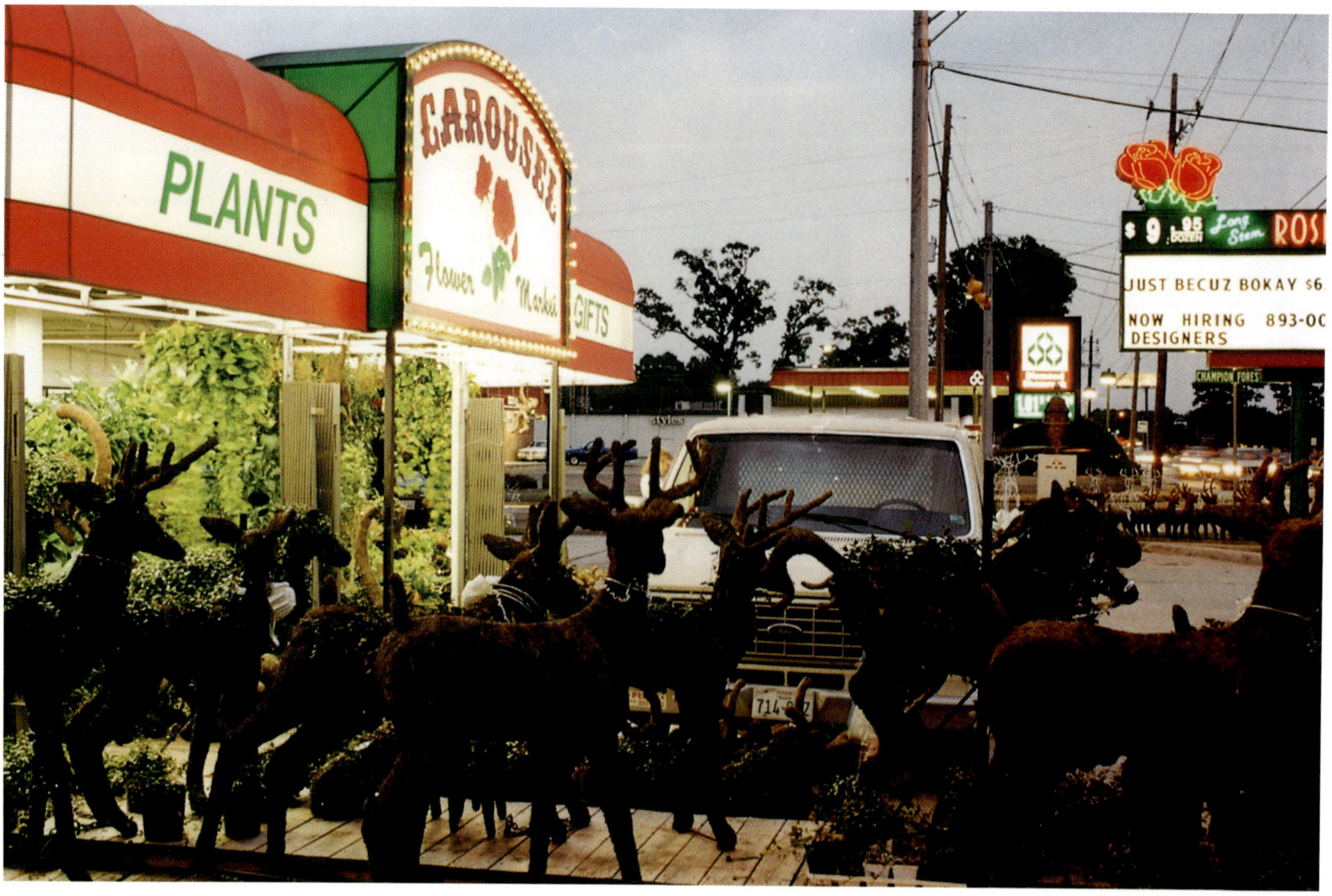

DESIGNER

Chris Suchko
Contemporary Sign
110 S. 2nd St.
W. Newton, PA 15089
(412) 872-0456

FABRICATOR

Contemporary Sign

This 40-ft. awning features a center peak that measures 15 x 10 x 4 ft. Comprised of an all-aluminum frame, the awning uses eggcrates, a John Boyle Starlit #630 yellow cover and airbrushed vinyl lettering. The logo itself has been designed on a Macintosh® using Adobe Illustrator®. Although not pictured in the photo, teal and purple flags have been added to this awning.

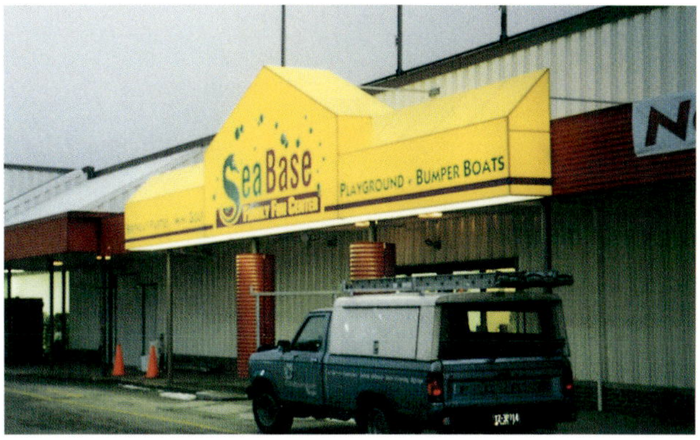

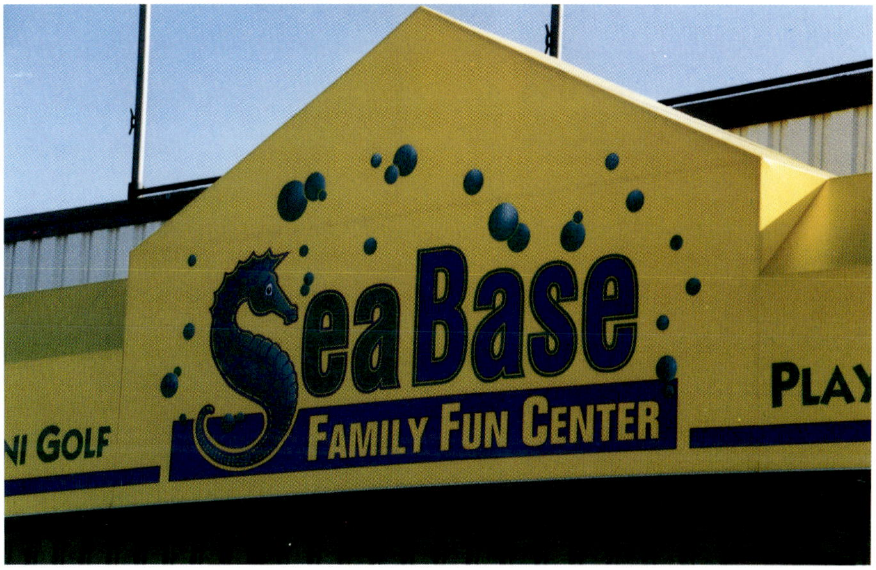

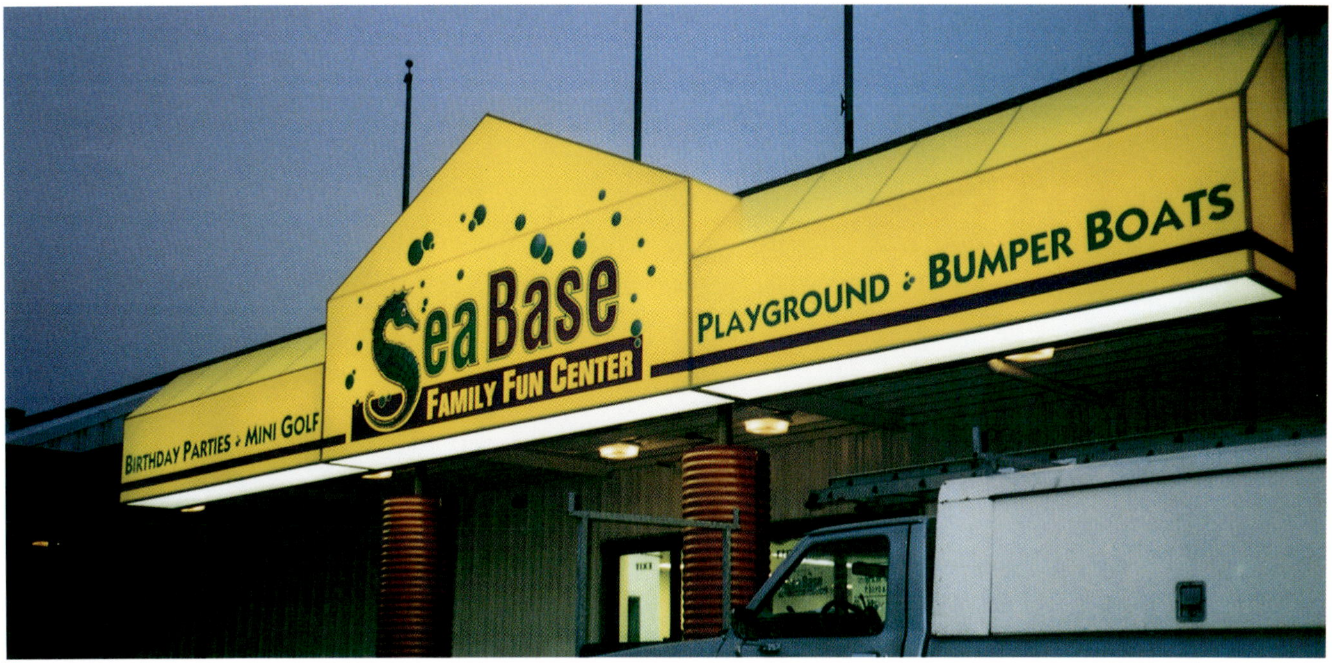

EXPOSED NEON

ELECTRIC

DESIGNER

Elvia's Cantina

FABRICATOR

Awnings & Such/Accent Signs
9000 Daffodil
Houston, TX 77063
(713) 780-1151

The painted aluminum background is outlined with exposed neon.

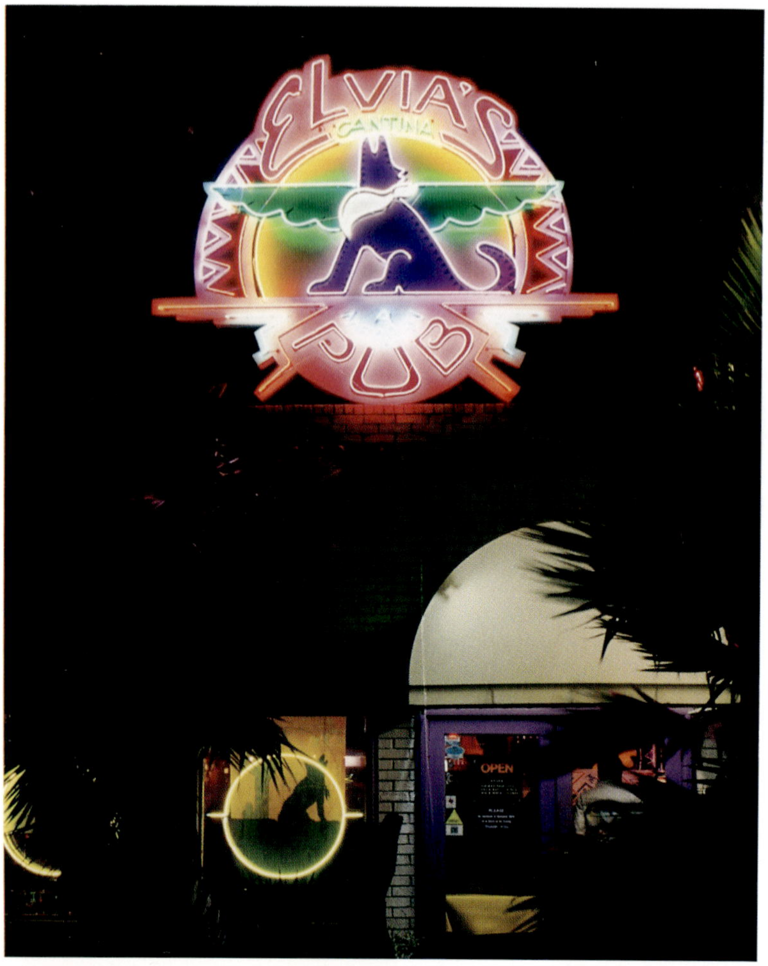

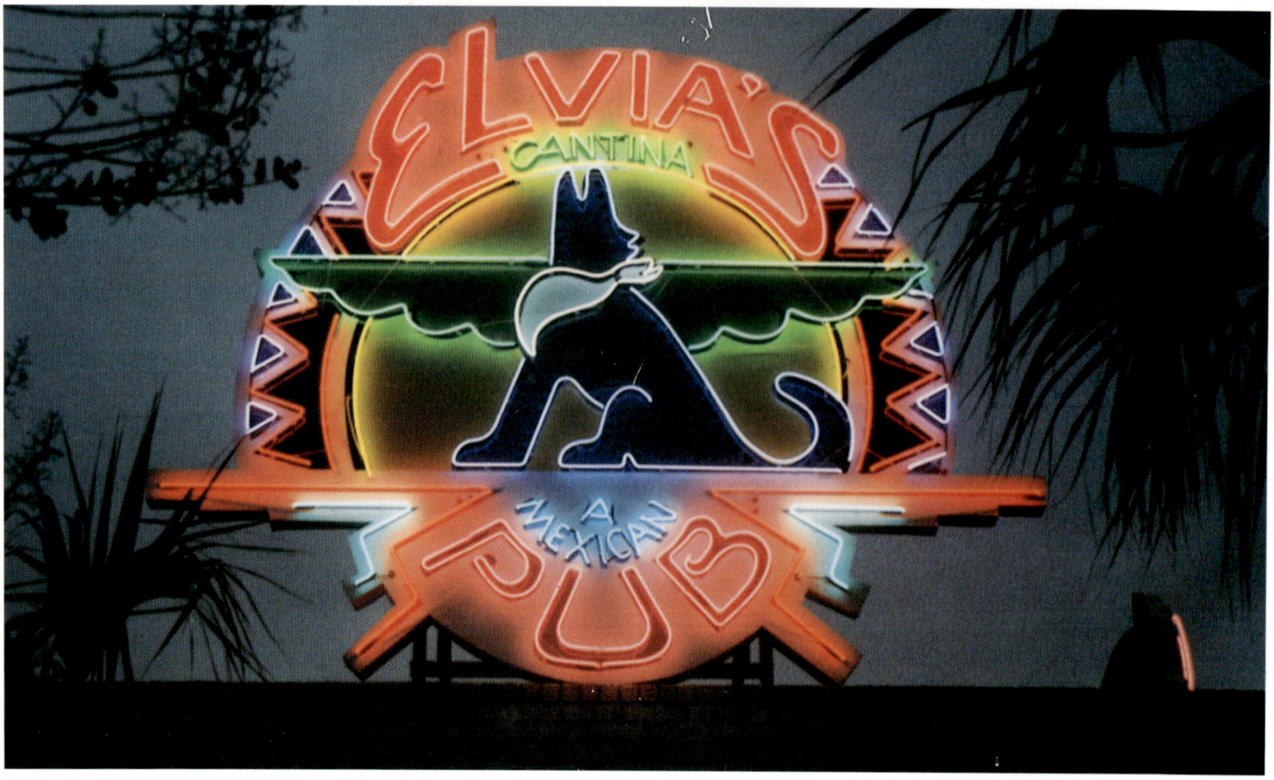

DESIGNER

Finito Art & Design, Ltd.
Christchurch, New Zealand

FABRICATOR

Sign Adv.
31 Dundas St.
Christchurch, New Zealand
3662-106

This sign has a powder-coated, aluminum sign case with an internal steel frame bolted to a concrete wall. The graphics are hand-painted in enamel and illuminated with 12mm glass tubing. The bottom panel is backlit with fluorescent tubing.

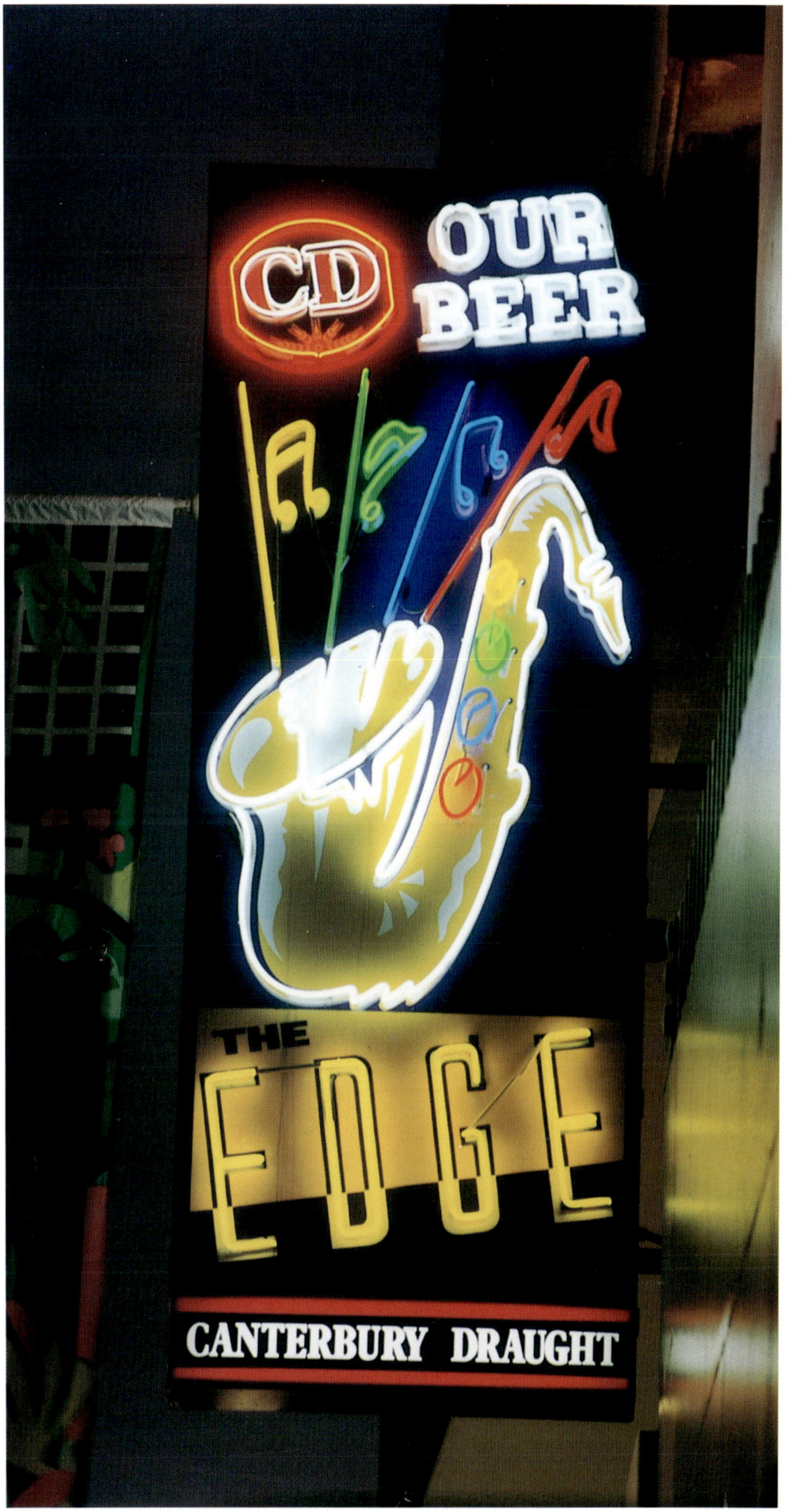

EXPOSED NEON ELECTRIC

DESIGNER

Charlie Stroud
Arrow Sign Co.
1051 46th Ave.
Oakland, CA 94601
(510) 533-7693

FABRICATOR

Arrow Sign Co.

Warm white neon dips behind the pegged-off acrylic letters. Plate graphics are acrylic with turquoise halo illumination.

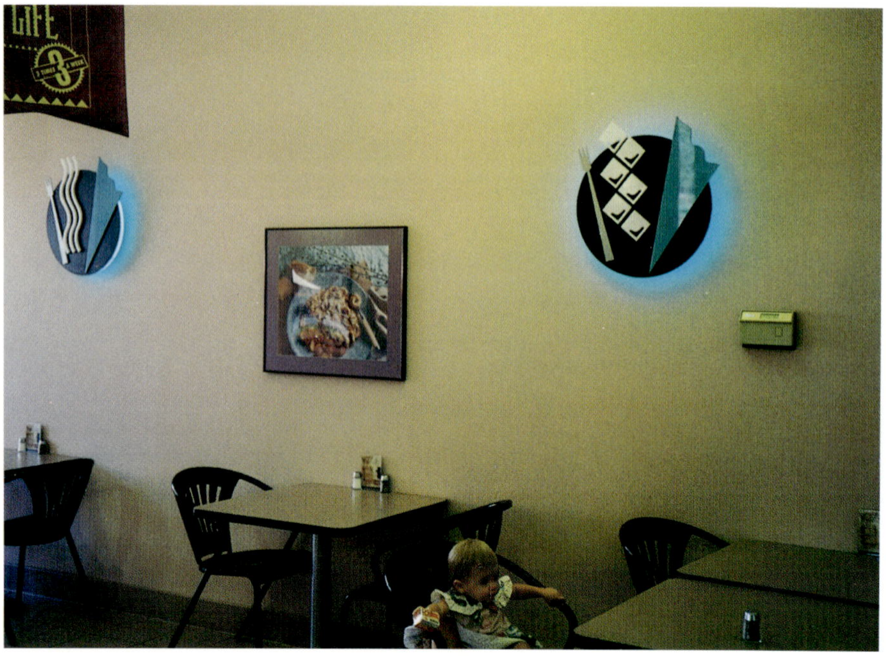

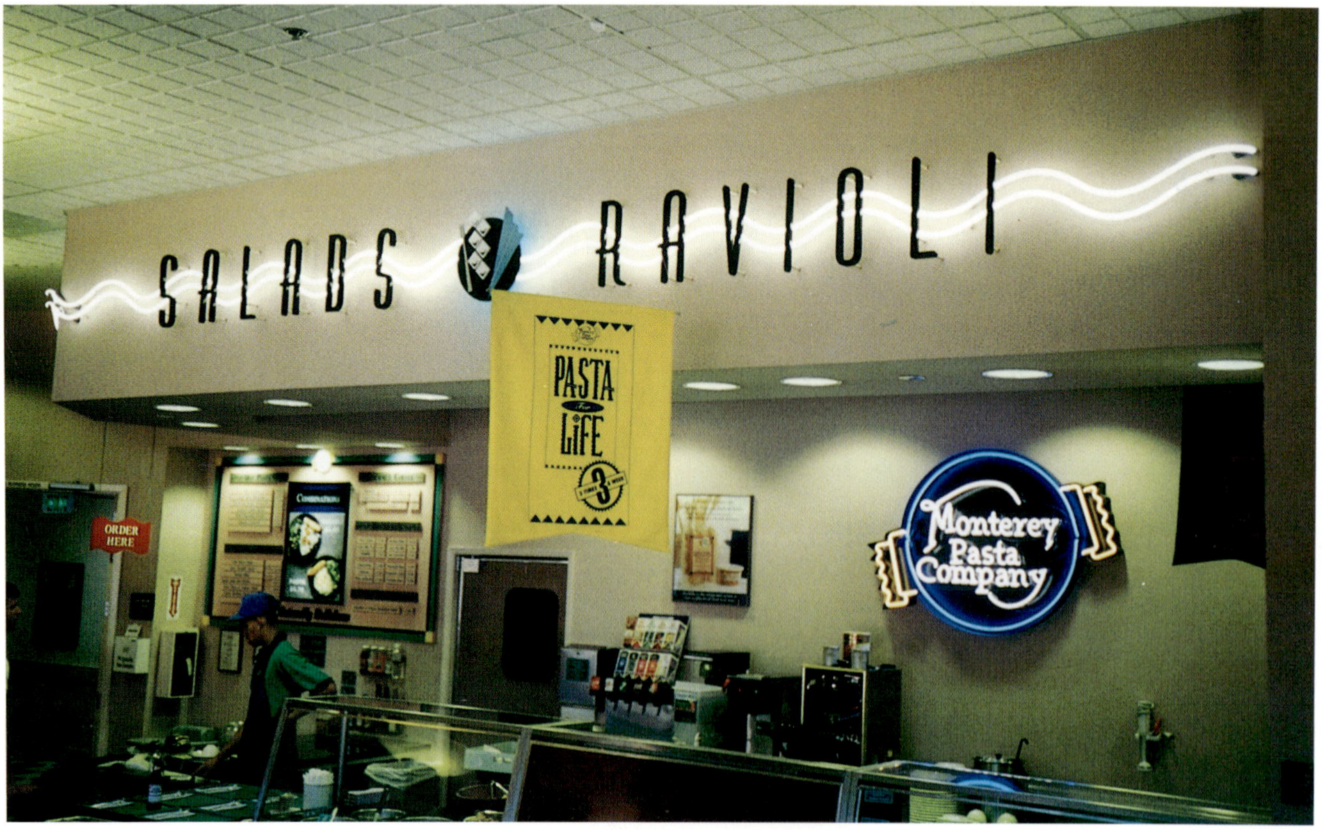

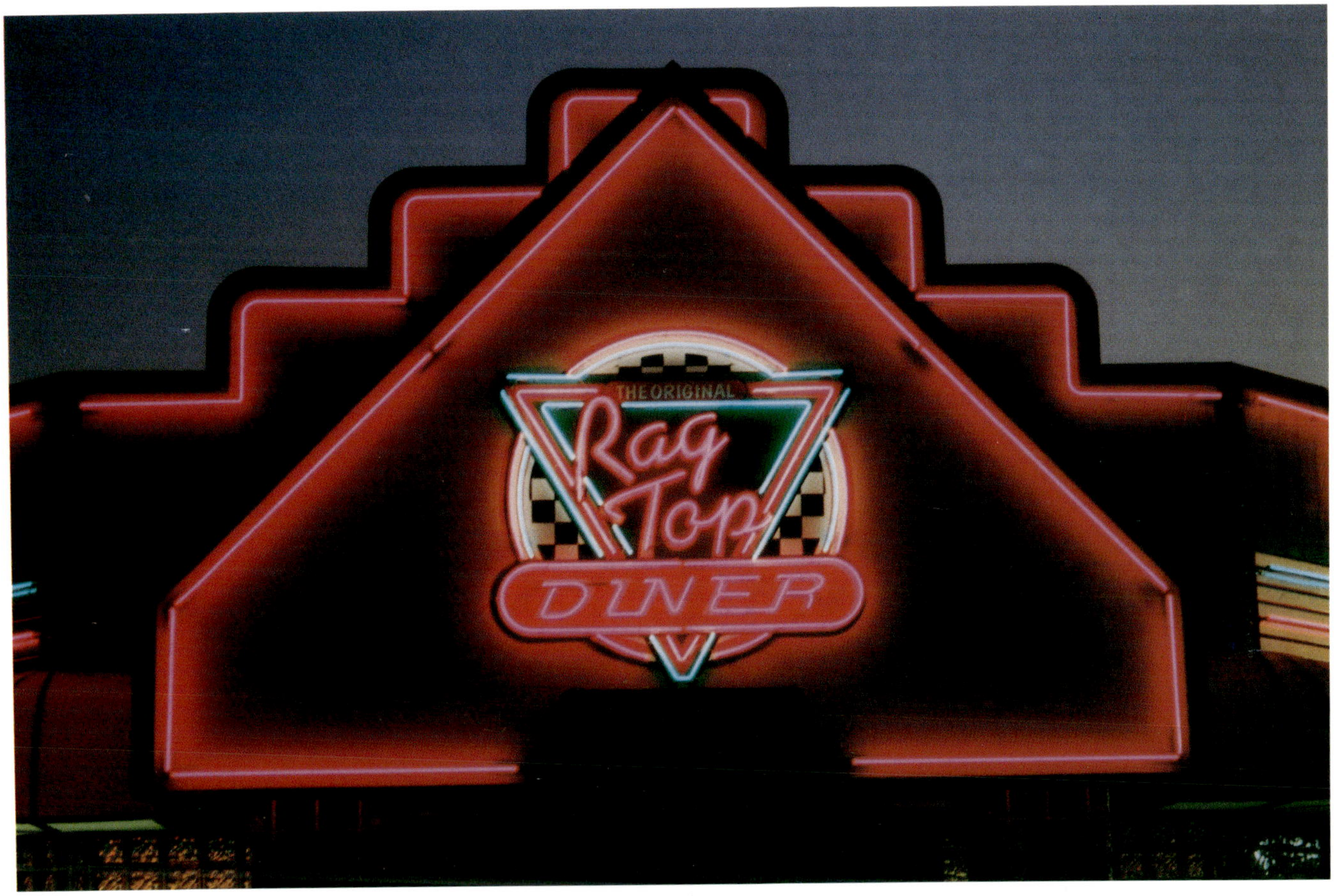

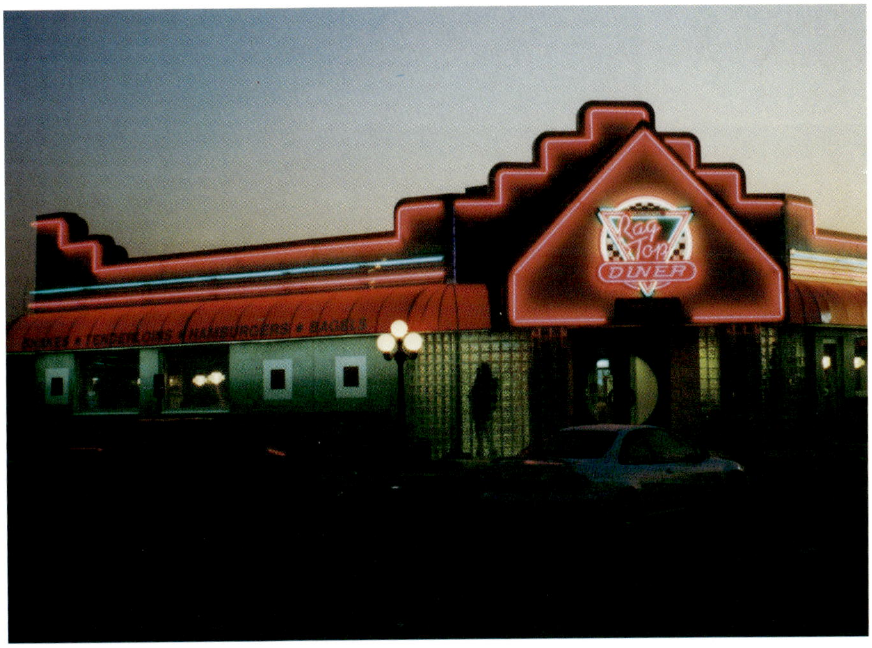

DESIGNER

John Hawn Graphic Design
Cedar Rapids, IA

FABRICATOR

Sign Productions, Inc.
1010 First Ave. NW
Cedar Rapids, IA 52405
(319) 364-6697

This 6-ft.-diameter logo uses magenta and aqua neon. The aluminum background is painted with automotive enamel and decorated with vinyl graphics.

EXPOSED NEON

ELECTRIC

DESIGNER

Finito Art & Design, Ltd.
Christchurch, New Zealand

FABRICATOR

Sign Adv.
31 Dundas St.
Christchurch, New Zealand
3662-106

For "Lochinvar's" Bar, the sign utilizes 3.6 x 1.2m, double-sided neon. There are powder-coated aluminum cases, top and bottom, with internal steel frames bolted to the wall. The 12mm exterior treated ply Scotsman is an acrylic pictorial. Neon tubes 12 mm thick feature a kilt lifted, held, and lowered movement, every three seconds.

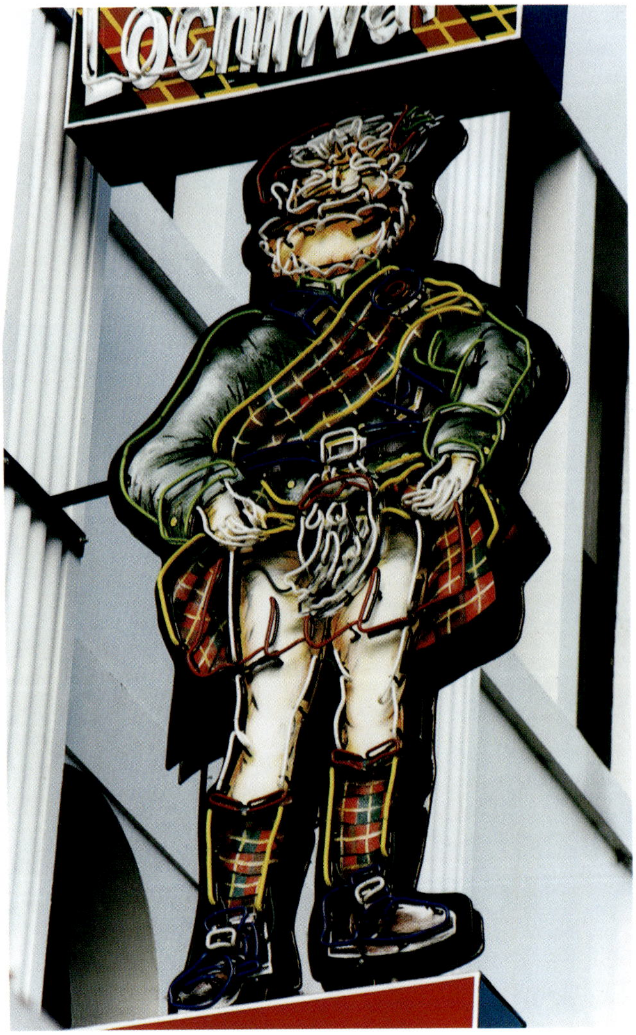

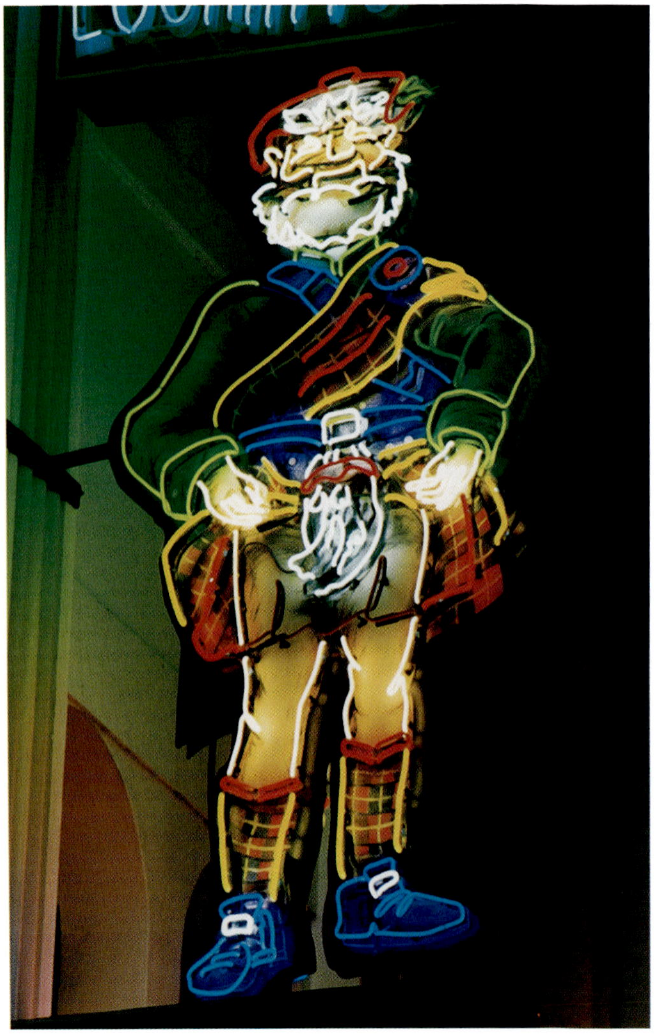

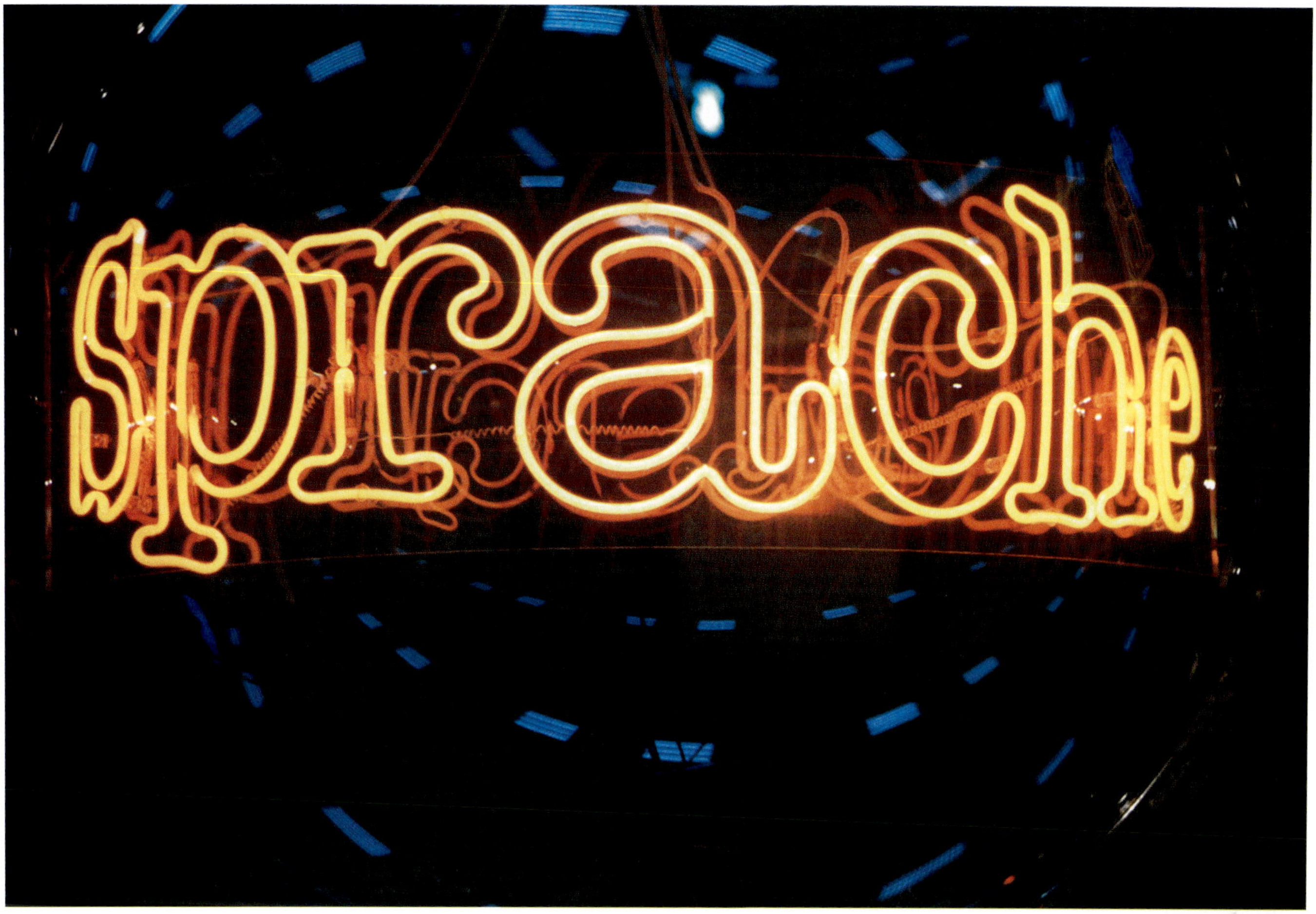

DESIGNERS

Alexander Novotny, project director
Siemens Exhibit-Fair Dept.
(concept)

D.J. Sprengnagel
Herwig Kucera
NeonLine Werbedesign GmbH
Obere Donaustrasse 45a
Vienna, Austria 1020
431 332-0607

FABRICATOR

NeonLine Werbedesign GmbH

Semi-circular neon logos and lettering were installed inside 4-ft. 6-in. diameter transparent acrylic spheres suspended from the roof.

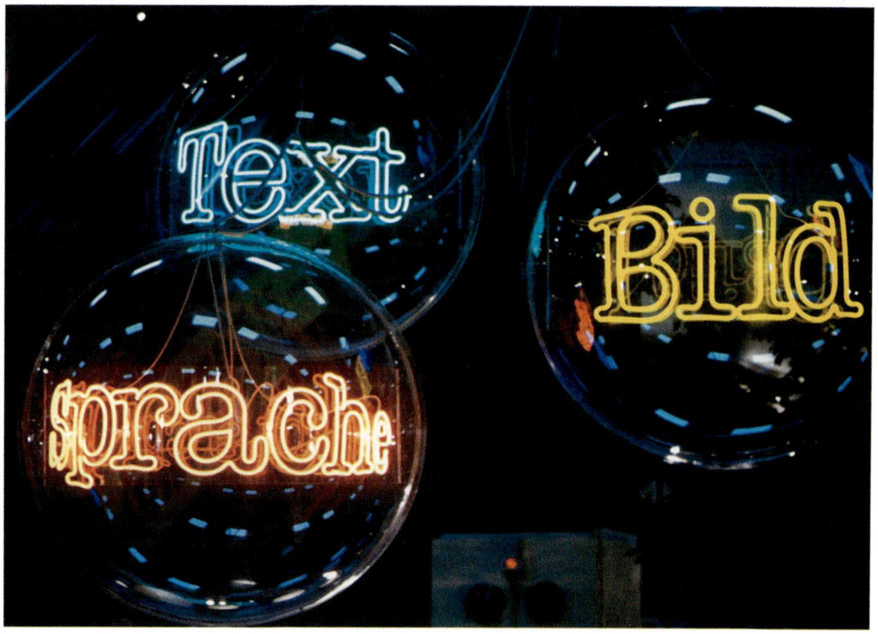

EXPOSED NEON
ELECTRIC

DESIGNERS

Elektro Haas (graphic)

Markus Lang
Herwig Kucera
D.J. Sprengnagel
NeonLine Werbedesign GmbH
Obere Donaustrasse 45a
Vienna, Austria 1020
431 332-0607

FABRICATOR

NeonLine Werbedesign GmbH

Comic drawings executed in neon installed in standard aluminum boxes on the awning.

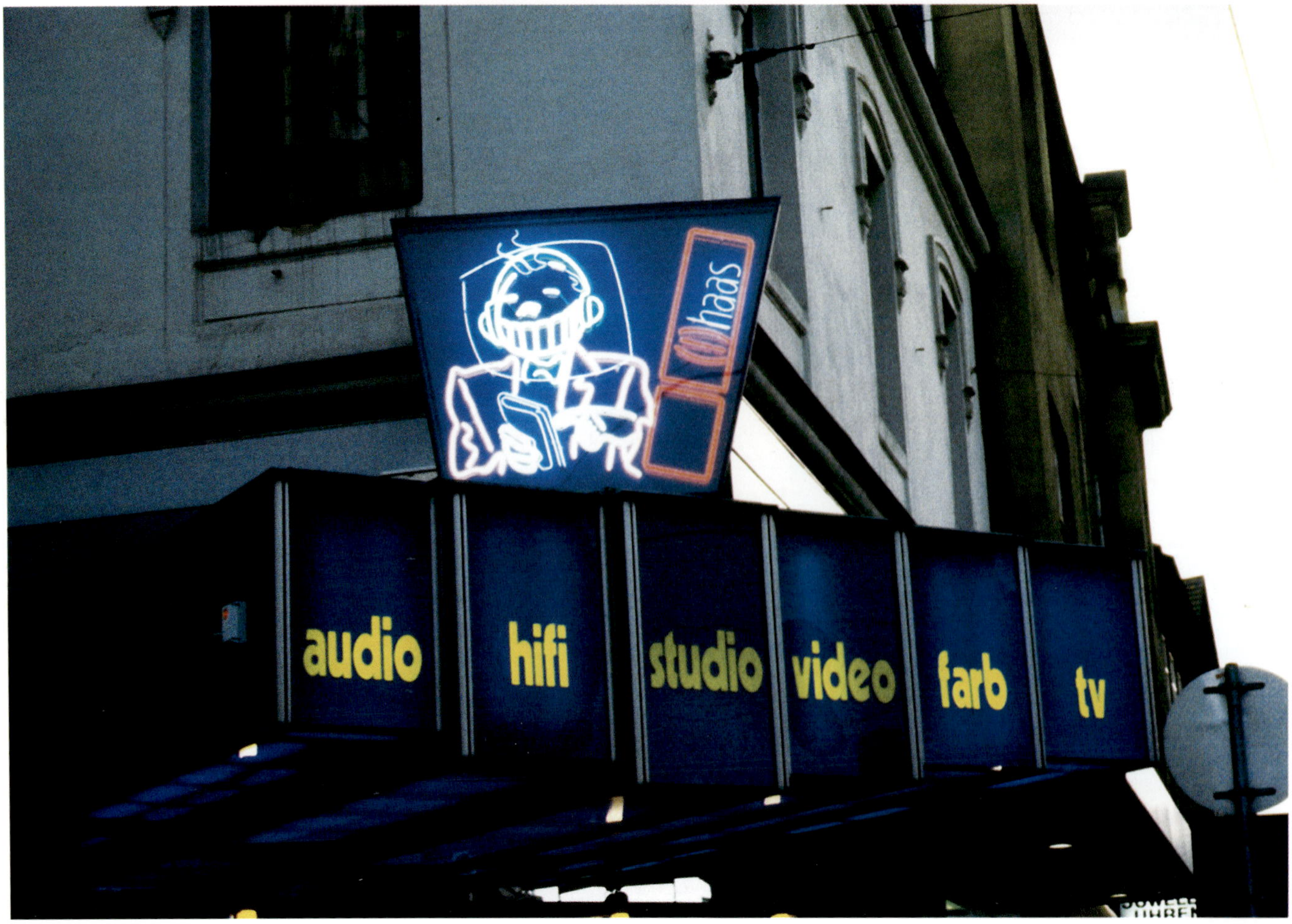

DESIGNERS

Kevin Stirnweis
Light Design Neon
118 Winnisimmet St.
Chelsea, MA 02150
(617) 884-0507

Bill Mitchell
Ed Knudson
National Amusement, Inc.
200 Elm St.
Dedham, MA 02026
(617) 461-1306

FABRICATOR

Light Design Neon

Color-changing welds and 10-25mm European and US glass add interest to this cinema neon display. The drywall-mounted display measures 9 x 85 ft. Its design minimizes GTO connections; transformers are concealed above a drop ceiling.

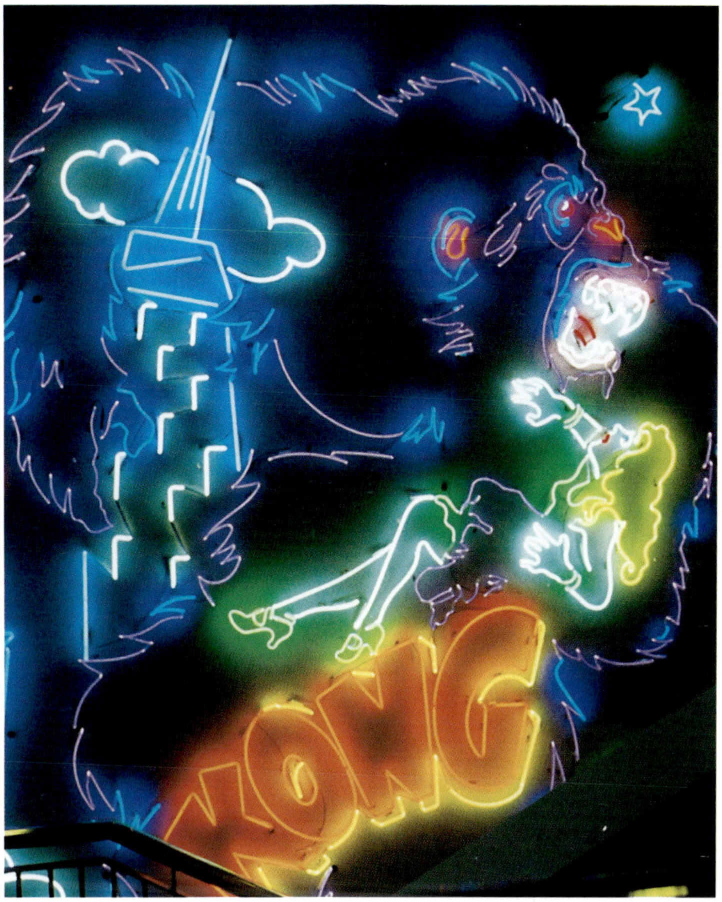

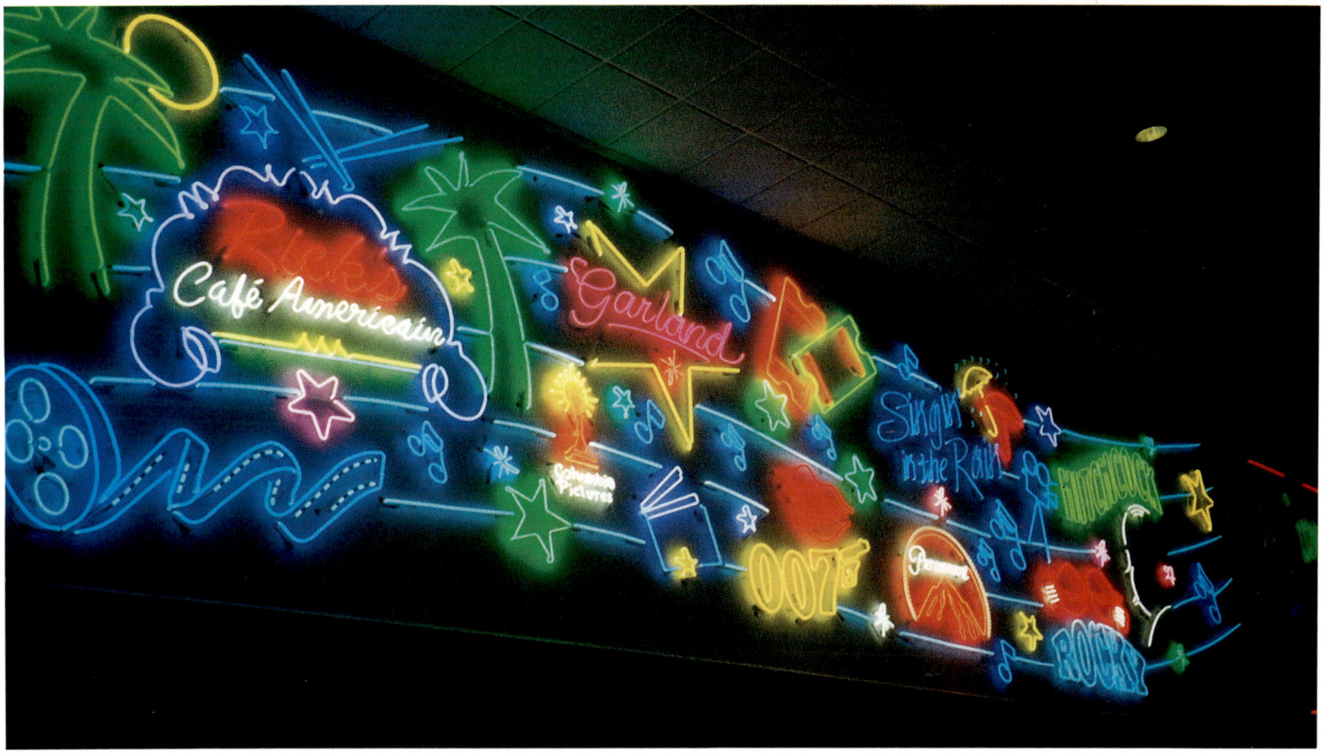

ELECTRIC

DESIGNER

Lawrin Rosen
ARTeffects, Inc.
27 Britton Dr.
Broomfield, CT 06002
(203) 242-0031

FABRICATOR

ARTeffects, Inc.

Lawrin Rosen says the design concept for this 15mm neon window display came to him in 30 seconds — "It took a lot longer to figure out how to hang it," he adds. ARTeffects erected scaffolding to install two of these 70-lb., 20-ft.-high displays, attaching them to the window mullions with neon posts; secondary support and spacing is with 7mm clear-glass tubing. The six-color displays are GTO-wired; no permit was required for the interior installation.

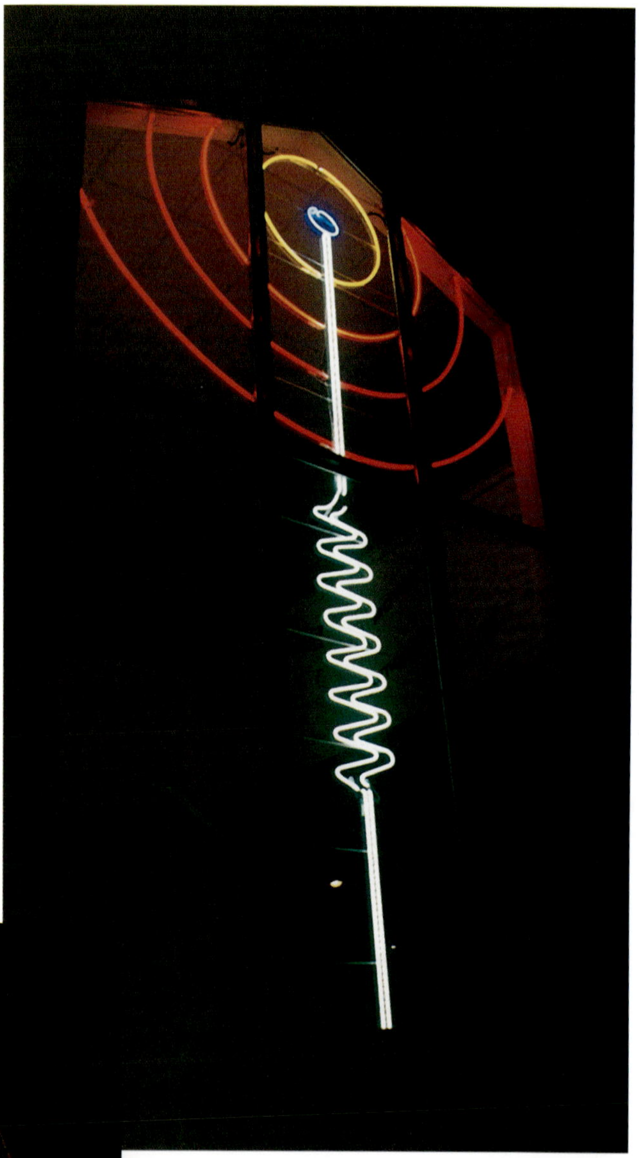

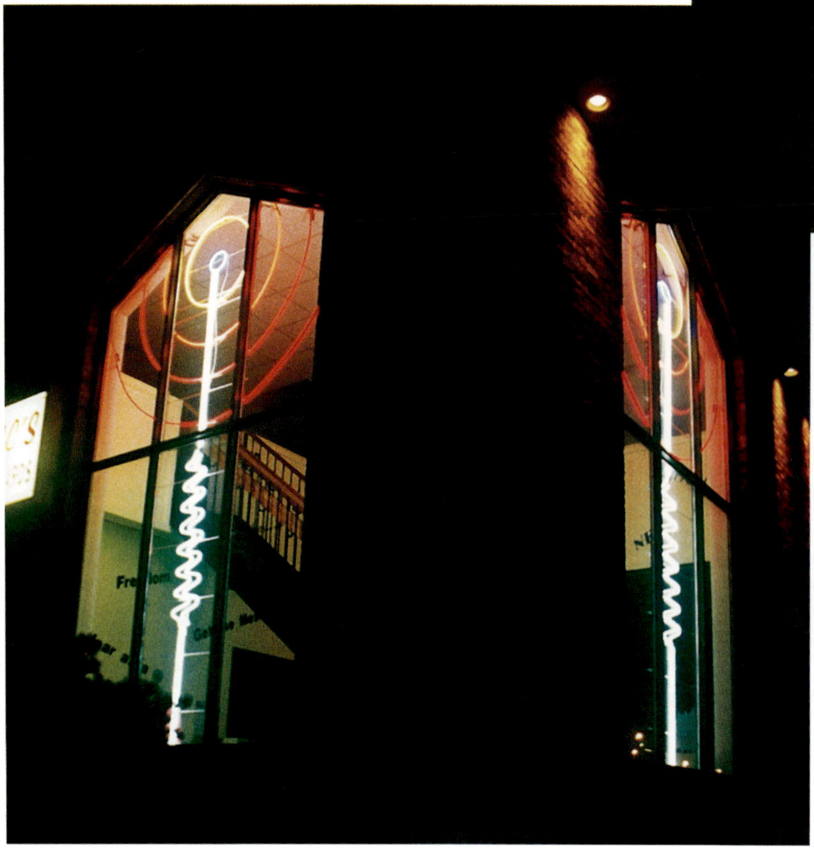

DESIGNERS

Eric Flynn
Bud J. Lawson
Sign Designs, Inc.
204 Campus Way
Modesto, CA 95352
(209) 524-4484

FABRICATOR

Sign Designs, Inc.

Wall-mounted mirrors double the length of this 480-ft. interior neon lighting installation; another 60 ft. of purple tubing outline the mirror. Coordination with the contractor allowed overhead (PK) wiring and transformers to be installed during construction of the stepped ceiling. The neon lighting is 15mm Voltarc® purple pumped red.

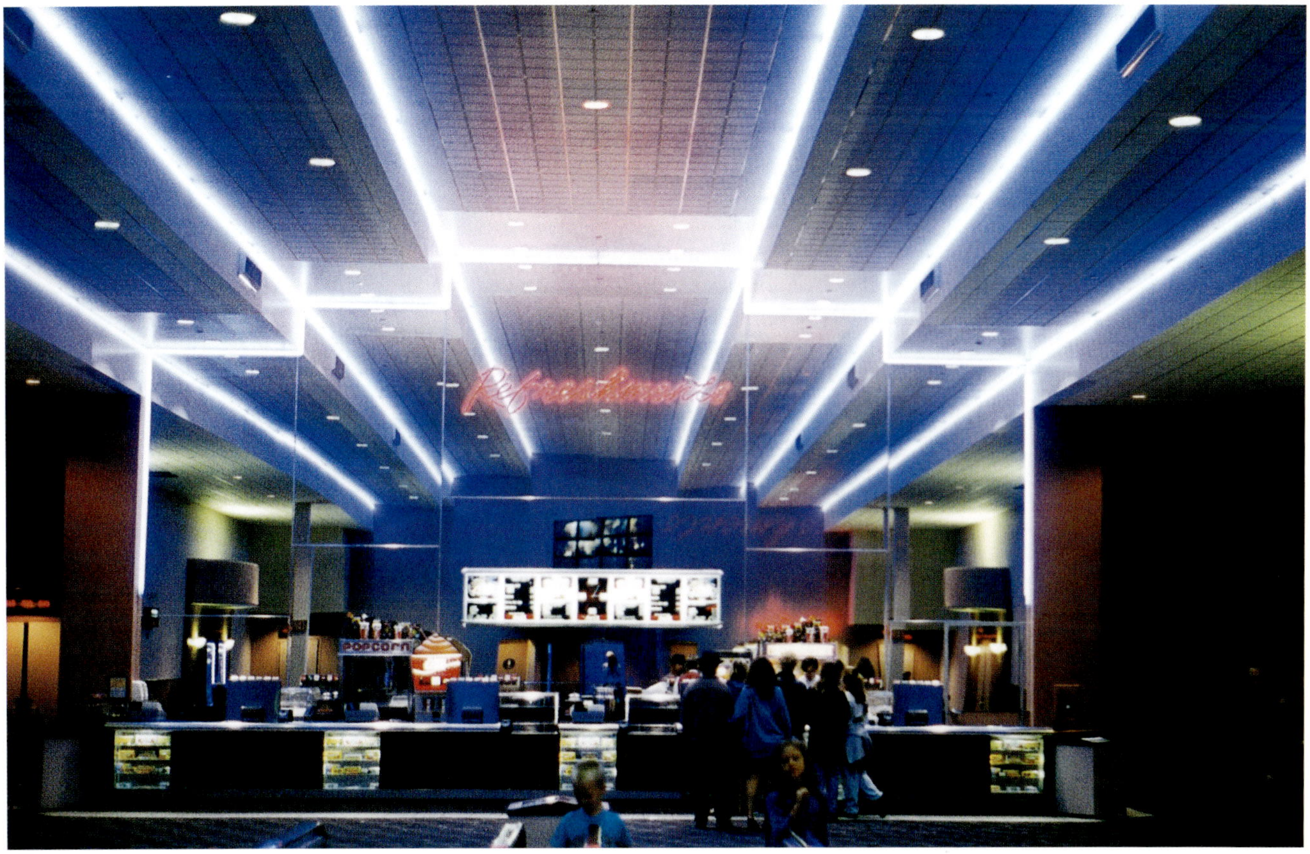

ELECTRIC

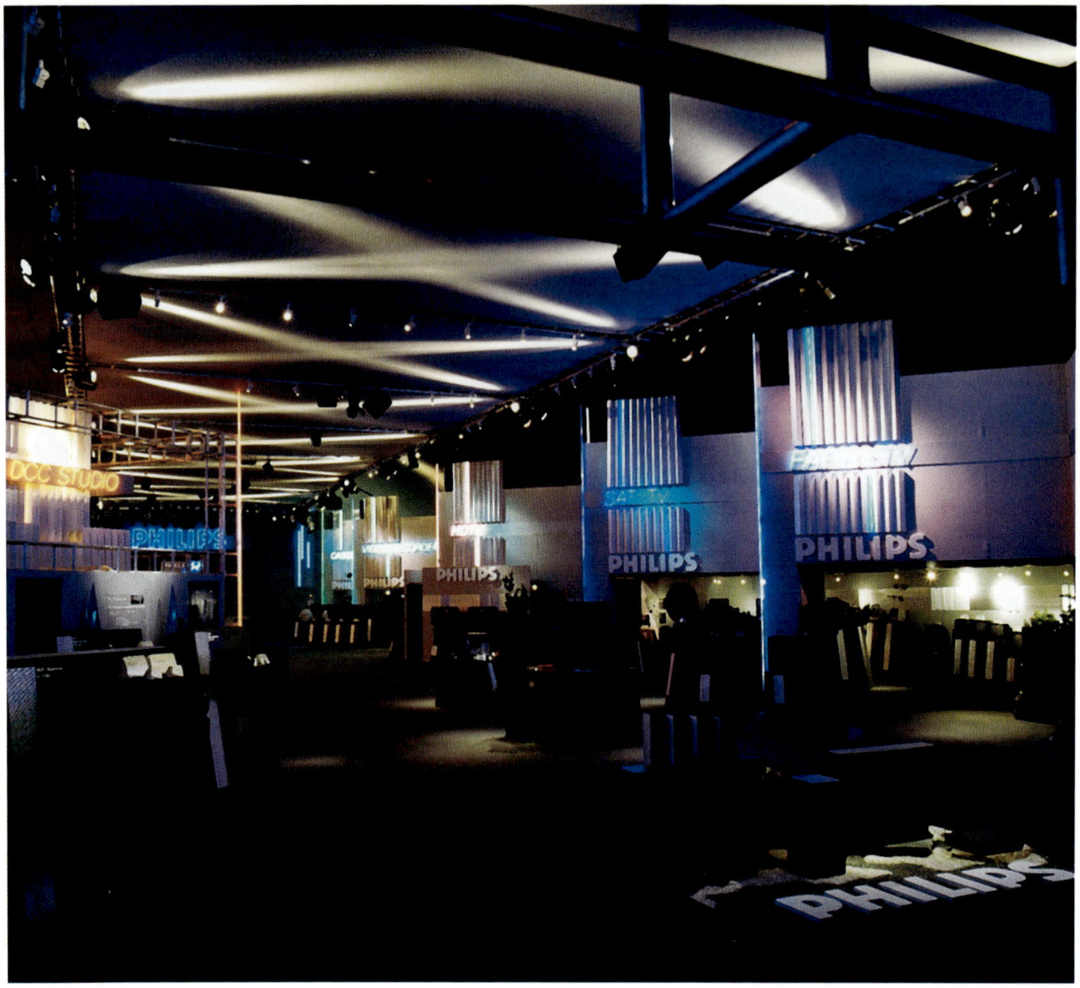

DESIGNERS

Atelier Hutter
H. Kernreuther
K+P Marketing Communication
Kolpingstr. 19
Vienna, Austria 1230
16155200

Architekturburo Duniezki
Bosendorfer Str. 6
Vienna, Austria 1010
15054142

D.J. Sprengnagel
NeonLine Werbedesign GmbH.
Obere Donaustrasse 45a
Vienna, Austria 1020
431 332-0607

FABRICATOR

NeonLine Werbedesign GmbH.

Neon logos, lettering and tubing are in place for signage and interesting light effects in this 10,000-sq.-ft. exhibition area. One-piece, 20-ft.-high, vertical neon tubes (left of center) help customer wayfinding.

DESIGNERS

Damir Krizmanic
D. J. Sprengnagel
Alfred Hager
NeonLine Werbedesign GmbH.
Obere Donaustrasse 45a
Vienna, Austria 1020
431 332-0607

FABRICATOR

NeonLine Werbedesign GmbH.

The neon pull-lever on this animated one-armed bandit lights in three positions. With the third lighting, the winning sevens turn on and illuminated gold coins "tumble" from below. After this, the entire sign flashes on-and-off five times, and the cycle repeats. The background graphics are screen printed.

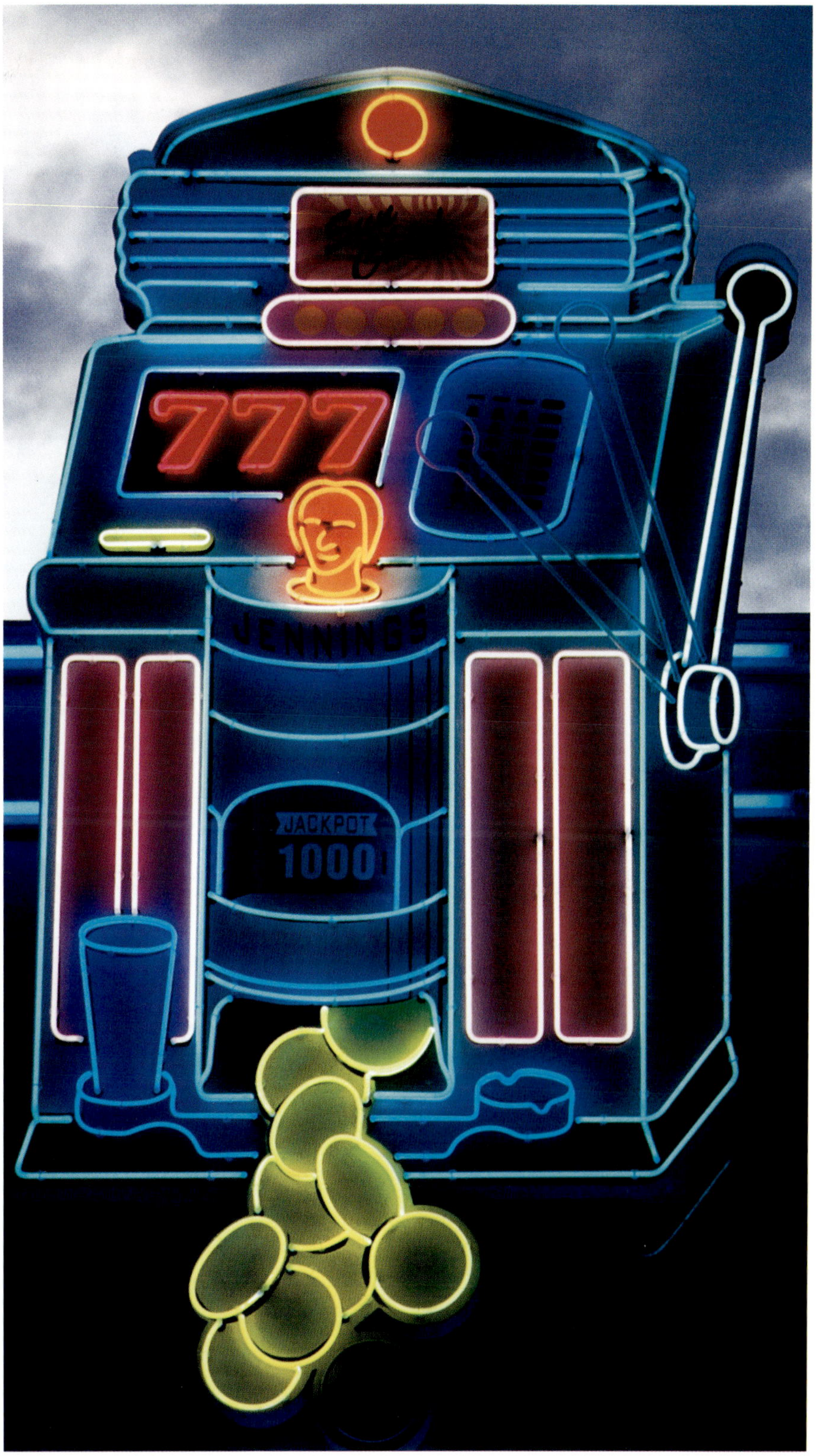

MULTI-TENANT ELECTRIC

DESIGNERS

Gary "Peewee" Ward
Bob Dail
Oklahoma Sign Co., Inc.
2720 East King Pl.
Tulsa, OK 74110
(918) 835-5581

Becky Hyman
1721 W. 7th
Joplin, MO 64801
(417) 782-1702

FABRICATOR

Oklahoma Sign Co., Inc.

An illuminated directory with translucent vinyl copy, exposed neon, backlit reveals, routed letters and reverse channel letters are packaged in this 35-ft.-high, freestanding sign. Vertical rows of illuminated glass blocks rise on each side; ceramic tiles dress the bottom panels.

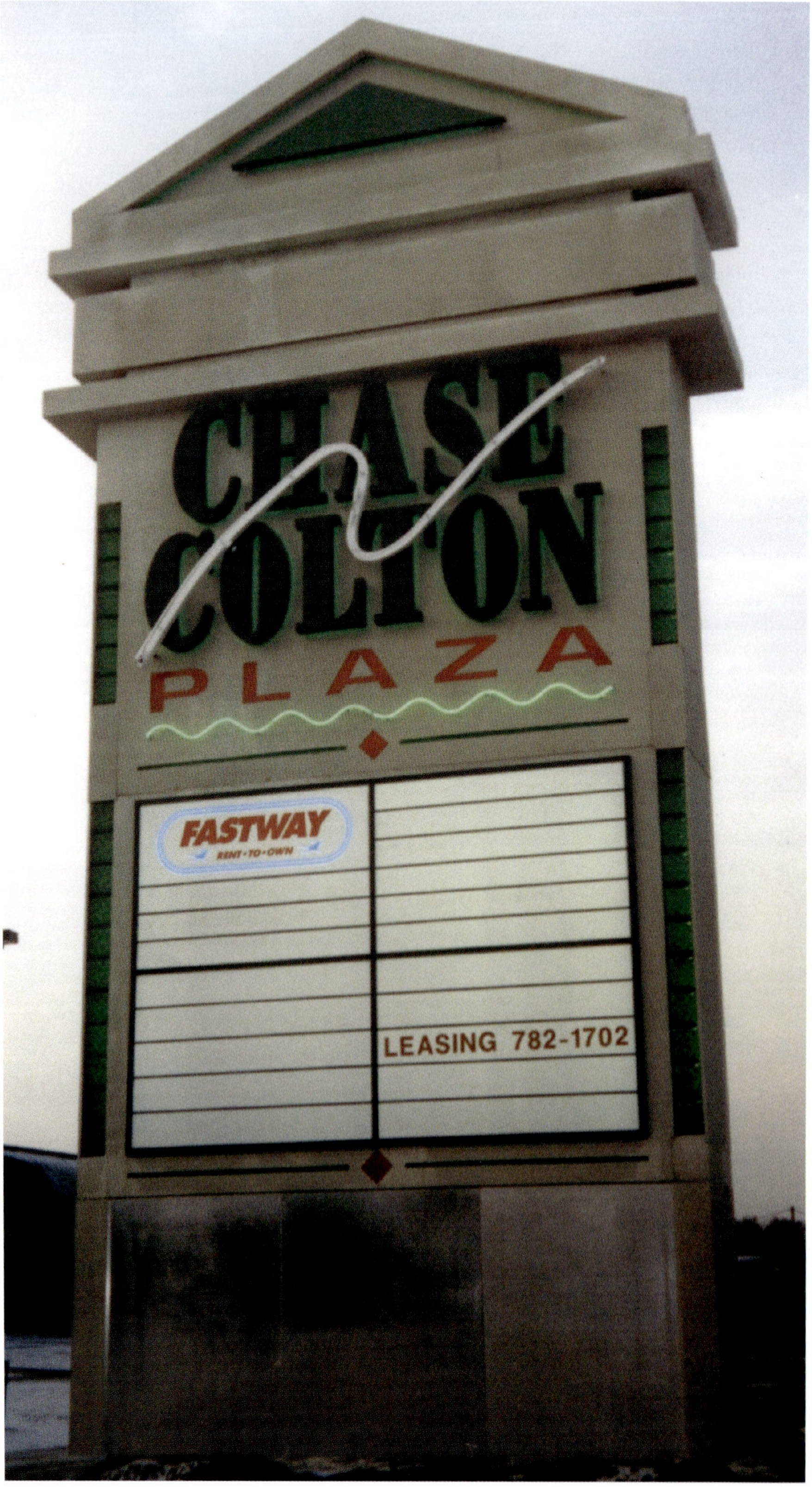

DESIGNER

Graphic Solutions
1750 Kettner Blvd.
San Diego, CA 92107
(619) 239-1335

FABRICATOR

Ad-Art Electric Sign Corp.
3133 N. Ad-Art Rd.
Stockton, CA 95215
(204) 931-0860

Bigger than you may first think, this illuminated, double-face, free standing sign measures 80 ft. to the top. The multi-surfaced crowning logo is 18 ft. high, and each wedge-shaped panel measures 9½ x 22 ft. The sign faces are Lexan® polycarbonate with vinyl colors and graphics.

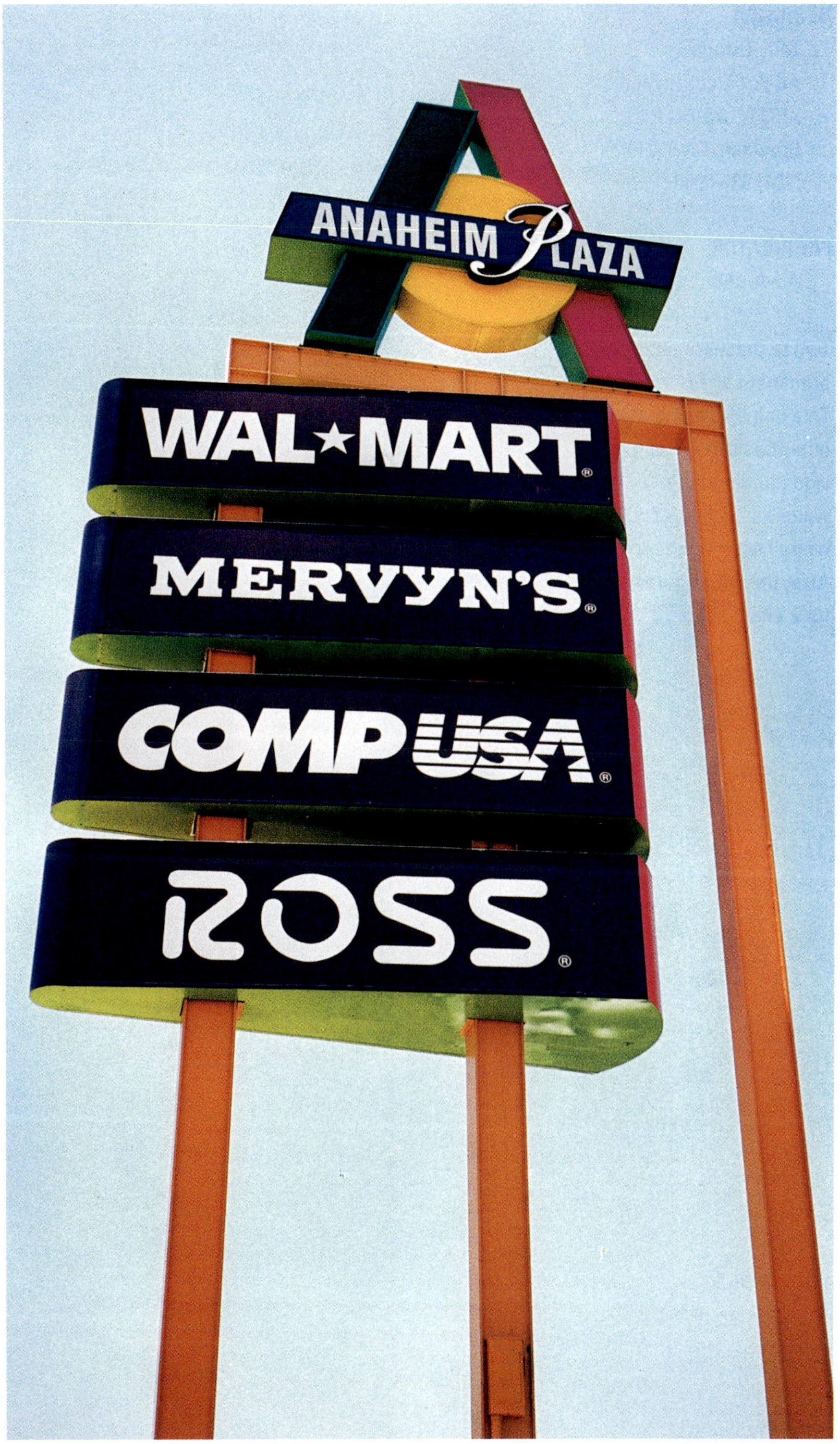

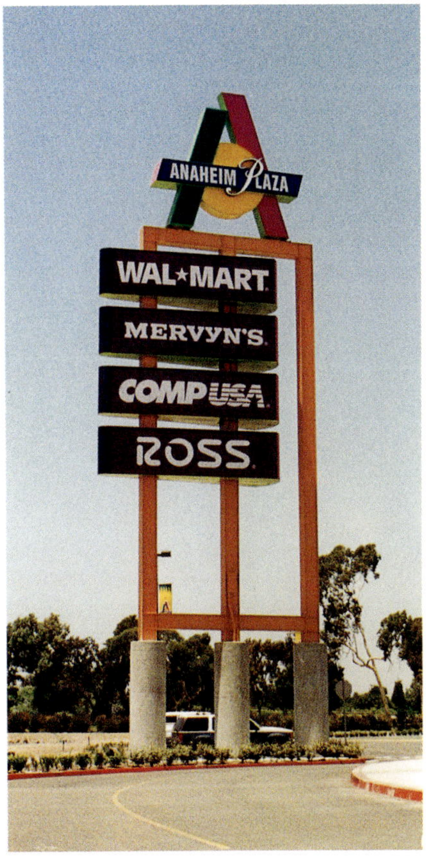

MULTI-TENANT

ELECTRIC

DESIGNER

Tony Ortega
Ad-Art Electric Sign Corp.
3133 N. Ad-Art Rd.
Stockton, CA 95215
(204) 931-0860

FABRICATOR

Ad-Art Electric Sign Corp.

Two of these freestanding signs are prominent at a Chico, CA, shopping center. This one displays tenant panels, and the other has cinema marquees. The upper sign panels are routed aluminum with white acrylic letters; the tenant panels are white Lexan® with reverse-cut vinyl film. Also, the upper reveals contain single-tube white neon.

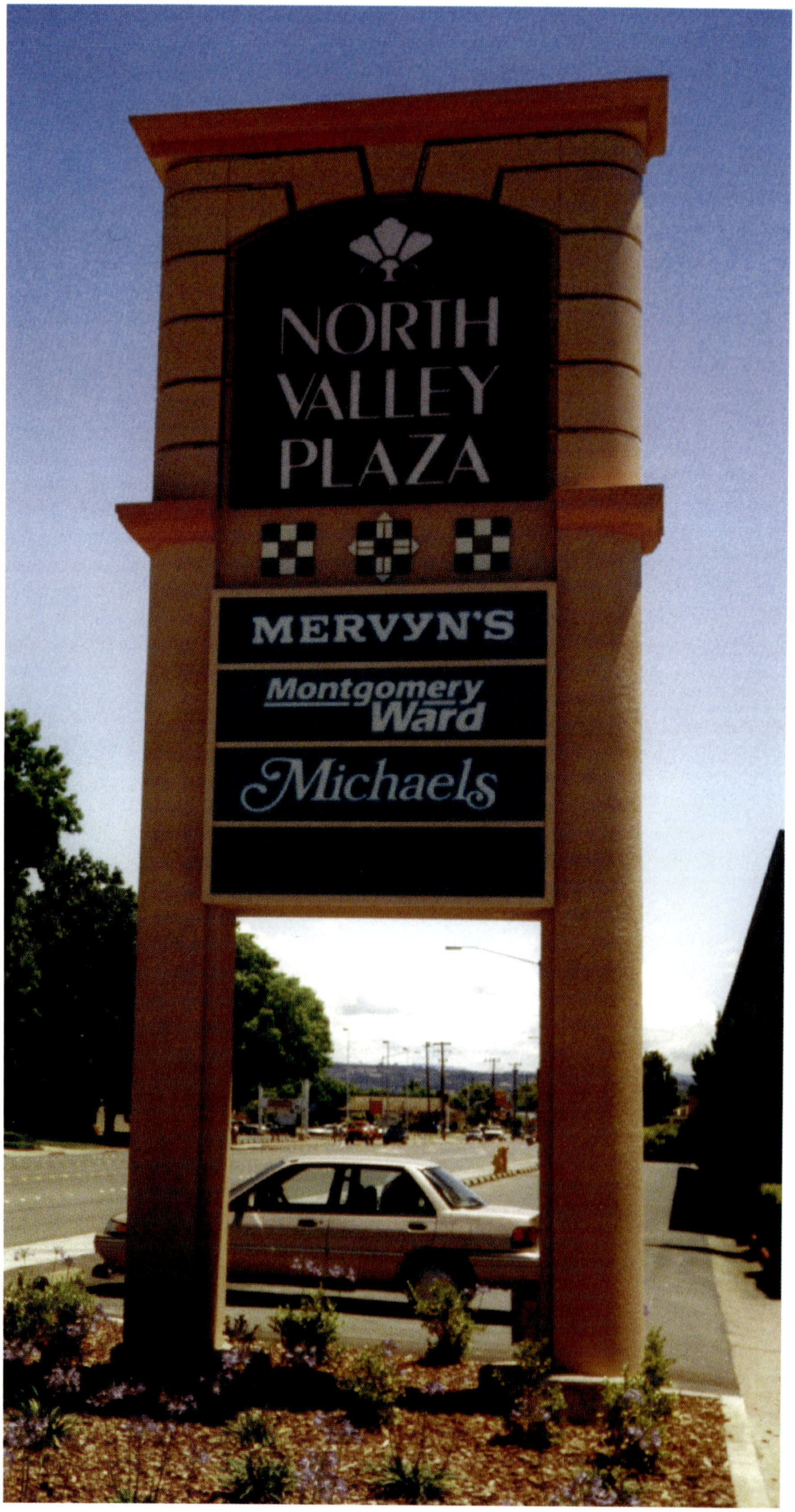

DESIGNER

Ultraneon Sign Co.
5458 Complex St. #401
San Diego, CA 92123
(619) 569-6716

FABRICATOR

Ultraneon Sign Co.

Bold colors to match the buildings were teamed with art-deco neon to create this 30-ft.-high, main-ID sign; the Camelot flags add merriment.

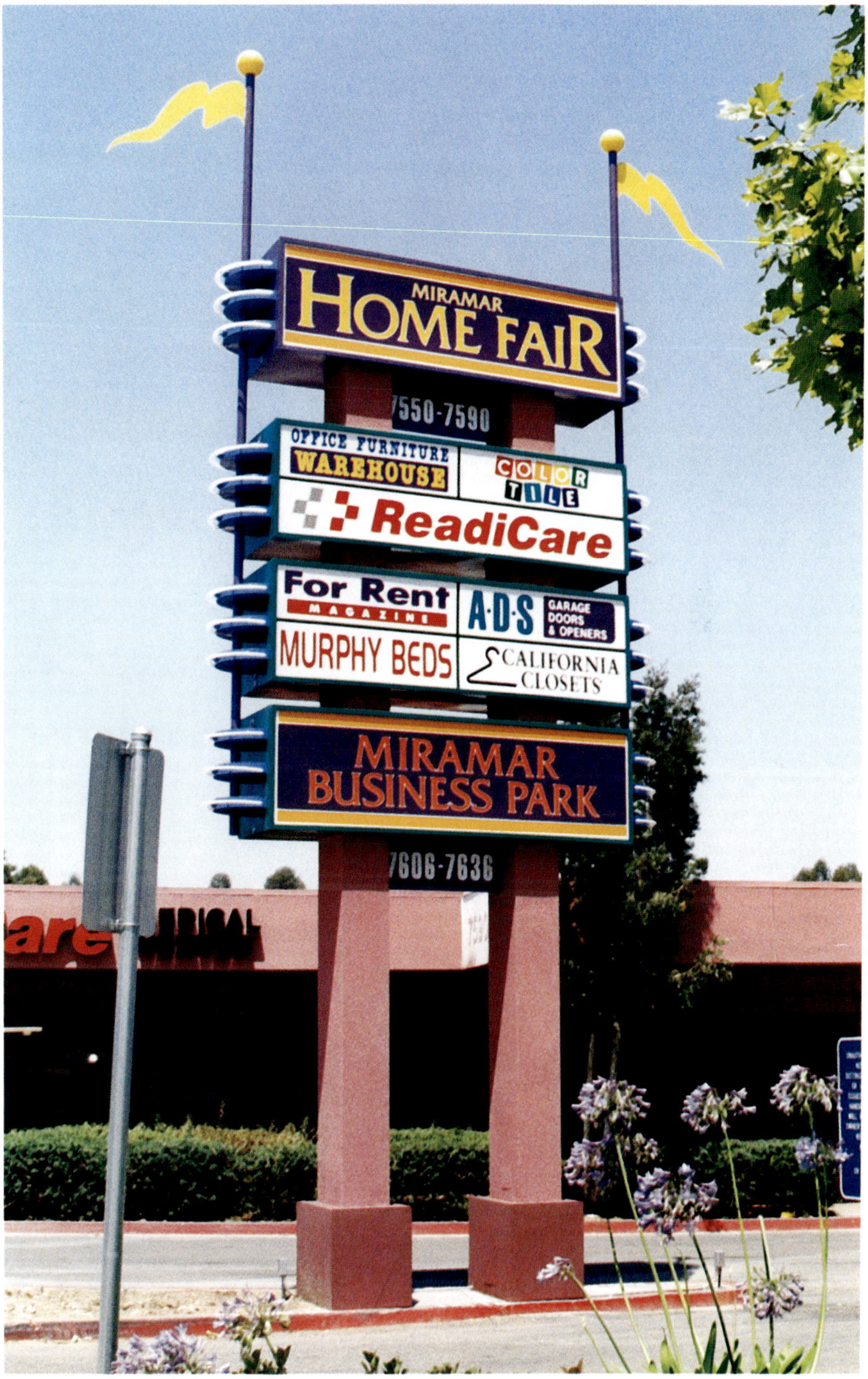

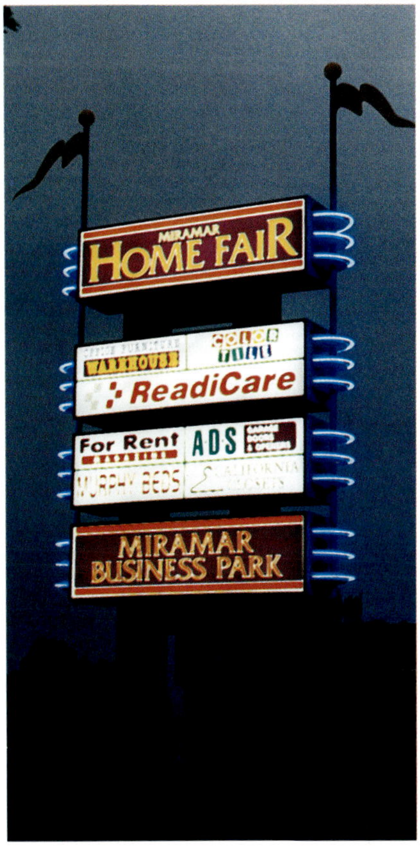

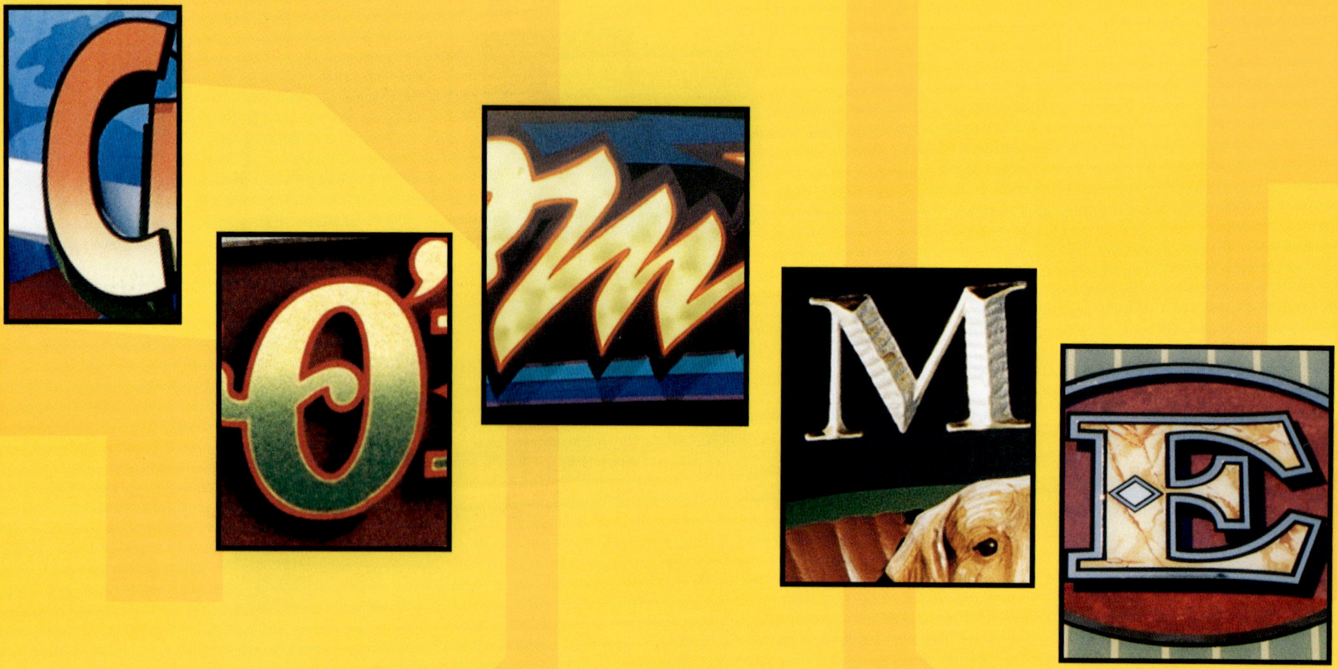
COMME

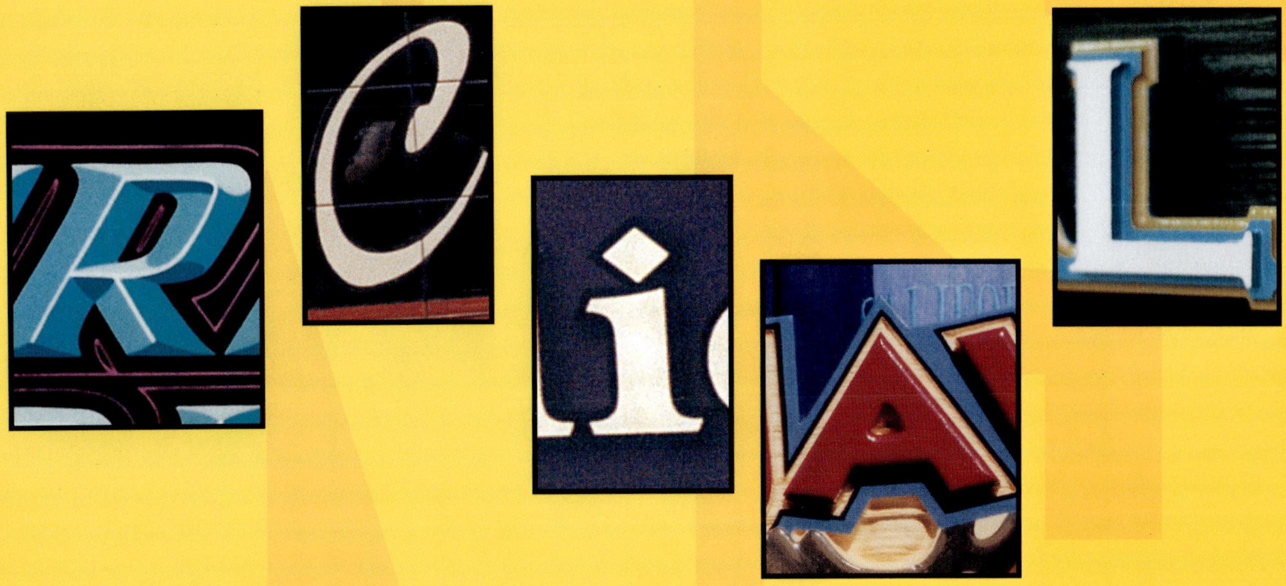

The commercial sign industry has been affected by the same technological advances as the electric side. Specifically, images output directly to computer-cut vinyl have decreased the time required executing a design, thereby creating a new niche within the industry of "fast signs" offering one-day or same-day delivery. Practically every commercial signshop uses vinyl, and many have begun to incorporate digital imaging on vinyl with more traditional methods of painting, carving and gilding signs. Vinyl has incorporated even goldleaf, in the form of Signgold®. Nevertheless, materials and methods apart from vinyl are still demanded, particularly for custom-made signs. This section features a couple of signs finished with copper leaf and variegated leaf. Others have details fabricated by "halo sandblasting," a subtle sandblasting technique for multi-dimensional wood signs. While there is no denying the emergence of vinyl in commercial signmaking, traditional techniques as well as good design will always be necessary to create unique signs.

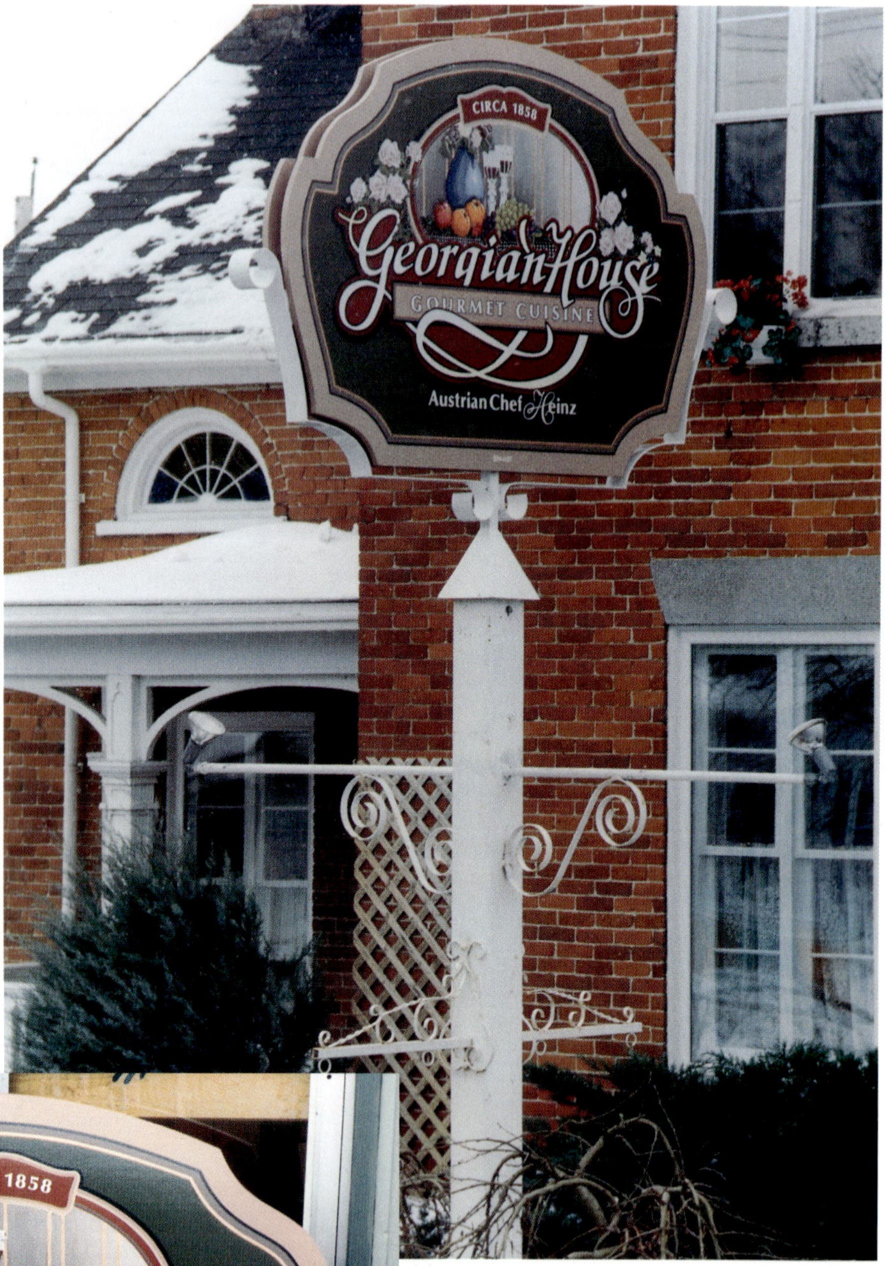

DESIGNERS

Nancy Beaudette
Noëlla Cotnam
Sign It
812-33 Pitt St.
Cornwall, ON, Canada K6J 5R2
(613) 933-7447
Fax: (613) 933-3480

FABRICATOR

Sign It

This 4 x 6-ft. flat sign is fabricated from MDO. The sign is all hand-painted and features blended pictorials and copper-leaf striping.

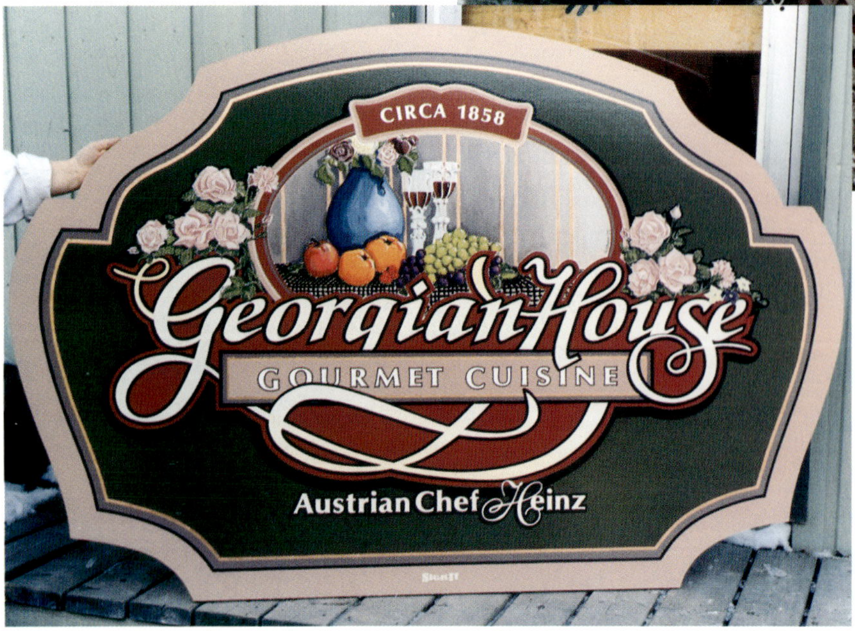

DESIGNER

Claire Lemieux
Miller Graphiste
115 Abraham Martin
Quebec, PQ, Canada G1K 7K7
(418) 692-2642
Fax: (418) 692-1746

FABRICATOR

Atelier des Champs de Bataille
390 Ave. de Bernieres
Quebec, PQ, Canada G1K 7K7
(418) 692-2642
Fax: (418) 692-1746

This is one of 10 structures fabricated from aluminum. The four-color illustration is screen printed, and the frame includes forged baguettes and ornaments.

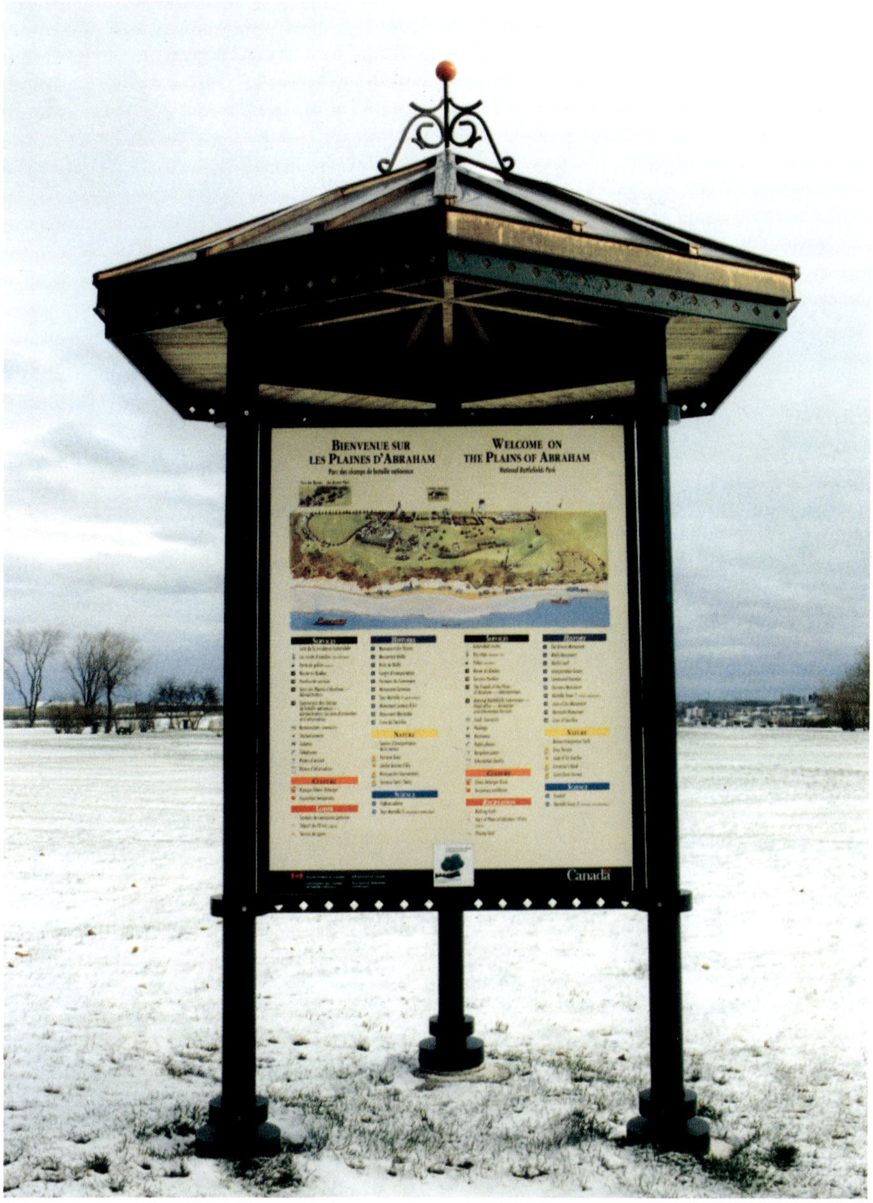

DESIGNERS

Nancy Beaudette
Noëlla Cotnam
Sign It
812-33 Pitt St.
Cornwall, ON, Canada K6J 5R2
(613) 933-7447
Fax: (613) 933-3480

FABRICATOR

Sign It

This 3 x 4-ft. sign is fabricated using ¾-in. MDO. All the graphics are hand-painted. The outline is airbrushed, and the pictorial is created using a dry-brush technique.

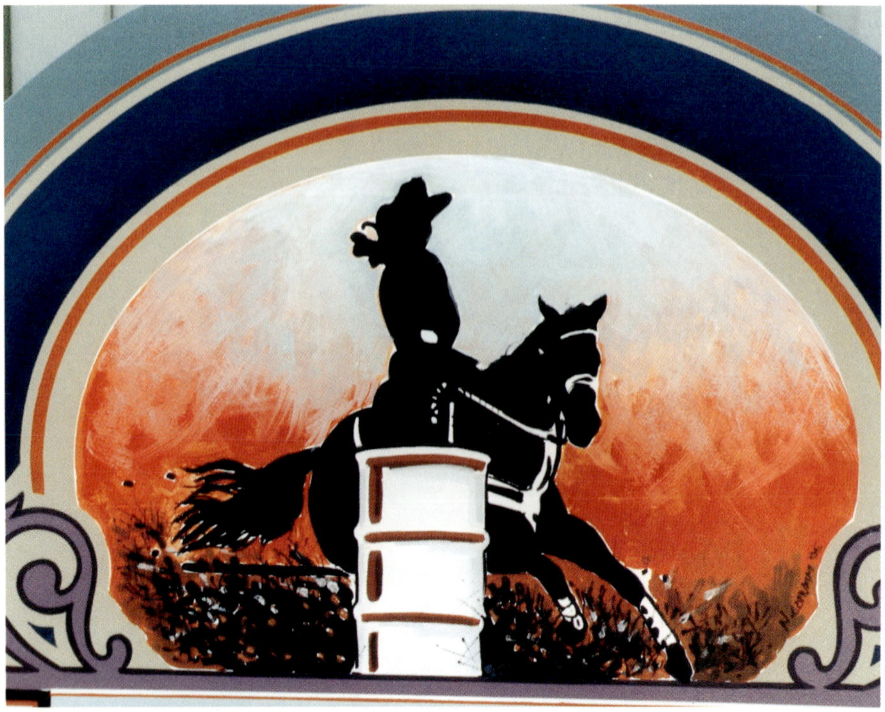

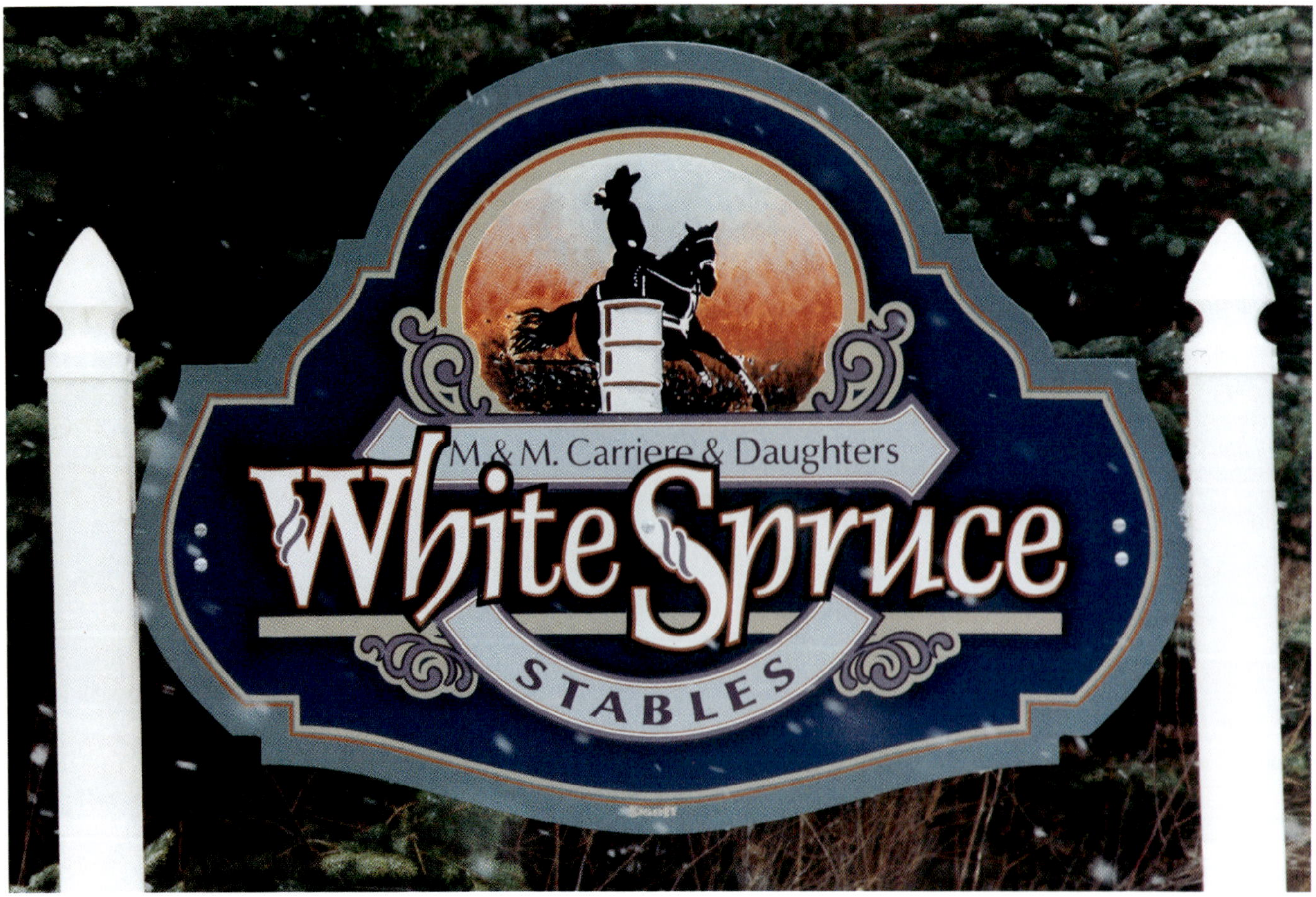

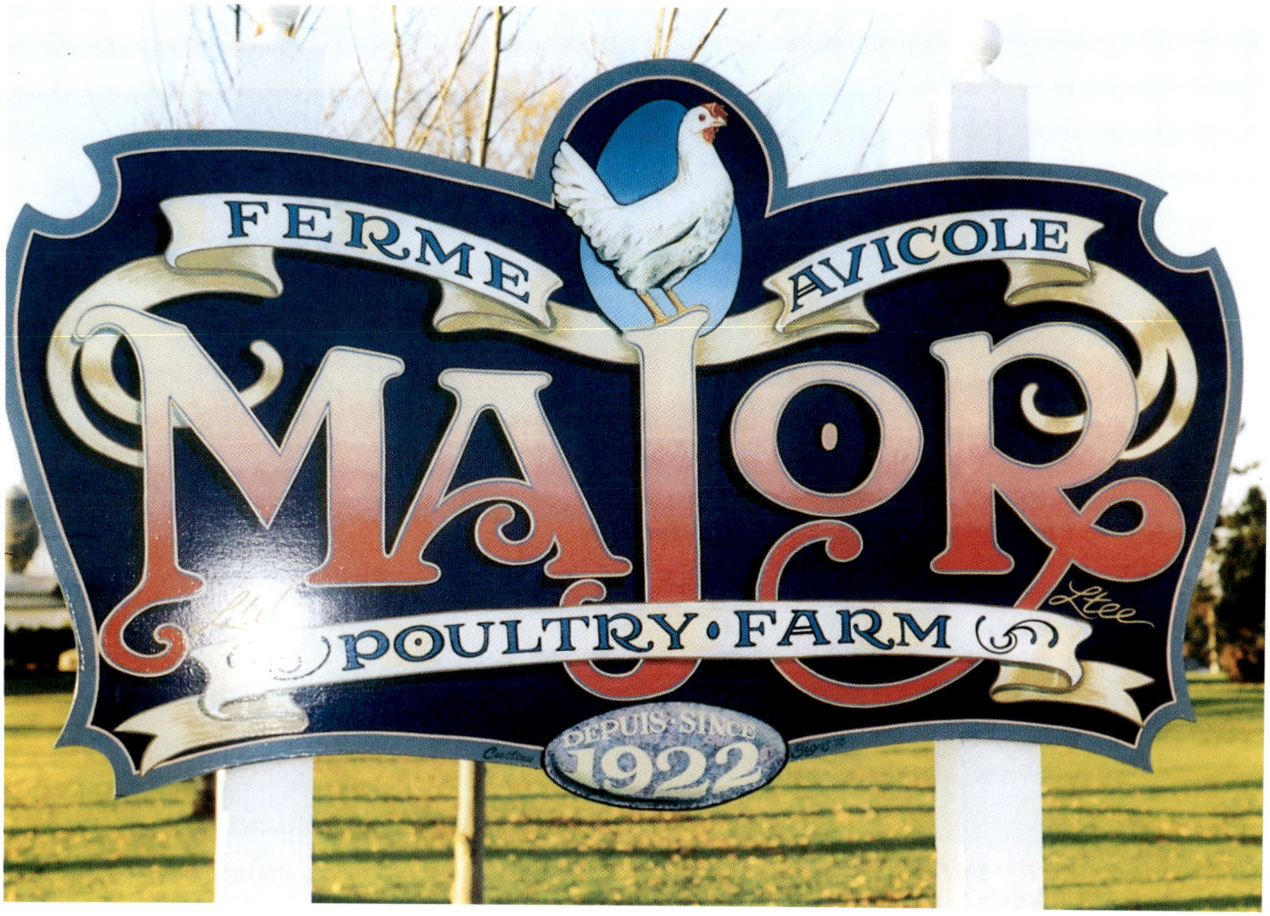

DESIGNER

Louise Macaulay
Custom Signs
304 Military Rd.
Lancaster, ON, Canada K0C 1N0
(613) 347-7405
Fax: (613) 347-1206

FABRICATOR

Custom Signs

This single-sided sign is constructed from ¾-in. MDO and measures 4 x 6½ ft. The background is created using the "sponge" technique. Everything is hand-lettered and illustrated.

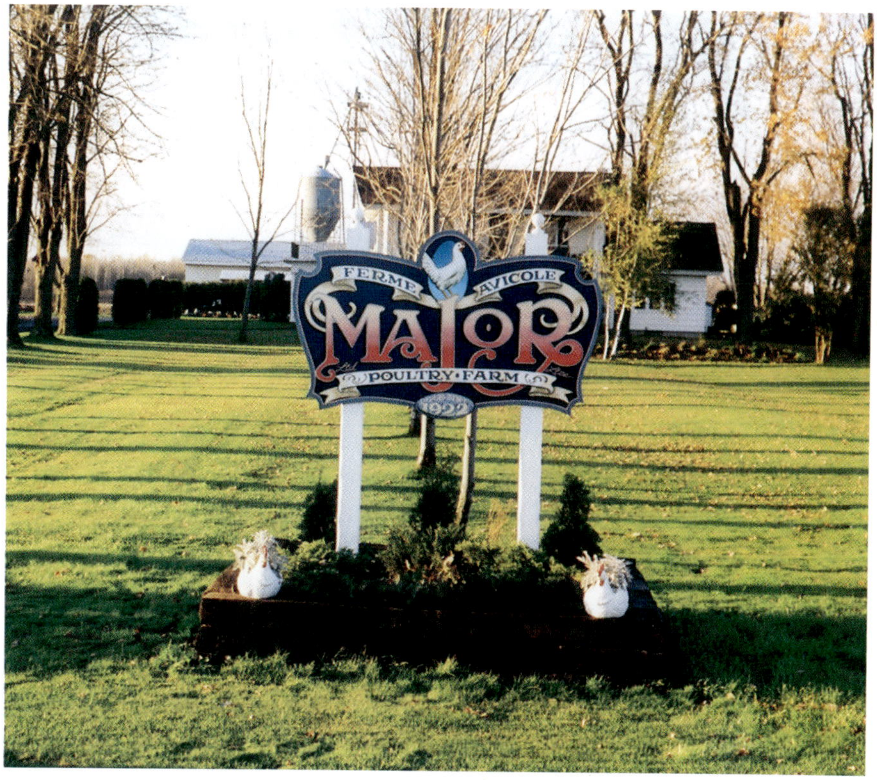

DESIGNERS

Nancy Beaudette
Noëlla Cotnam
Sign It
812-33 Pitt St.
Cornwall, ON, Canada K6J 5R2
(613) 933-7447
Fax: (613) 933-3480

FABRICATOR

Sign It

This 3 x 8-ft. MDO sign features composition leaf with variegated scrolls and stripes. The background is painted flat using a dry-brush technique. The pictorial is blended with sign-lettering enamels. The frame is a combination of panfiber and molding. The "chili pepper" corners are hand-carved high-density urethane.

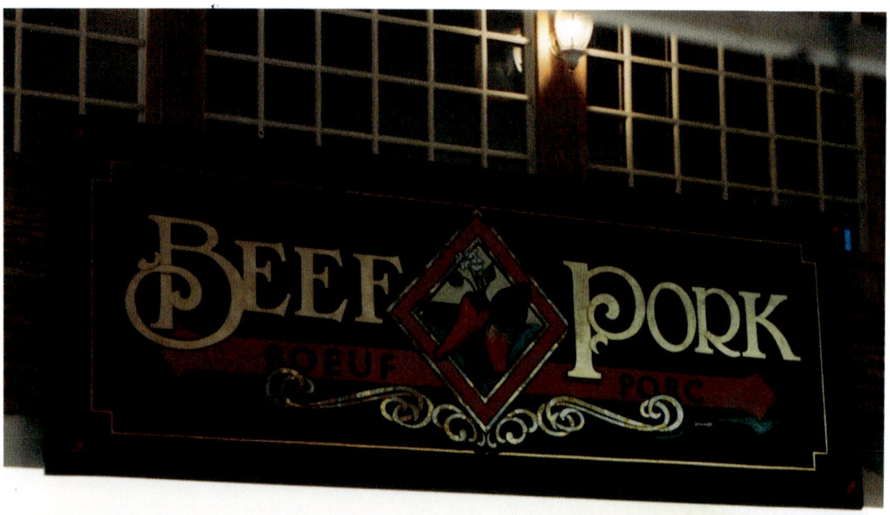

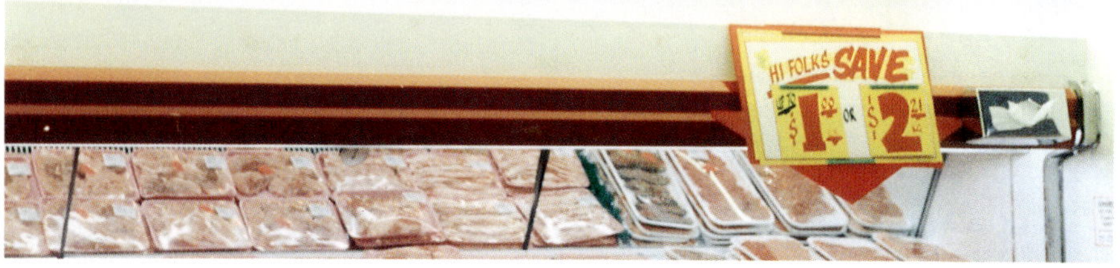

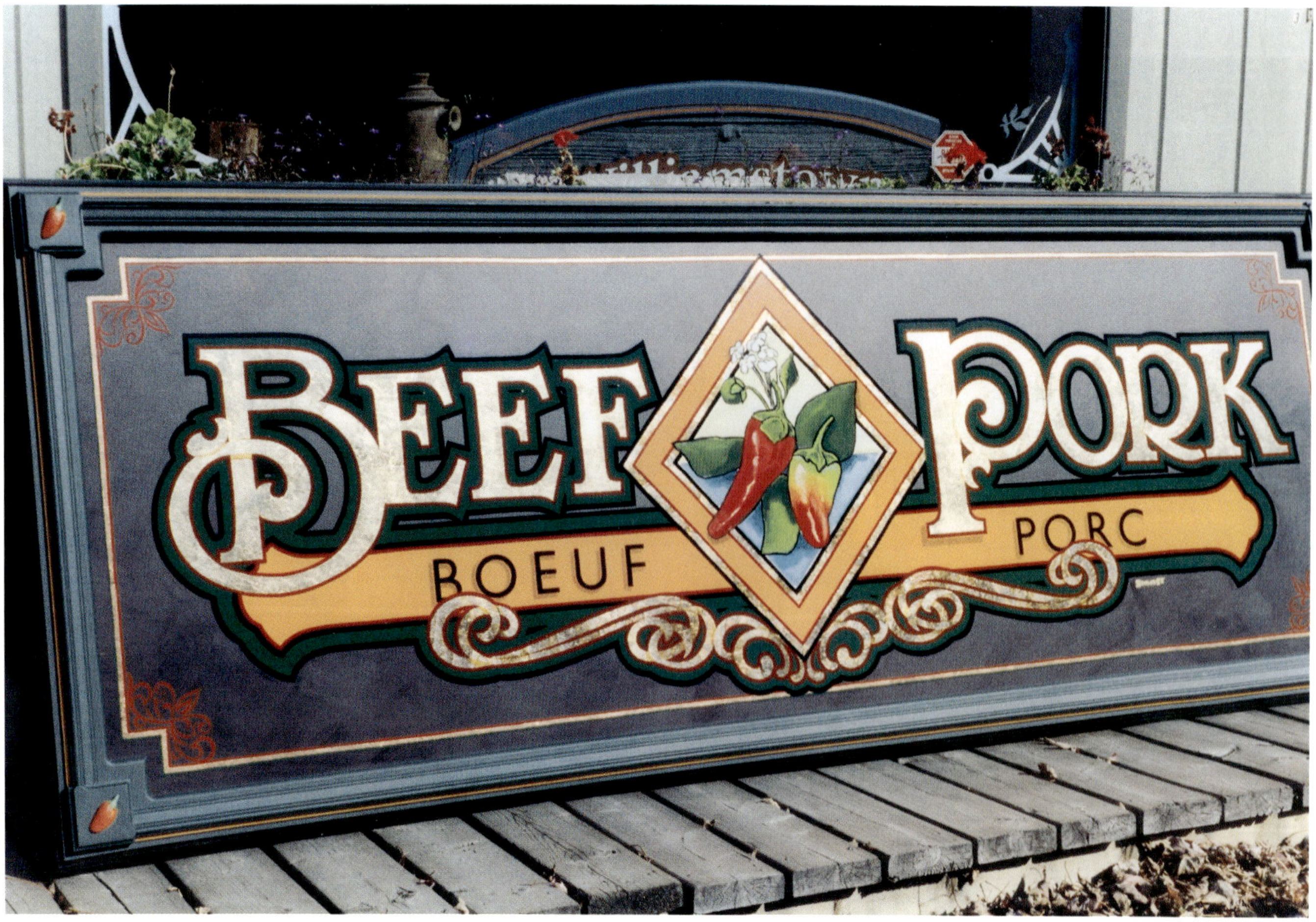

DESIGNER

Jeff Douglas
Douglas Signs
413 14th Ave. E.
Ashland, WI 54806
(715) 682-2160
Fax: (715) 682-6680

FABRICATORS

Tony Dietz
Jeff Douglas
Douglas Signs

This 8 x 4-ft. sign projects 5 ft. from the building. It is fabricated from MDO, which is attached to steel tubing and a mounting plate with a cut-out of a coffee cup. The MDO faces are painted with lettering enamel along with black glass smalt. The sign is lit from above with quartz floods.

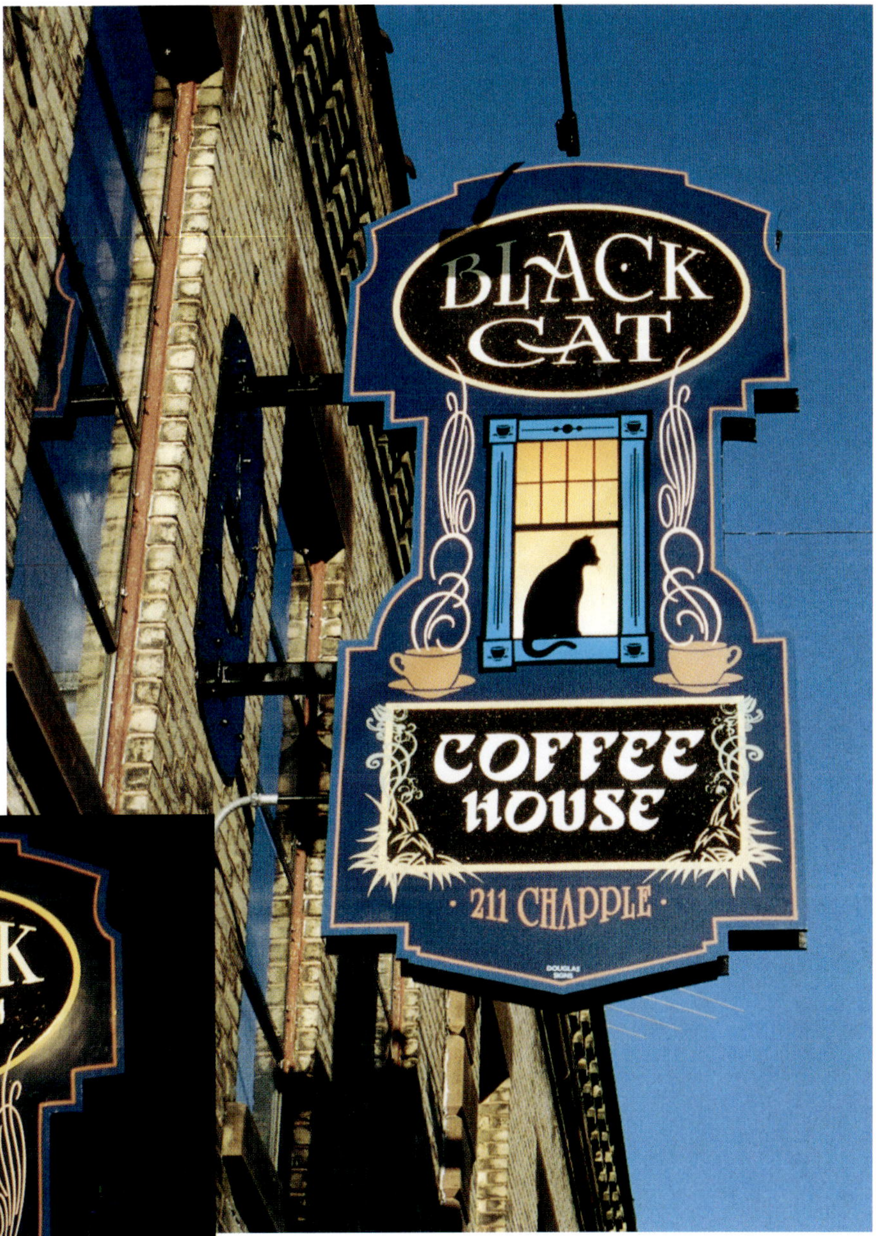

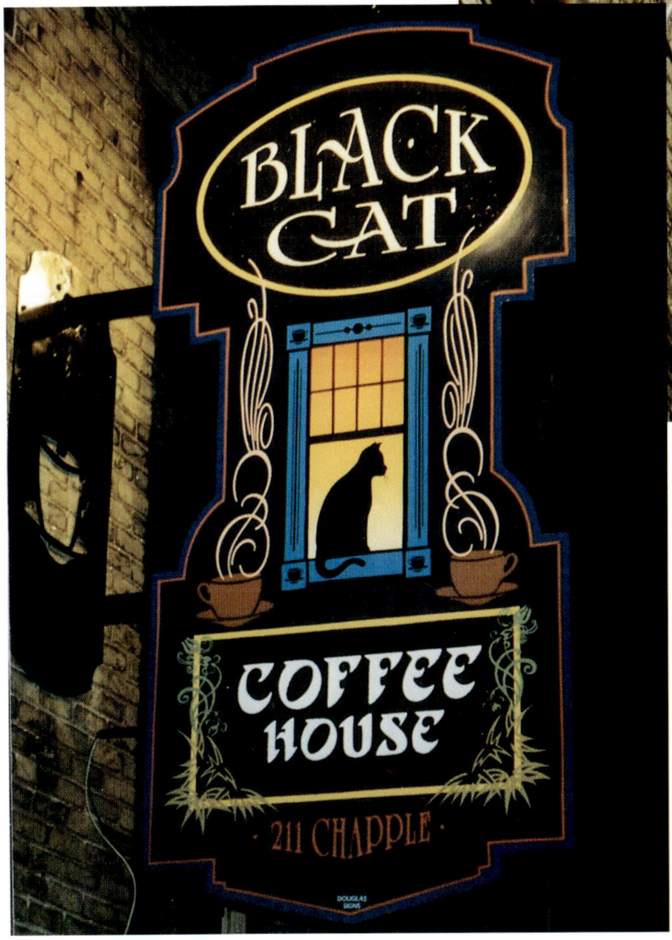

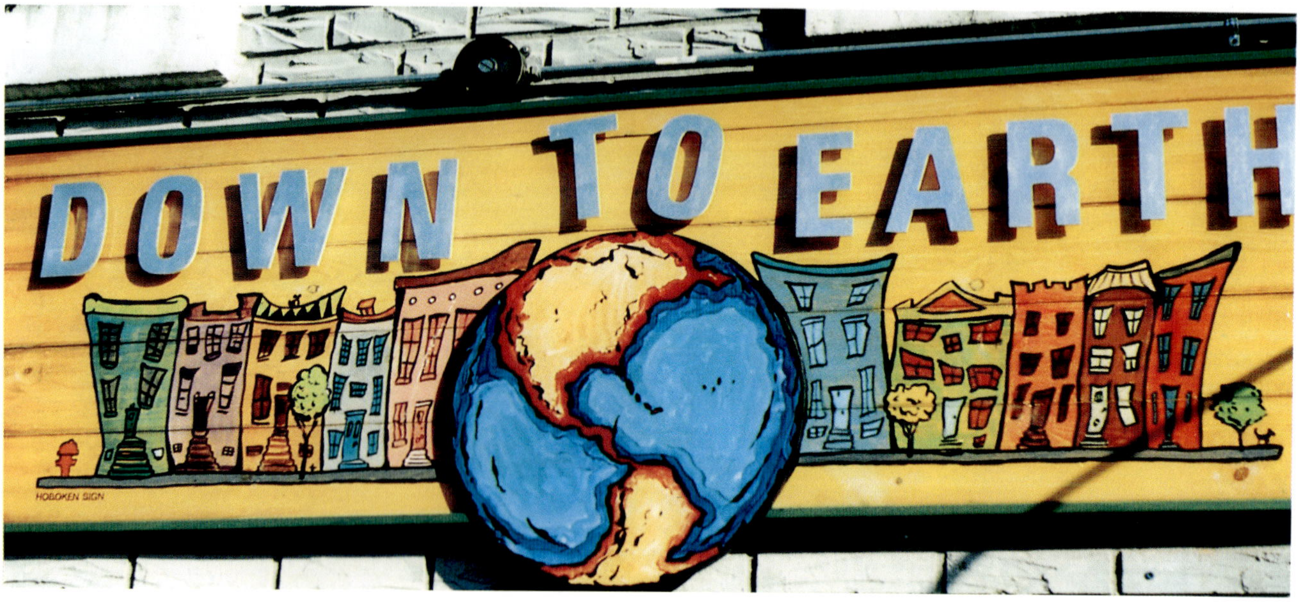

DESIGNERS

Ray Guzman
Hoboken Sign
108 Jefferson St.
Hoboken, NJ 07030
(201) 798-0688
Fax: (201) 798-8405

Chris Nyien (logo design)

FABRICATOR

Hoboken Sign

This 2 x 7-ft. sign's pine panels incorporate a "washed and stain" effect on acrylics. The sign is finished in water-based urethane. The letters are flat-cut, finished with silver leaf, and clear-coated.

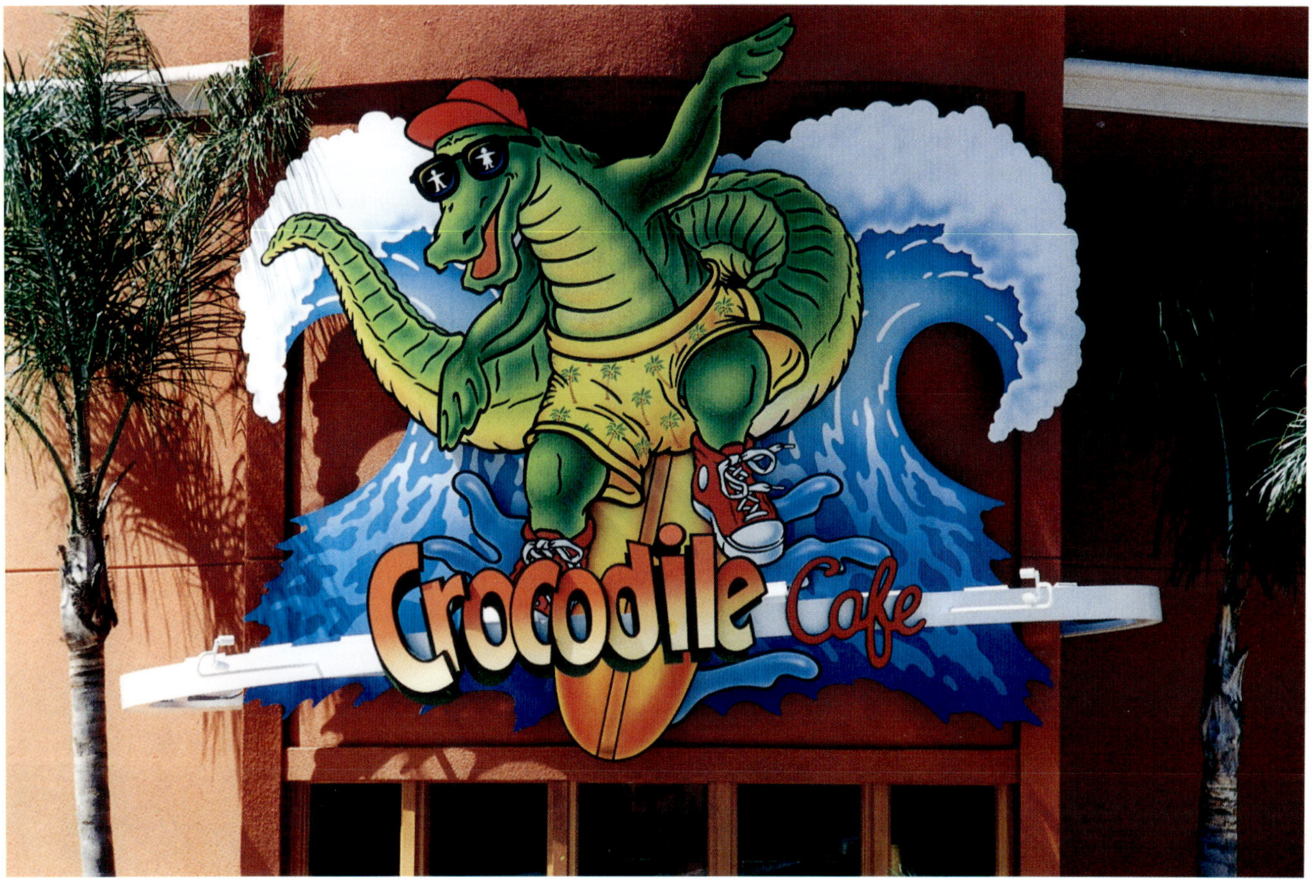

DESIGNER

John Hyatt Retail Design
2217 Canyon Dr.
Los Angeles, CA 90068
(213) 463-0868
Fax: (213) 463-0859

FABRICATORS

Dick Brokaw
Pino Signs
12024 F Centralia Rd.
Hawaiian Gardens, CA 90716
(310) 924-5353
Fax: (310) 924-5849

Rembrandt Graphics
720-G N. Valley St.
Anaheim, CA 92801
(714) 535-6600
Fax: (714) 535-6703

This 20 x 15-ft. 3M Scotchprint® graphic is applied over ⅛-in.-radius aluminum plate welded to an aluminum-tube frame. The wave projects 12-18 in. and conforms to a radiused wall. The crocodile, surfboard and splash project out from the wave in successive layers. The letters are separate, flat cut-outs projecting from an elliptical band.

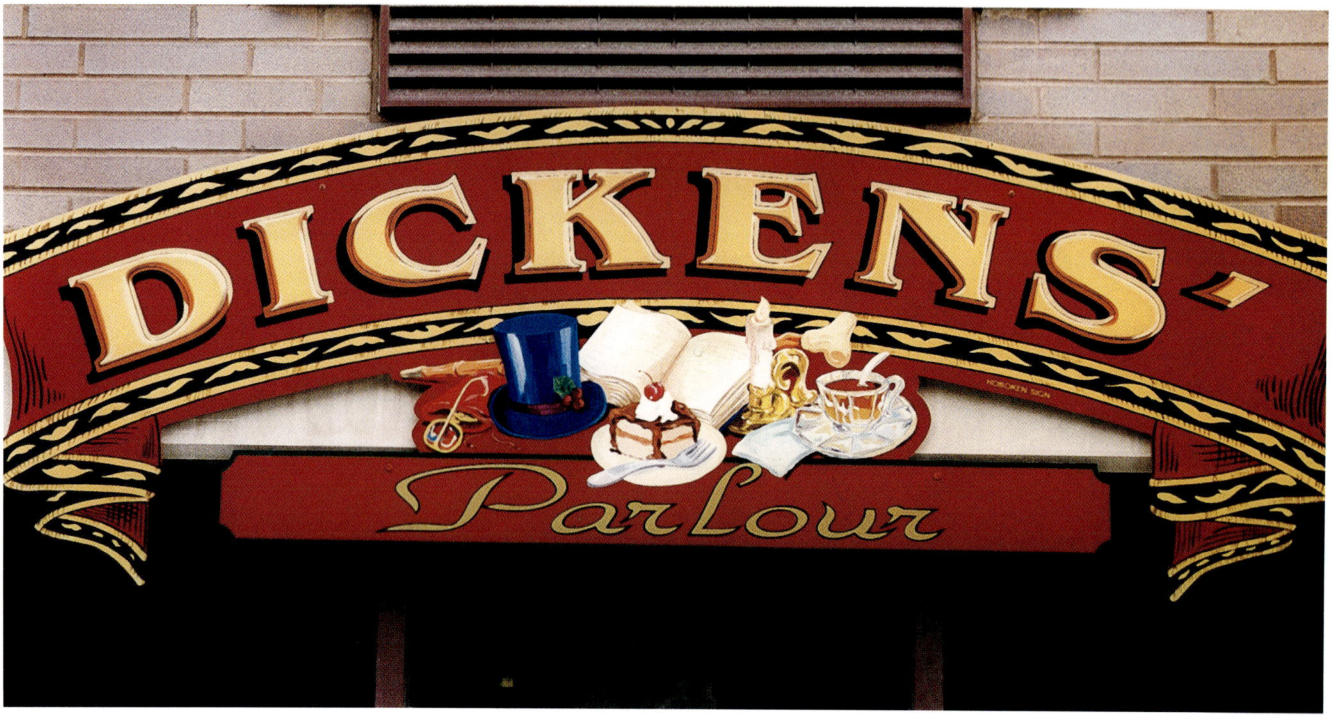

DESIGNERS

Ray and Renata Guzman
Hoboken Sign
108 Jefferson St.
Hoboken, NJ 07030
(201) 798-0688
Fax: (201) 798-8405

FABRICATOR

Hoboken Sign

The sign for this coffee, tea and dessert parlor measures 30 in. x 8 ft. The MDO sign blank is fully painted with enamel.

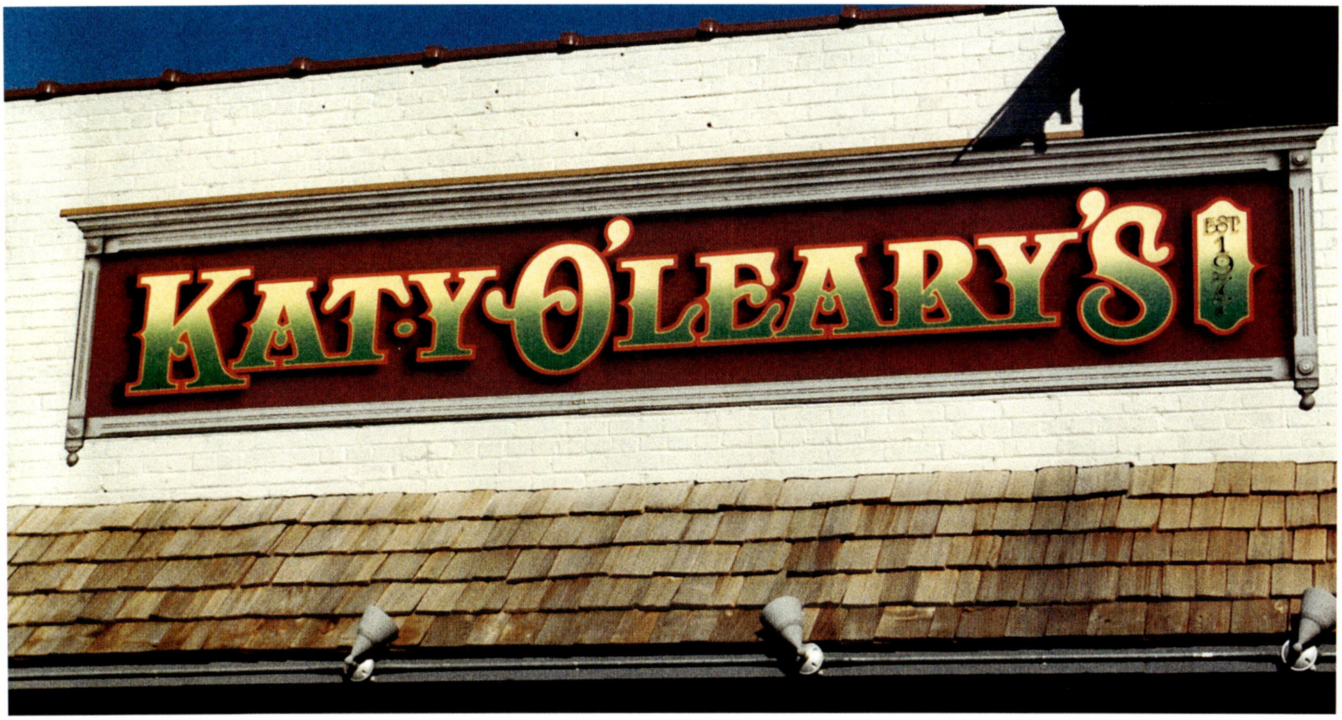

DESIGNER

Carousel Signs & Designs, Inc.
7202 Brook Rd.
Richmond, VA 23227
(804) 262-3497
Fax: (804) 262-9073

FABRICATOR

Carousel Signs & Designs, Inc.

The entire sign is comprised of ½-in. MDO board. It is airbrushed with enamel to depict the molding and for dimension.

COMMERCIAL

DESIGNERS

Al Malave
Jo Ann Malave
Design Quest Inc.
2950 Aloma Ave., Ste. 200
Winter Park, FL 32792
(407) 678-5520

FABRICATOR

Don Bell Industries, Inc.
365 Oak Place
Port Orange, FL 32127
(904) 788-8084

These six signs are each approximately 3-ft. square, and routed out of ⅛-in. aluminum.

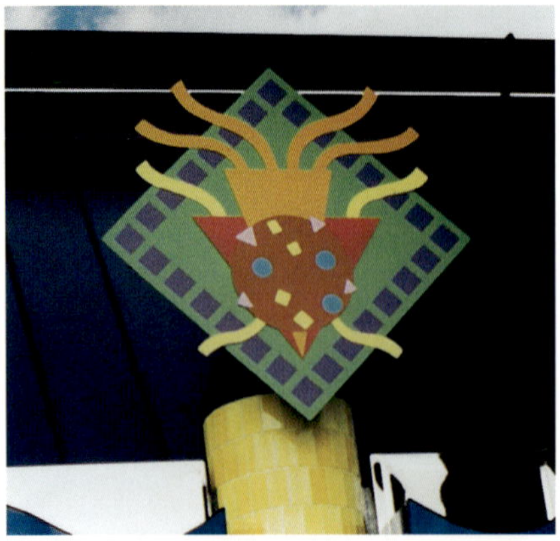

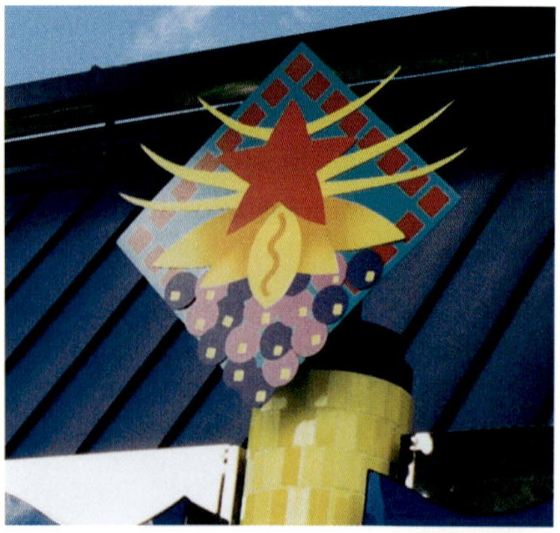

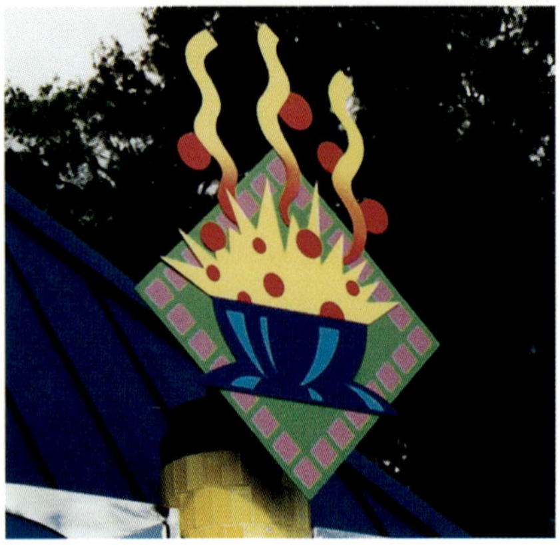

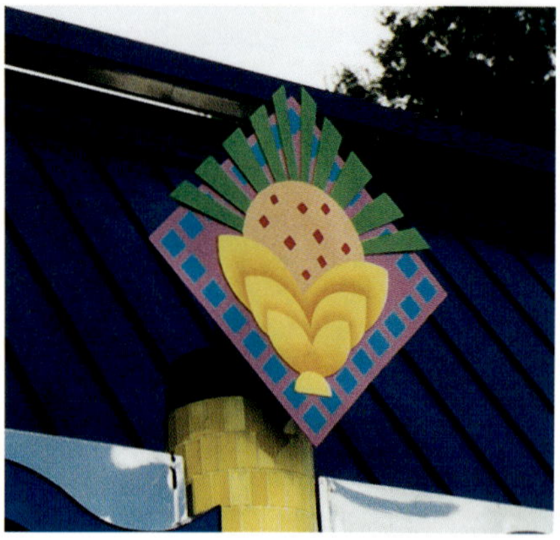

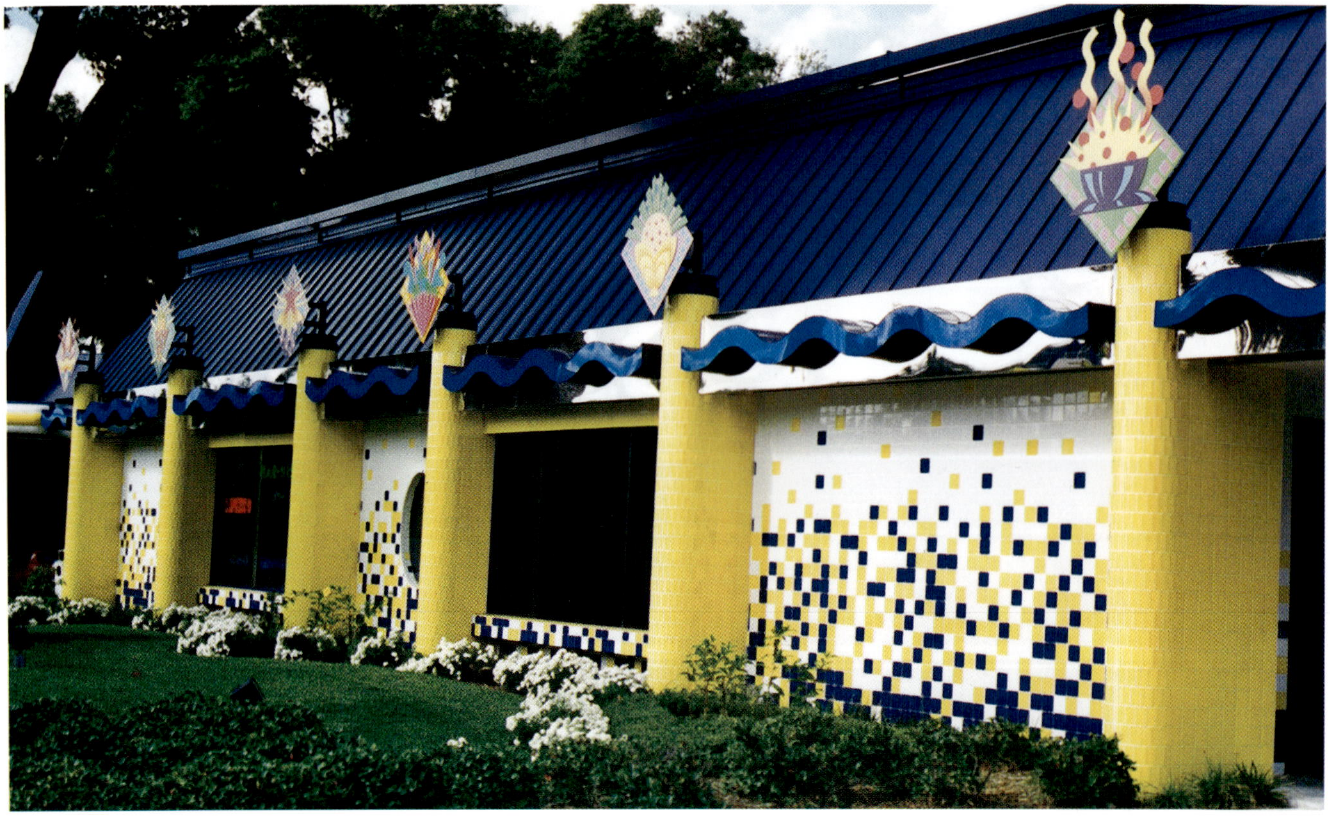

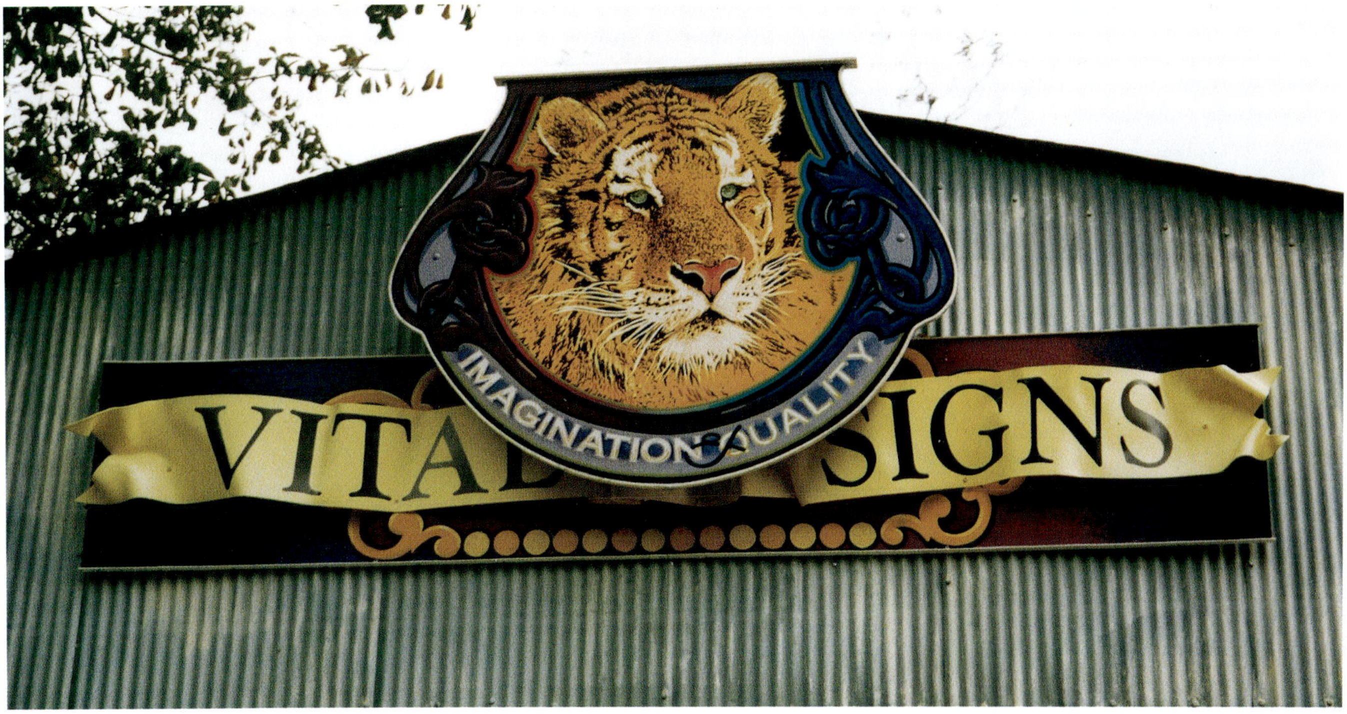

DESIGNER

Chip Spirson
Vital Signs
606 N. Davis St.
Pensacola, FL 32501
(904) 434-6364

FABRICATOR

Vital Signs

This sign for a signshop is 96 x 52-in., constructed of MDO,and painted in lettering enamel.

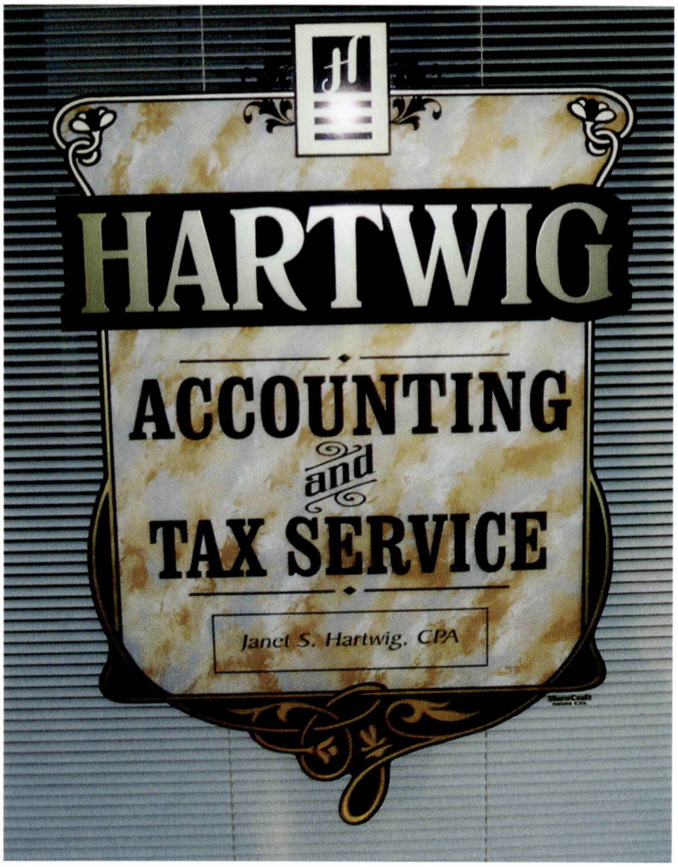

DESIGNERS

Jay Allen
Joe Marshall
Shawcraft Sign Co.
7727 Burden Rd.
Machesney Park, IL 61115
(815) 282-4105
Fax: (815) 282-4147

FABRICATOR

Shawcraft Sign Co.

This 36 x 48-in. window graphic is fabricated from black, high-performance vinyl with gold-enamel border highlights. "Hartwig" is created in reverse-cut matte using 22K SignGold® vinyl. The background is marbleized with lettering enamels.

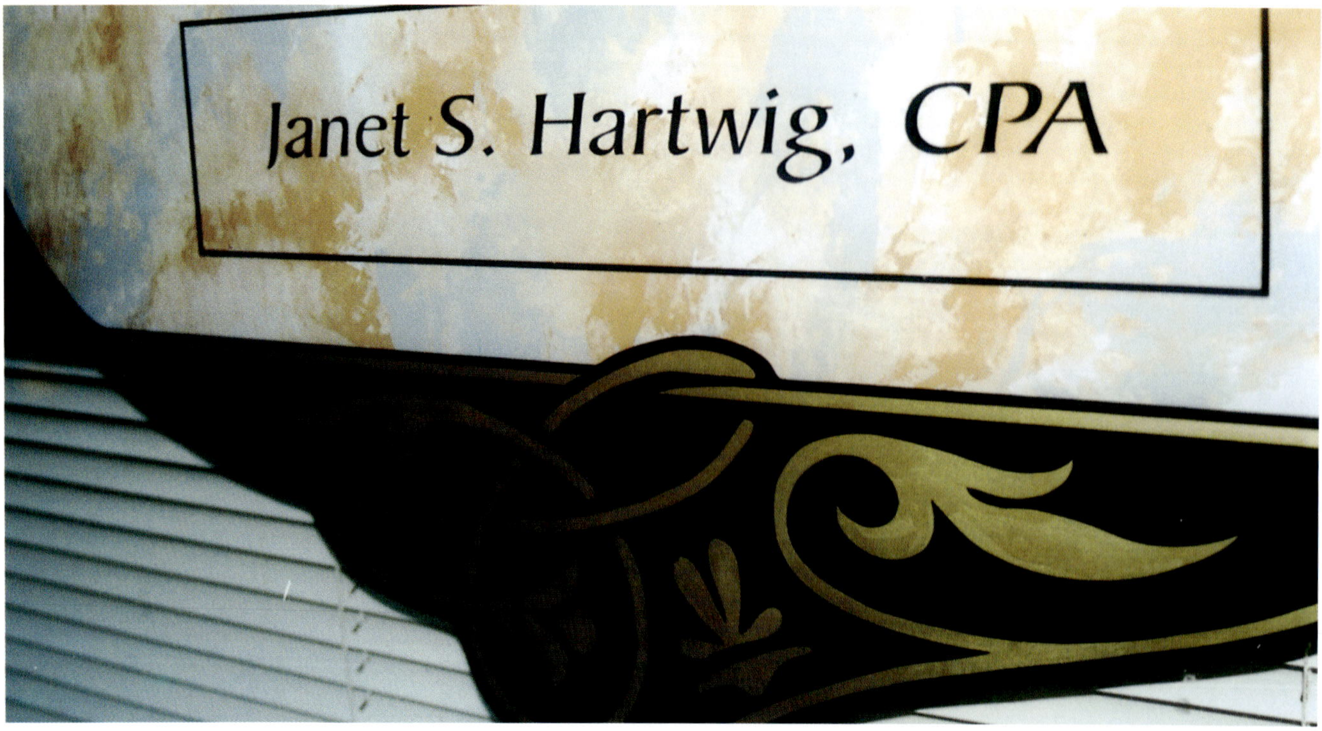

DESIGNERS

Ray and Renata Guzman
Hoboken Sign
108 Jefferson St.
Hoboken, NJ 07030
(201) 798-0688
Fax: (201) 798-8405

FABRICATOR

Hoboken Sign

This window sign incorporates vinyl graphics, gold vinyl and handpainted images.

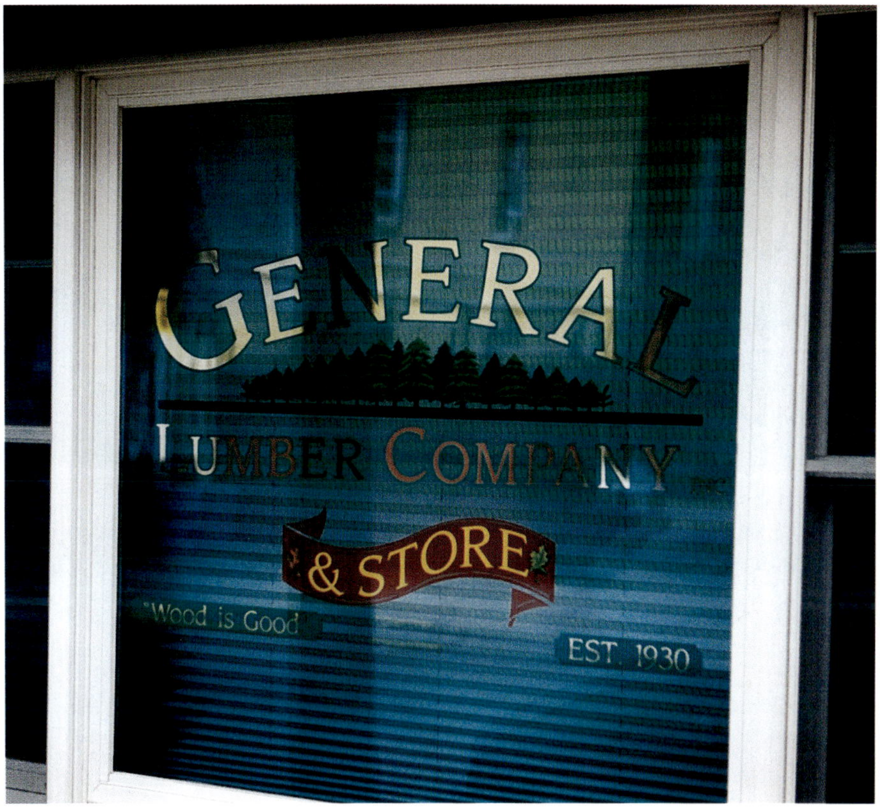

DESIGNER

Lynn Wilkerson
Austin Sign & Pictorial
500 A. East St. Elmo
Austin, TX 78745
(512) 443-5566
Fax: (512) 443-9699

FABRICATORS

Mario Muñoz
Lynn Wilkerson
Austin Sign & Pictorial

Textured drywall with Drivit® painted and stained to look like stone, hand-painted hieroglyphics and faux-marble columns give this movie theatre its Egyptian look. The pharaoh head capitals atop the columns are sculpted from Celluclay®. Muslin drops in the rear of the theatre, and trompe l'oiel statues align the entrance.

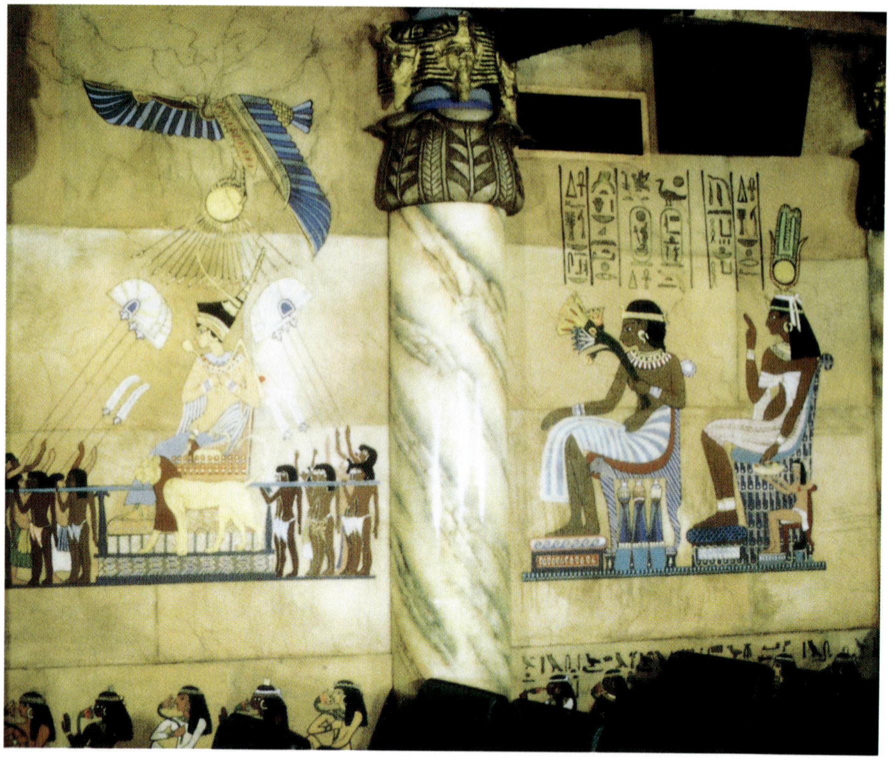

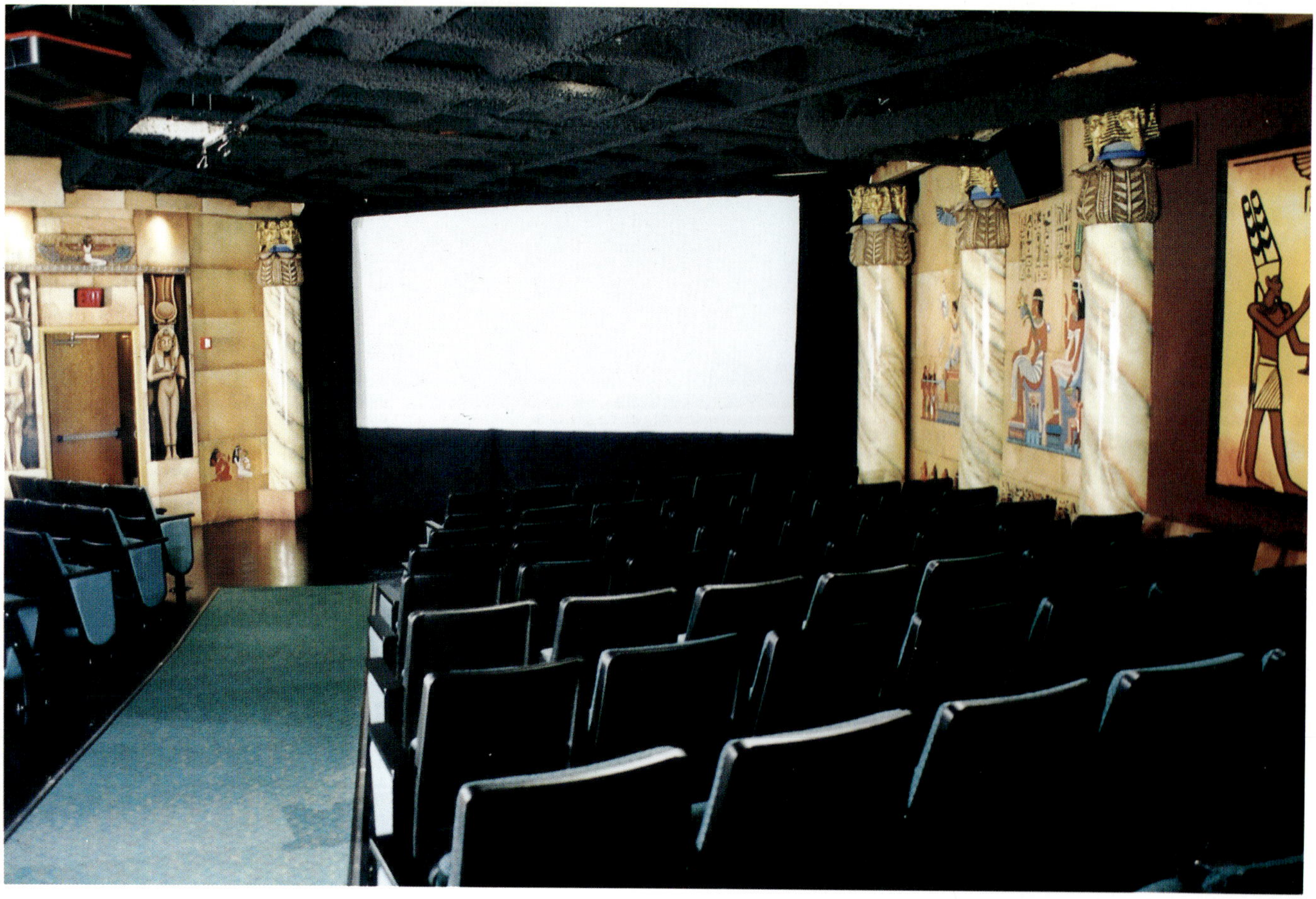

DESIGNER

Dunn Reber Glenn Marz Adv.
1221 Town Center Dr., Ste. B
Las Vegas, NV 89134

FABRICATOR

Larger than Life, Inc.
330 S. Decatur, Ste. 231
Las Vegas, NV 89107
(702) 259-1936
Fax: (702) 259-1936

This wall graphic — located near the monorail system that connects the hotels at the MGM Grand Adventures Theme Park — measures 20 x 90 ft. Painted with enamels, the sign's background has been blended from blue to purple with an airless sprayer; hand blending, however, has been used for the film strip. The copy is hand-lettered.

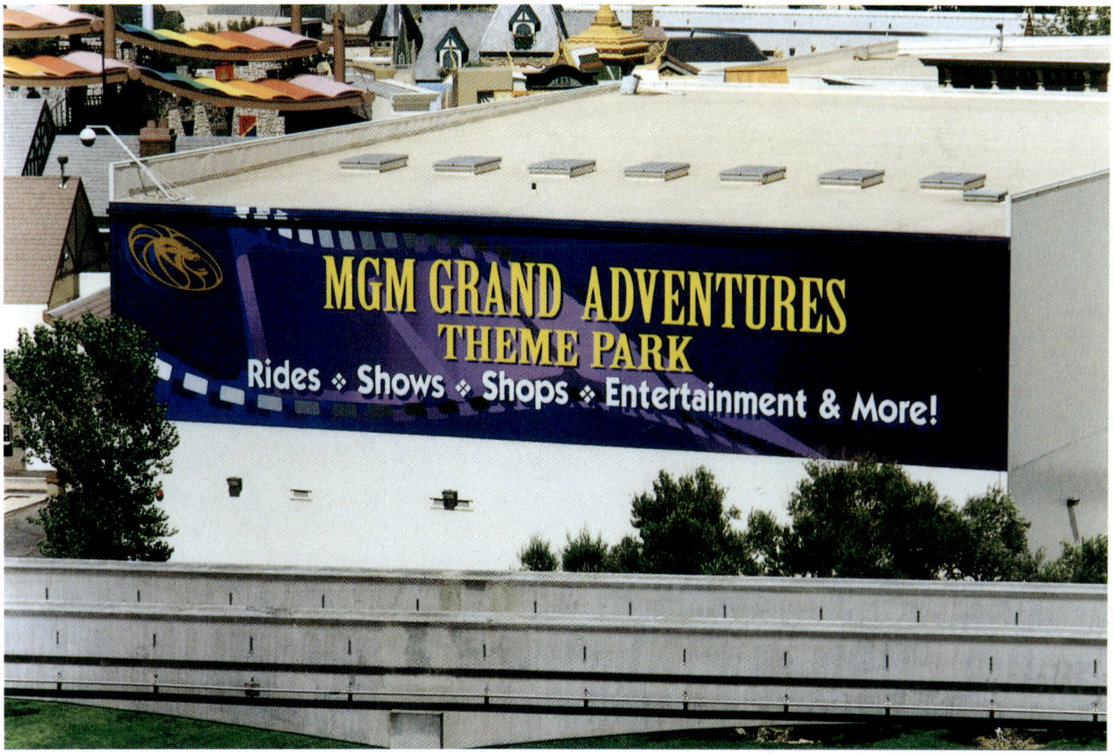

DESIGNER

Larger than Life, Inc.
330 S. Decatur, Ste. 231
Las Vegas, NV 89107
(702) 259-1936
Fax: (702) 259-1936

FABRICATOR

Larger than Life, Inc.

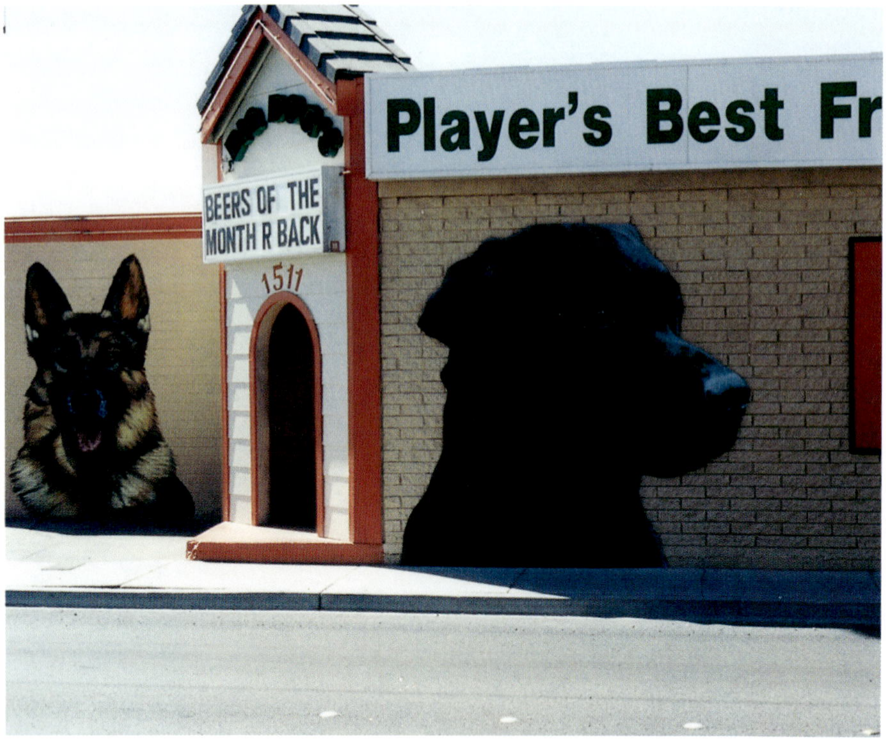

Patrons of Big Dog's — a restaurant that features specialty beers — are greeted by these two oversized canine murals. Both dogs' heads are 10 ft. tall and painted with enamels. The German shepherd is painted directly onto the wall surface, while the black Labrador retriever is painted on cut-out Medex® panels, mounted to the rough brick.

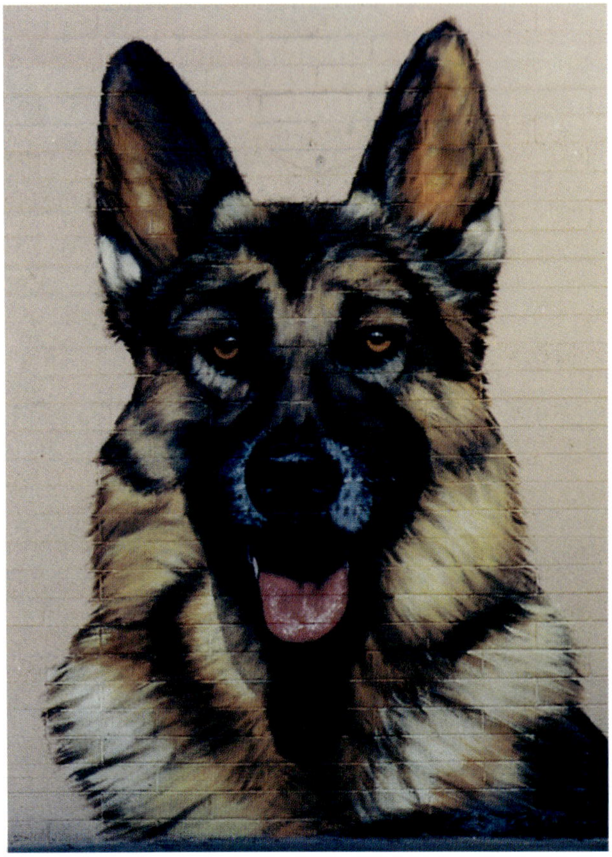

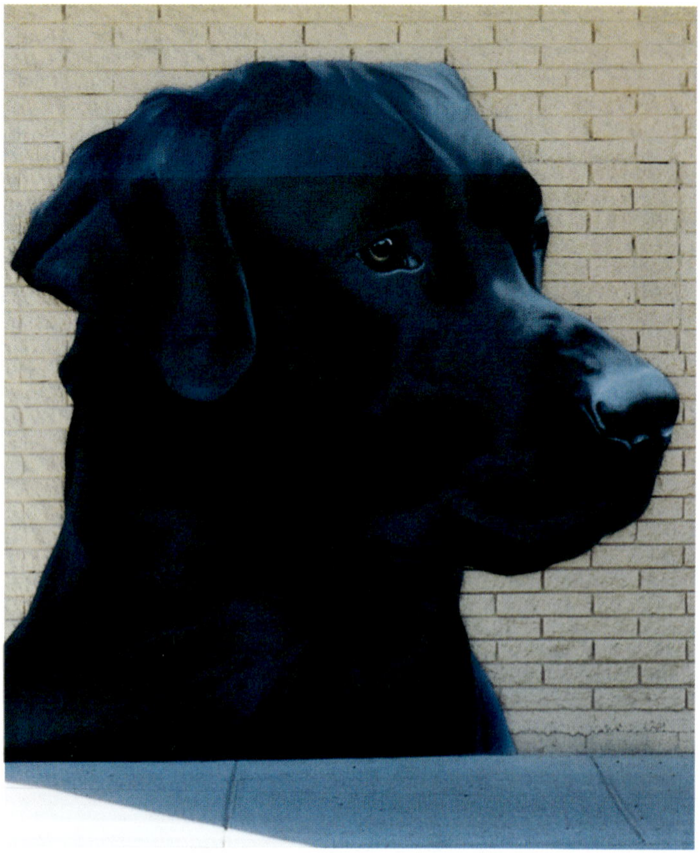

DESIGNER

Lynn Wilkerson
Austin Signs & Pictorial
500 A. East St. Elmo
Austin, TX 78745
(512) 443-5566
Fax: (512) 443-9699

FABRICATORS

Lynn Wilkerson
Mario Muñoz
Timothy Wilkerson
Sharon Cozad
Austin Signs & Pictorial

The walls of this theatre are hand-painted to look like stone. Trompe l'oiel arches and coves further contribute to the Gothic effect. Faux-marbling is used on the columns, and the gargoyles are sculpted. Stained glass is featured at the tops of the archways.

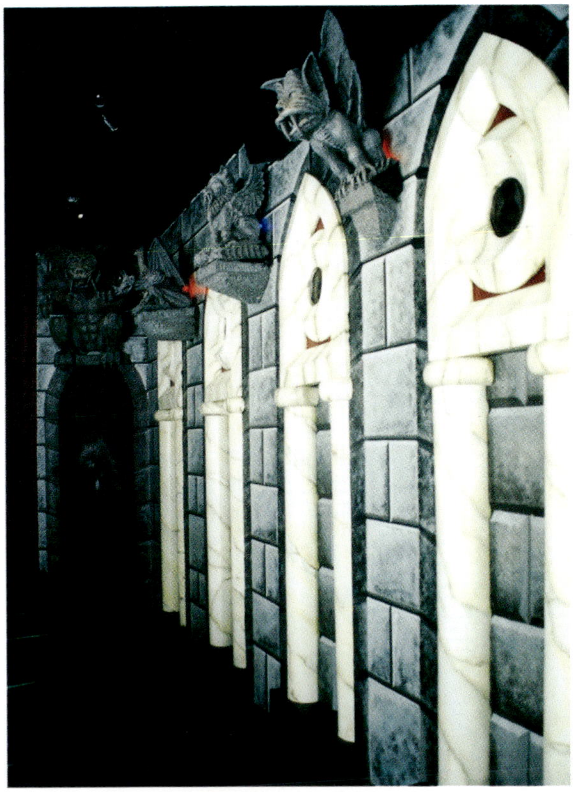

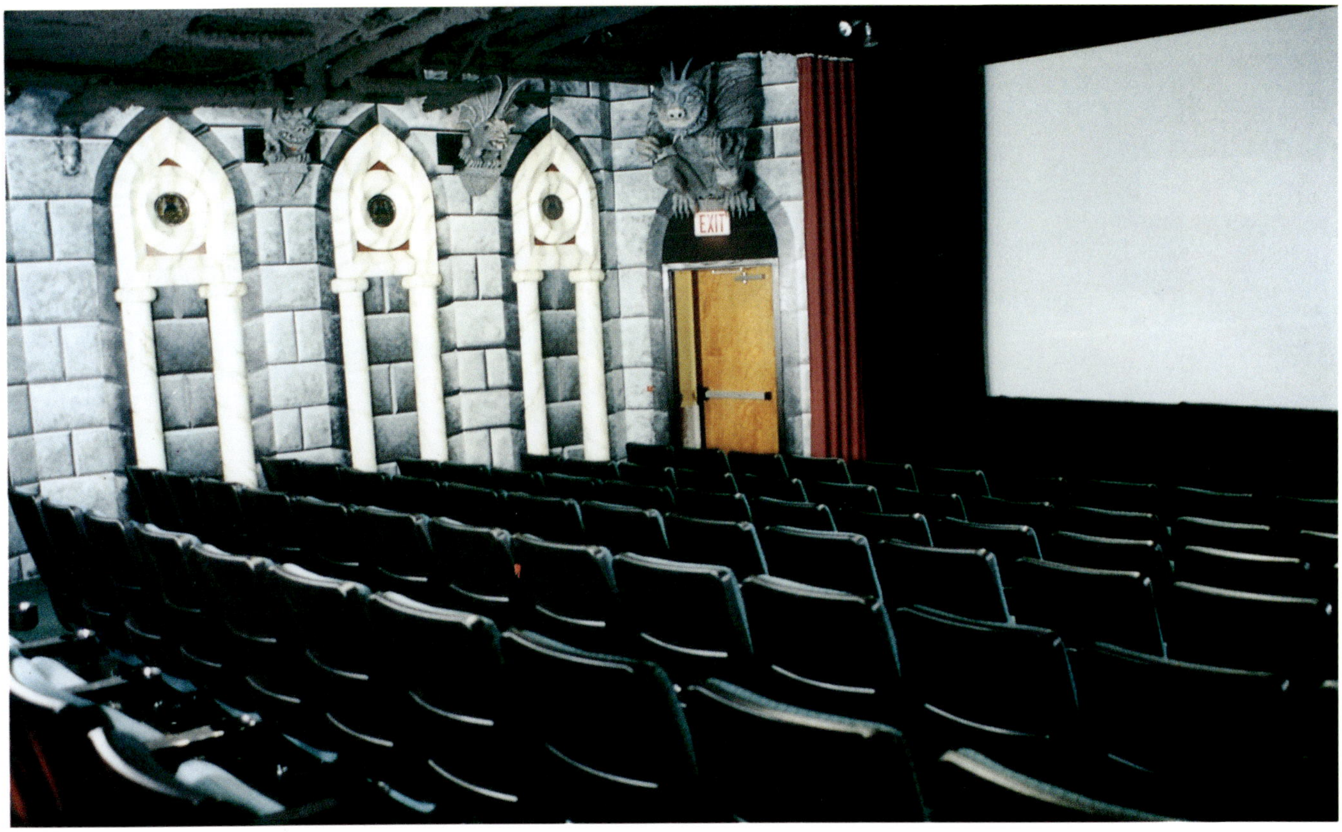

COMMERCIAL

DESIGNER

Bert Graphix
7 Ivy St.
Pompton Lakes, NJ 07442
(201) 835-2040
Fax: (201) 835-3341

FABRICATOR

Bert Graphix

Hand painting and airbrushing are used to create this pickup graphic.

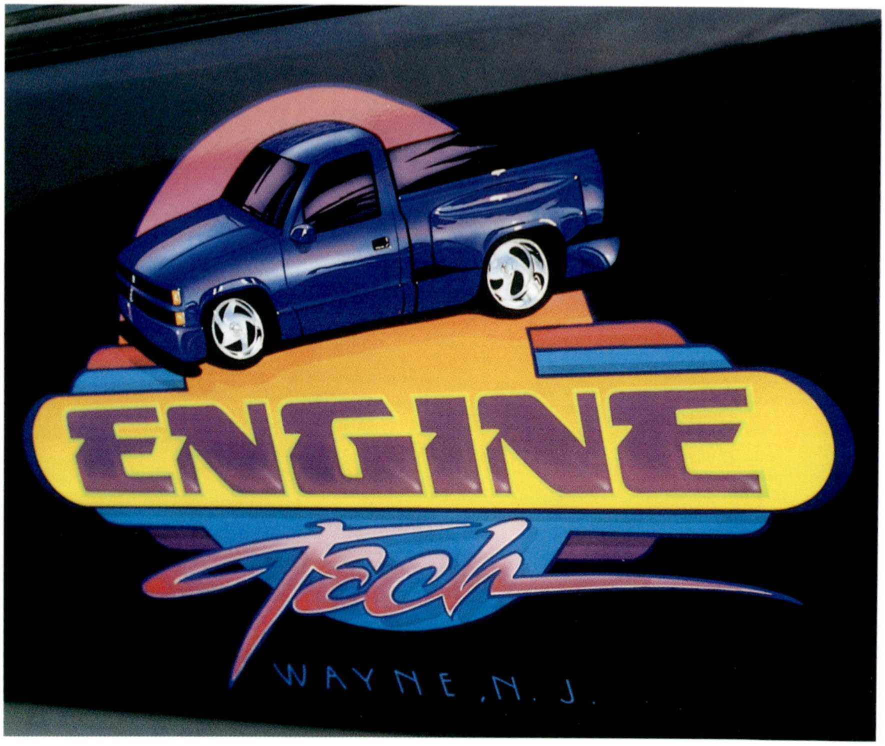

DESIGNER

Bert Graphix
7 Ivy St.
Pompton Lakes, NJ 07442
(201) 835-2040
Fax: (201) 835-3341

FABRICATORS

Bert Graphix

This graphic for a landscaping company is hand-lettered and airbrushed.

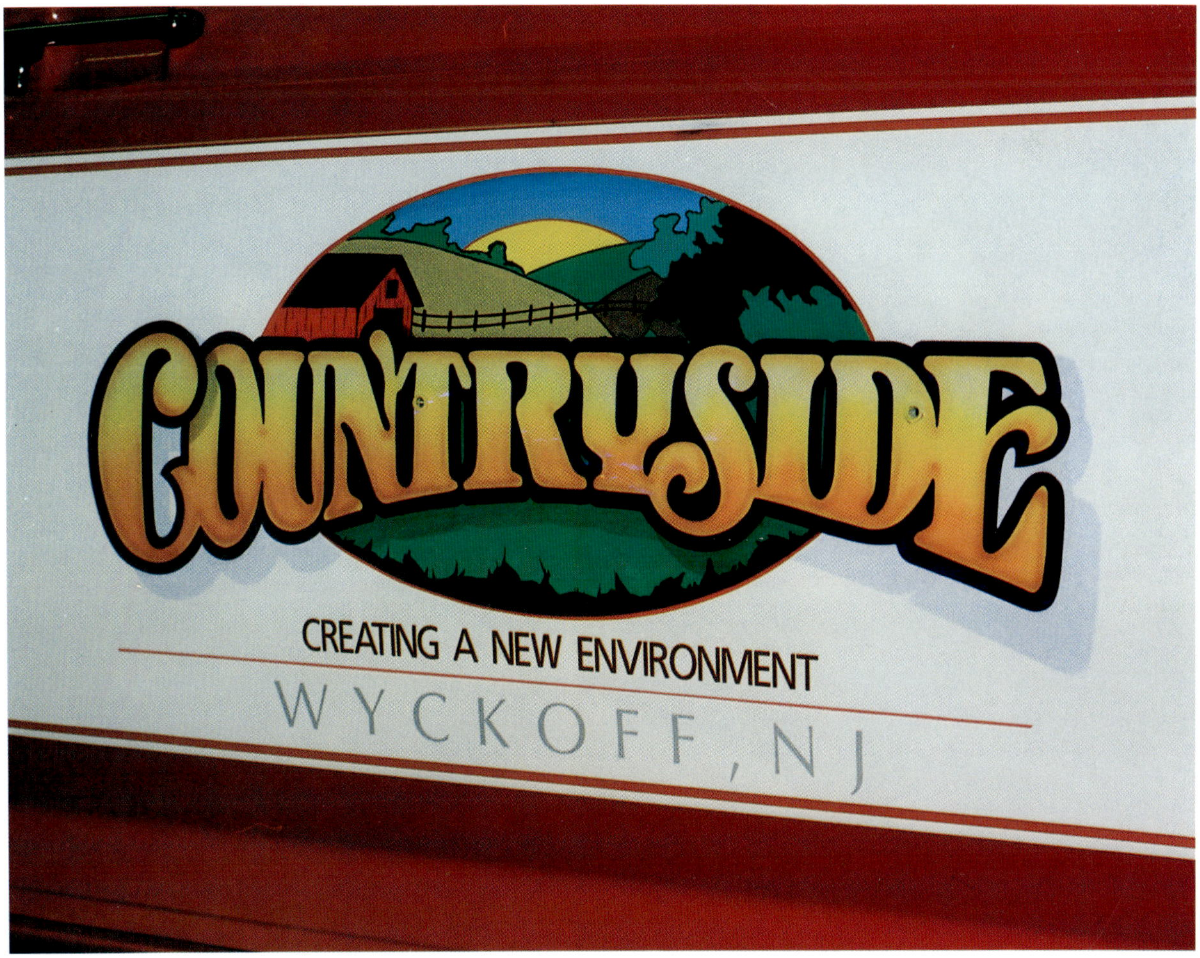

DESIGNER

Bert Graphix
7 Ivy St.
Pompton Lakes, NJ 07442
(201) 835-2040
Fax: (201) 835-3341

FABRICATORS

Bert Graphix

Although the secondary copy — "Commercial/Residential Sales & Service" — is made of vinyl, the remainder of this company's logo is airbrushed.

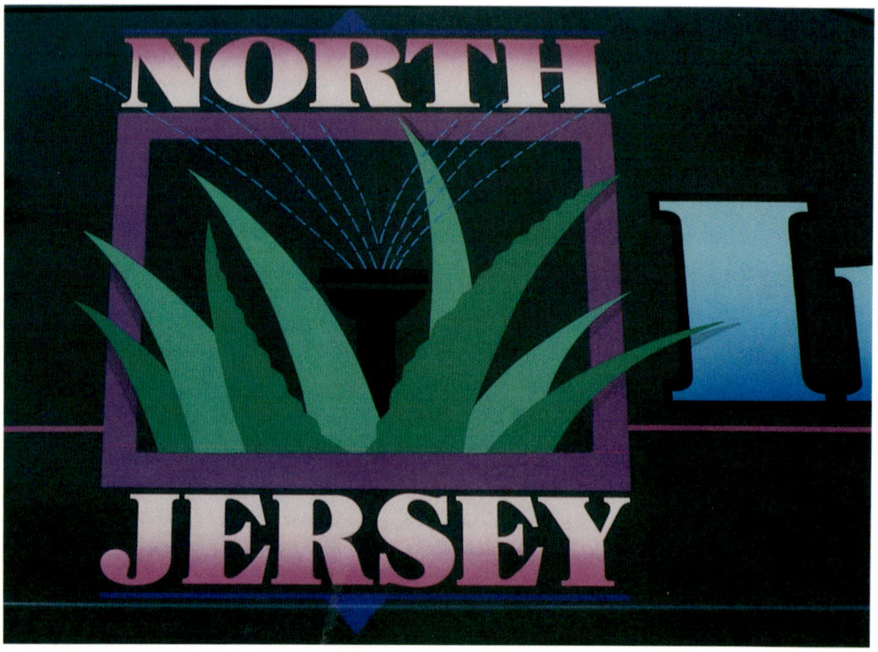

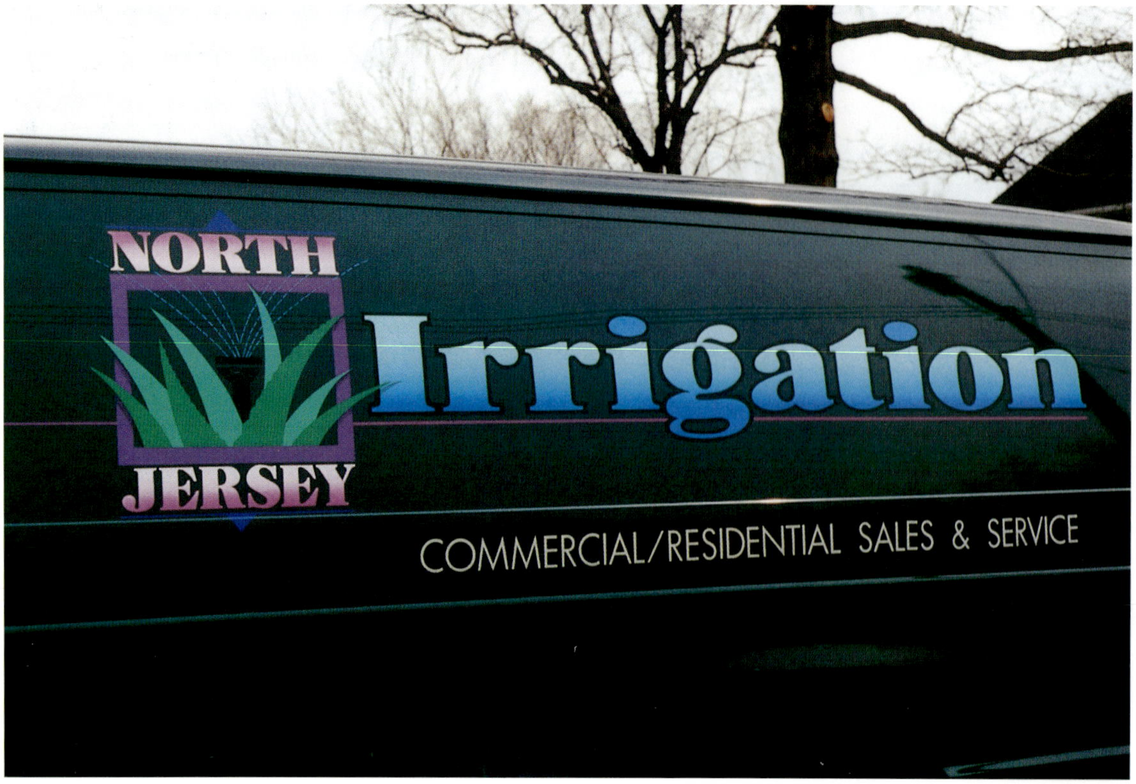

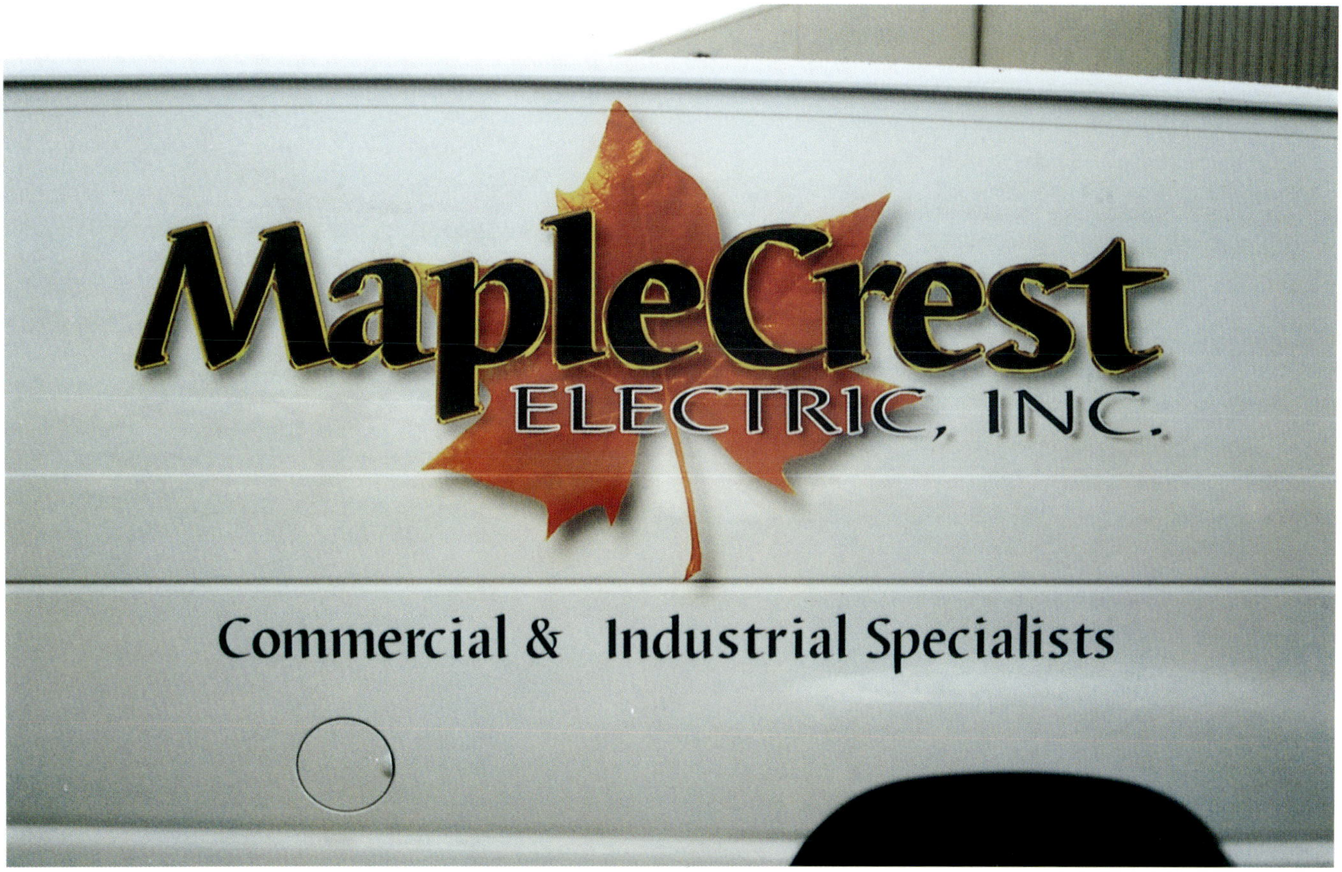

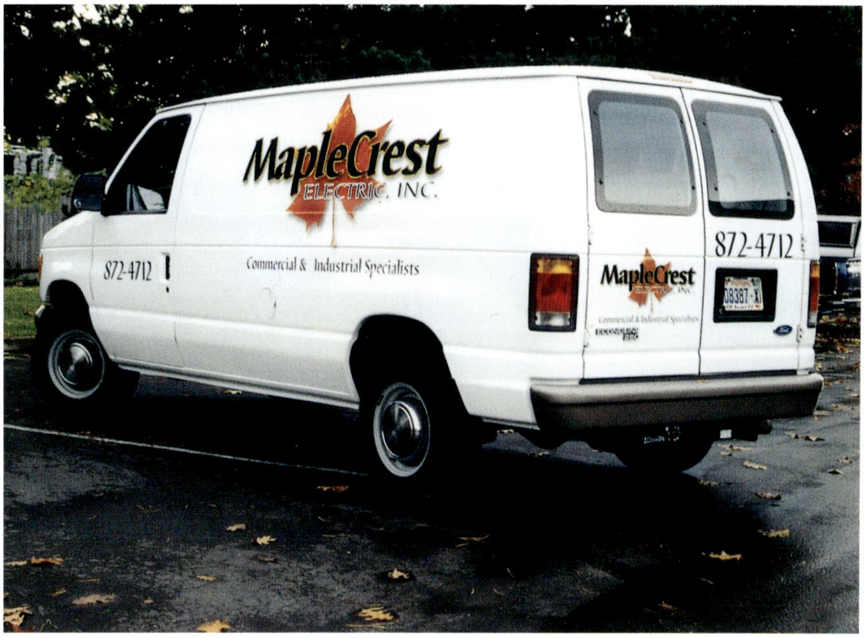

DESIGNER

Phil Martins
Karagrafic
22412 72nd Ave. S.
Kent, WA 98032

FABRICATOR

Karagrafic

Created on a computer using Pixar Typestry® and Photoshop® software, this 28 x 66-in. graphic has been reproduced for the sides of four vans. The images are printed on clear 3M Scotchprint® 180-114 vinyl, and cut to shape on a flatbed plotter.

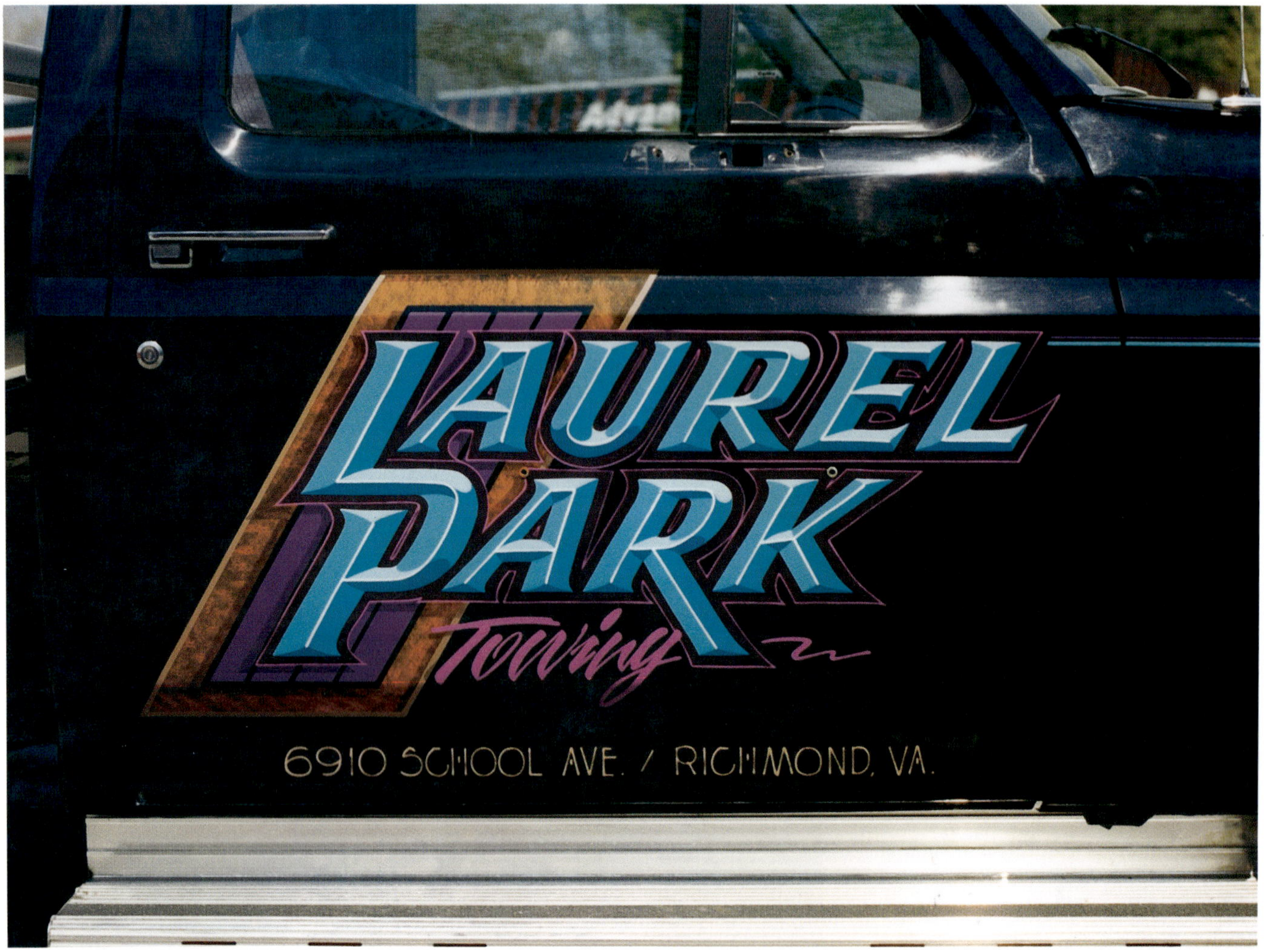

DESIGNER

Carousel Signs & Designs, Inc.
7202 Brook Rd.
Richmond, VA 23227
(804) 262-3497
Fax: (804) 262-9073

FABRICATOR

Carousel Signs & Designs, Inc.

This truck for Laurel Park Towing Services is hand painted using convex letters. The orange panel is sponge stippled.

DESIGNER

Carousel Signs & Designs, Inc.
7202 Brook Rd.
Richmond, VA 23227
(804) 262-3497
Fax: (804) 262-9073

FABRICATOR

Carousel Signs & Designs, Inc.

All black and white copy for this beer truck is computer-cut vinyl. The ribbon and eagle are airbrushed. The lettering on the truck doors is 23K spun goldleaf.

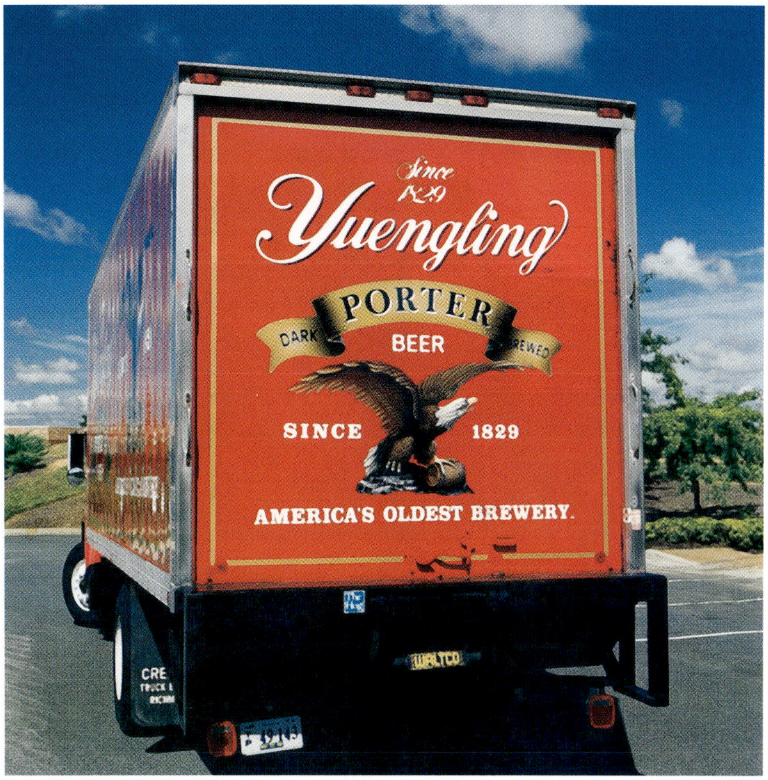

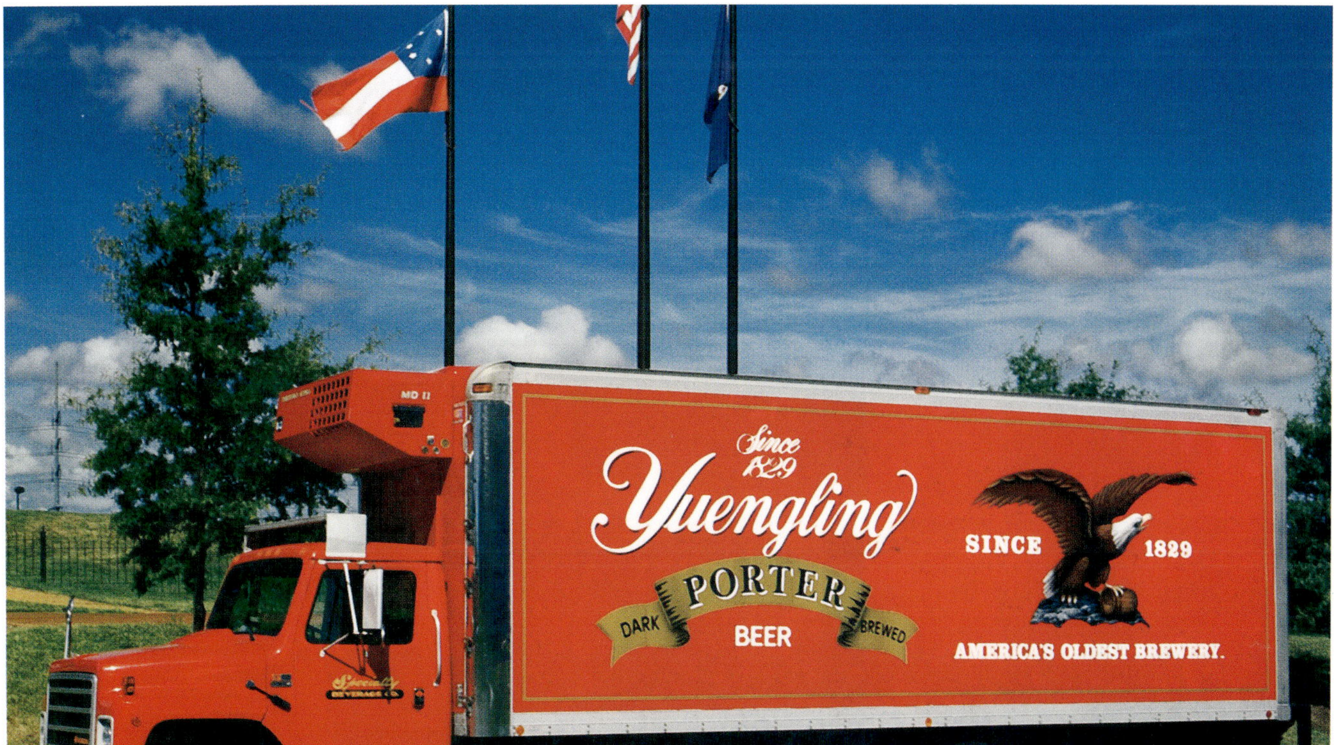

DESIGNER

Chip Spirson
Vital Signs
606 N. Davis St.
Pensacola, FL 32501
(904) 434-6364

FABRICATOR

Vital Signs

This Shriner's parade car — for "De Lunatics Order of Tristan" — has a refabricated carriage. The base coat of paint is purple-blue lacquer with aqua fenders. All other paint is lettering enamel.

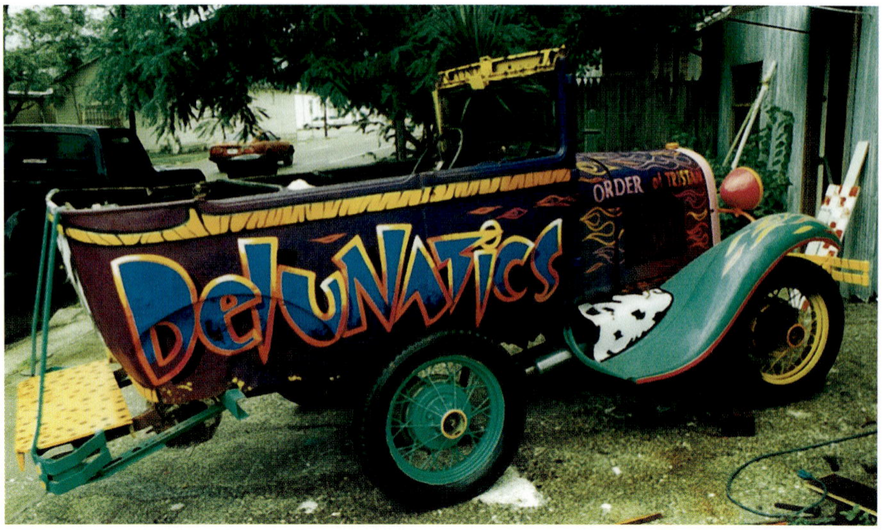

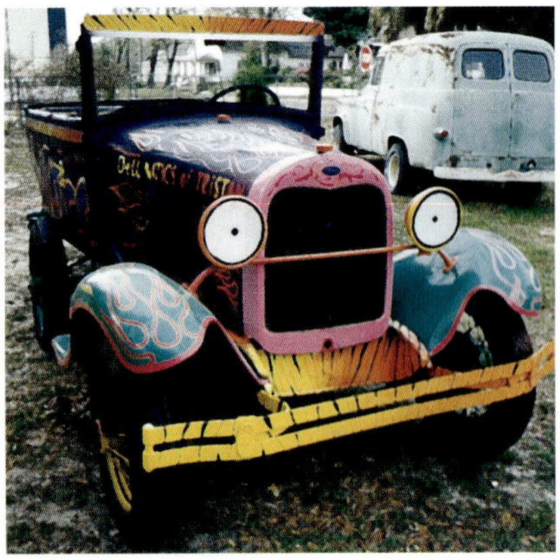

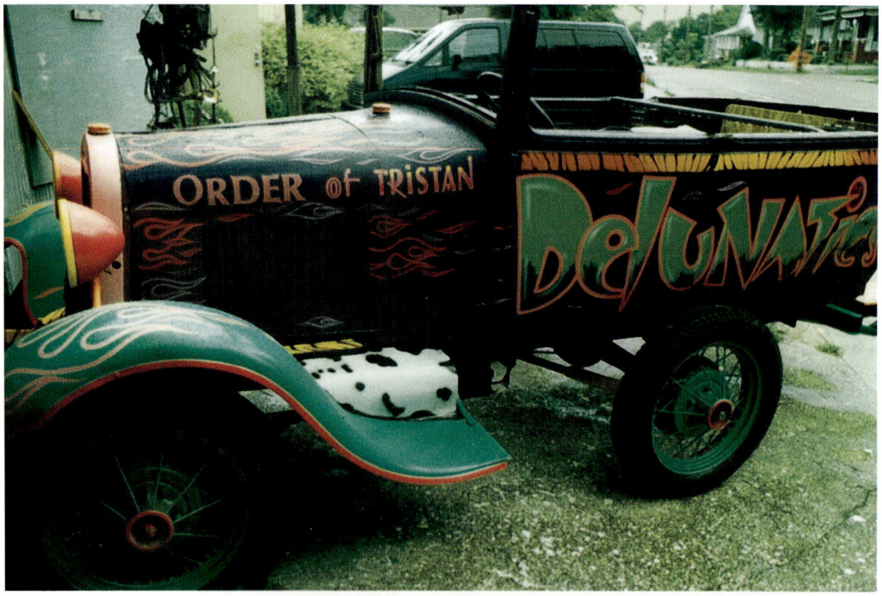

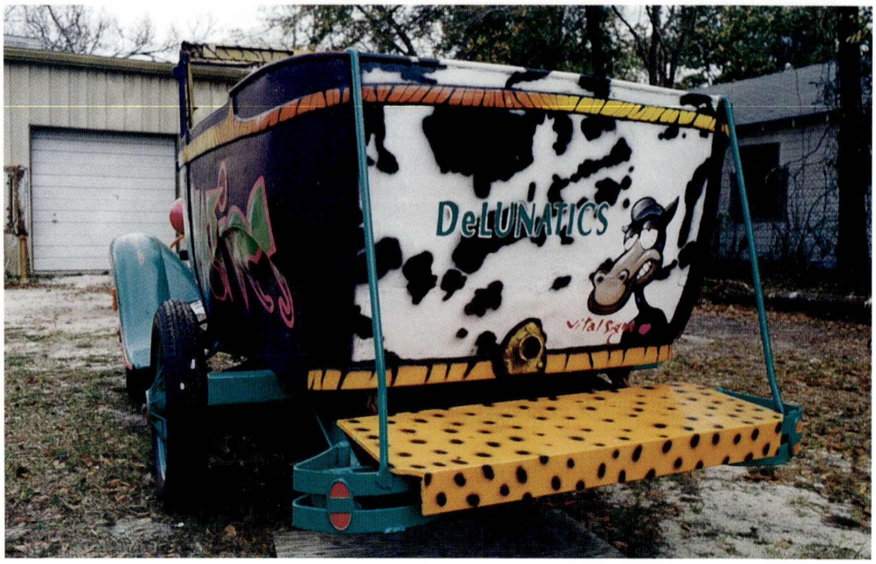

DESIGNER

Bishop Museum
1525 Bernice
Honolulu, HI 96819
(808) 536-7351

FABRICATOR

Signs, Inc.
531 Puuhale Rd.
Honolulu, HI 96819
(808) 848-5666
Fax: (808) 847-5444

A combination of painted graphics and CAD-cut vinyl is used on this 24 x 16-ft. banner. The project took two days to complete.

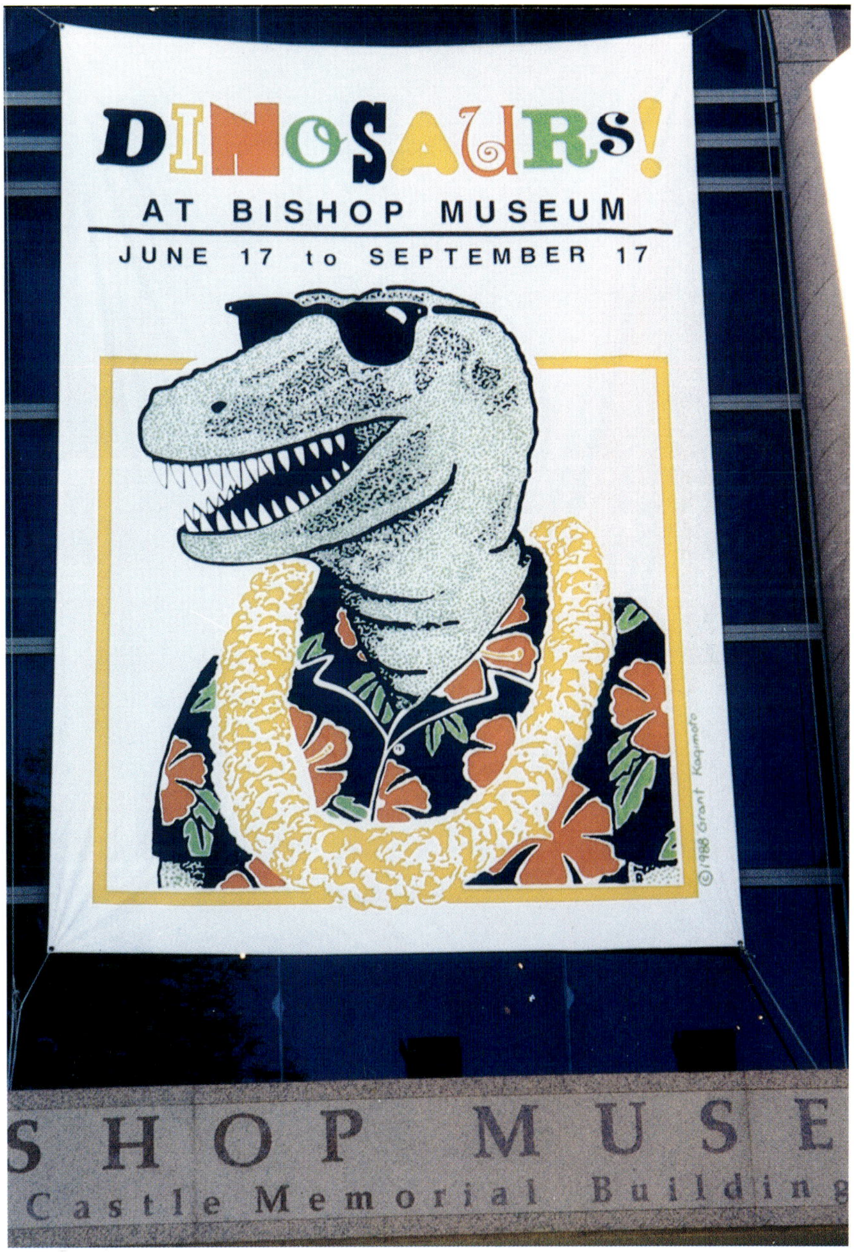

DESIGNER

Bishop Museum
1525 Bernice
Honolulu, HI 96819
(808) 536-7351

FABRICATOR

Signs, Inc.
531 Puuhale Rd.
Honolulu, HI 96819
(808) 848-5666
Fax: (808) 847-5444

Fabricated in two days, this 24 x 16-ft. heavy-duty banner features airbrushed artwork and CAD-cut vinyl copy.

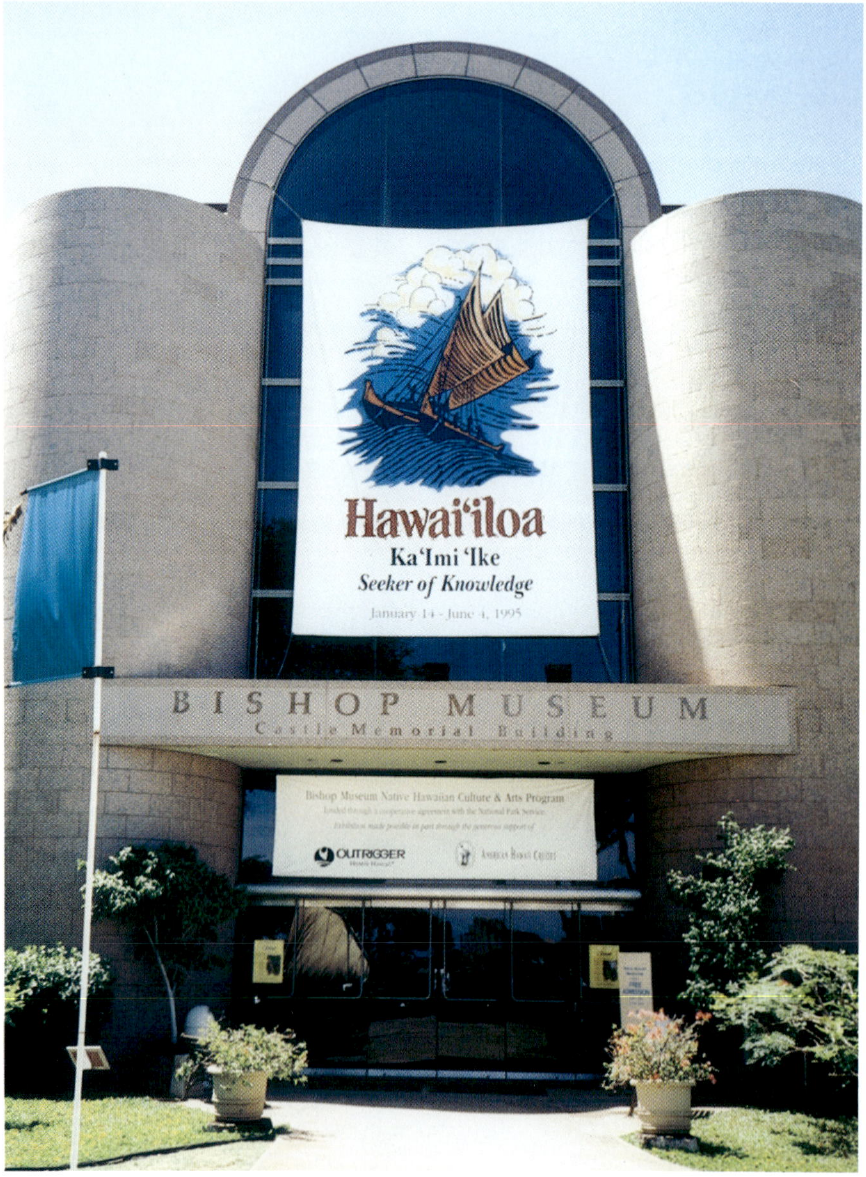

DESIGNER

Butch Anton
Superfrog Enterprises
116 21st St. S.
Moorhead, MN 56560
(218) 236-7000
Fax: (218) 236-1379

FABRICATOR

Superfrog Enterprises

Designed for use at a tradeshow booth, this 2 x 10-ft. banner is made from US Banner Corp.'s Regal Banner material. Deka® water-based background/enamel paints are used for the background, all blended shades, outlines and the purple splatter panel. During fabrication, Cal-Mask® was used to mask off the word "Signgold," which was filled in with Florentine swirl, and airbrushed with Deka transparent glass paints (lemon yellow and emerald green). The border stripe and corner designs feature Signgold 22®, matte-finish; the bottom line of copy is made from Signsilver® material.

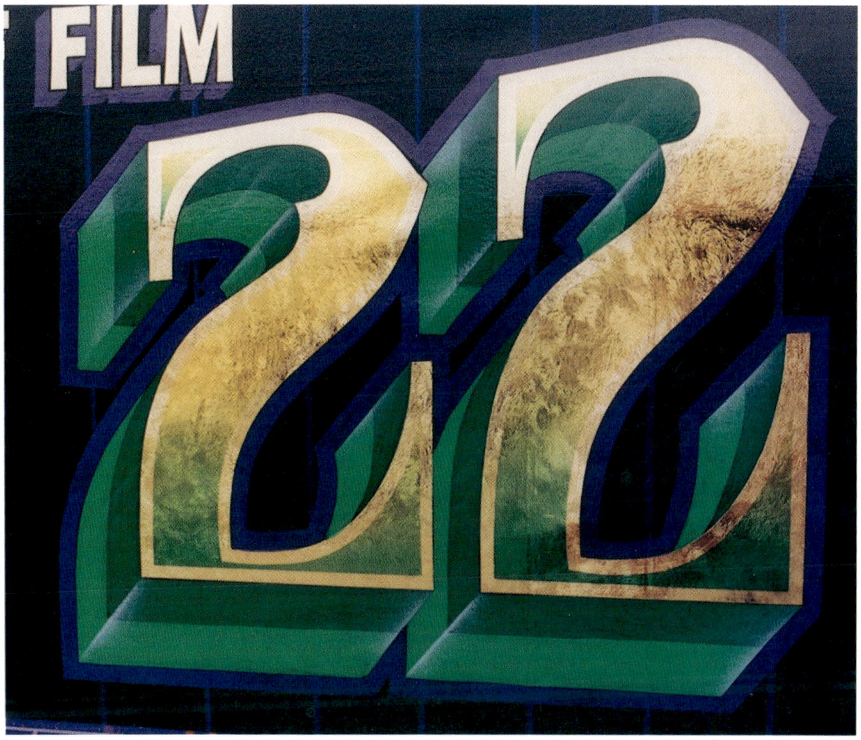

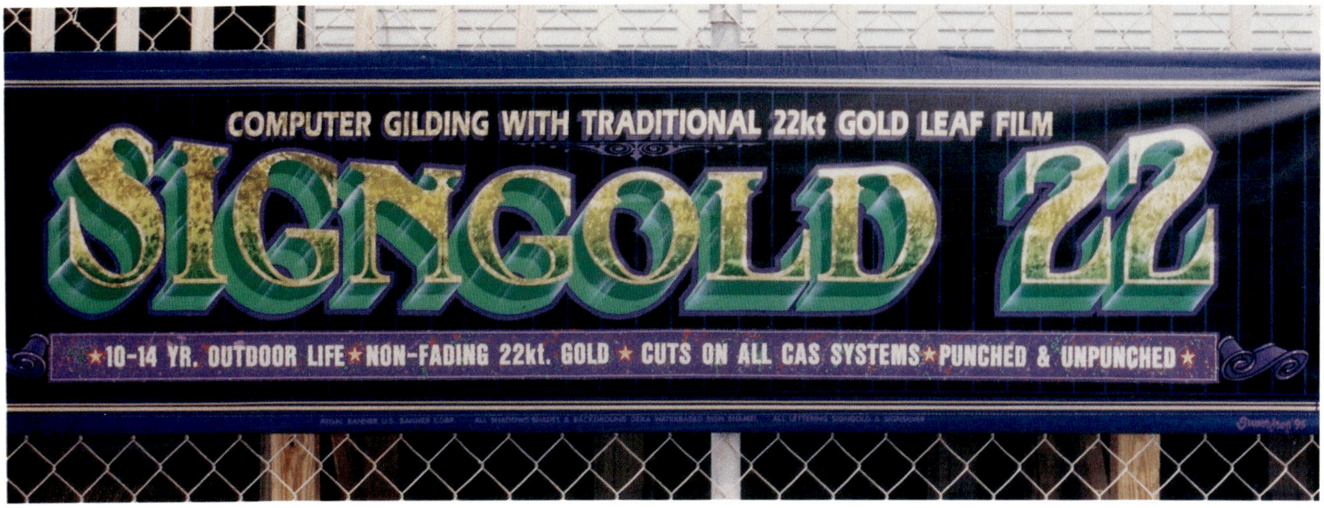

FLAT / BANNERS
COMMERCIAL

DESIGNERS

Marty Winters
Don Browning
Banner Signs
570 E. 9 Mile Rd.
Ferndale, MI 48220
(810) 545-5888
Fax: (810) 545-0742

FABRICATOR

Banner Signs

Created for the Michigan Thanksgiving Parade, these banners are fabricated using pieces of 30 x 94-in., 12-oz. vinyl. Screen printed on two sides with five colors, each banner features a computer-generated gradient background and metallic gold stars. Banner Flex® bracketing systems hold the banners to the light-poles; built-in vertical tensioning systems keep the banners taut.

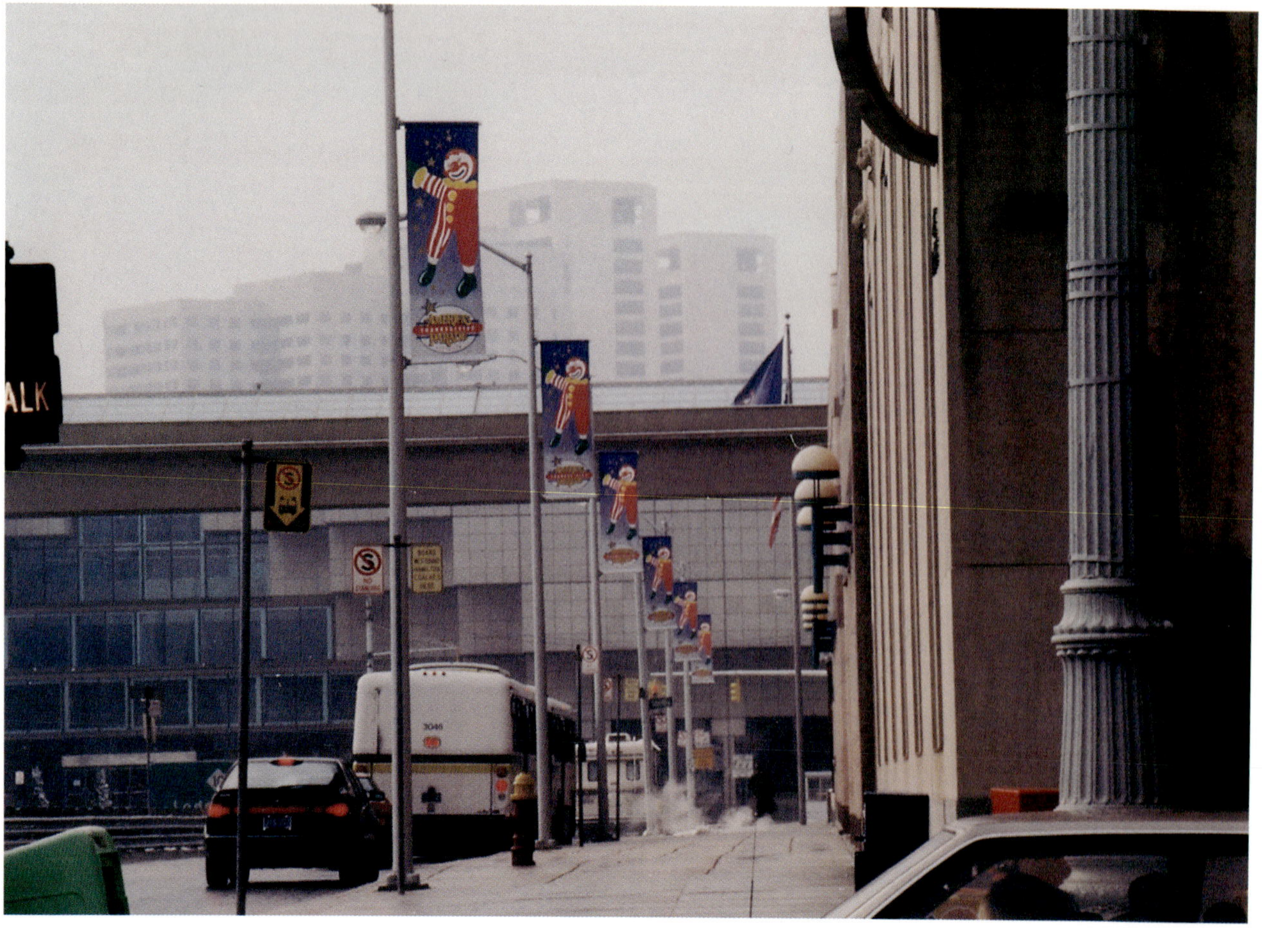

DESIGNER

Michael Wismer
1-Hour Signs
London, ON, Canada N5W 3L1
(519) 659-8846
Fax: (519) 659-9166

FABRICATOR

1-Hour Signs

This banner, used to promote a hotel volleyball tournament, measures 13 x 1 ft.; an identical banner, twice as large, was created for outdoor use. On each sign, seven layers of different-colored 2-mil vinyl are used to achieve special color blends and shadow effects.

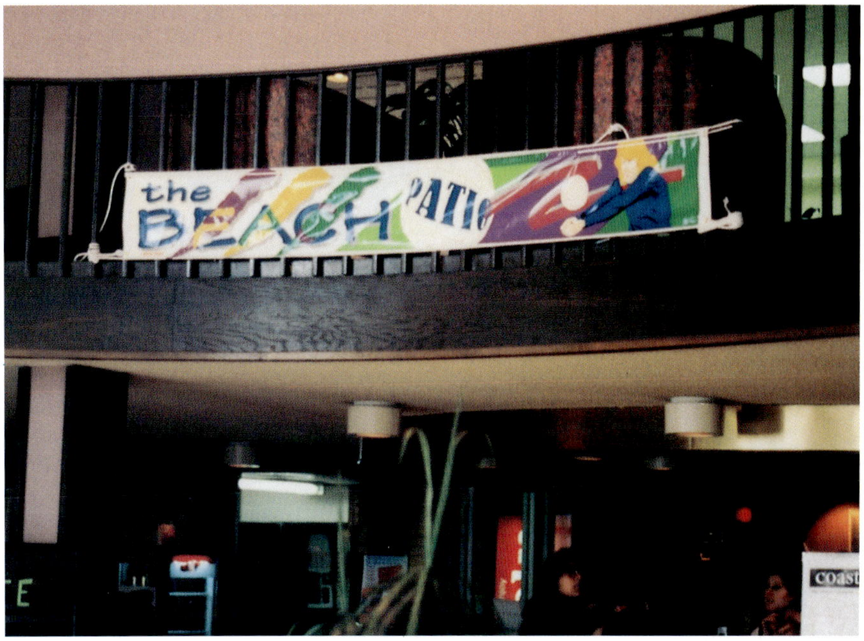

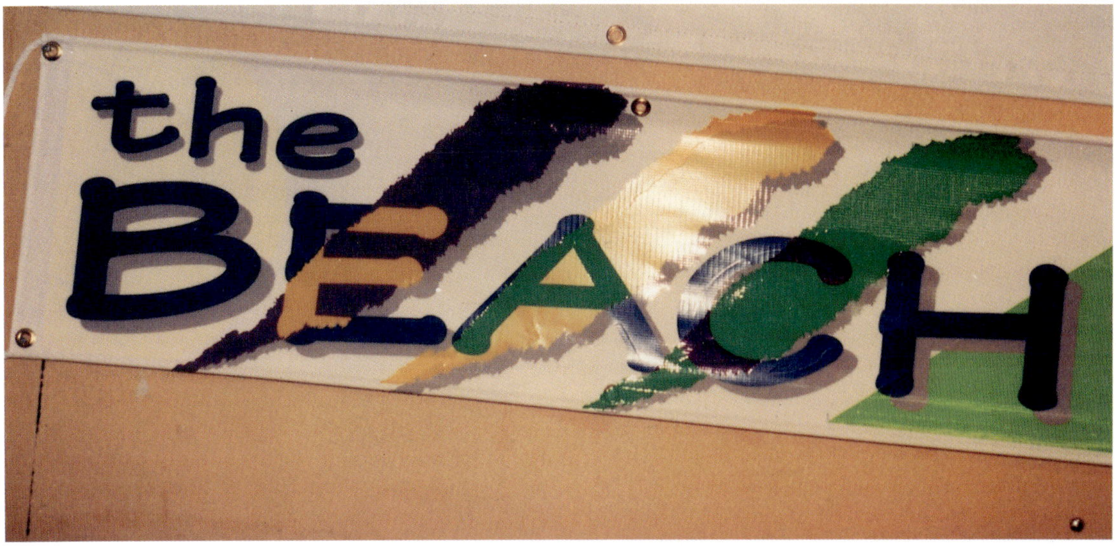

COMMERCIAL

DESIGNER

Kraig Yaseen
Yaseen Design Studio
434 Turner Dr.
Durango, CO 81301
(970) 247-4467
Fax: (970) 385-4005

FABRICATORS

Leon Newman
Al Lowrie
Brian Ballard
Kraig Yaseen
Yaseen Design Studio

This sign measures 110 in. high x 112 in. long and incorporates hand-carved spiral pillars. The prismatic hand-carved primary copy is created from high-density urethane and mounted to redwood sign blanks. The embossed copper "fan" is created using verde green patina. The decorative metal brackets are fabricated from aluminum. The sign's base is cultured stone.

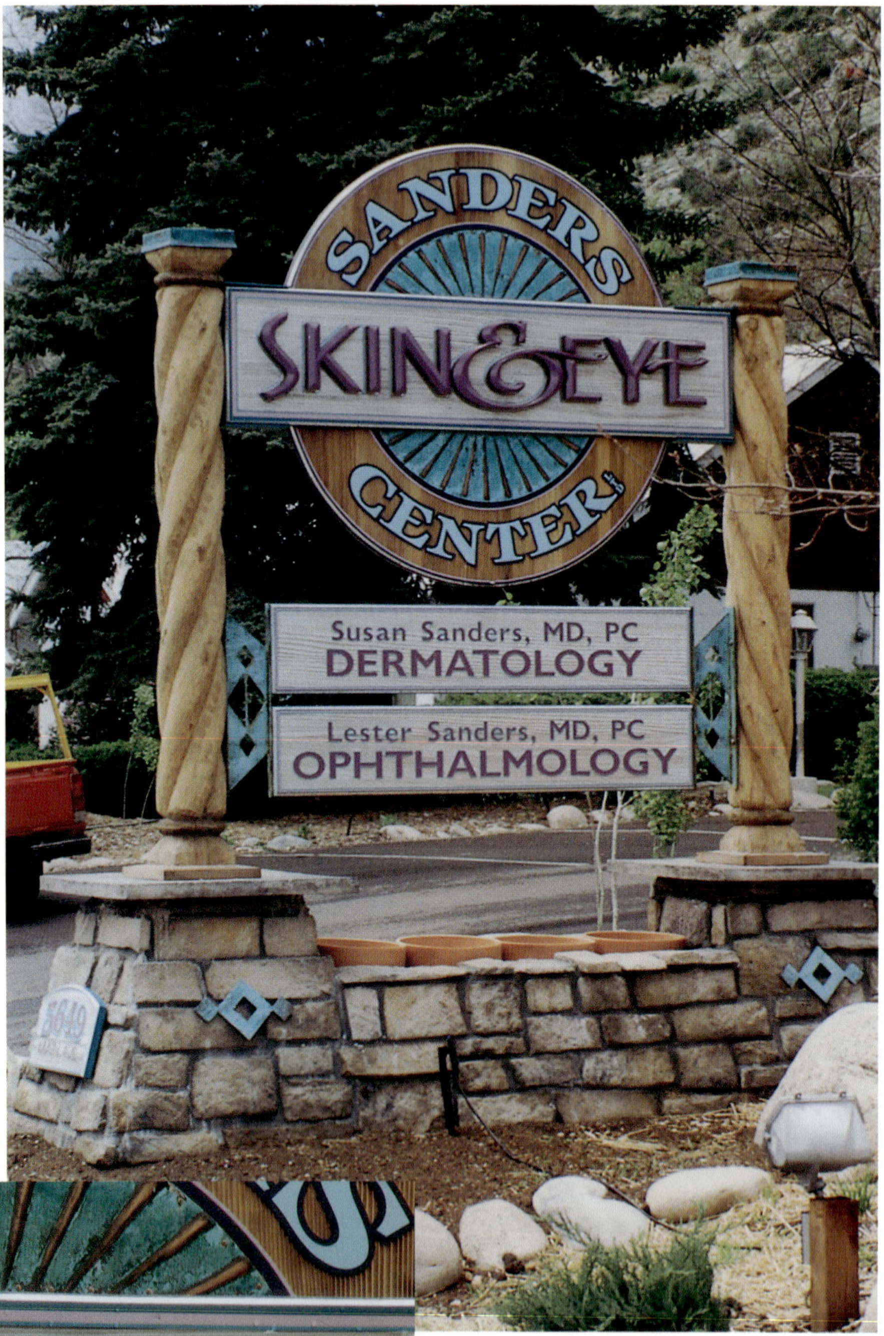

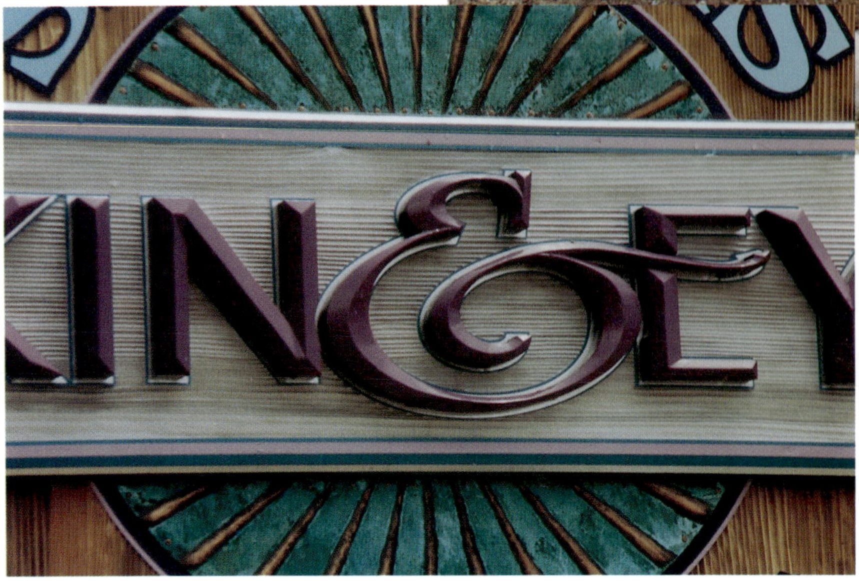

DESIGNERS

Gary Whitman
Donna Whitman
Mountain Signs
P.O. Box 98
Ripton, VT 05766
(802) 388-2271
Fax: (802) 388-2271

FABRICATOR

Mountain Signs

This double-faced 34 x 49-in. sign is fabricated from hand-carved redwood. The applied panel is made from mahogany with glass smaltz and accented with hammered copper leaves. All lettering and stripes are 23K goldleaf.

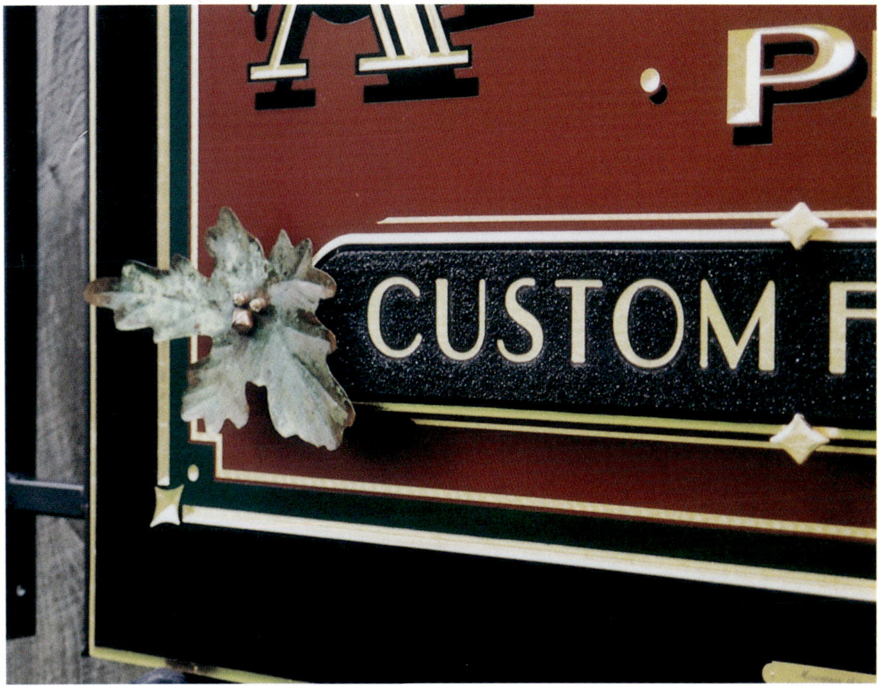

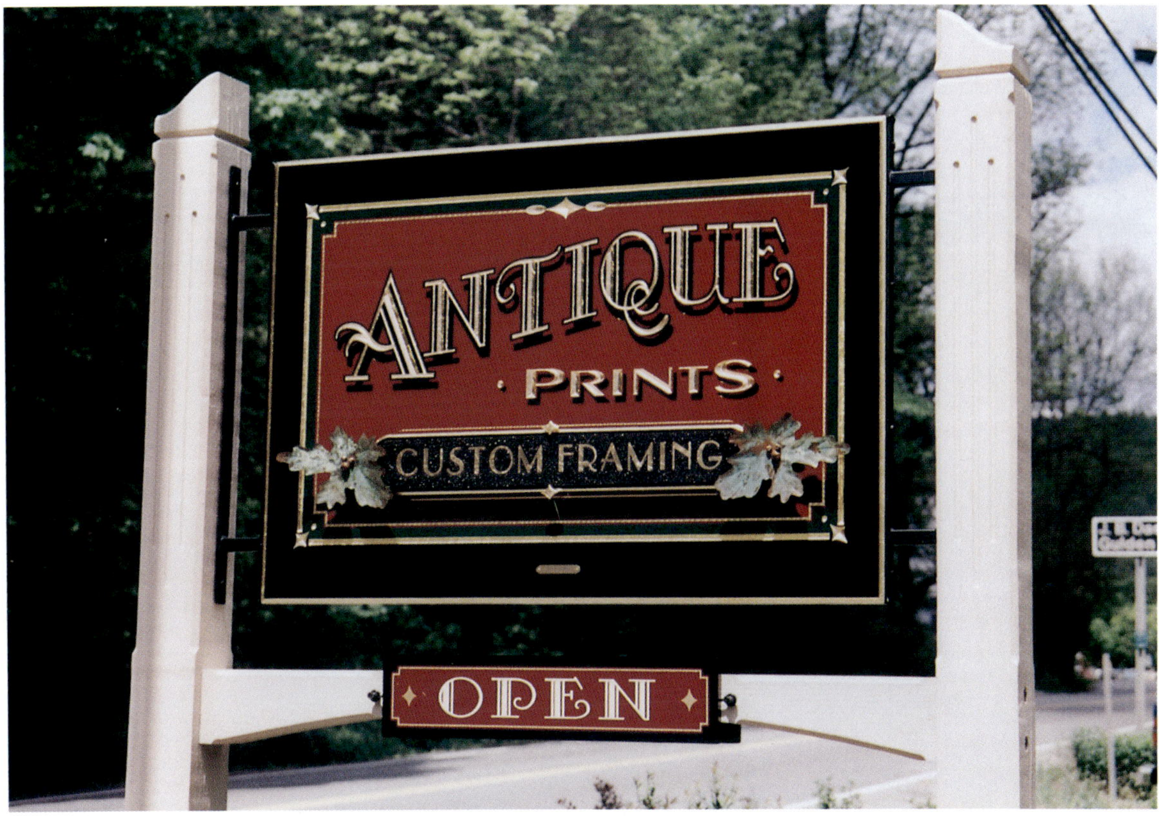

DESIGNERS

Carousel Signs & Designs Inc.
7202 Brook Rd.
Richmond, VA 23227
(804) 262-3497
Fax: (804) 262-9073

Higgins Assoc.
8501 Patterson Ave.
Richmond, VA 23229
(804) 740-7500
Fax: (804) 740-1620

FABRICATOR

Carousel Signs & Designs Inc.

This is a 3 x 4-ft. sign created using 1½-in. high-density urethane. The background and inset stripes are sandblasted. The leaves are hand-carved and gilded using 23K goldleaf. The tree is hand-painted. All other "gold" is created using enamel. The 8 x 8-in. sign post has a 1½-in. redwood wrap at the bottom and a gilded redwood acorn at the top.

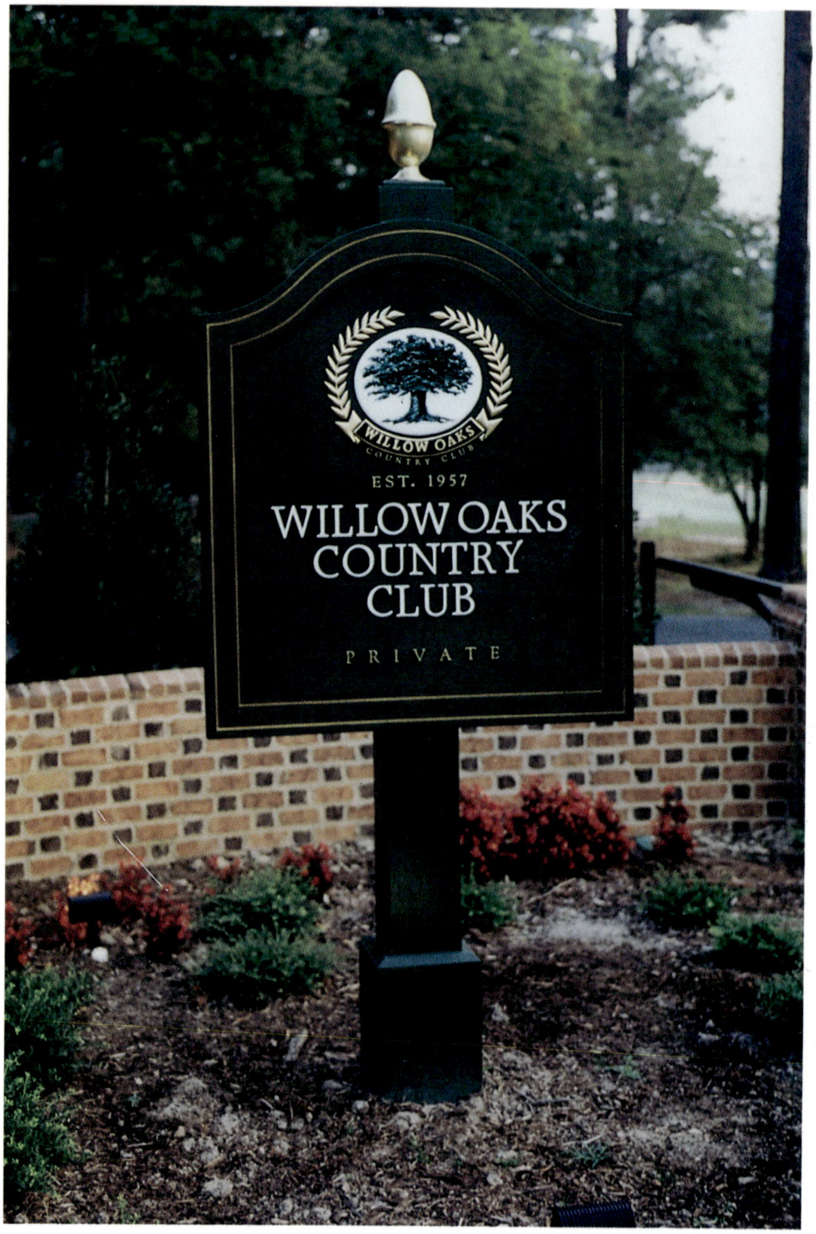

DESIGNERS

Nancy Beaudette
Noëlla Cotnam
Sign It
812-33 Pitt St.
Cornwall, ON, Canada K6J 5R2
(613) 933-7447
Fax: (613) 933-3480

FABRICATOR

Sign It

This 6-ft. x 42-in. sandblasted redwood sign (one of four) is finished on one side. It features a high-density urethane crest applique, blended scrolls and a halo sandblasting technique around the crest and scroll areas.

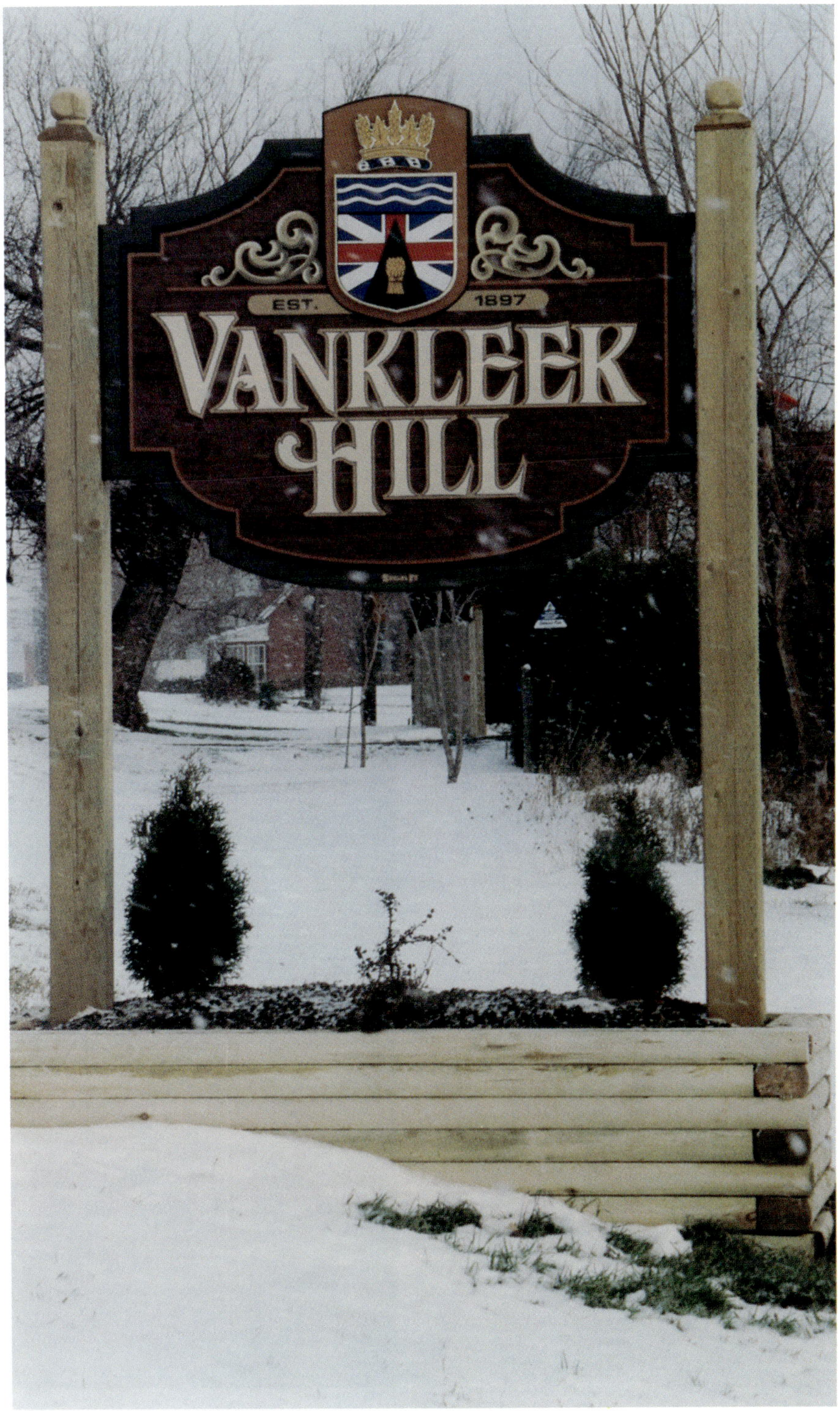

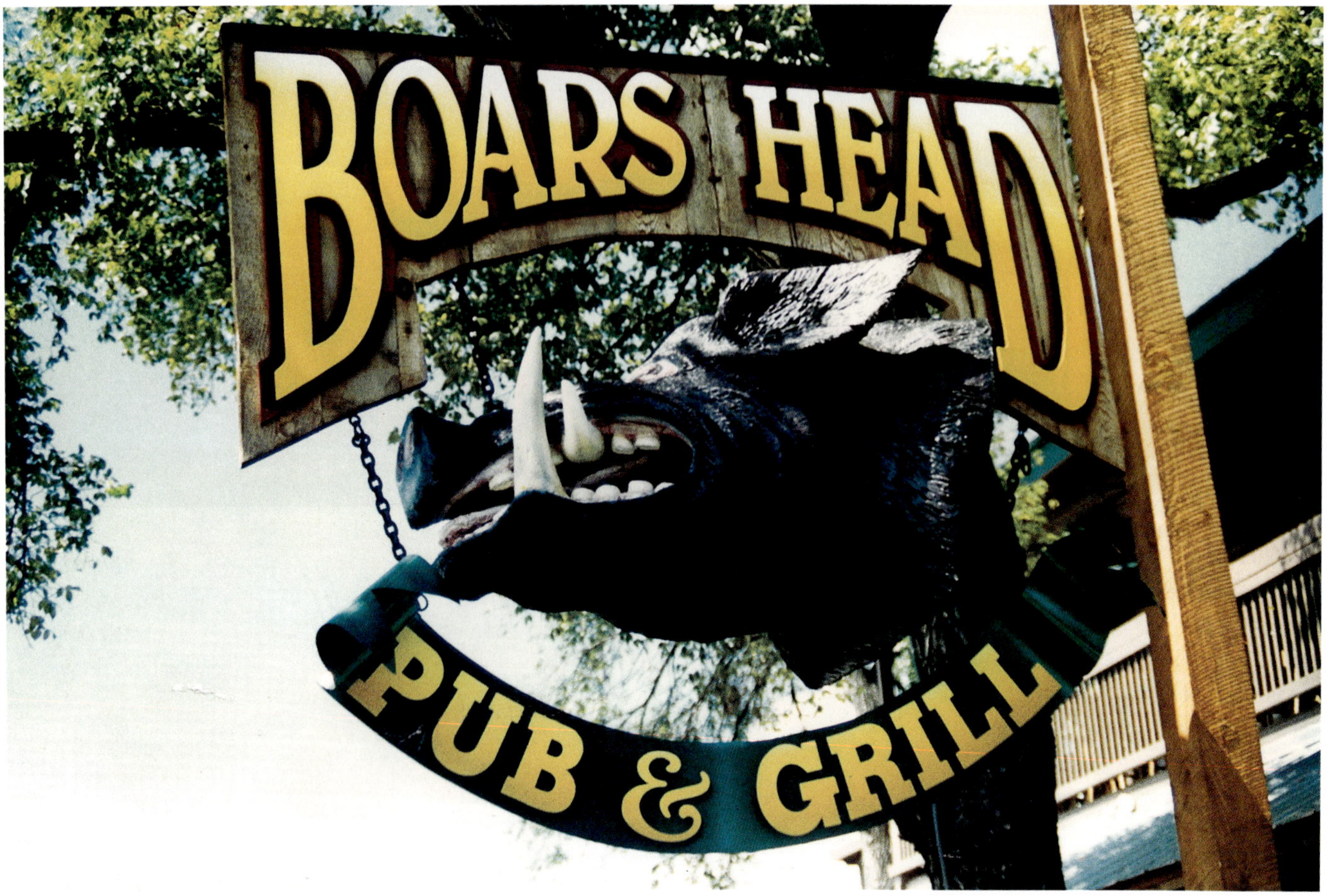

DESIGNER

Lynn Wilkerson
Austin Sign & Pictorial
500 A. East St. Elmo
Austin, TX 78743
(512) 443-5566
Fax: (512) 443-9699

FABRICATOR

Austin Sign & Pictorial

The boar's head is sculpted from beaded Styrofoam®. It has a finish of Foamcote® and is painted with One Shot® enamel paint. It measures 5 x 8 ft. The top panel is fabricated of 2-in. rough-cut sandblasted cedar, glued and clamped, and bolted in a metal bracket at the top. The bottom ribbon is made of ⅛-in. aluminum, hand-cut and bent to shape. The lettering and background are airbrushed.

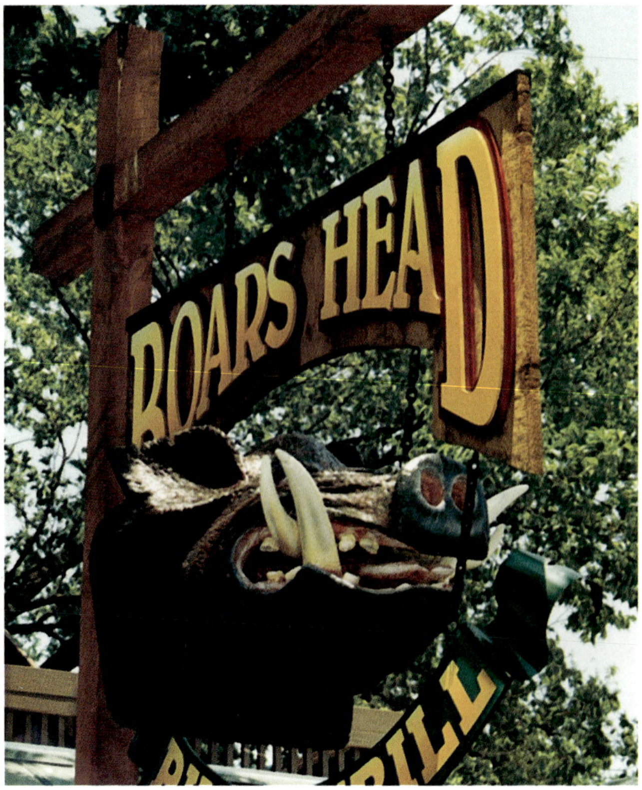

DESIGNER

Susan Bemel
Bemel Carved Sign
Cty. Rt. 1 & Schoolhouse Rd.
Pine Island, NY 10969
(914) 258-6000
Fax: (914) 258-4023

FABRICATOR

Bemel Carved Sign

This is a 7 ft. x 3 ft. 4 in. double-sided sign, handcarved of 2-in. redwood. The animals are built up with an extra 2-in. of wood and carved. The letters and incline are 23K gold leaf.

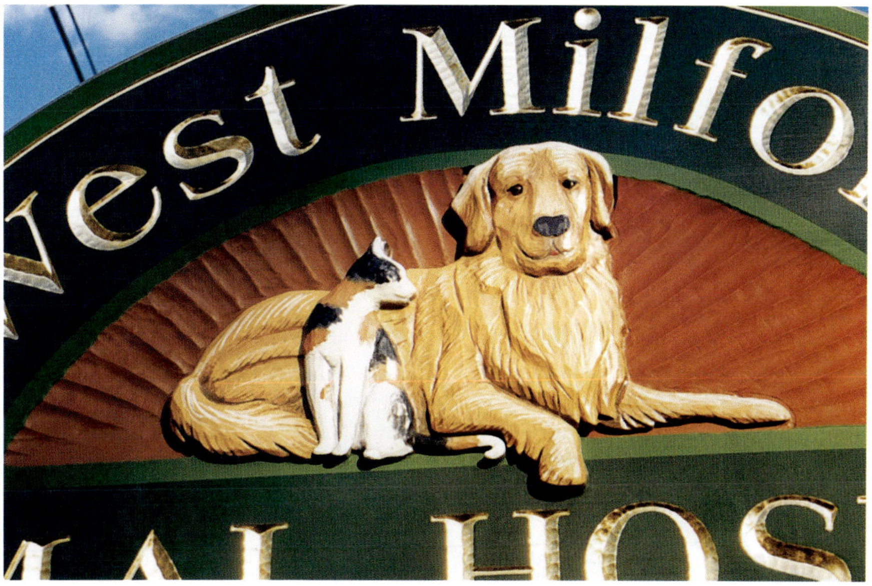

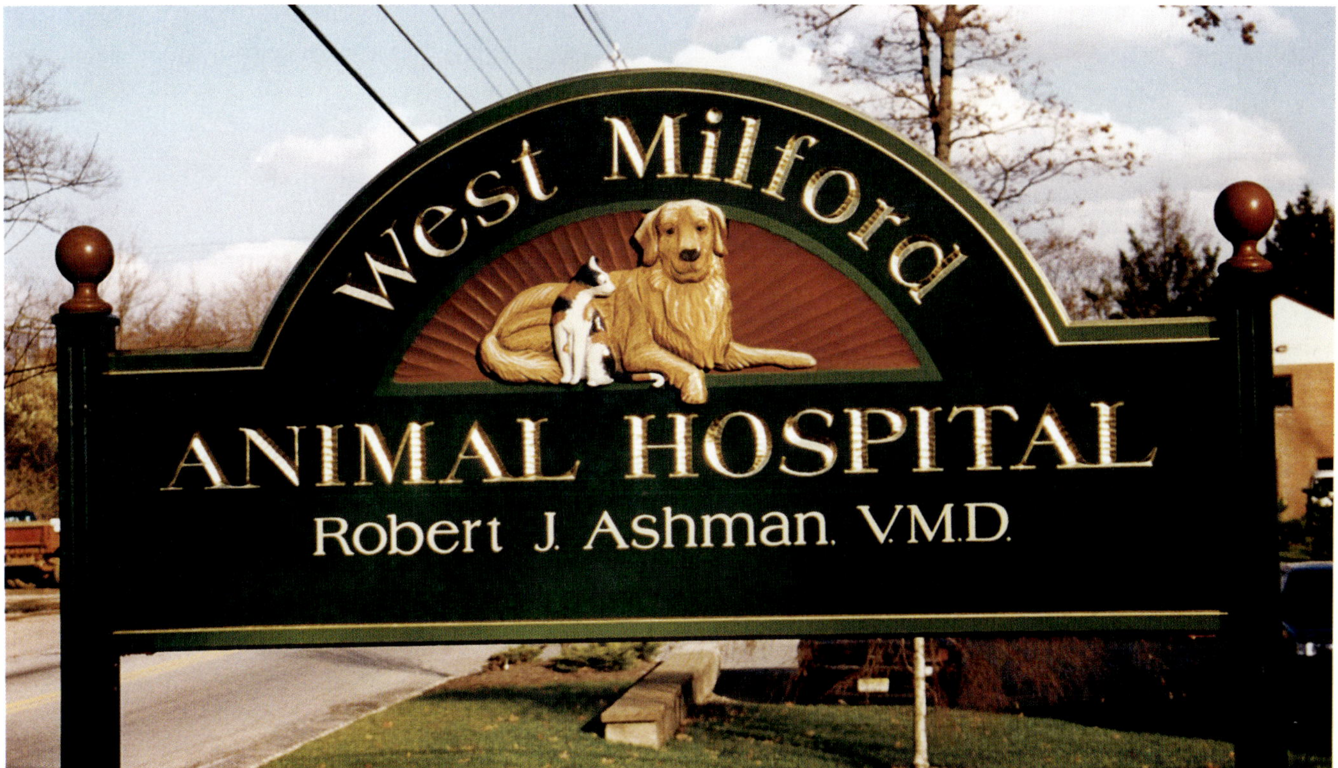

DESIGNERS

Chip Carter
Randy Tuthill
Island Designs
P.O. Box 114
Captiva, FL 33924
(813) 395-2222

FABRICATORS

Chip Carter
Marilyn Carter
Island Designs

This 3 ft. 9 in. x 8 ft. sign is fabricated of 2-in. rigid urethane, redwood backbraces and cedar posts. The area behind the rounded and outlined main copy is sand-blasted, and the copy is finished with 23K patent gold leaf. The sign is painted with latex and lettering enamel.

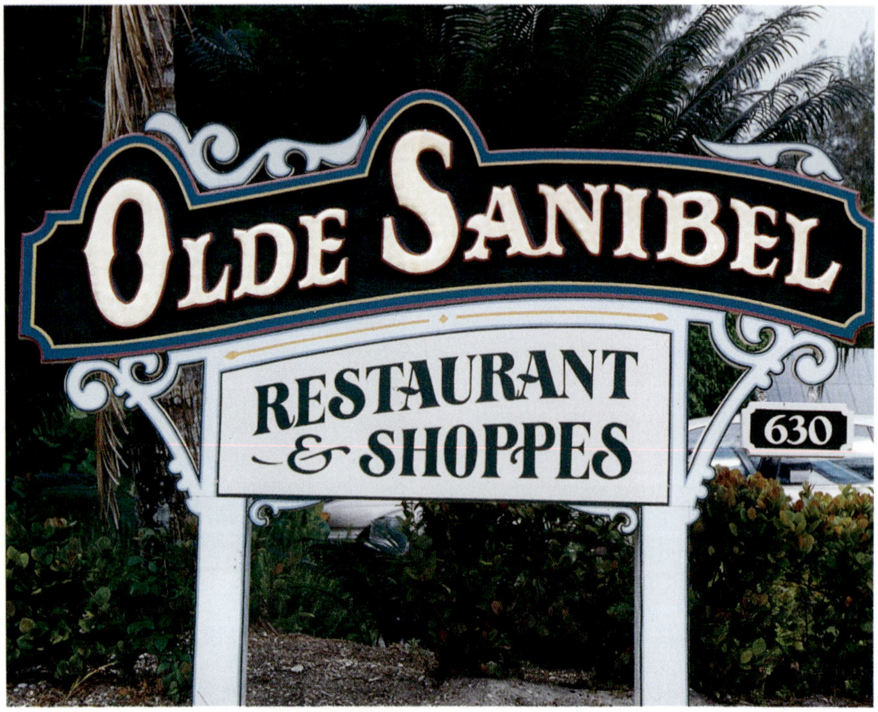

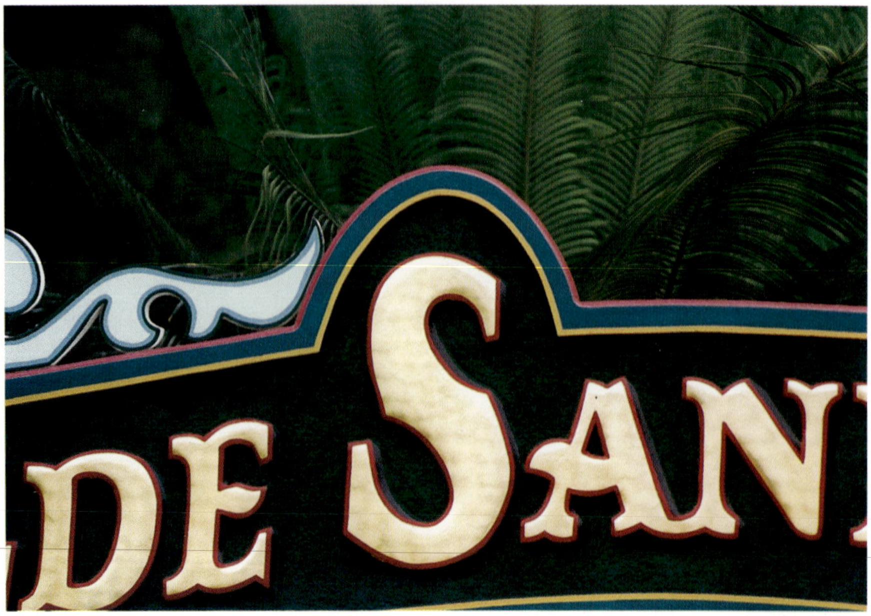

DESIGNER

Chip Carter
Island Designs
P.O. Box 114
Captiva, FL 33924
(813) 395-2222

FABRICATOR

Island Designs

This private residence has an 18 x 28-in. redwood panel sandblasted sign. The edges are cove routed and the background is painted with latex. The copy is epoxy poured on raw letters to create a rounded face. When hardened, the epoxy was sanded and gilded.

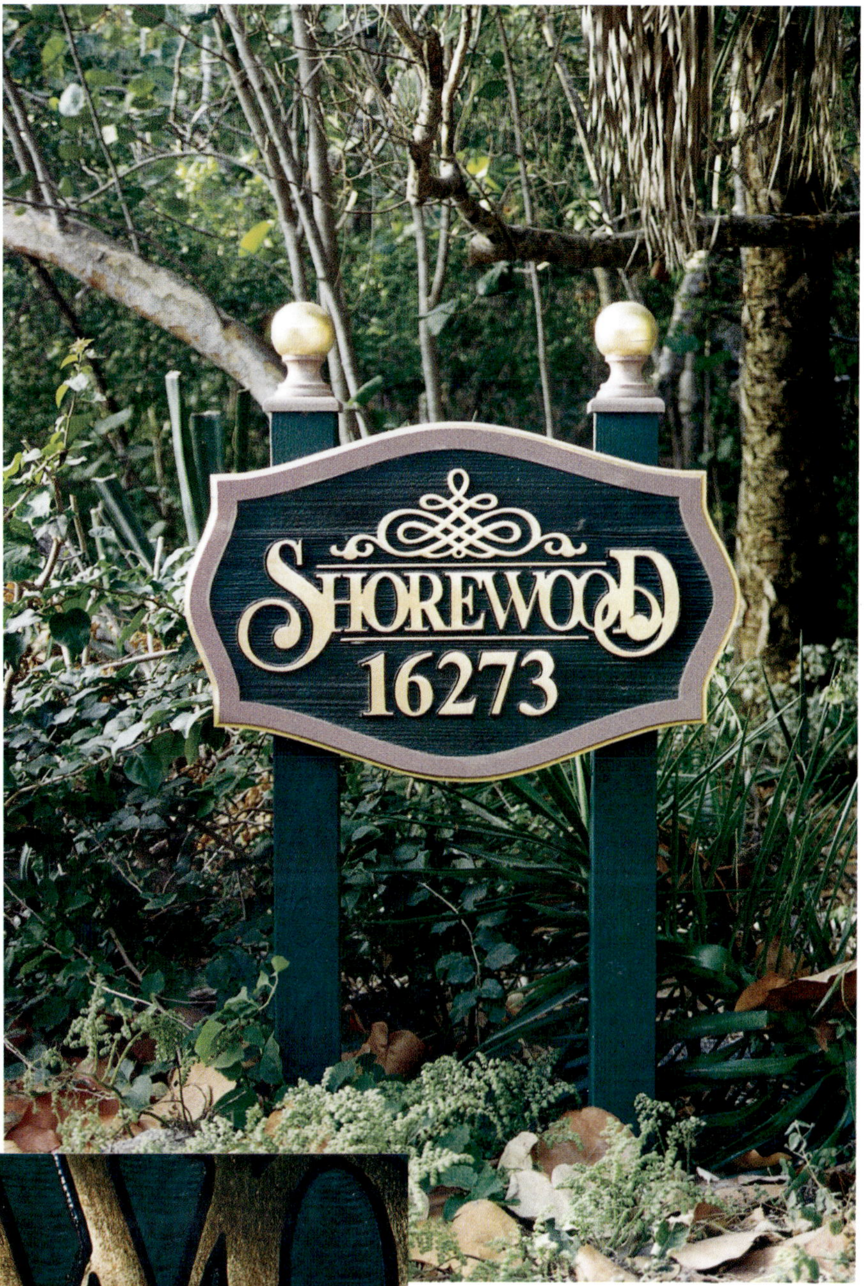

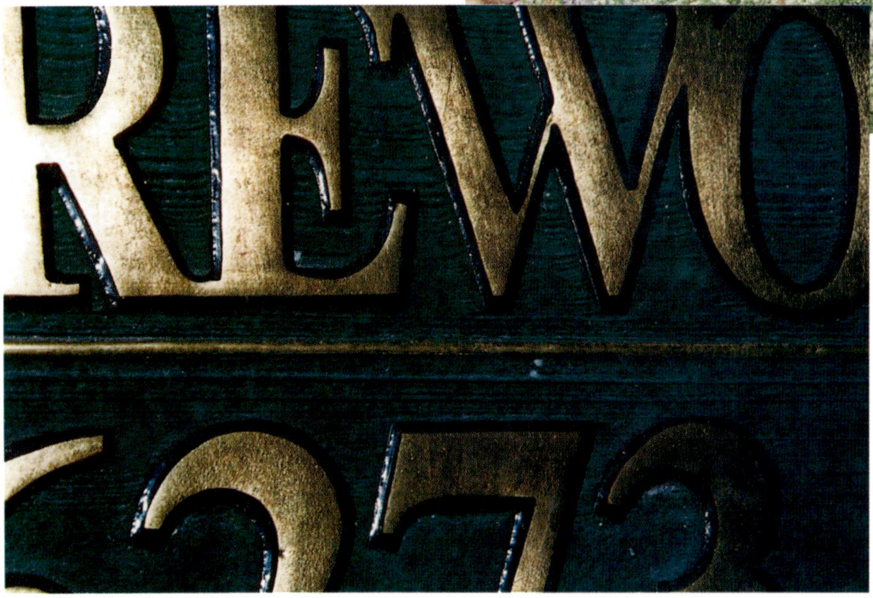

DESIGNER

Matt Zudweg
2900 Chicago Dr. SW
Grandville, MI 49418
(616) 532-2034
Fax: (616) 532-8109

FABRICATOR

Matt Zudweg

The sandblasted cypress sign measures approximately 20 x 31 x 1½ in. The bluegill, banner and lettering are carved from high-density urethane.

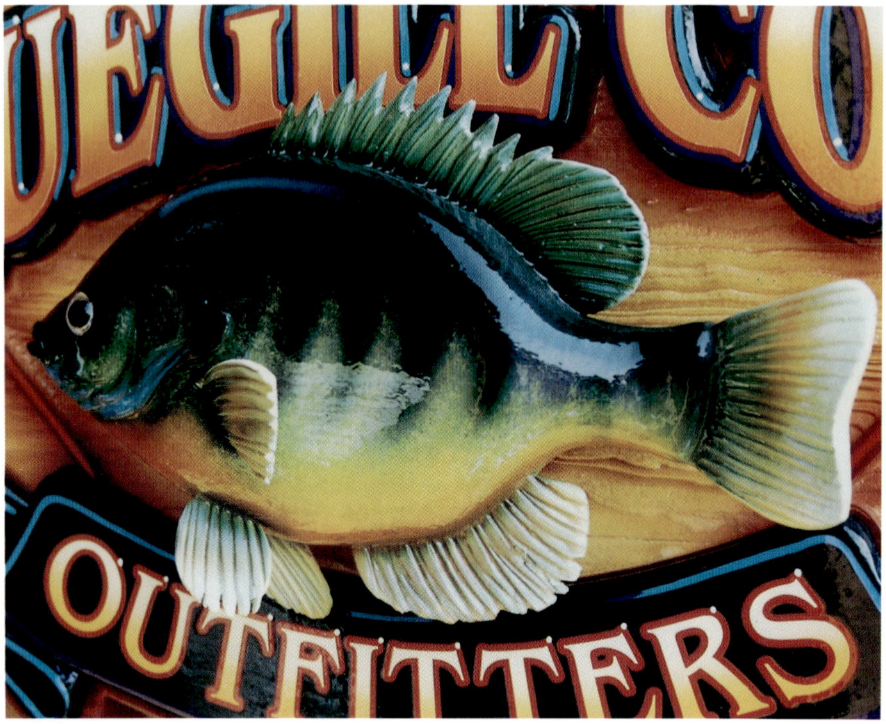

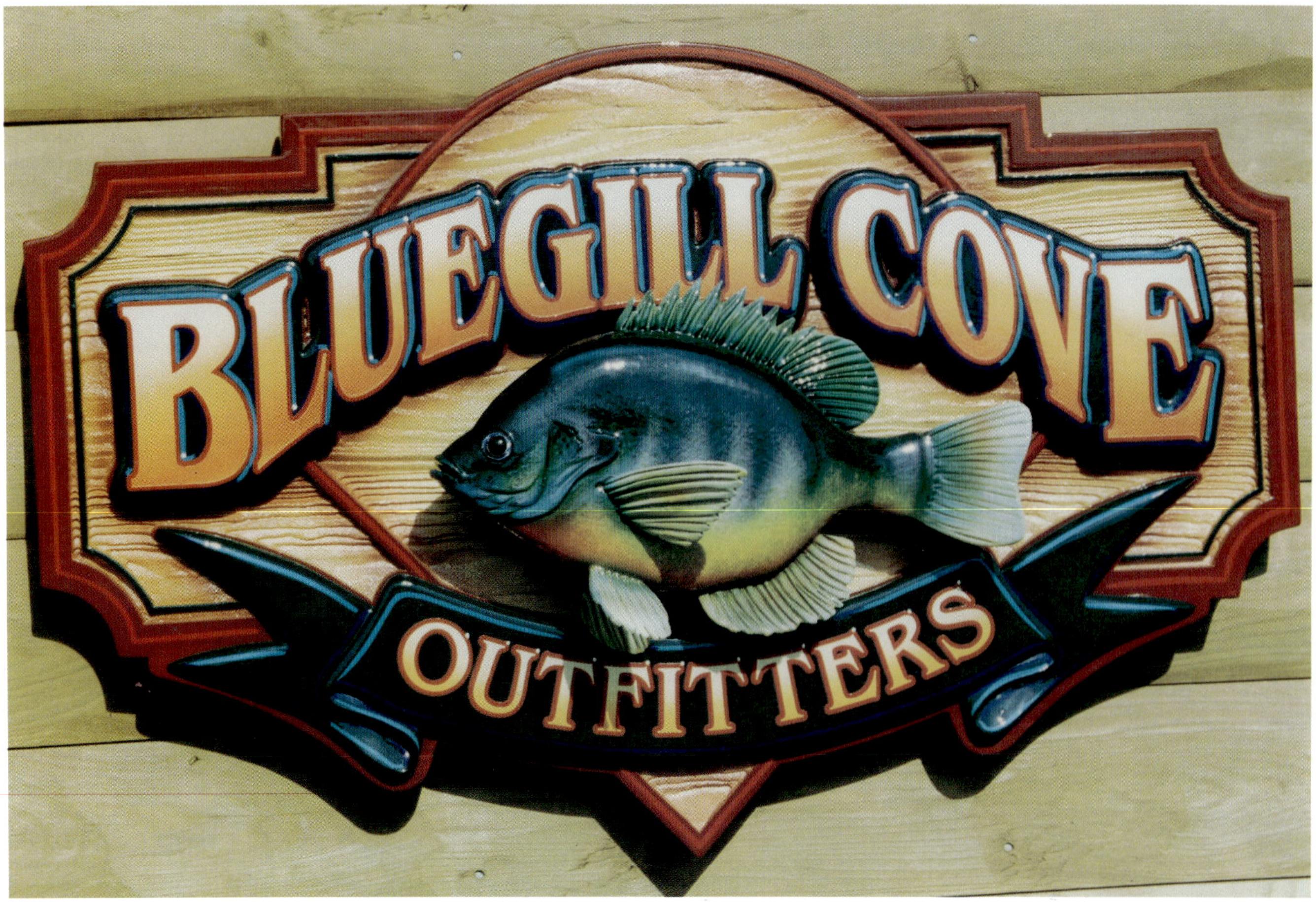

DESIGNERS

Nancy Beaudette
Noëlla Cotnam
Sign It
812-33 Pitt St.
Cornwall, ON, Canada K6J 5R2
(613) 933-7447
Fax: (613) 933-3480

FABRICATOR

Sign It

This 30 x 30-in. sandblasted sign includes high-relief carving. "Java" is raised high-density urethane; the moose is hand-carved; the beans are carved and finished with copper leaf, and the falling beans are held on with Plexiglas® acrylic. This sign is one of a larger sign package.

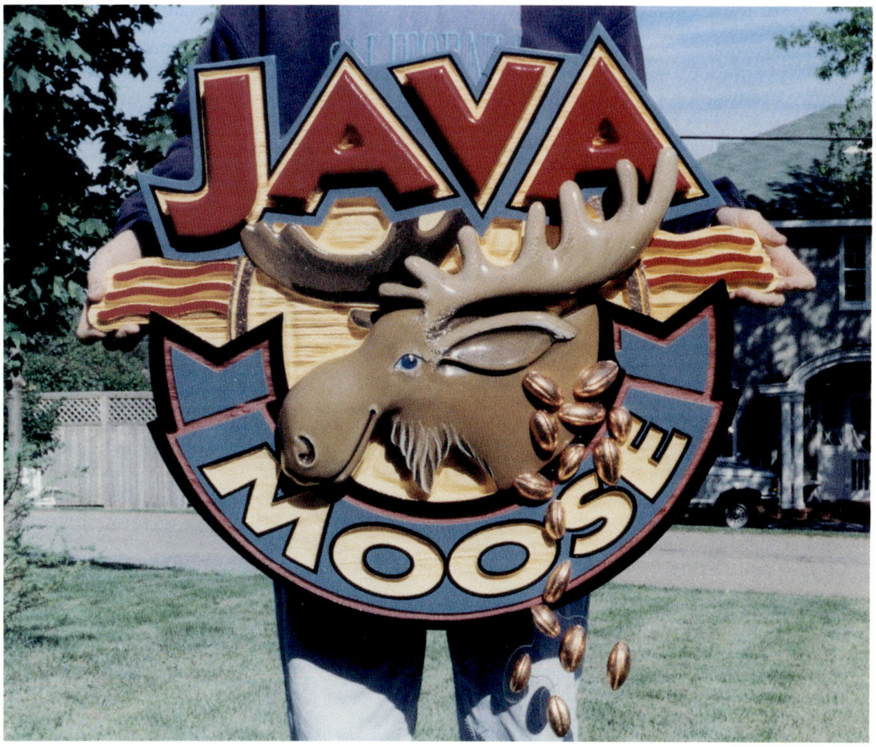

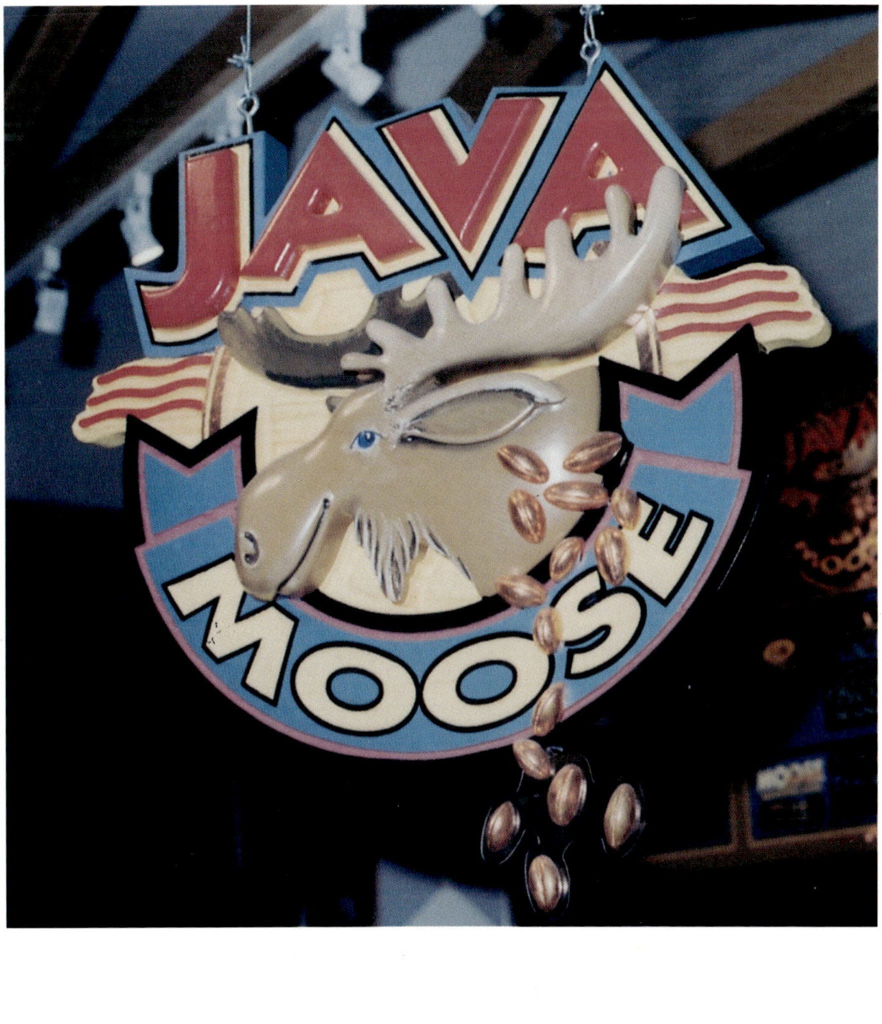

DESIGNER

Scott Owen
Sign Graphics
670 Highway 70
Columbiana, AL 35051
(205) 669-9700
Fax: (205) 669-9700

FABRICATOR

Sign Graphics

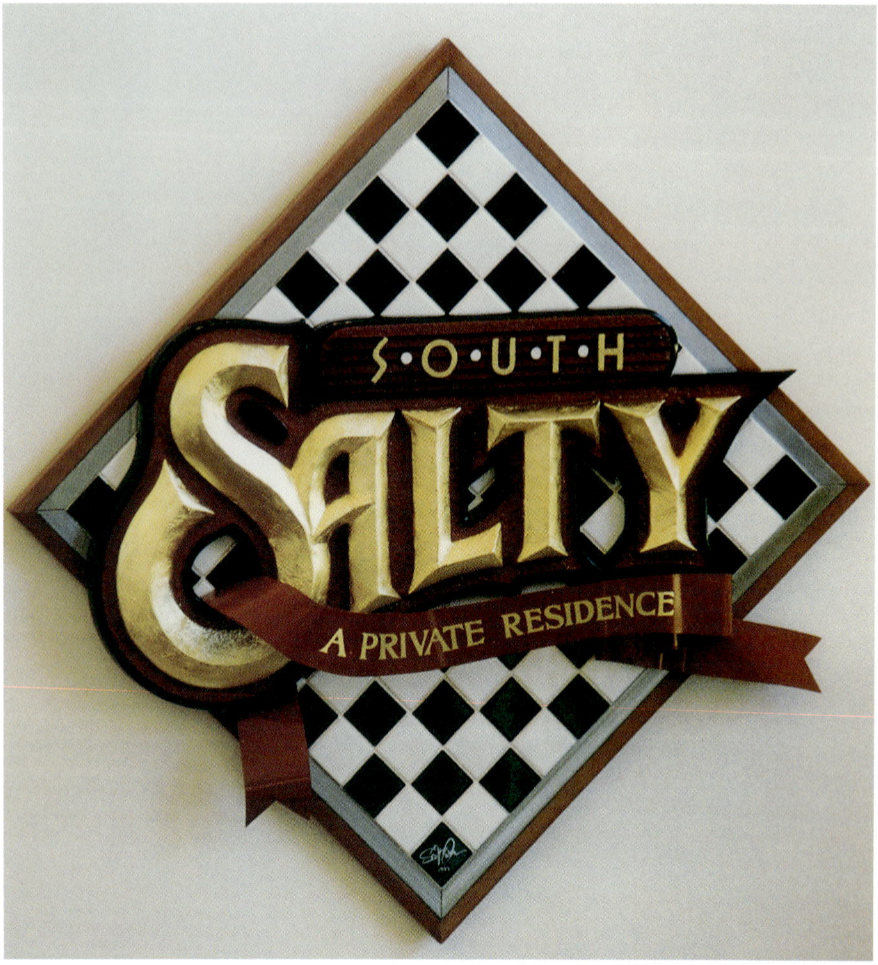

This 40 x 40-in. sign is fabricated around a piece of ¾-in. MDO. The edges are redwood with a 1-in. piece of polished aluminum inset between the redwood and the 2-in. ceramic tiles. A piece of 1-in. high-density urethane is sandblasted, and 1-in. hand-carved high-density-urethane letters are attached.

All the lettering is gilded using 23K goldleaf. The banner is hand-rolled .040 aluminum attached from the back of the sign.

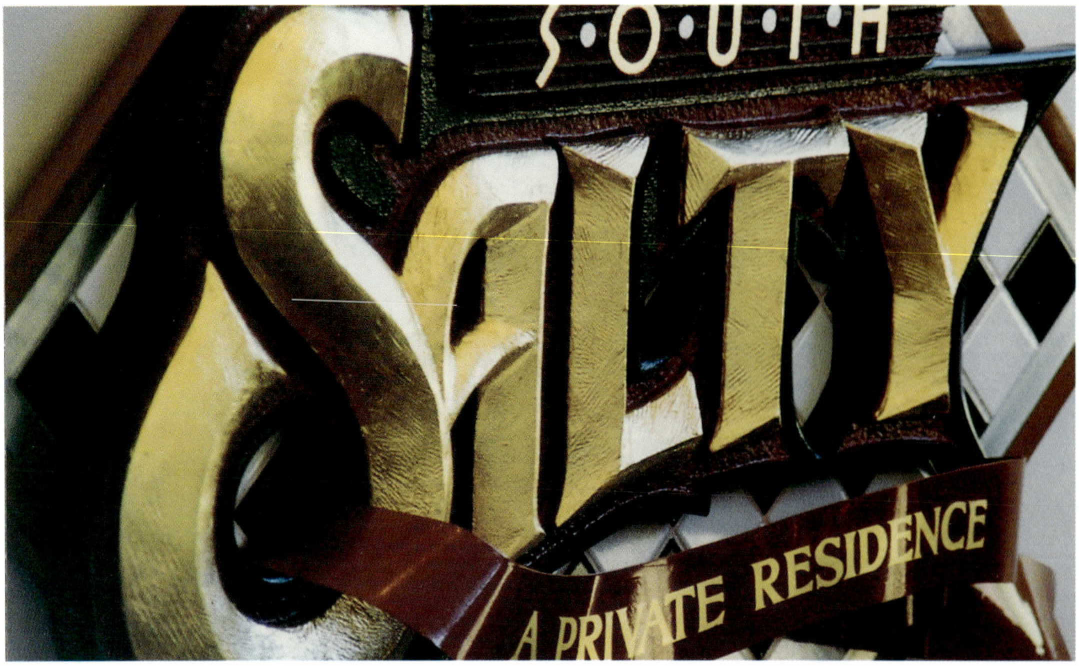

DESIGNER

Peter Poanessa
690 Court St.
Keene, NH 03431
(603) 358-1003

FABRICATOR

Peter Poanessa

The redwood main panel on this sign measures 20 ft. x 19 in. The background is sandblasted and carved; gilded high-density letters are applied. There is a ¼-in. shoulder between the cut-out letters and the blasted outline. The logo panel is fabricated from 18-lb. high-density urethane with applied raised letters and graphics. The background center of the panel has a sandblasted texture.

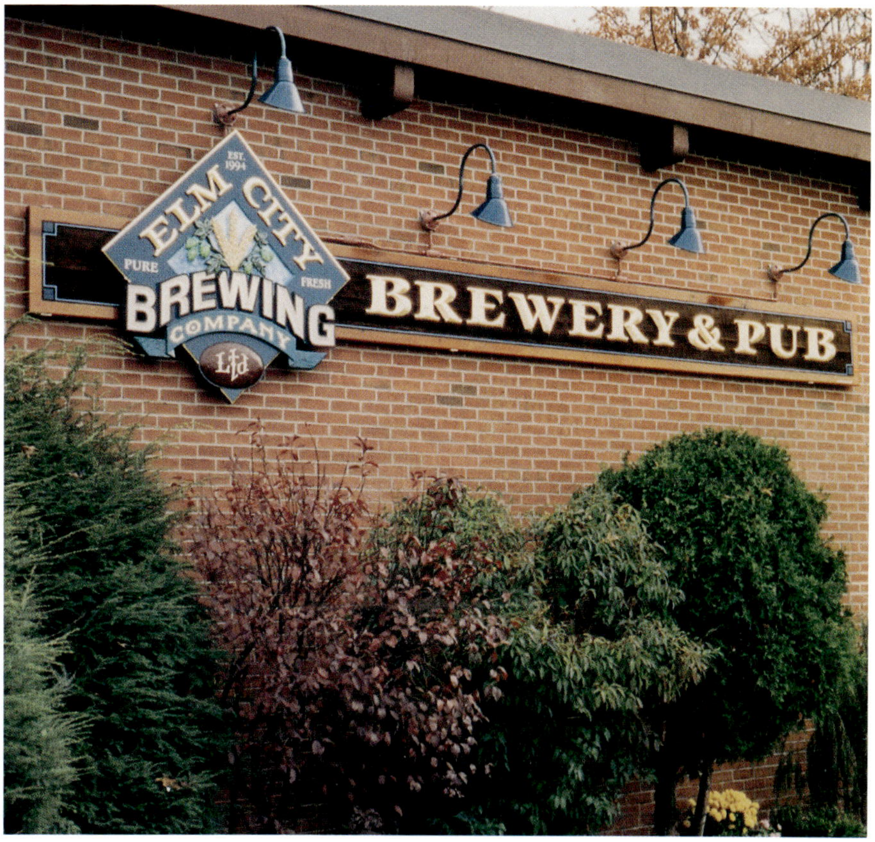

DESIGNER

Kraig Yaseen
Yaseen Design Studio
434 Turner Dr.
Durango, CO 81301
(970) 247-4467
Fax: (970) 385-4005

FABRICATORS

Leon Newman
Brian Ballard
Yaseen Design Studio

This 6-in. x 12-ft. high-density-urethane sign is hand-cut, bevel-carved and gilded using 23K goldleaf. The mountain elements are airbrushed, and the frame is stud-mounted into concrete block as one piece.

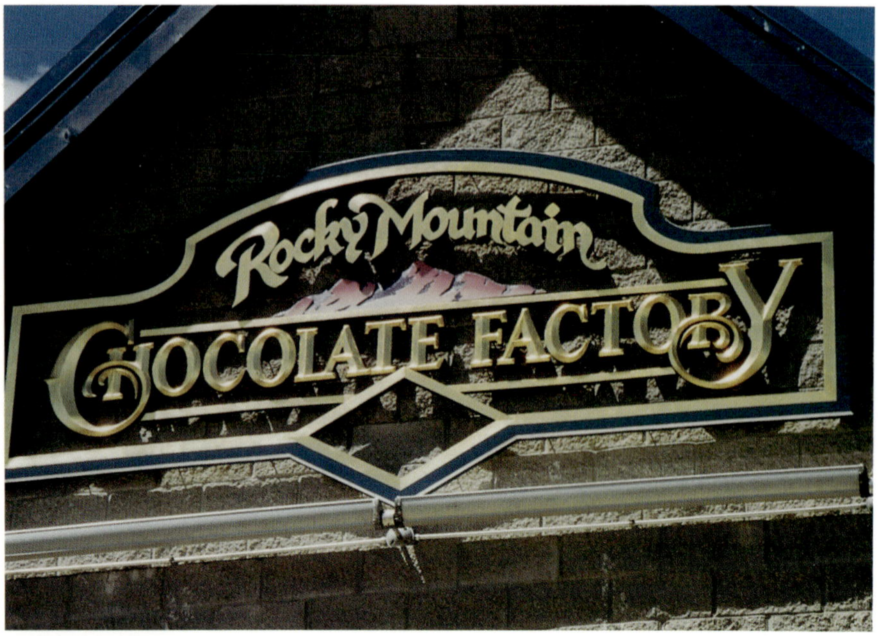

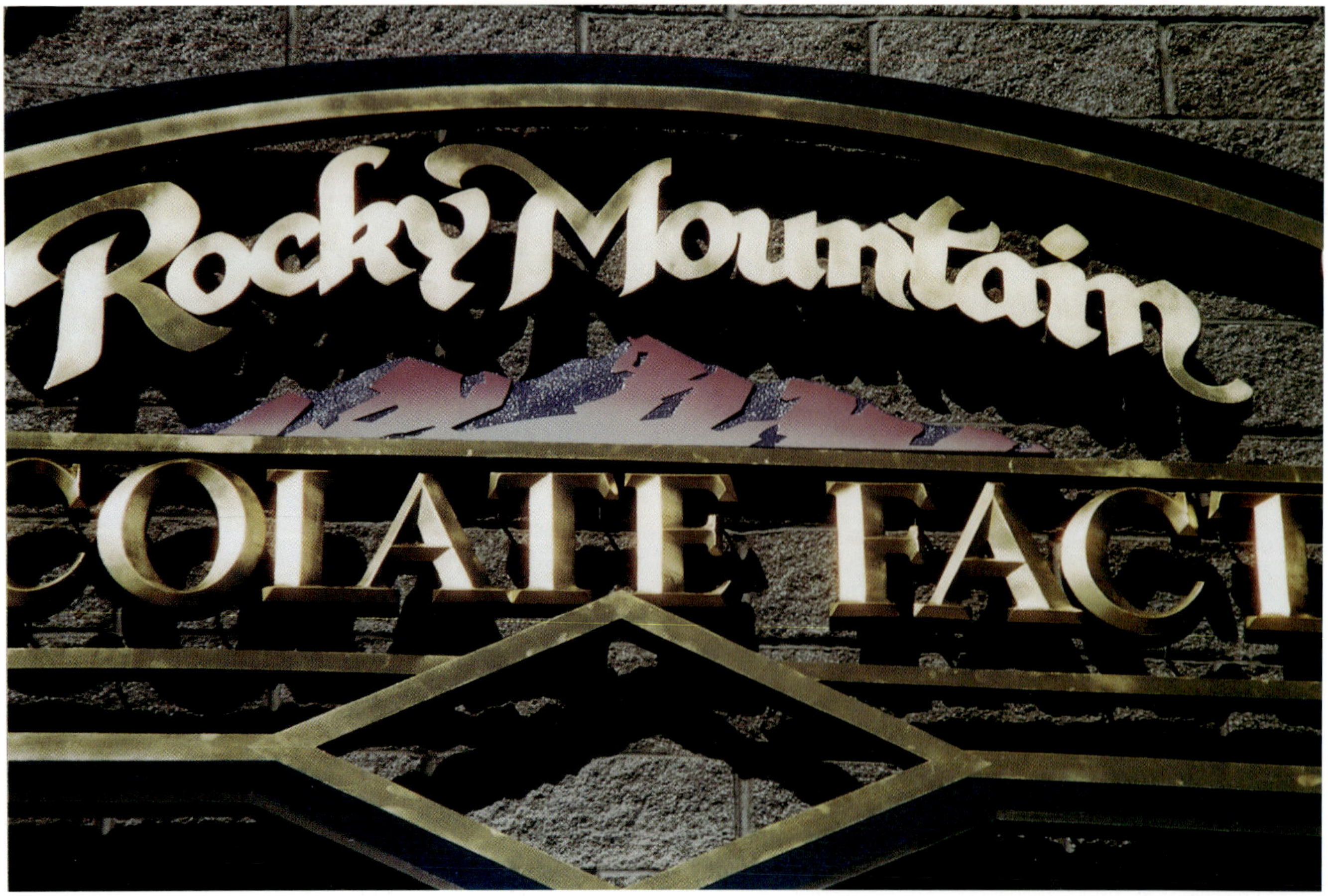

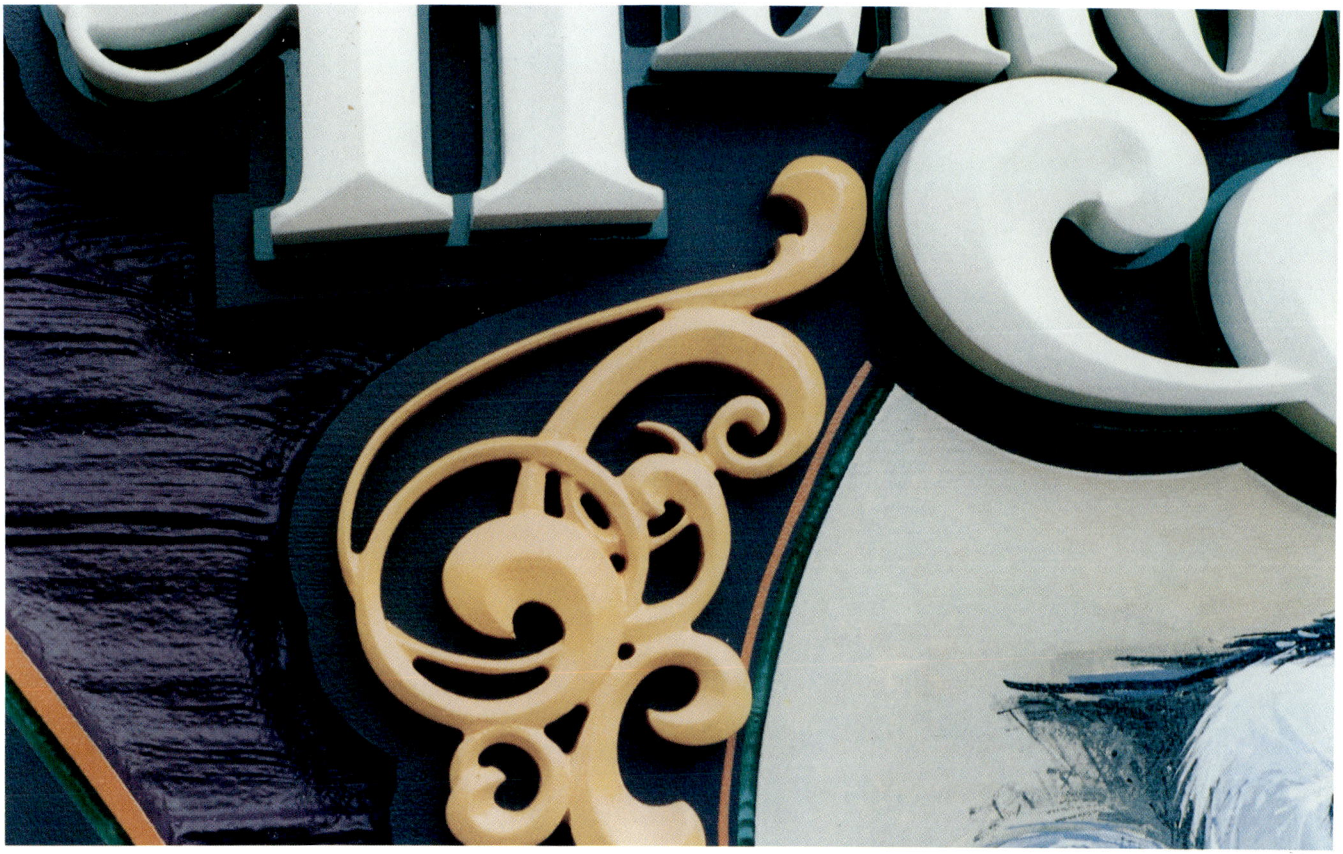

DESIGNERS

Nancy Beaudette
Noëlla Cotnam
Sign It
812-33 Pitt St.
Cornwall, ON, Canada K6J 5R2
(613) 933-7447
Fax: (613) 933-3480

FABRICATOR

Sign It

This 28 x 32-in. sandblasted redwood sign features raised 1-in. high-density-urethane letters as well as hand-carved convex letters and scrolls. The pictorial is hand-painted. There is also halo and contour sandblasting around the main silhouette. The outline around the main letters is created using ⅛-in. PVC.

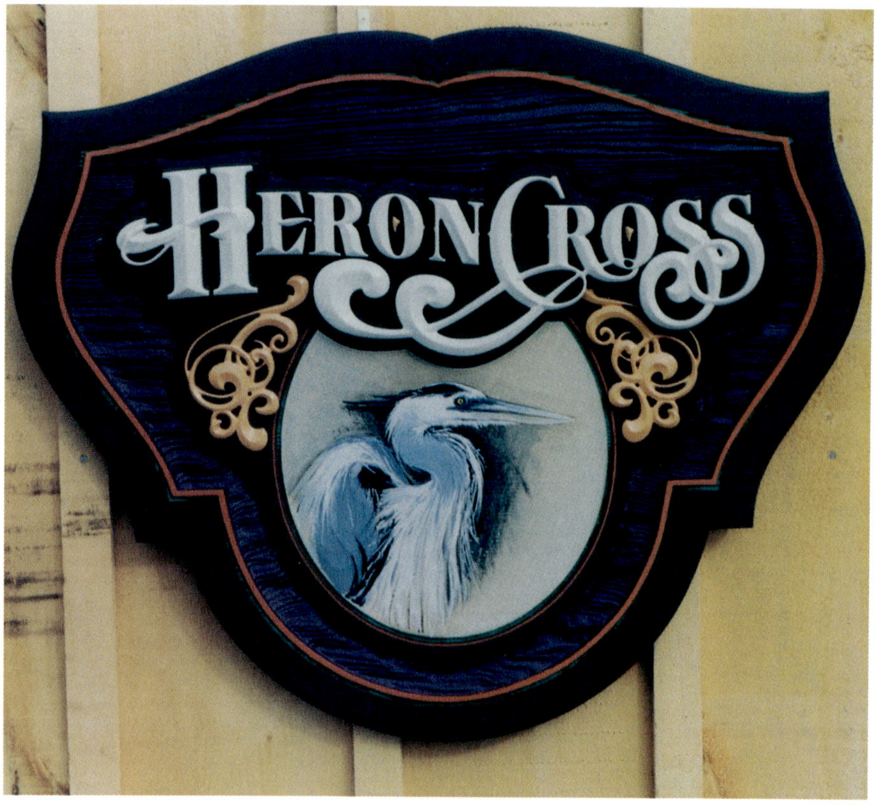

DESIGNER

Tim Hokes
123 Glacier Dr.
Box 875
Banff, AB, Canada T0L 0C0
(403) 762-8027
Fax: (403) 762-0617

FABRICATOR

Banff Sign Co., Ltd.
Box 2536
Banff, AB, Canada T0L 0C0
(403) 762-4945
Fax: (403) 762-8234

This 120 x 22-in. sign is fabricated from clear-heart cedar. The "Jump Start" copy is hand-carved. The secondary copy and logo are sandblasted. The coffee cup is sculpted from basswood and applied.

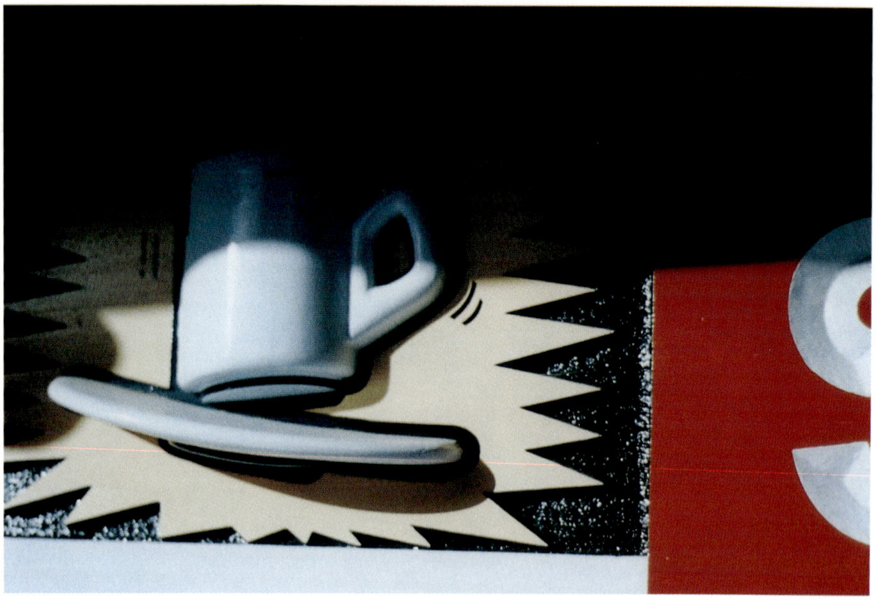

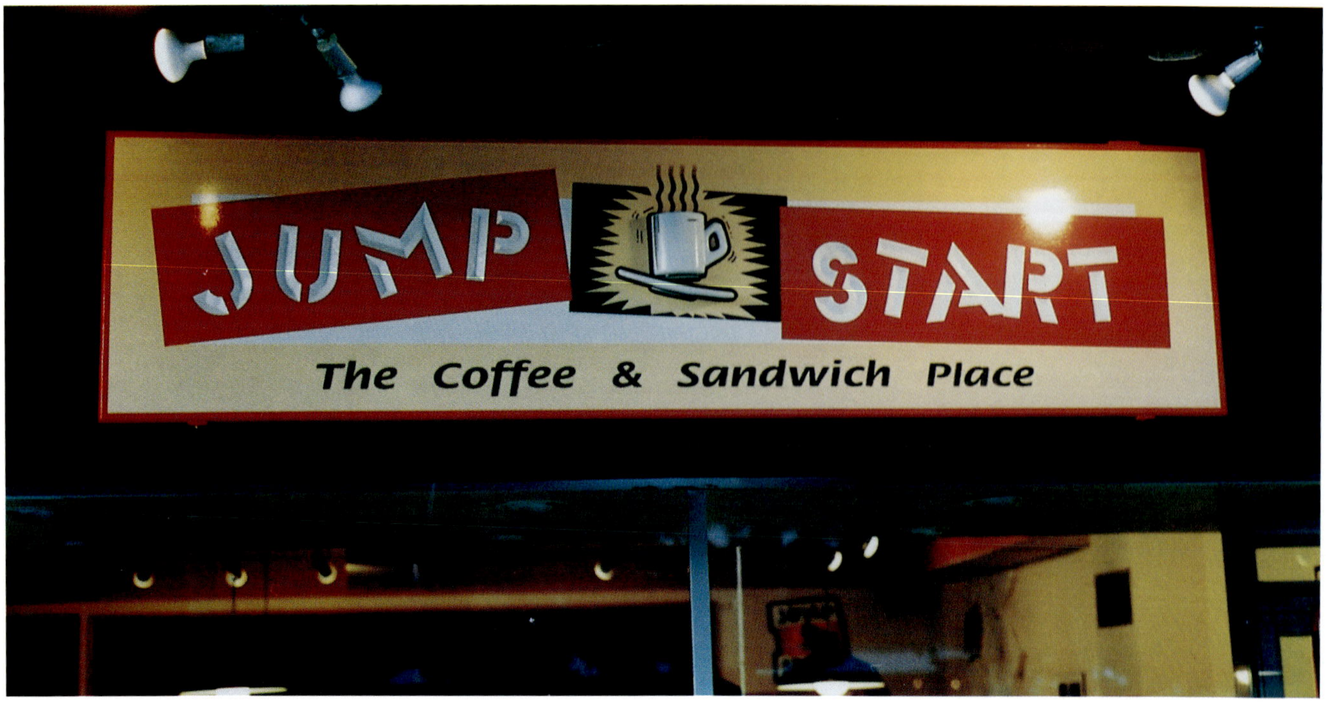

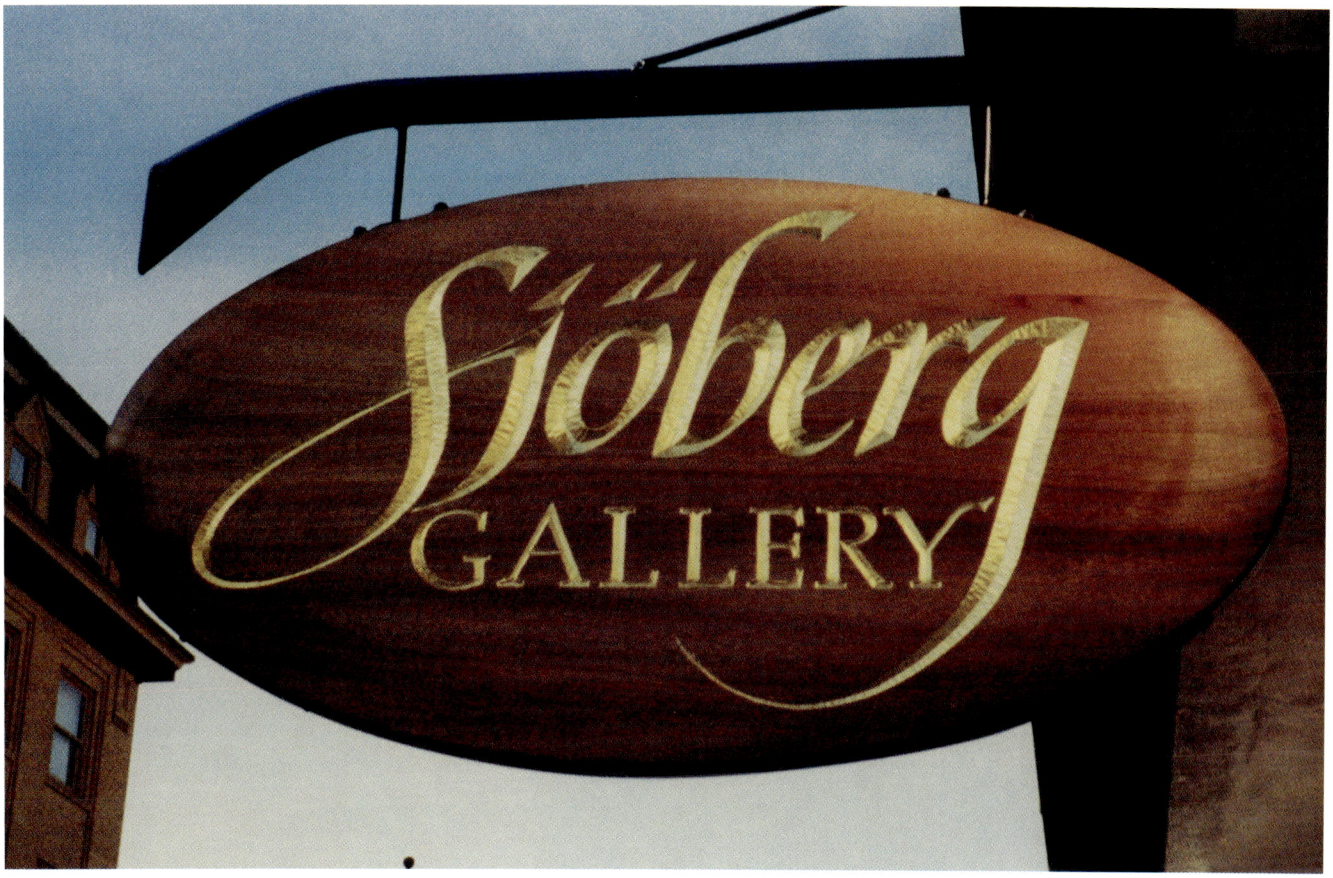

DESIGNER

Bill Blumberg
Signs & Art
109 Eel Lake Ln.
North Bend, OR 97459

FABRICATORS

Bill Blumberg
Joel Montgomery
Signs & Art

This double-faced 30 x 52-in. sign is created from 5-in.-thick mahogany shaped to 3 in. on the edge. The sign has carved incised lettering and is gilded using 23K goldleaf. The wood is covered with five coats of clear polyurethane. The sign is mounted to a sculpted 2-in.-sq. steel tube, with tempered ½-in. steel brackets. In addition, there is a 2-in. steel band around the entire sign.

DESIGNERS

Nancy Beaudette
Noëlla Cotnam
Sign It
812-33 Pitt St.
Cornwall, ON, Canada K6J 5R2
(613) 933-7447
Fax: (613) 933-3480

FABRICATOR

Sign It

This 24 x 48-in. sandblasted redwood sign incorporates raised high-density-urethane letters cut using a computerized router. The pictorial was roughed-out on the router, then hand-carved. The sign was installed at an angle on a brick wall.

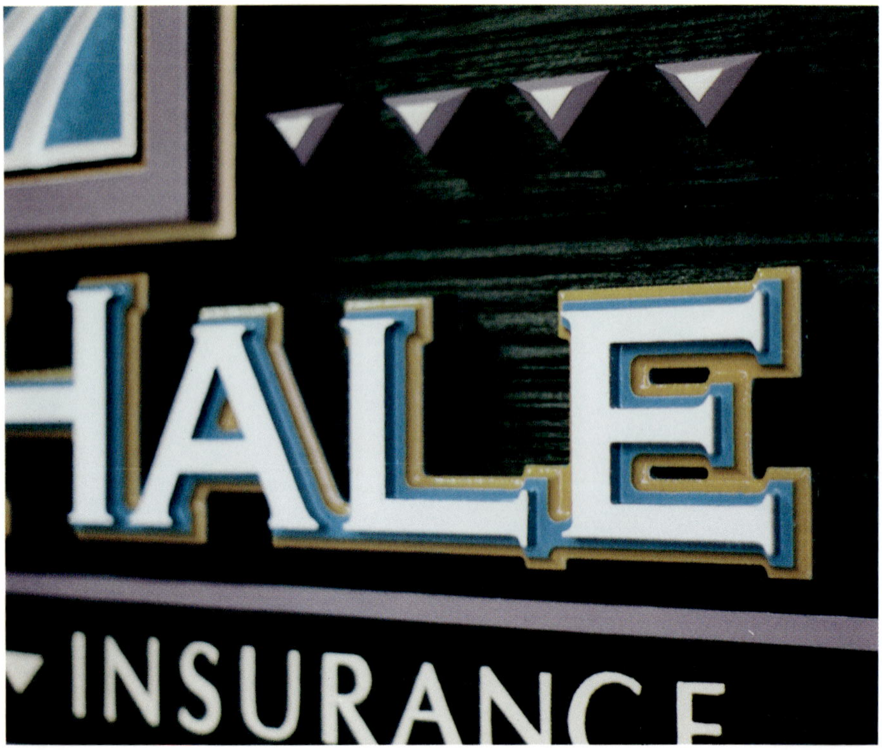

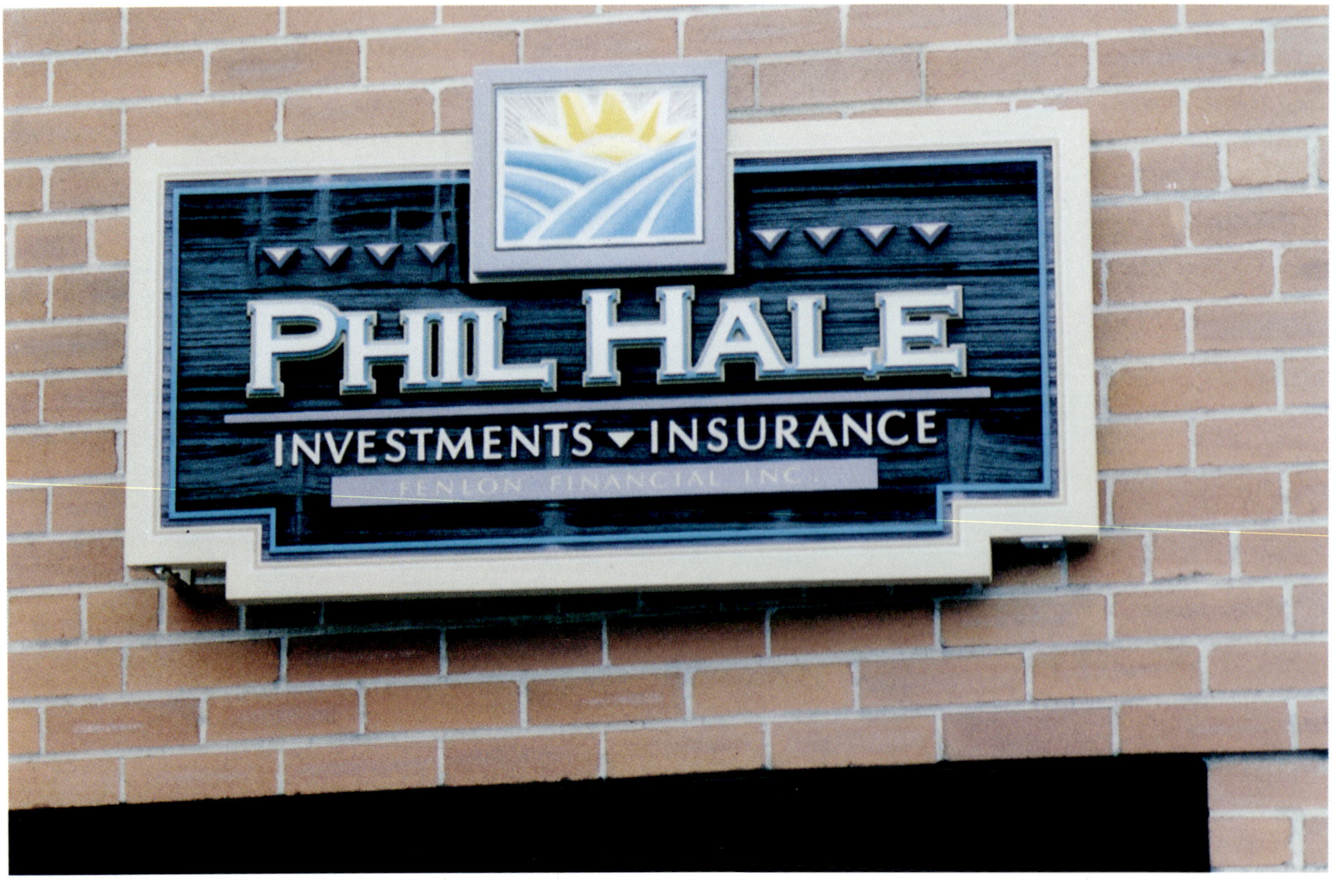

DESIGNER

Jeff Douglas
Douglas Signs
413 14th Ave. E.
Ashland, WI 54806
(715) 682-2160
Fax: (715) 682-6680

FABRICATORS

Jeff Douglas
Tony Dietz
Douglas Signs

This 3-ft.-high x 17-ft.-long MDO sign is painted using lettering enamels and gold acrylic polyurethane. The frame and mouldings are created from cedar. There are also pressed metal (zinc) dimensional pieces attached to the sign's face using brads. The pressed metal is painted with tinted acrylic polyurethane to enhance the sign's dimension.

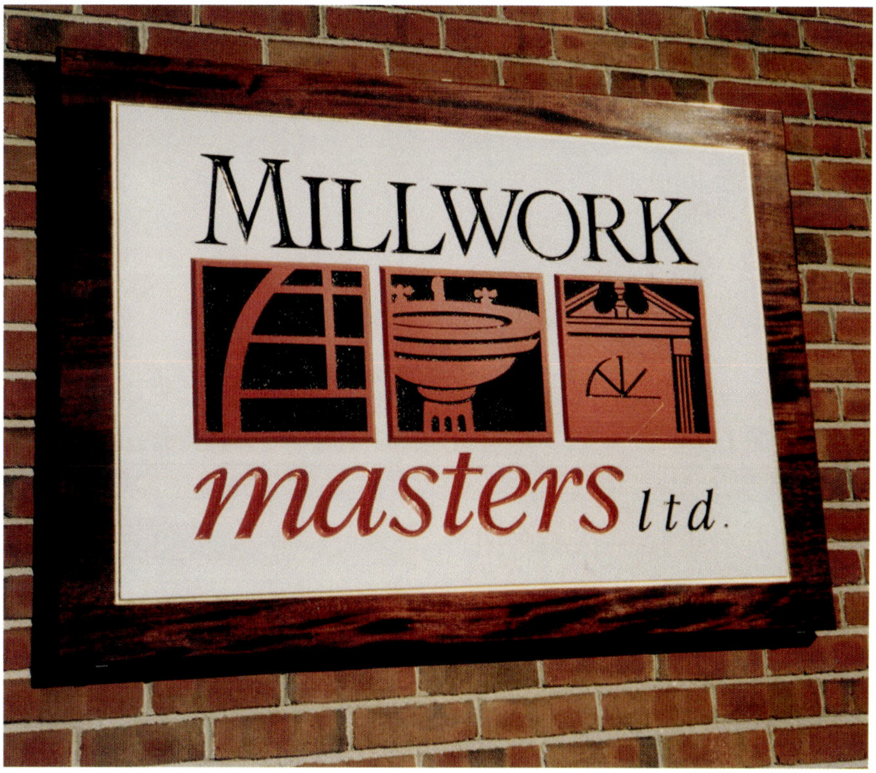

DESIGNER

Peter Poanessa
690 Court St.
Keene, NH 03431
(603) 358-1003

FABRICATOR

Peter Poanessa

This 3 x 4 ft. sign is fabricated from Brazilian mahogany. The sign's outer border is encapsulated with West Systems epoxy and then five coats of varnish. The inner border is routed and gilded. The letters are carved. The sign's graphics are created from raised, sandblasted high-density urethane.

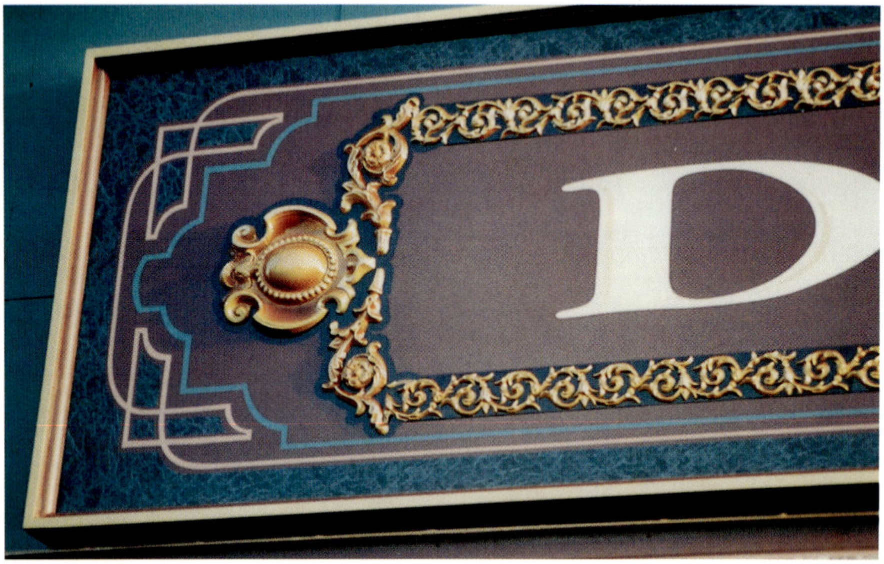

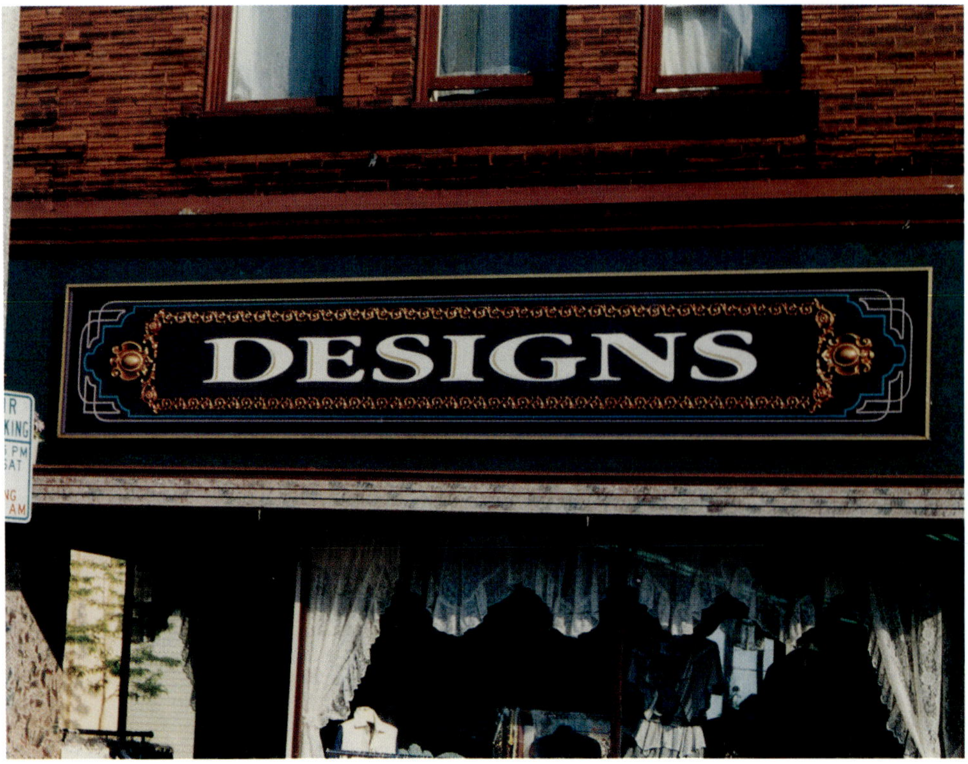

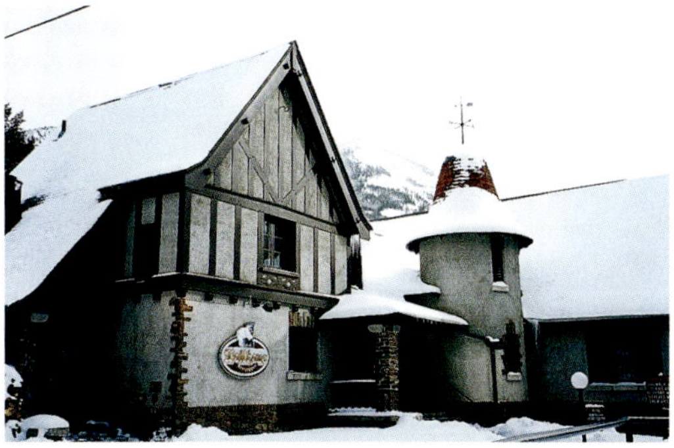

DESIGNER

Larry Whan
Banff Sign Co., Ltd.
Box 2536
Banff, AB, Canada TOL 0CO
(403) 762-4945
Fax: (403) 762-8234

FABRICATOR

Banff Sign Co., Ltd.

The sign blank for this German restaurant is clear cedar measuring 76 x 58 in. All copy and borders are hand carved and gilded with 23K gold leaf. The background and details are carved and painted foam. The bratwurst is sculpted of cedar and attached.

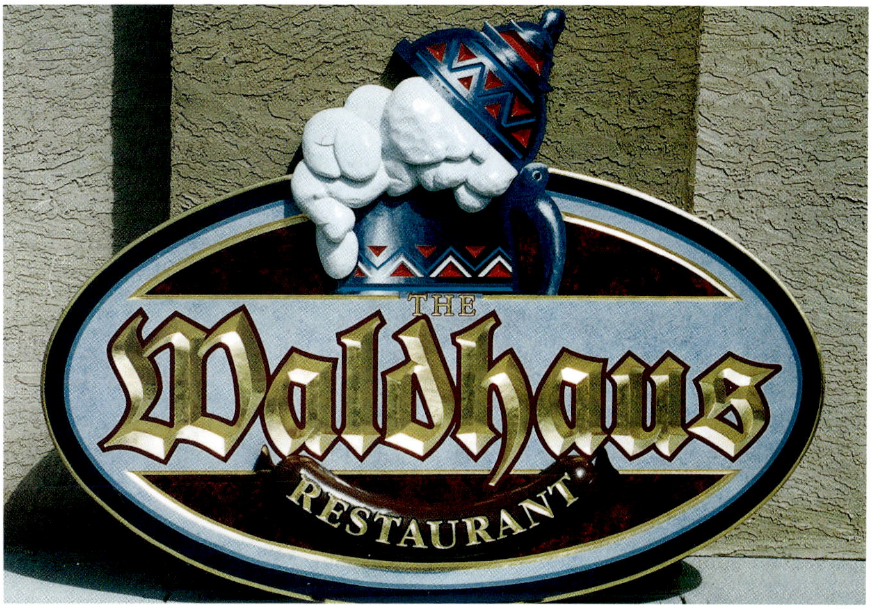

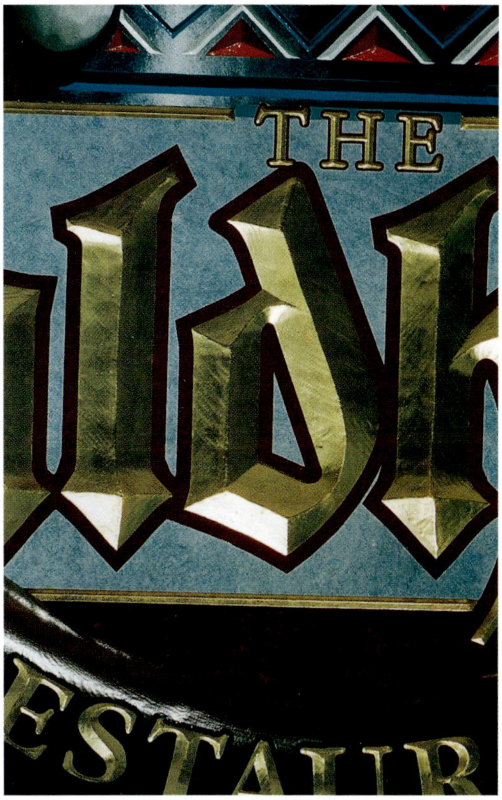

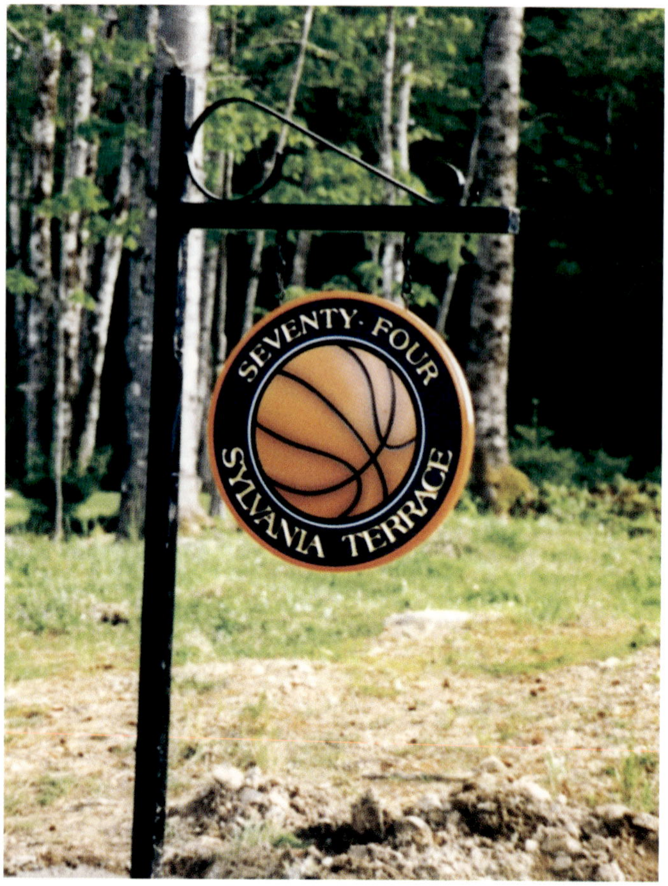

DESIGNER

Larry Whan
Banff Sign Co., Ltd.
Box 2536
Banff, AB, Canada T0L 0C0
(403) 762-4945
Fax: (403) 762-8234

FABRICATOR

Banff Sign Co., Ltd.

This 24-in. diameter double-sided sign is clear cedar with hand-carved copy, gilded with 23K gold. The basketballs are sculpted of Sign Foam® and airbrushed, and attached to each side. Primer is applied thick and bubbly to give the basketballs texture.

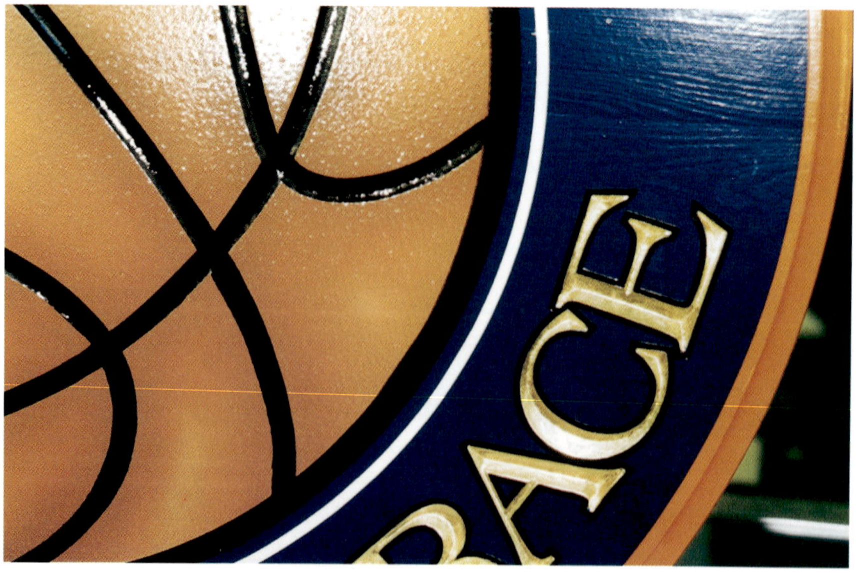

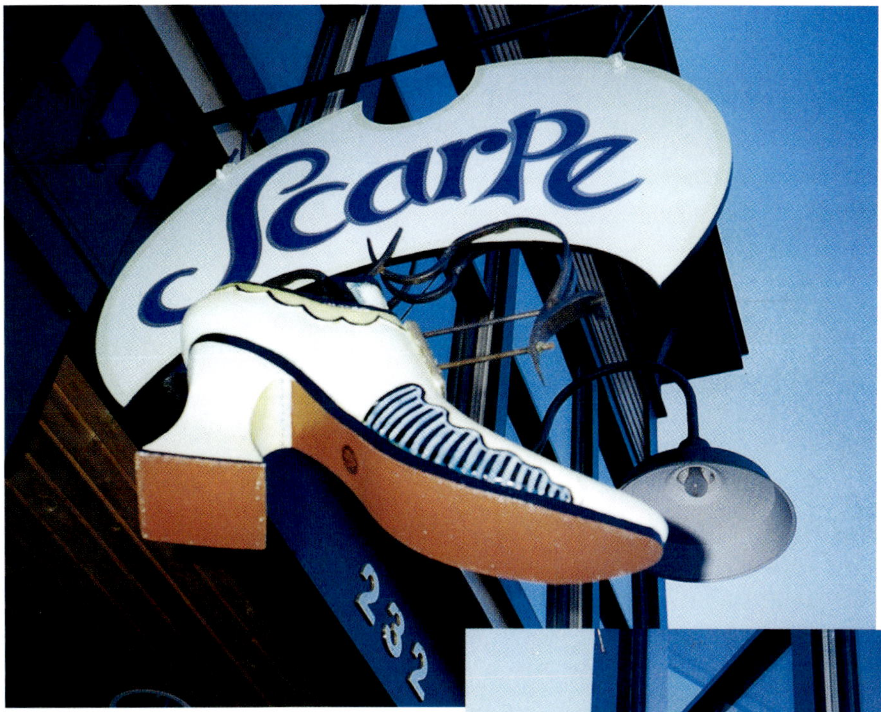

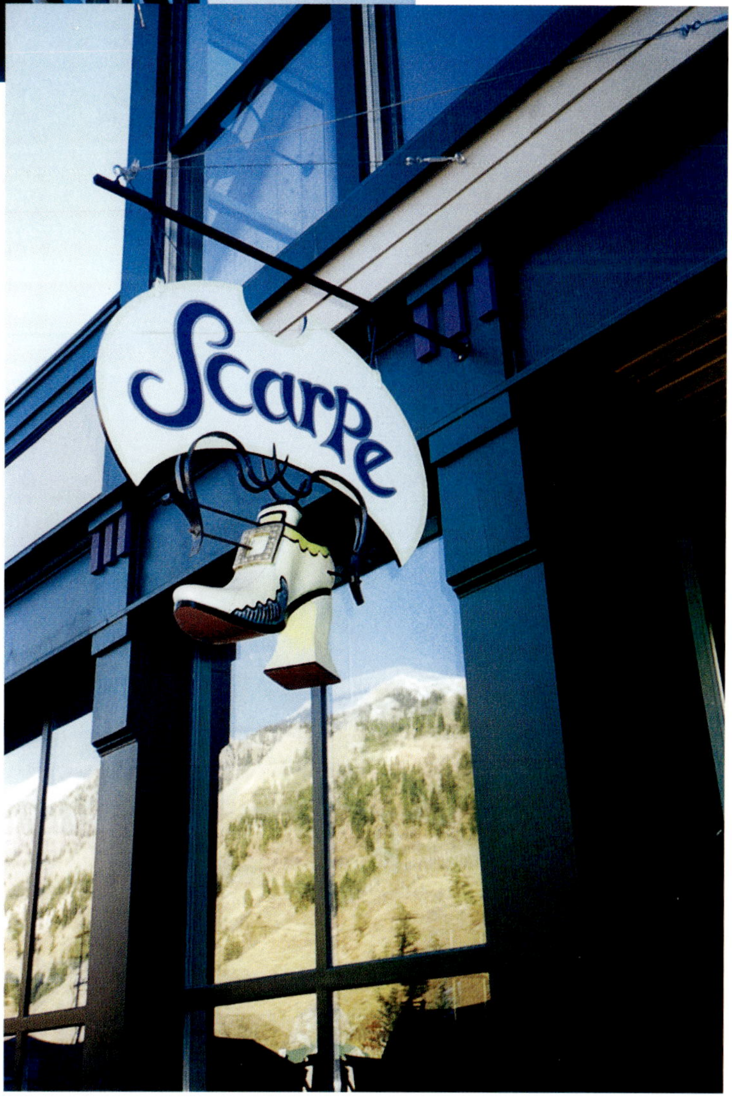

DESIGNER

Rod Pickett
Fordging Ahead
869 Florida Rd.
Durango, CO 81301
(970) 259-9706

FABRICATOR

Leon Newman
Yaseen Design Studio
434 Turner Dr.
Durango, CO 81301
(970) 247-4467
Fax: (970) 385-4005

This 6-ft.-tall sign is comprised of MDO signboard, laminated with an 18-lb. urethane foam shoe. Blacksmith-forged iron fastens the shoe to the signboard. The lettering is done in vinyl. The shoe is hand carved and painted with enamel.

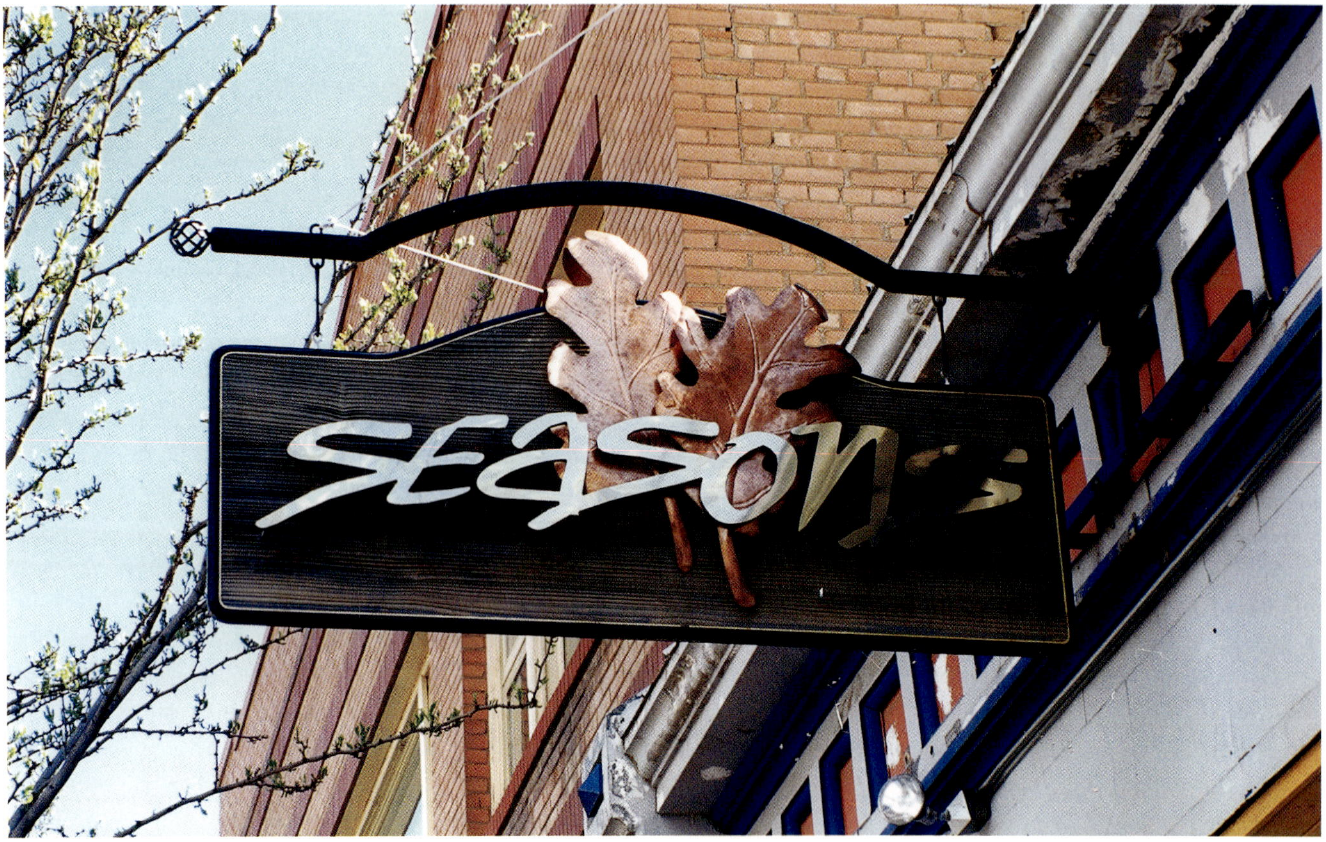

DESIGNERS

Kraig Yaseen
Leon Newman
Yaseen Design Studio
434 Turner Dr.
Durango, CO 81301
(970) 247-4467

FABRICATOR

Brian Ballard
Yaseen Design Studio

This sandblasted redwood backboard features a 23K inset pinstripe, and ½-in. aluminum letters with Brasstone® laminate. The oak leaves are hand embossed and sculpted from copper sheeting.

DESIGNER

Carousel Signs & Designs Inc.
7202 Brook Rd.
Richmond, VA 23227
(804) 262-3497
Fax: (804) 262-9073

FABRICATOR

Carousel Signs & Designs Inc.

This 24 x 36-in. sign's copy — "Rhett" and "Anita's" — is gilded and spun from behind. The "Place" copy is raised ½ in. from the glass and Sintra® expanded PVC panel. The sign's frame is made of redwood.

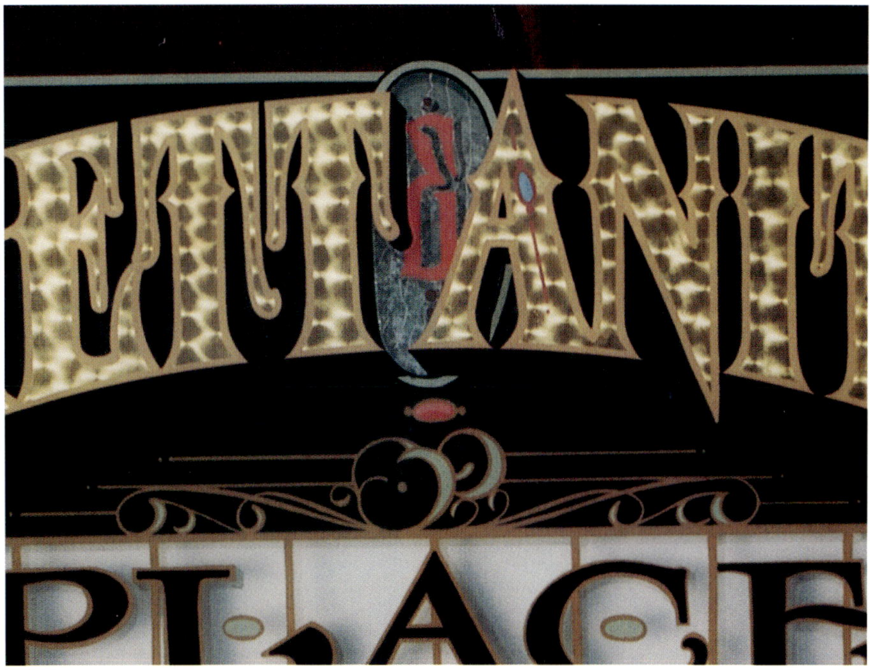

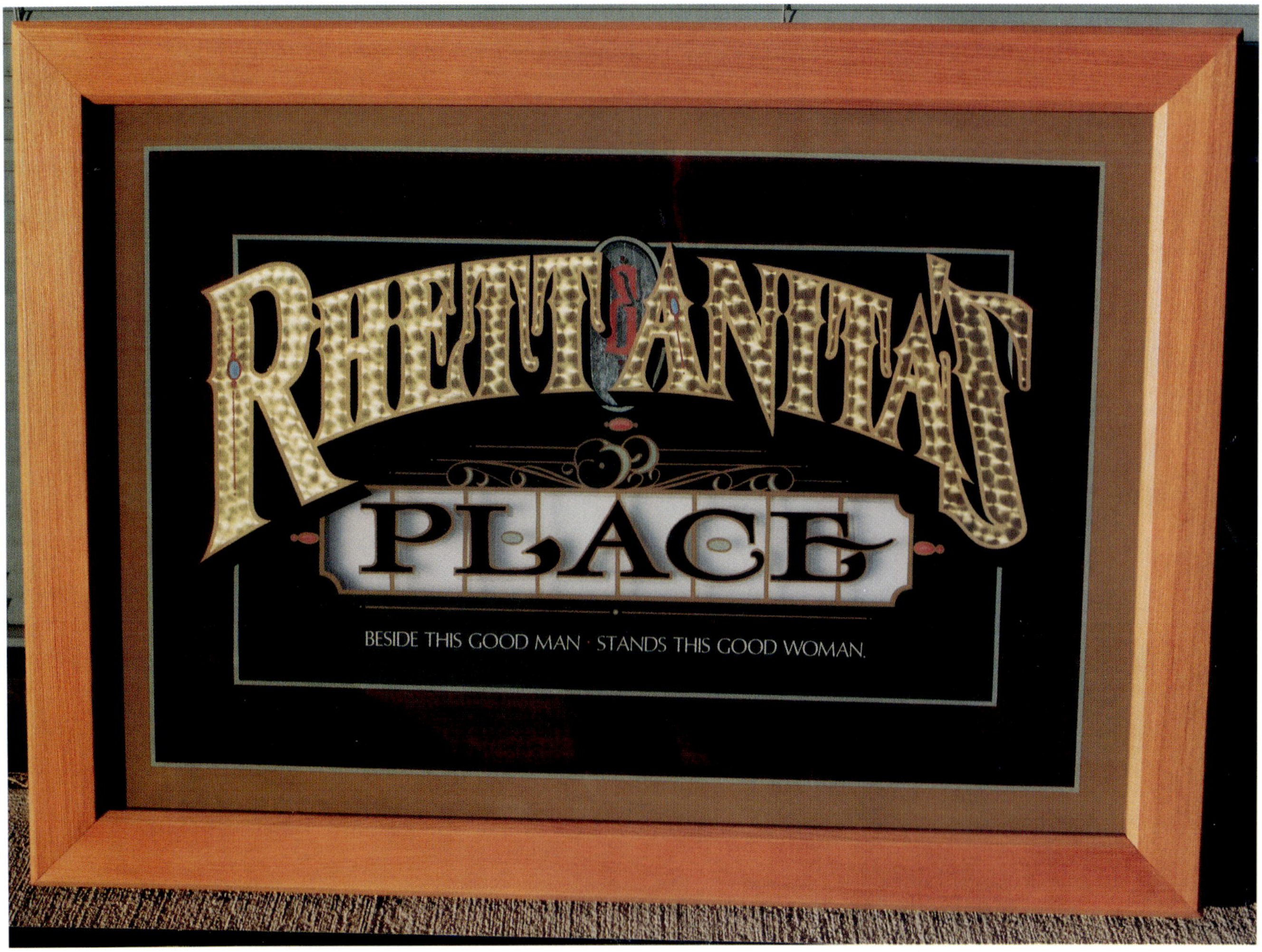

DESIGNER

Bill Blumberg
Signs & Art
109 Eel Lake Ln.
North Bend, OR 97459
(503) 759-4101

FABRICATOR

Bill Blumberg

This single-faced 30 x 42-in. sign has a glue-chip background and a mahogany frame. The "Village Candy Shoppe" copy is two-tone 23K water-size gilded over light-pink-glaze matte centers. The sign's outside and inside borders are deep sand-blasted from behind and pink glazed, backed with 12K goldleaf. The "Sweet tooth . . . " panel copy is water-size gilded using 23K goldleaf.

The candy jar is an actual candy jar sandblasted in half and attached with silicon to the front surface of the glass. The colored glass "globs" are attached with clear silicone inside and outside of the jar. The jar's lid is high-density urethane. The upper dome is surface gilded using 23K goldleaf. The bottom section of the dome is hand-painted to resemble cork.

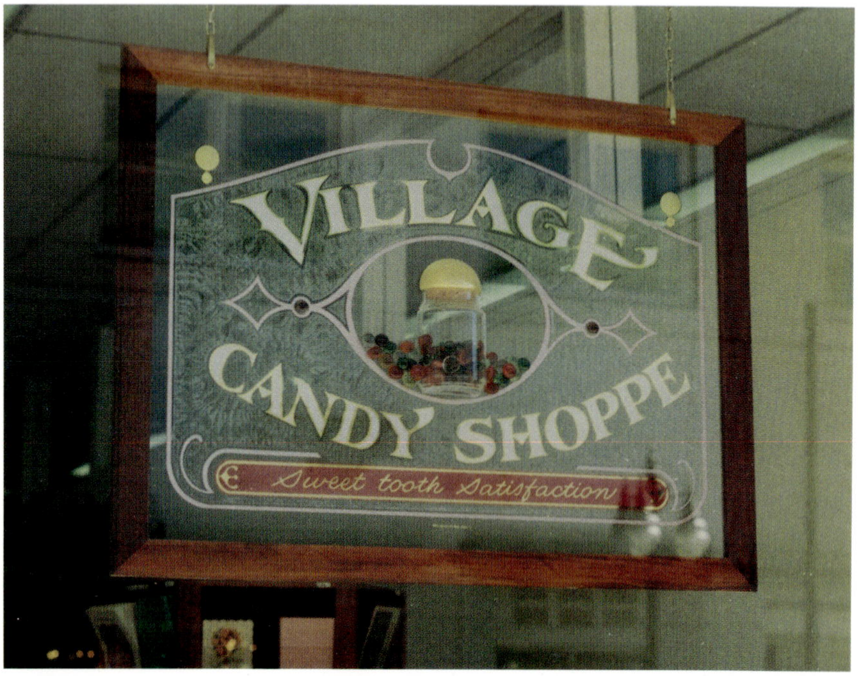

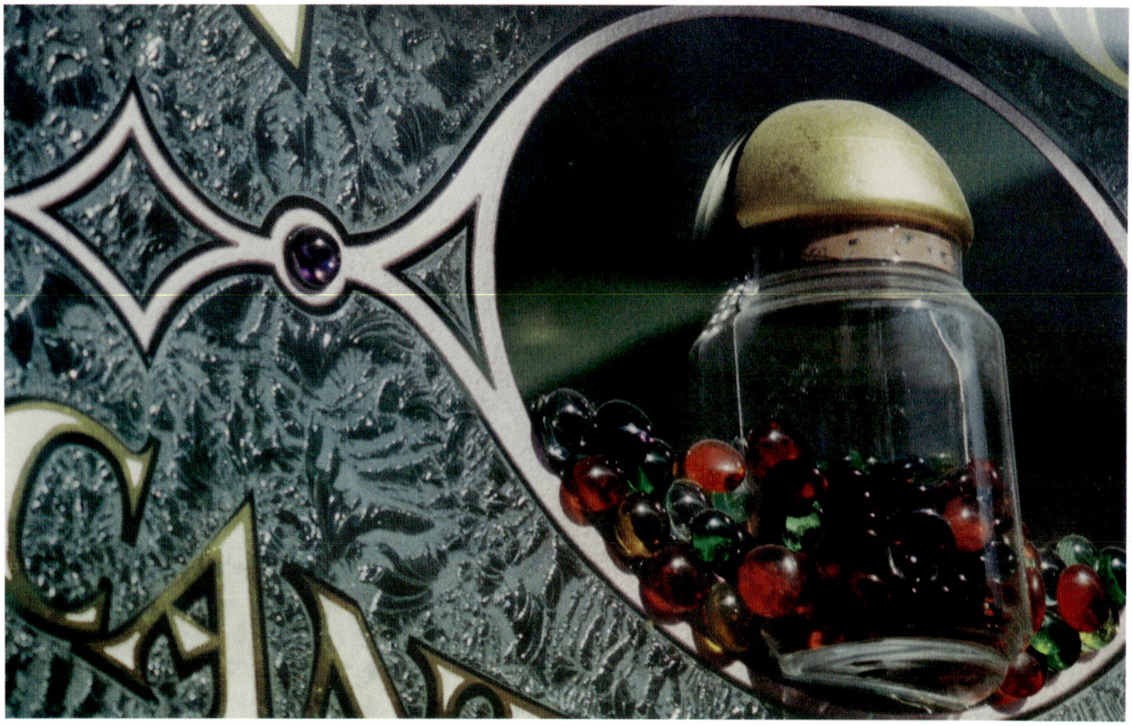

DESIGNER

Bill Blumberg
Signs & Art
109 Eel Lake Ln.
North Bend, OR 97459
(503) 759-4101
Fax: Same

FABRICATOR

Bill Blumberg

This is a single-faced 24 x 36-in. sign that incorporates a glue-chipped background. Also, 23K goldleaf is varnish-size gilded over asphaltum shades on "Books." The books are deep sandblasted and air-brushed. The "By the Bay" panel's 23K goldleaf, varnish-size gilded letters and border are deep sandblasted. The larger sign's frame is fabricated from ¾-in. Medex® wood composite painted with three colors of latex paint.

The 6 x 30-in. "New and Used" addition is fabricated from 3/16-in. glass with nipped edges. The lettering is deep-reverse sandblasted and varnish-size gilded using 23K goldleaf.

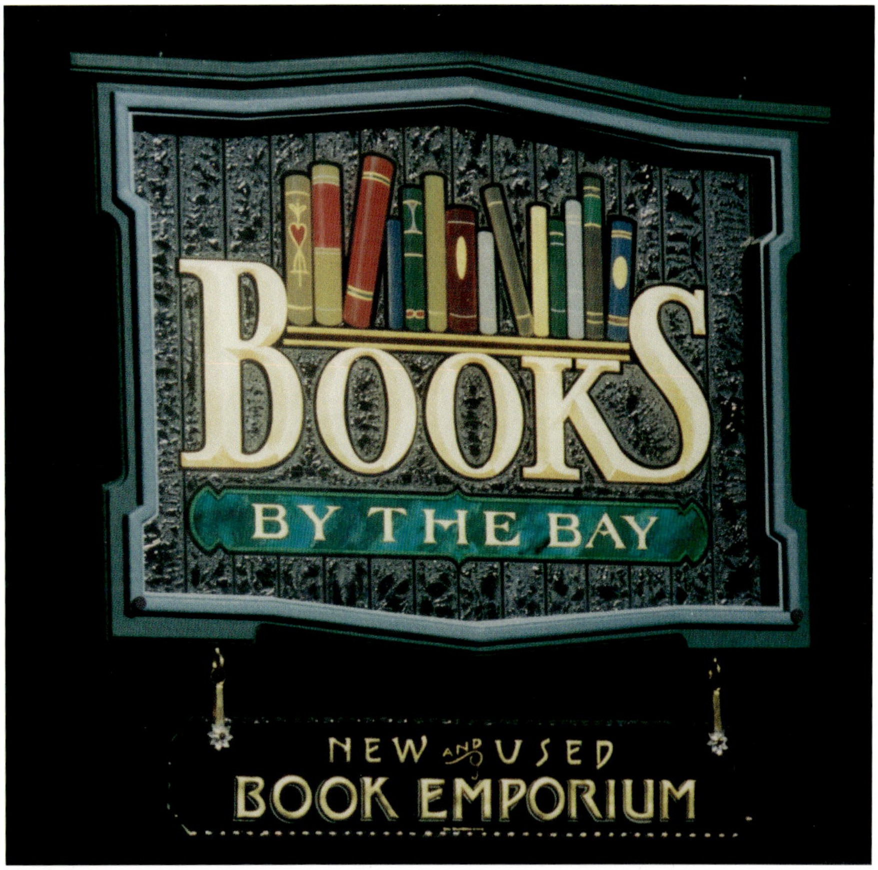

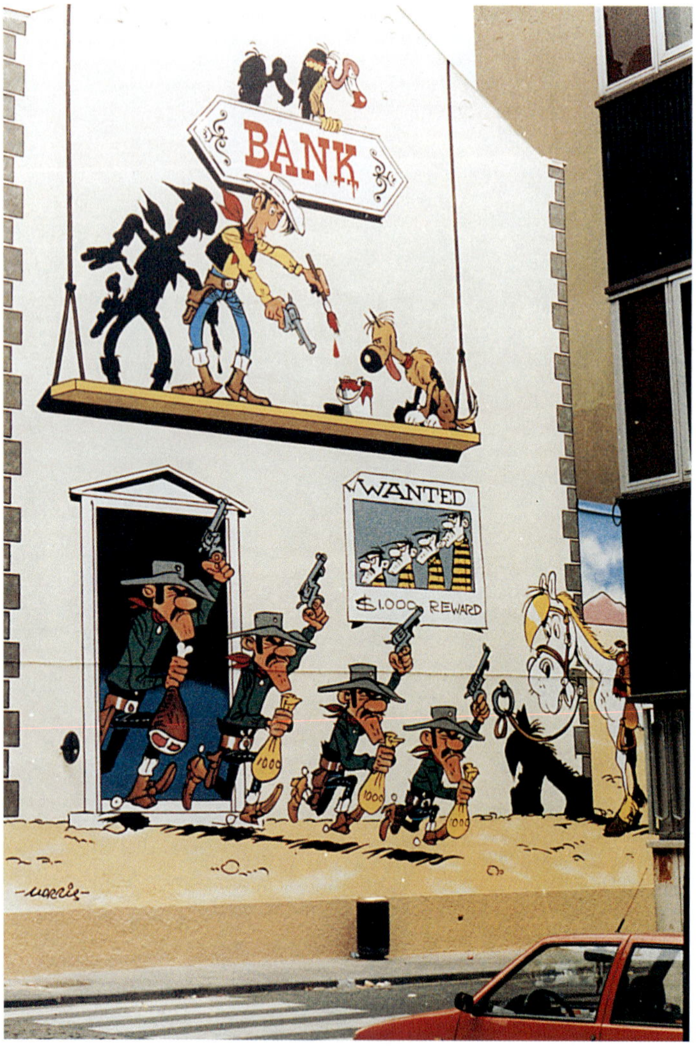

DESIGNERS (COMIC STRIP ARTISTS)
Dupa
Morris
Paul Geerts
Francois Schuiten
Marc Sleen
Willy Vandersteen
Tibet & Duchateau

FABRICATOR
Art Mural a.s.b.l.
Rue de L'Hotel des Monnaies, 167
1060 Brussels, Belgium
Phone: 02/538.24.58

This project, entitled "Comic Strip Journey," features the work of numerous Belgian comic-strip artists on 10 murals. They range in size from 20-180 sq. meters (215-1937 sq. ft.). Various techniques and products are used. Surface preparation is key to a technique called Sgraffite. A layer of Sikatop 121 black cement (a two-component cement and synthetic fiber) is applied to the wall. A 3-mil layer of Sikatop 121 white cement is applied on top. The drawing is then engraved to expose the black cement. Other synthetic cements used include Mineraaleschlam and Pegacrete. Herbofix and Primer 44 stabilizers are used, and the final surface preparation is a coat of structured paint called Armierungbasis or an elastic paint called Murfill. Color is added using Pegacryl satin-gloss acrylic enamel.

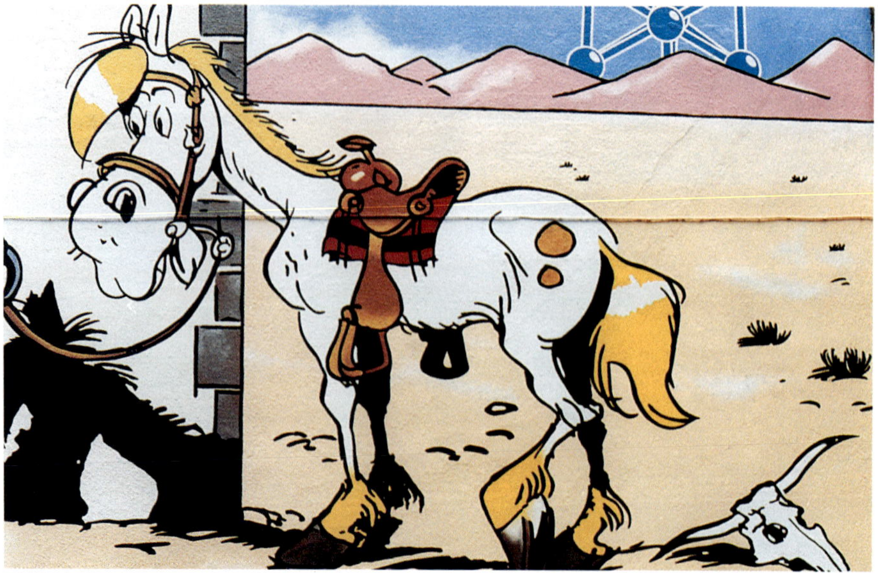

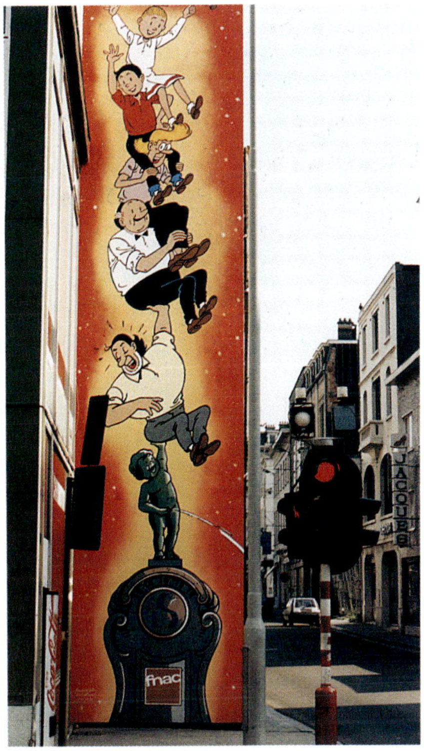
fnac
JACQUES
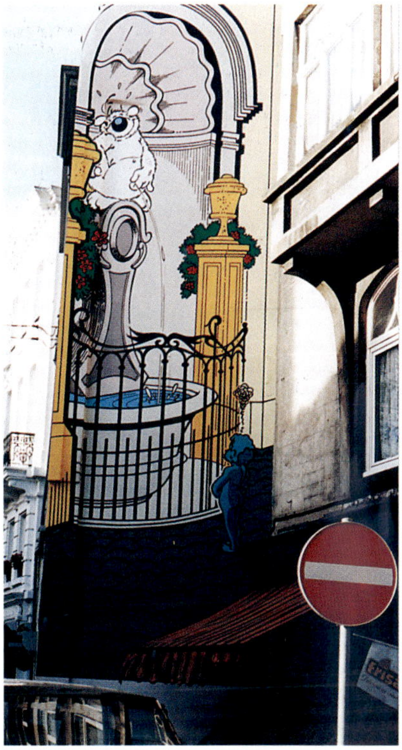
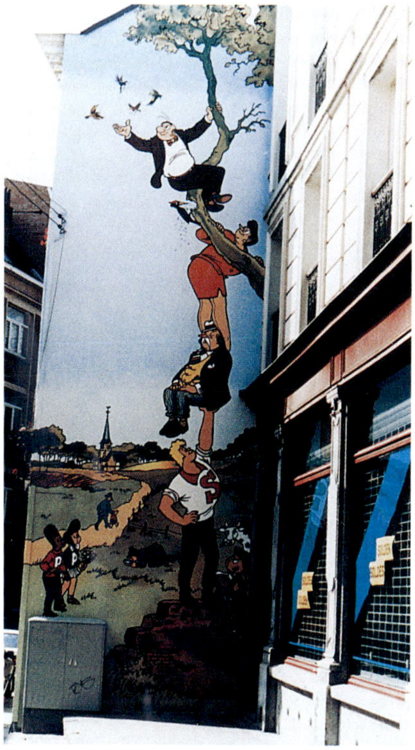
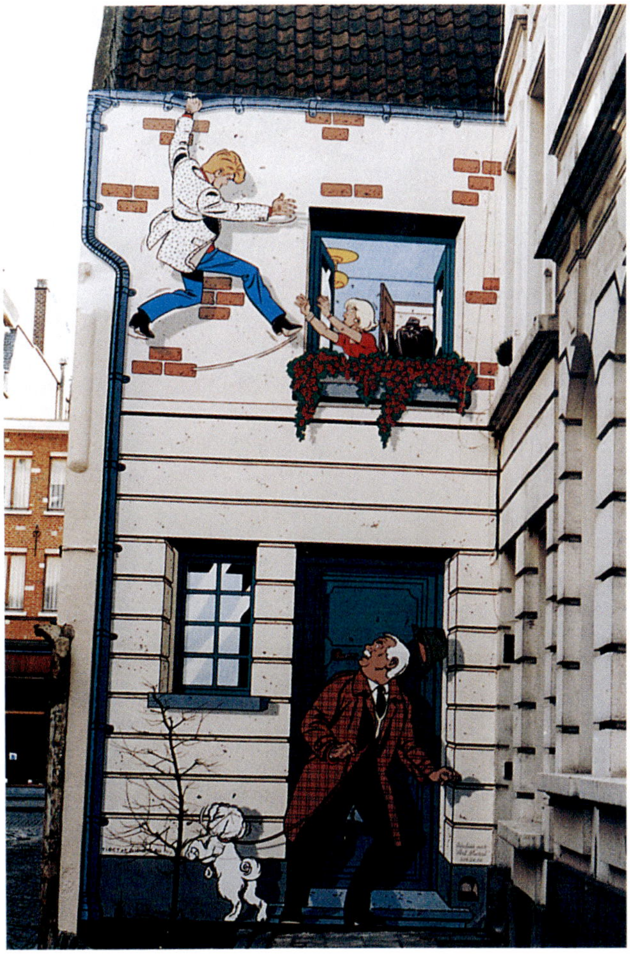
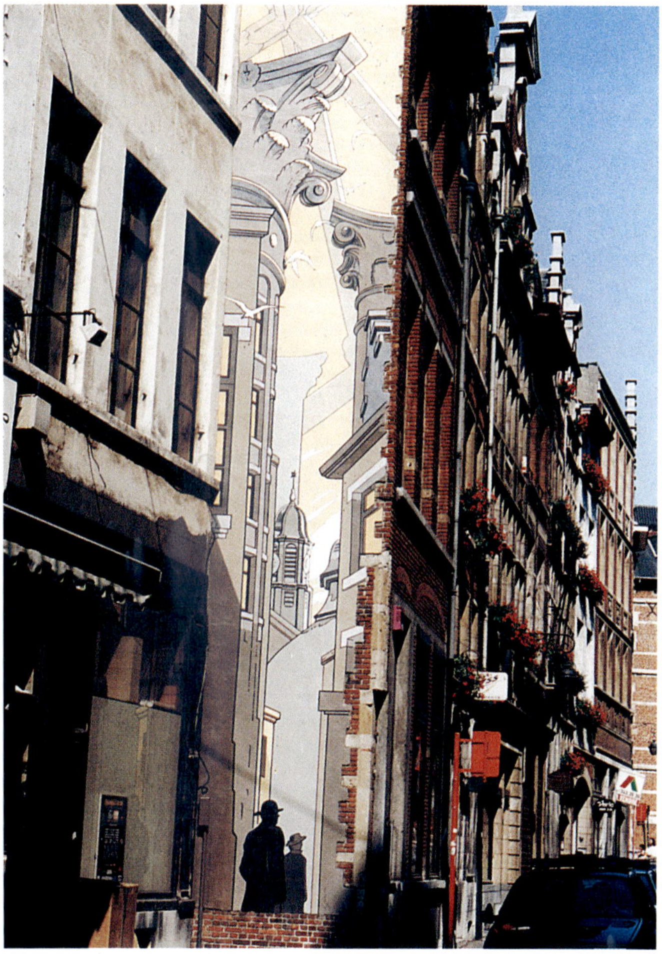

DESIGNER

Bailey Lauerman & Assoc.
900 NBC Center
Lincoln, NE 68508
(402) 475-2800
Fax: (402) 475-5115

FABRICATOR

The Wood Shop
111 East St.
Boyne City, MI 49712
(616) 582-9835
Fax: (616) 582-9868

This sign system includes 33 signs. Fourteen of these are the 2 x 3-ft. "field" signs; seventeen others are the shooting station signs. These 31 signs are all sandblasted redwood (cut from 2 x 6-ft. clear panels), with applied logos and brass. The brass trim is left unfinished to create a quick weathered look conducive to the natural surroundings. The logos are carved and sandblasted from cedar, molded with urethane and hand painted. Overall, the system includes 19 birds in flight that are hand-carved from Sign Foam® material and painted in acrylics. In addition, the 5-ft.-circle logo has a sandblasted redwood background to which carved, shaped and hand-painted Sign Foam material has been applied.

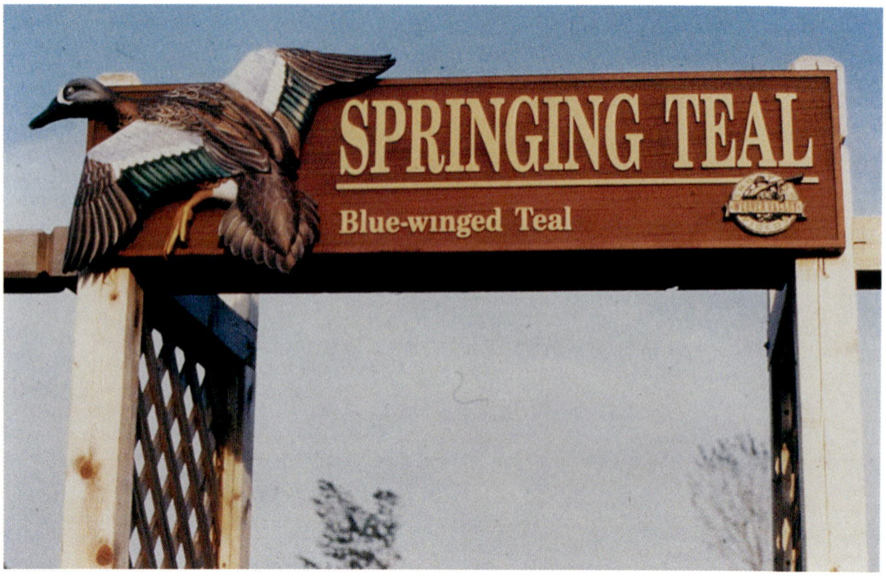

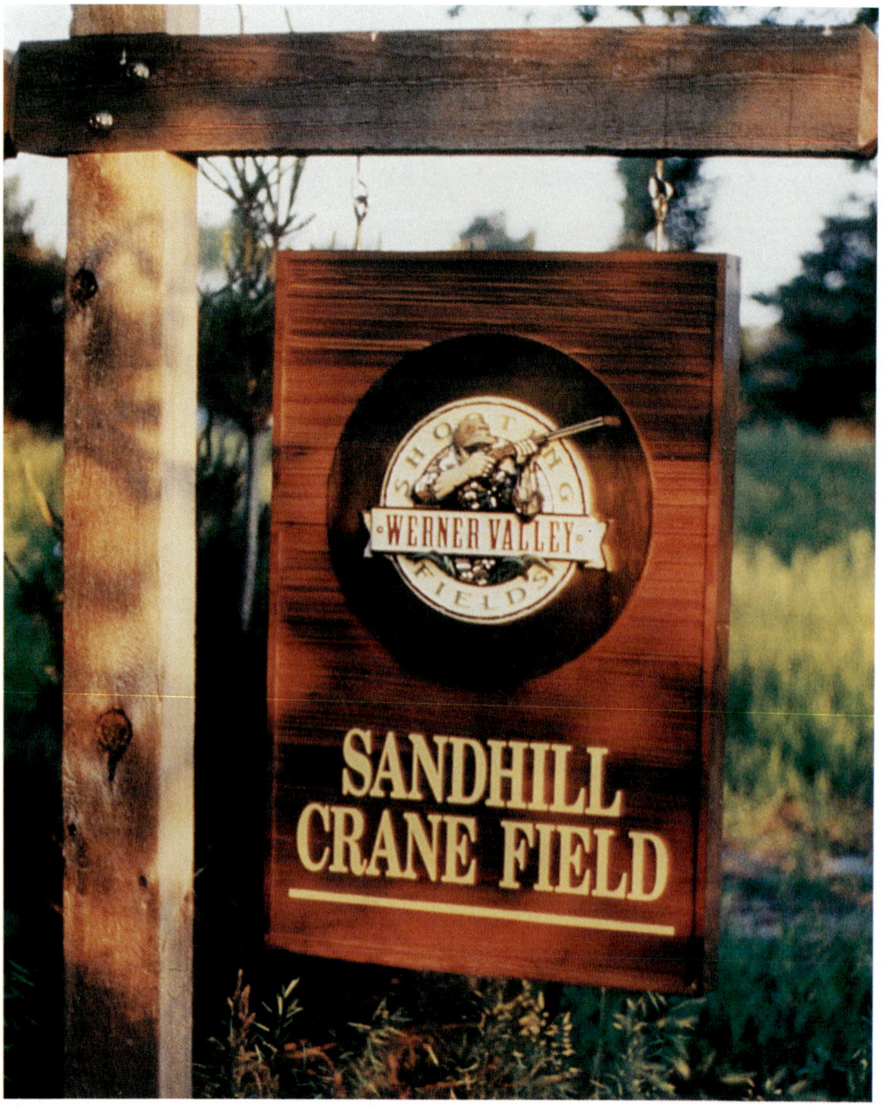

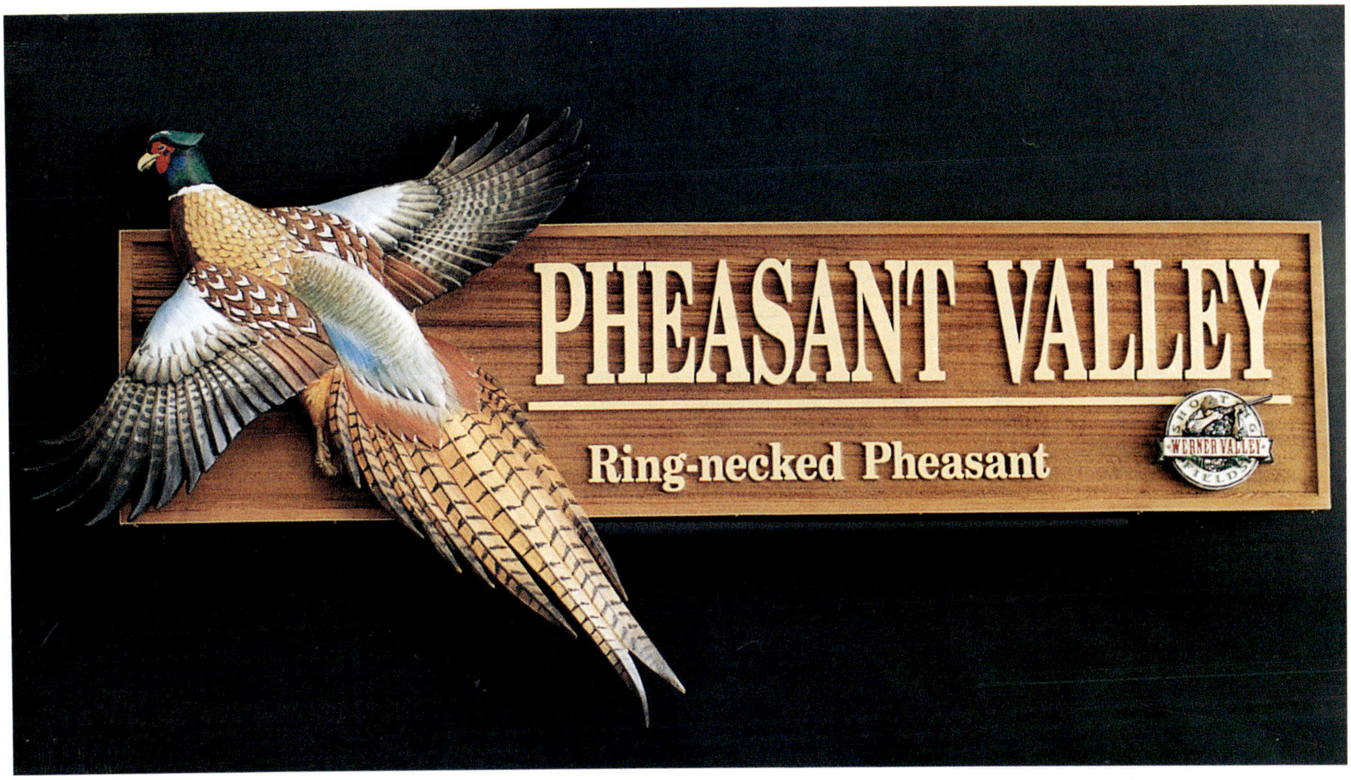
PHEASANT VALLEY
Ring-necked Pheasant
WERNER VALLEY

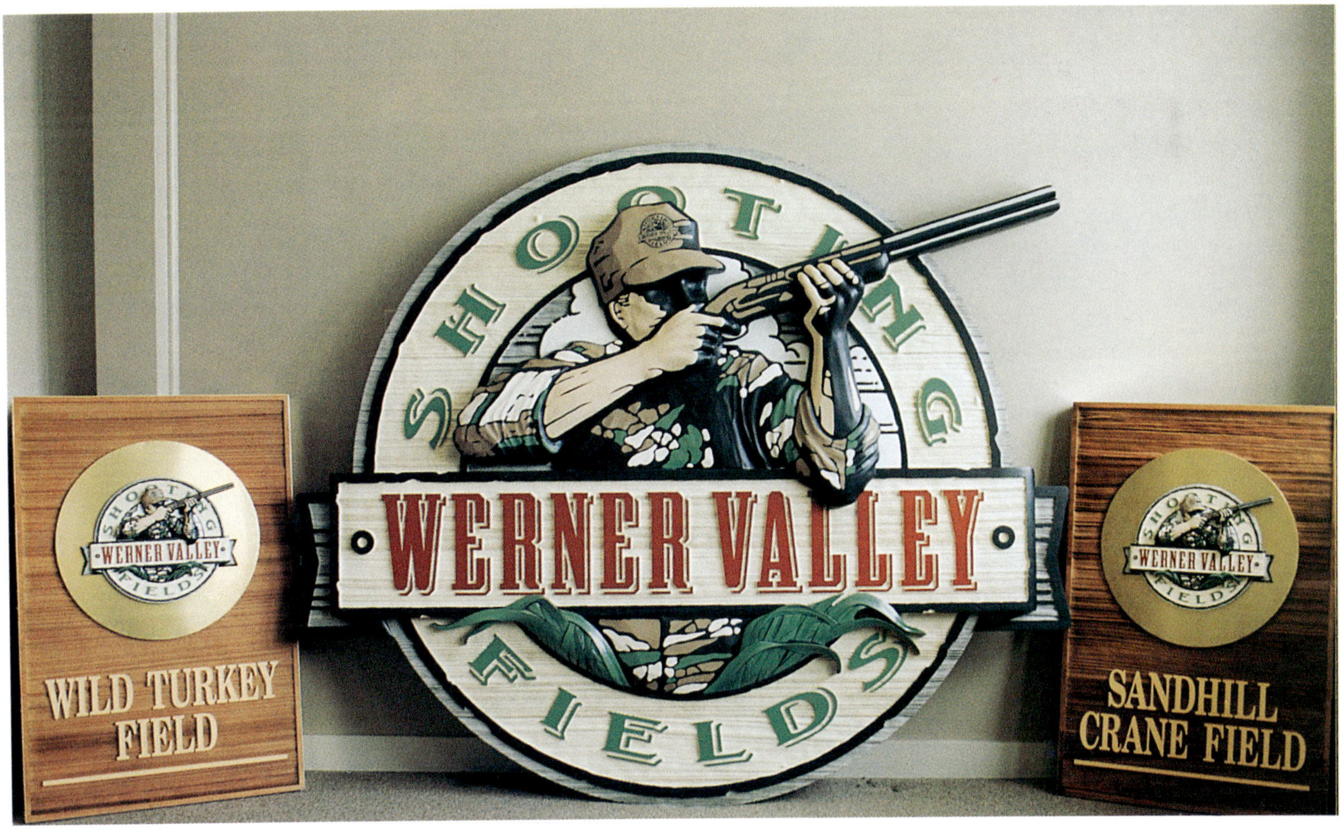
SHOOTING
WERNER VALLEY
FIELDS
WILD TURKEY
FIELD
SANDHILL
CRANE FIELD

DESIGNER

Anita R. Ambriz
Perkins & Will Environmental
Graphic Design
330 N. Wabash
Chicago, IL 60611
(312) 755-4614
Fax: (312) 755-0775

FABRICATORS

Brilliant Electric Signs
4811 Van Epps Rd.
Cleveland, OH 44131
(216) 741-3800
Fax: (216) 741-8733

Poblocki & Sons Co.
P.O. Box 1541
922 S. 70th St.
Milwaukee, WI 53201
(414) 453-4010
Fax: (414) 453-3070

Eder Flag Mfg. Co., Inc.
1000 W. Rawson Ave.
Oak Creek, WI 53154
(414) 764-3522
Fax: (414) 764-1039

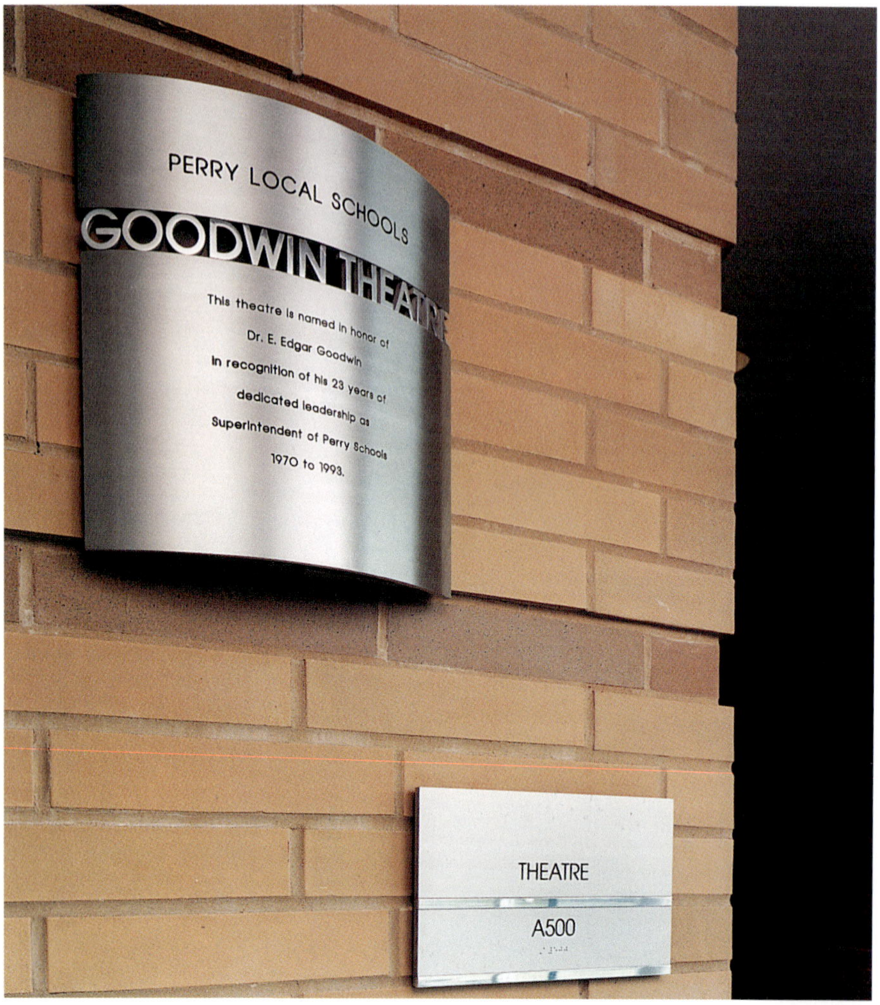

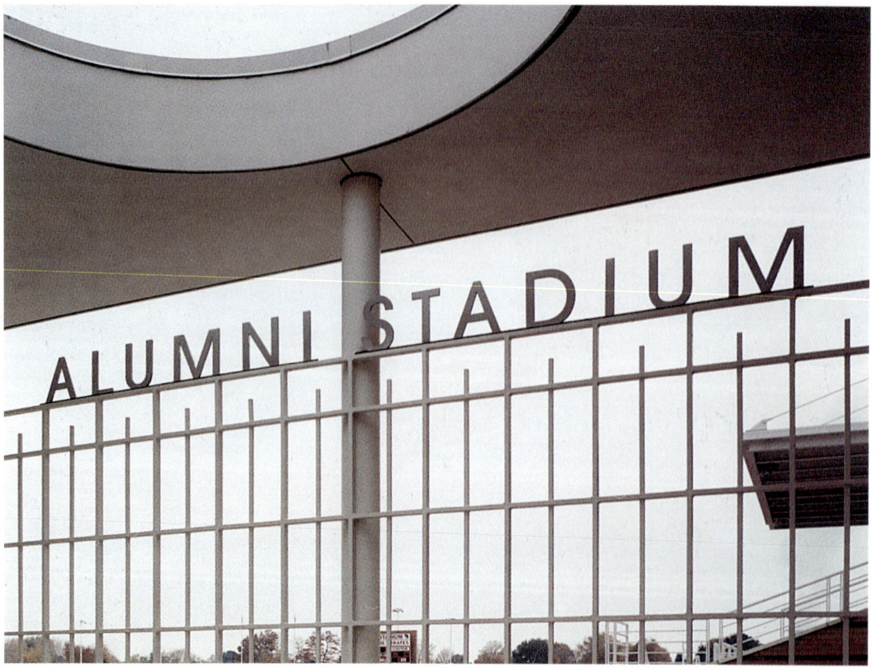

This interior/exterior system has many facets. Starting from the outside, the pin-mounted satin aluminum letters are ½-in.-thick rendered in Avant Garde. Stadium letters are the same except for being screw-mounted. The exterior directional signage is painted aluminum attached to a simple post-and-panel system. The interior cafeteria/vending signage is Celtec PVC decorated with painted, die-cut vinyl. The typical room signs are 3/16-in. zinc plate painted silver with a matte finish. All copy, symbols and braille are photochemically raised 1/32 in. from the sign surface. The dedication plaque is ¼-in. curved satin aluminum plate with ¼-in.-thick polished aluminum letters. The text is acid-etched and filled, and the sign is pin-mounted ½ in. off the wall. The interior banner system features two-sided, 13 ft. 9 in. x 1 ft. nylon with appliqued or machine-sewn graphics.

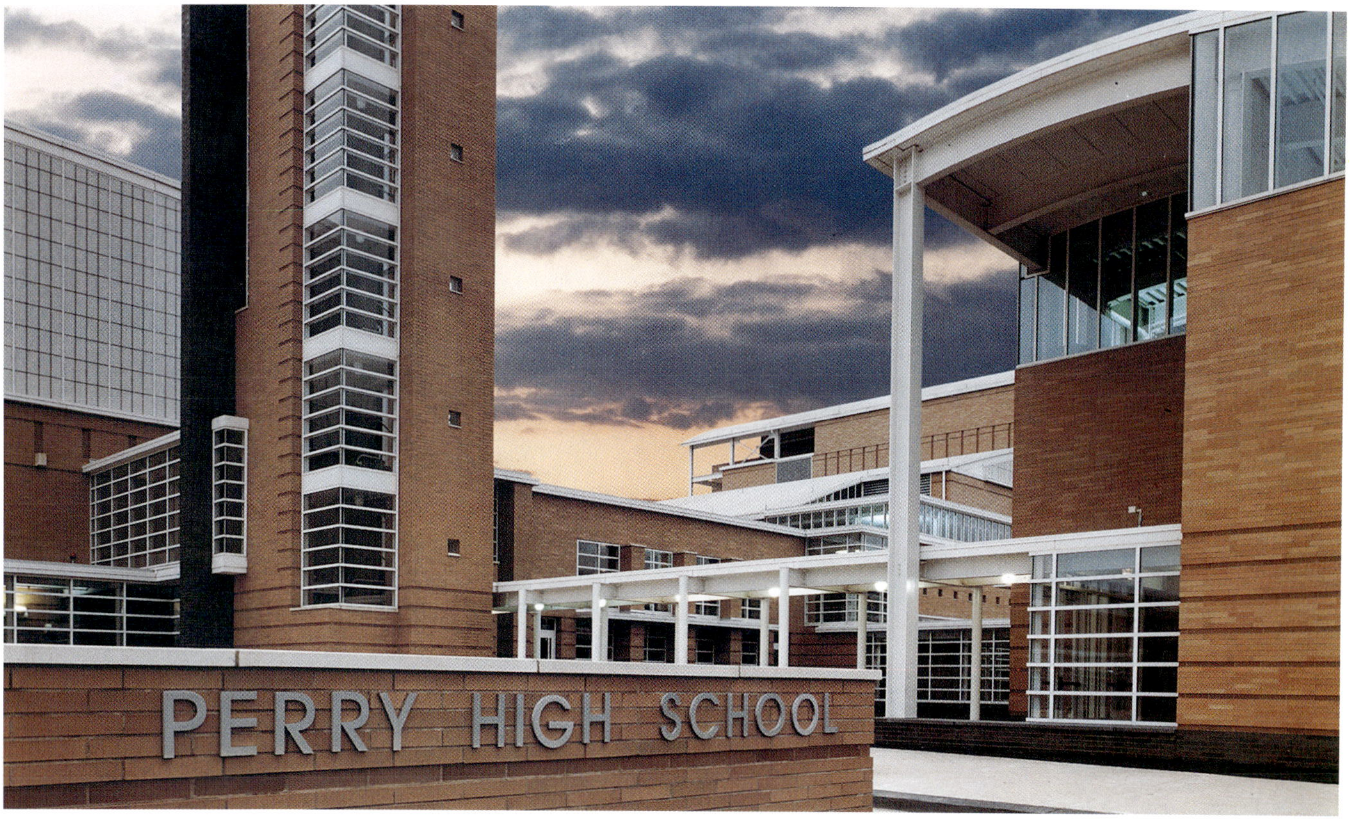
PERRY HIGH SCHOOL

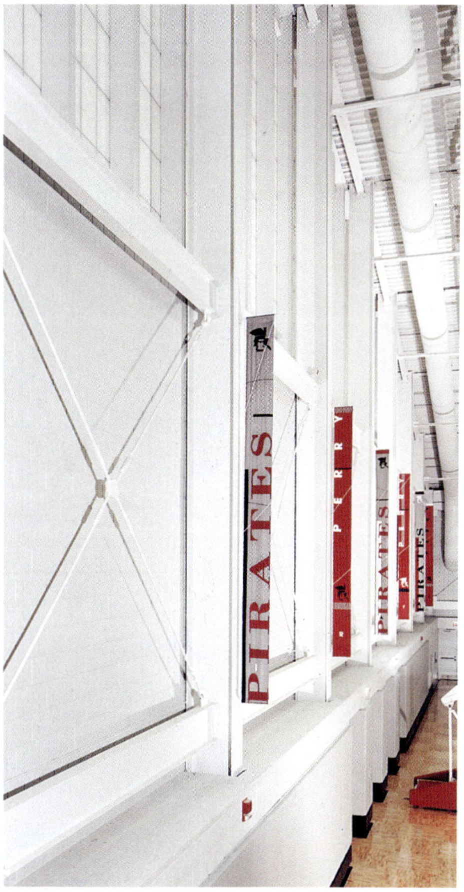
PIRATES
PERRY
PIRATES

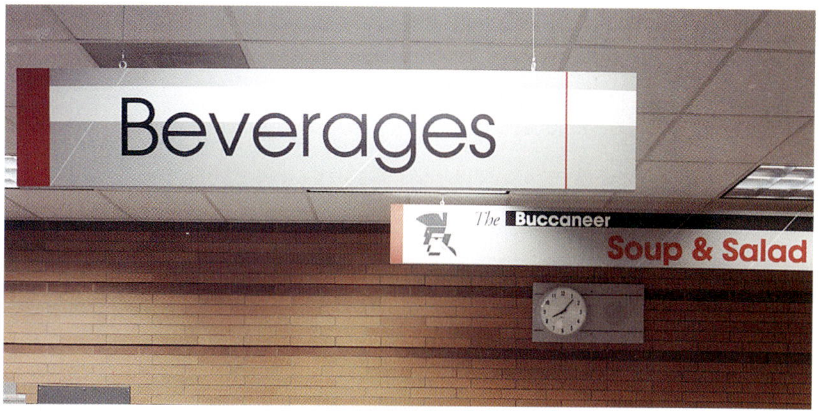
Beverages
The Buccaneer
Soup & Salad

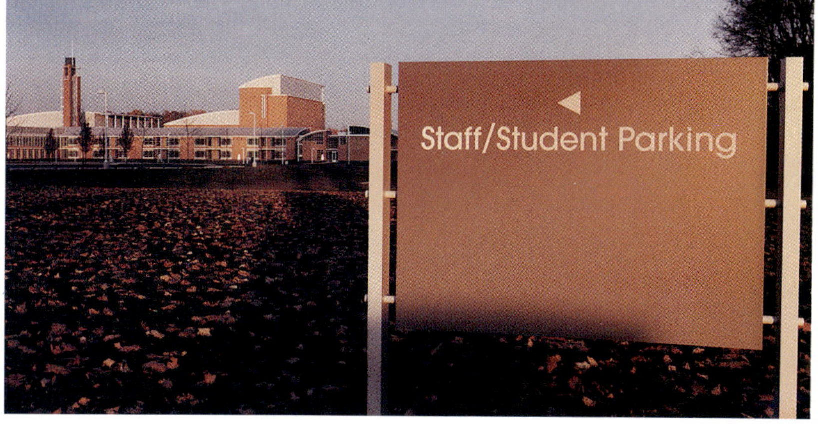
Staff/Student Parking

DESIGNER

Nelson McDonald Design
#540 2424 4th St. SW
Calgary, AB, Canada T2S 2T4
(403) 228-9010
Fax: (403) 229-3849

FABRICATOR

Banff Sign Co. Ltd.
Box 2536
Banff, AB, Canada T0L 0C0
(403) 762-4945
Fax: (403) 762-8234

This mall comprises four retail outlets and a restaurant. The wall signs are 10 x 1⅓ ft.; the exterior hanging signs are 32 x 14 in. The front of the directory signs spans 36 x 42 in. Various materials are used: cedar, pine, mahogany, Medex® composite wood panel, Sign Foam® high-density urethane, rundle rock and smaltz. All the copy is hand-carved and gilded. The hanging signs are double-faced with pine frames. Fabrication techniques used include blending, painting, gilding, sculpting, carving and sandblasting.

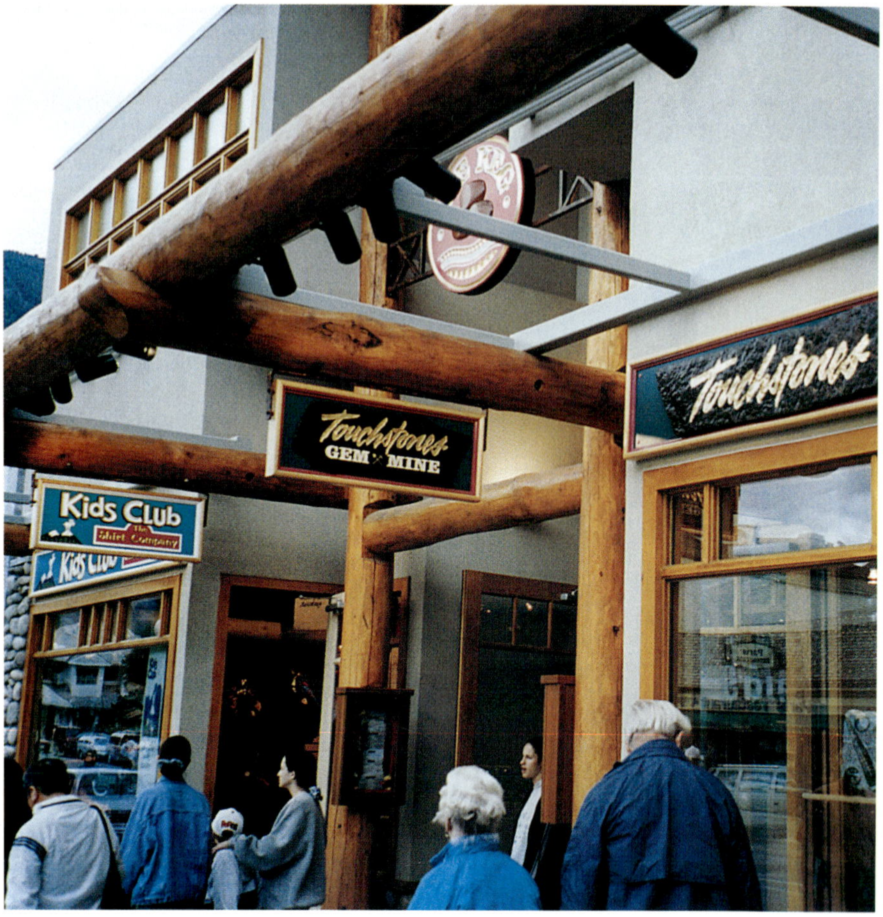

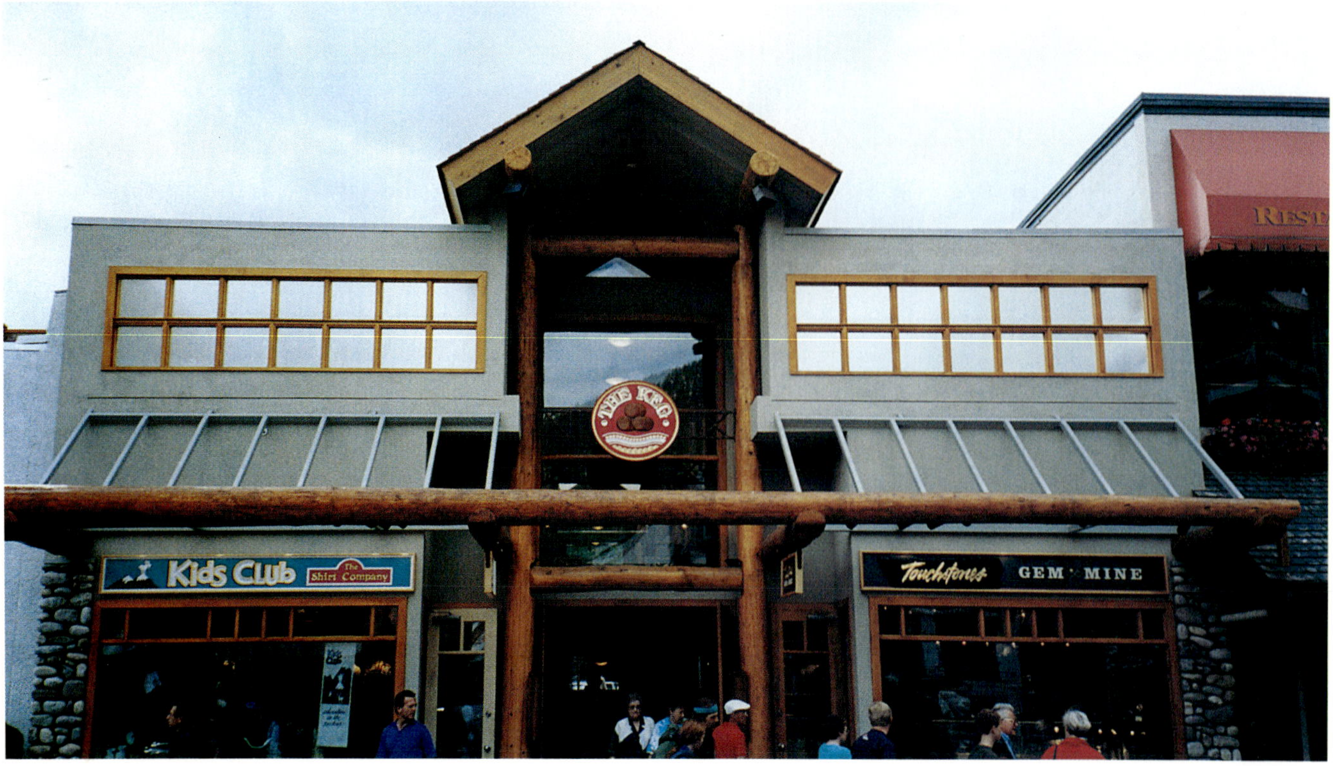

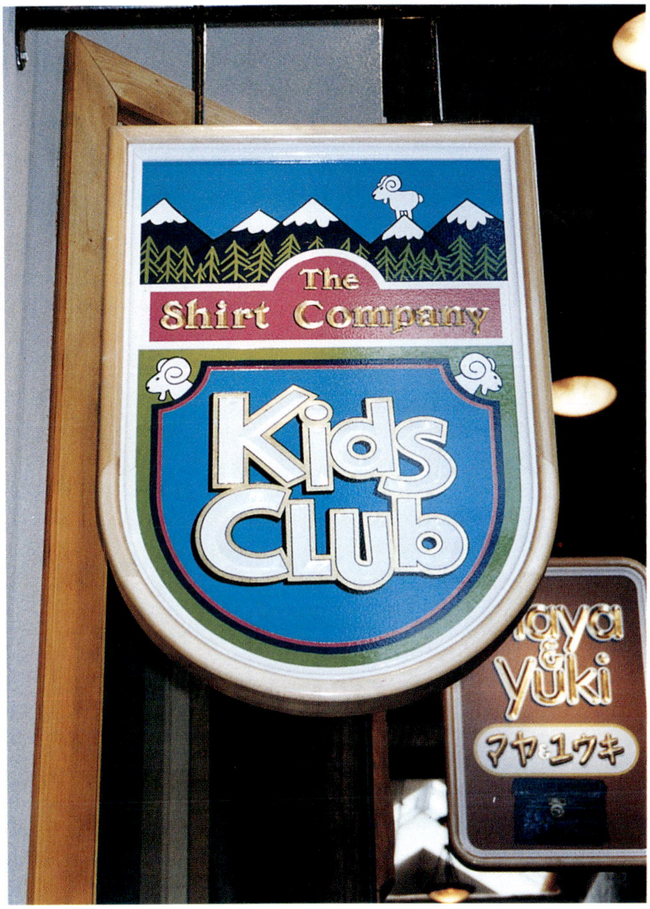
The
Shirt Company
Kids
Club

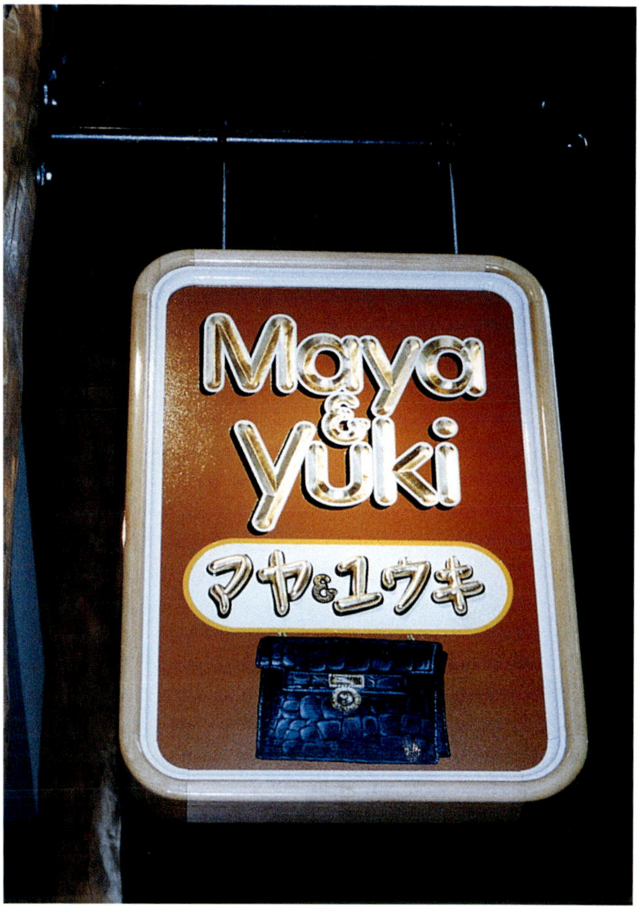
Maya
&
yuki
マヤ&ユウキ

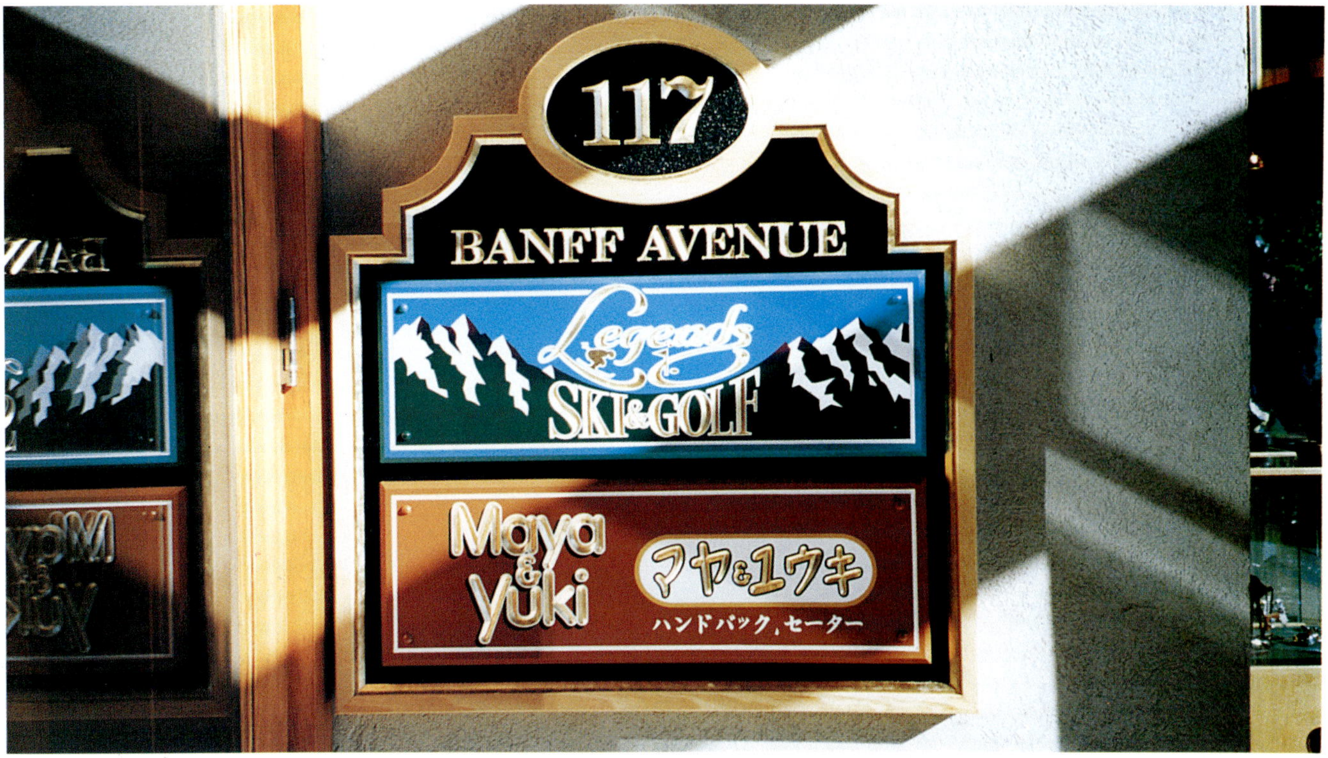
117
BANFF AVENUE
Legends
SKI&GOLF
Maya
&
yuki
マヤ&ユウキ
ハンドバック、セーター

DESIGNER

Larry Whan
Banff Sign Co. Ltd.
Box 2356
Banff, AB, Canada TOL 0C0
(403) 762-4945
Fax: (403) 762-8234

FABRICATOR

Banff Sign Co. Ltd.

All of these directory door signs are 16 x 16 in. The glass panels have a ¾-in. bevel on the edge. The logo is sandblasted with a border, and the inside panels are glue-chipped. All the copy is vinyl applied to the face. The directory signs are 24 x 32 in.

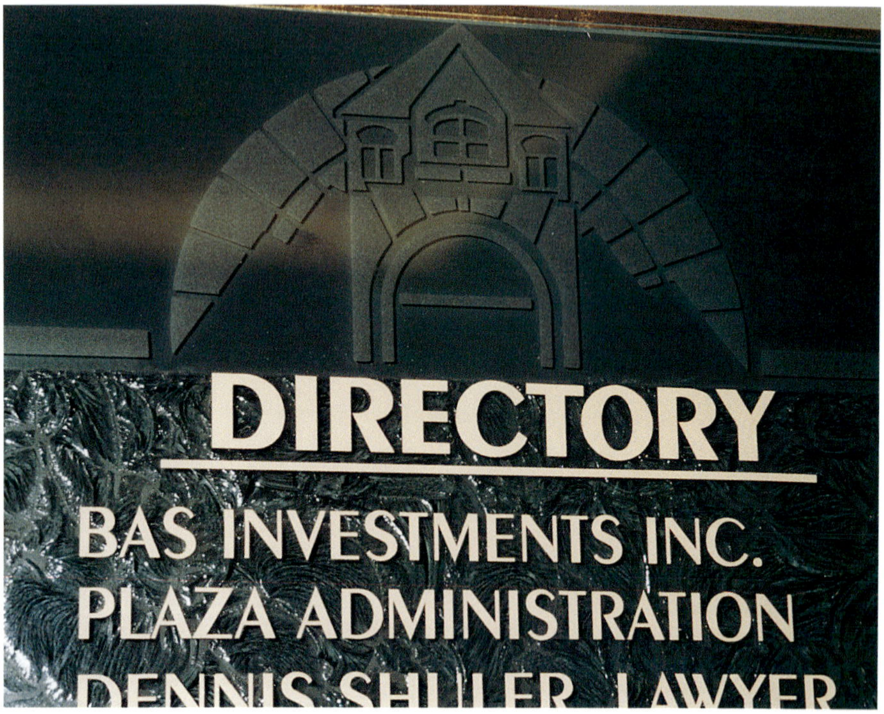

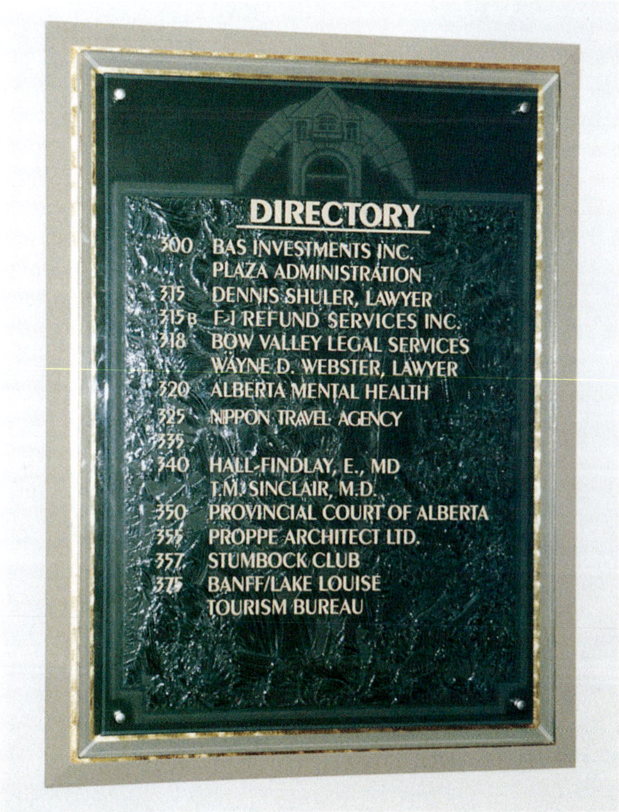

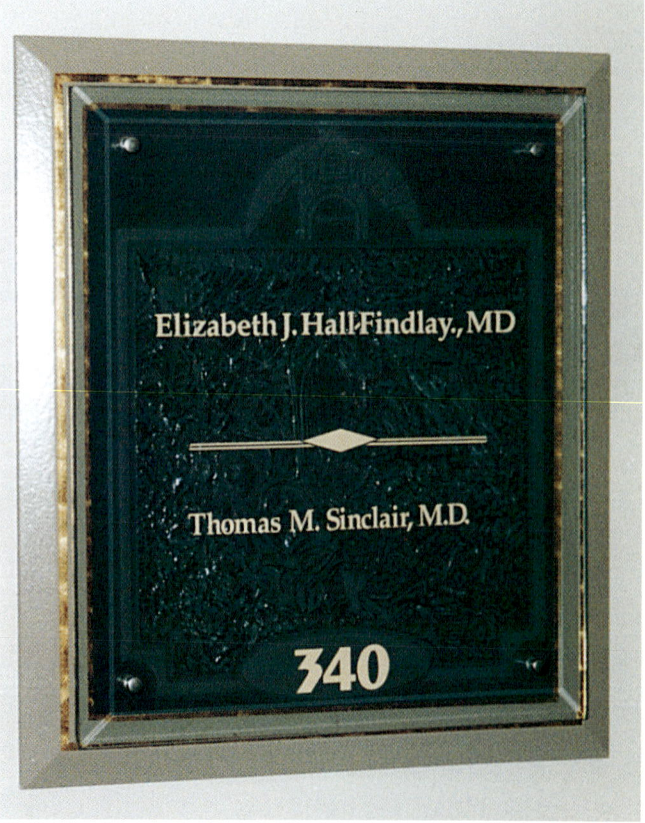

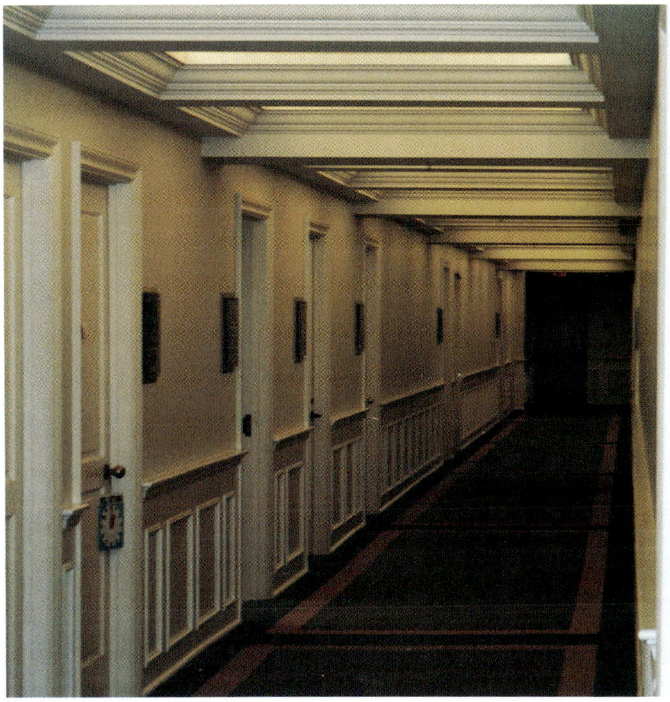

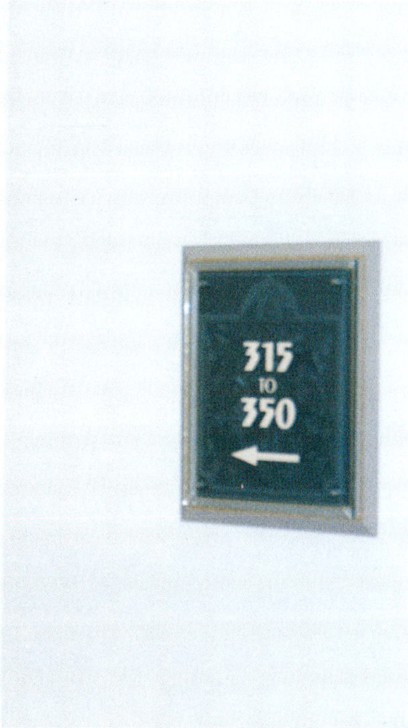

315
TO
350

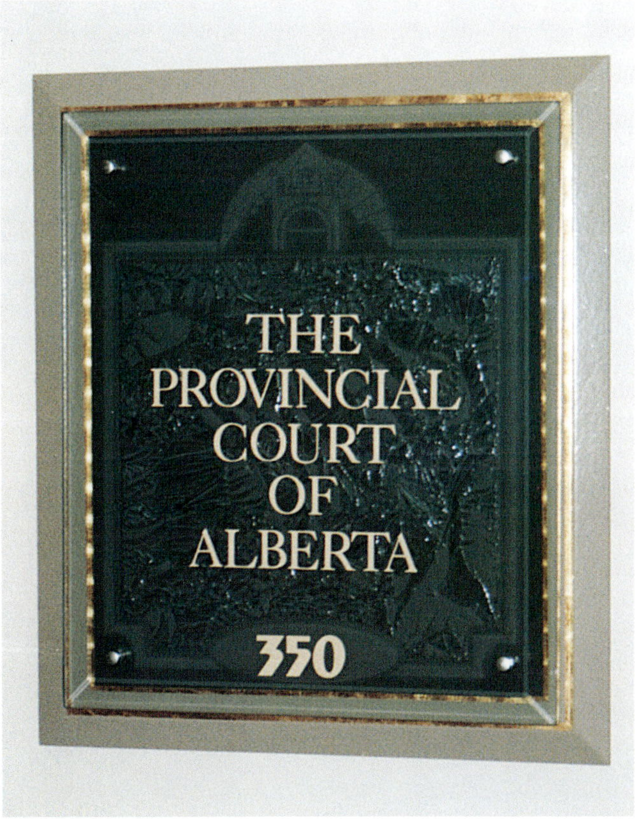

THE PROVINCIAL COURT OF ALBERTA
350

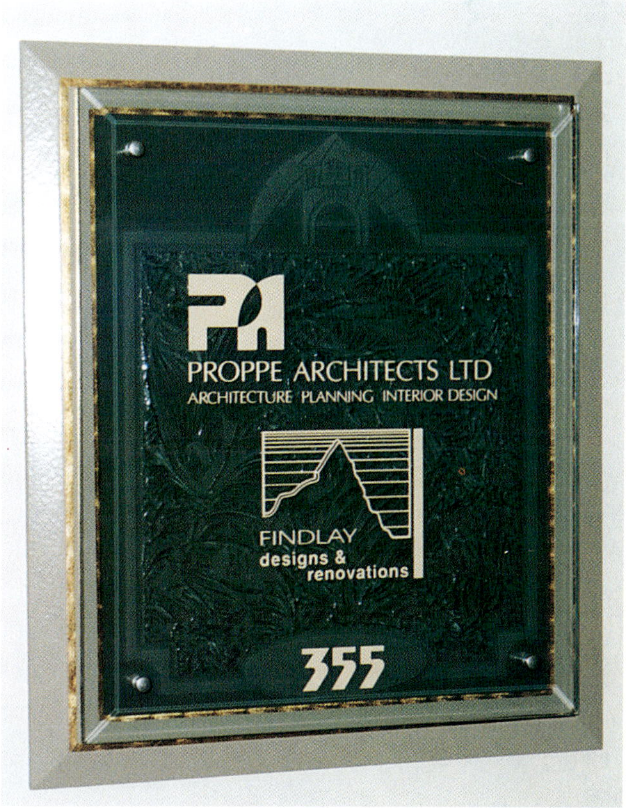

PROPPE ARCHITECTS LTD
ARCHITECTURE PLANNING INTERIOR DESIGN
FINDLAY
designs &
renovations
355

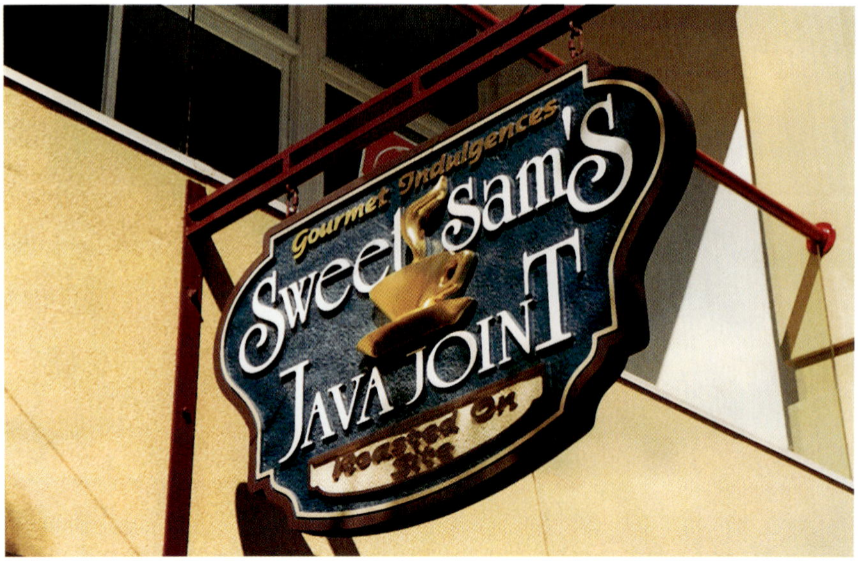

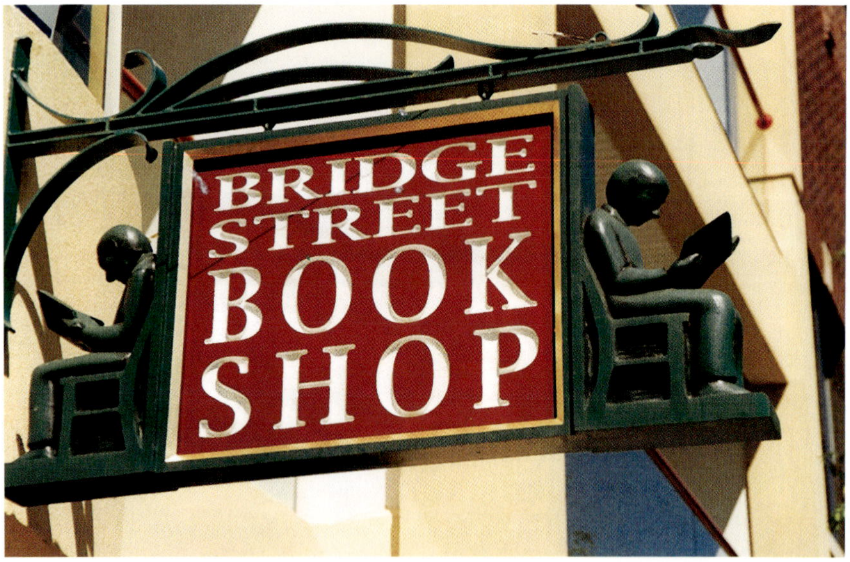

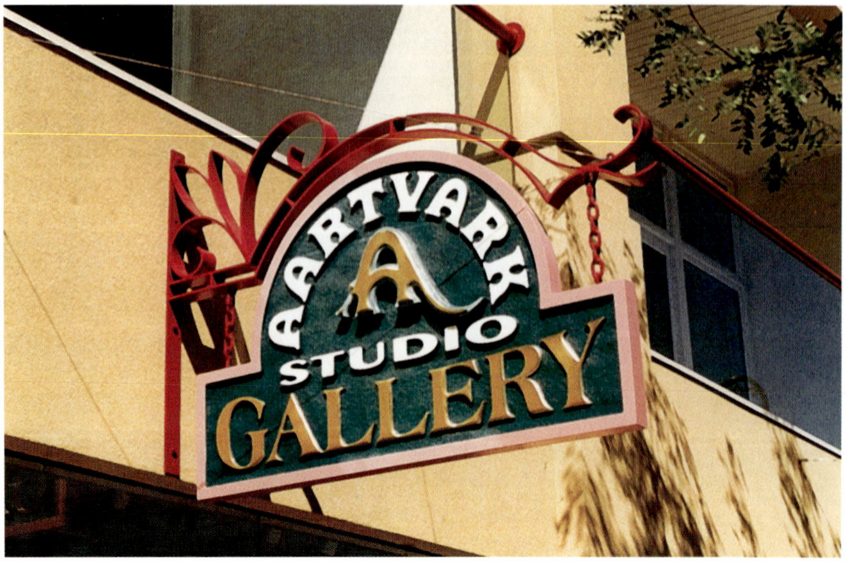

DESIGNER

Martha Avery
12250 Rd. 90
Elbert, CO 80106
(303) 648-3289

FABRICATORS

Bruce Janssen
The Wood Shop
111 East St.
Boyne City, MI 49712
(616) 582-9835
Fax: (616) 582-9868

Wally Barkley
04796 Old Horton Bay Rd.
Boyne City, MI 49712
(616) 582-7528
(steel brackets)

In order to have projecting signs on this remodeled building, and to meet the zoning requirements, the signs with brackets had to remain within a 33-in. height limit. All the signs are approximately 8 sq. ft., or 42-48 in. wide by 24 in tall. The signs are constructed of 2-in. high density urethane, sandblasted and carved to detail, and finished with water-based enamels and 23K gold leaf. The brackets are cold rolled and welded from 2-in. flat steel, with enamel finish.

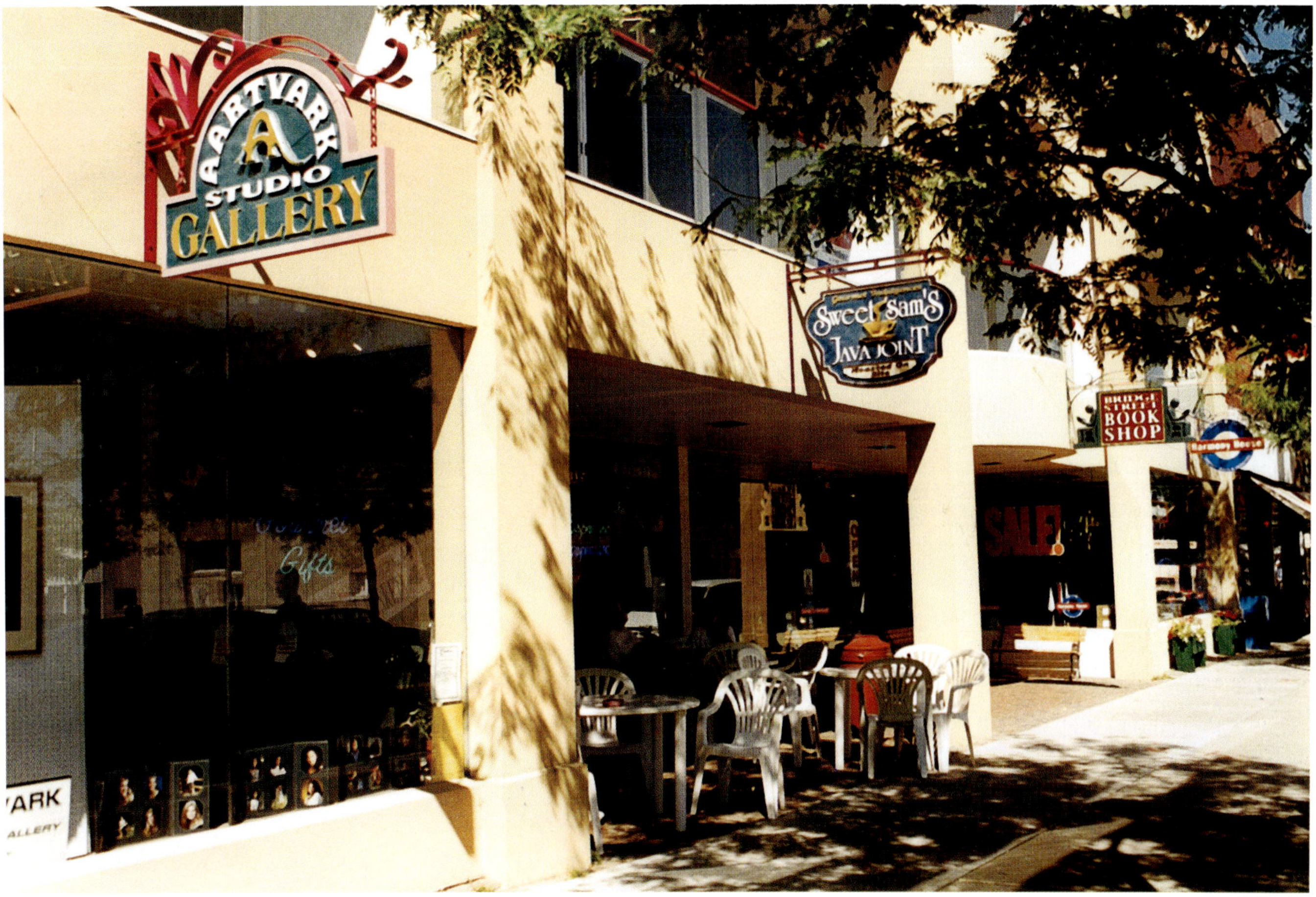
AARTVARK
STUDIO
GALLERY
Sweet Sam's
JAVA JOINT
BRIDGE STREET
BOOK
SHOP
SALE!
Gifts

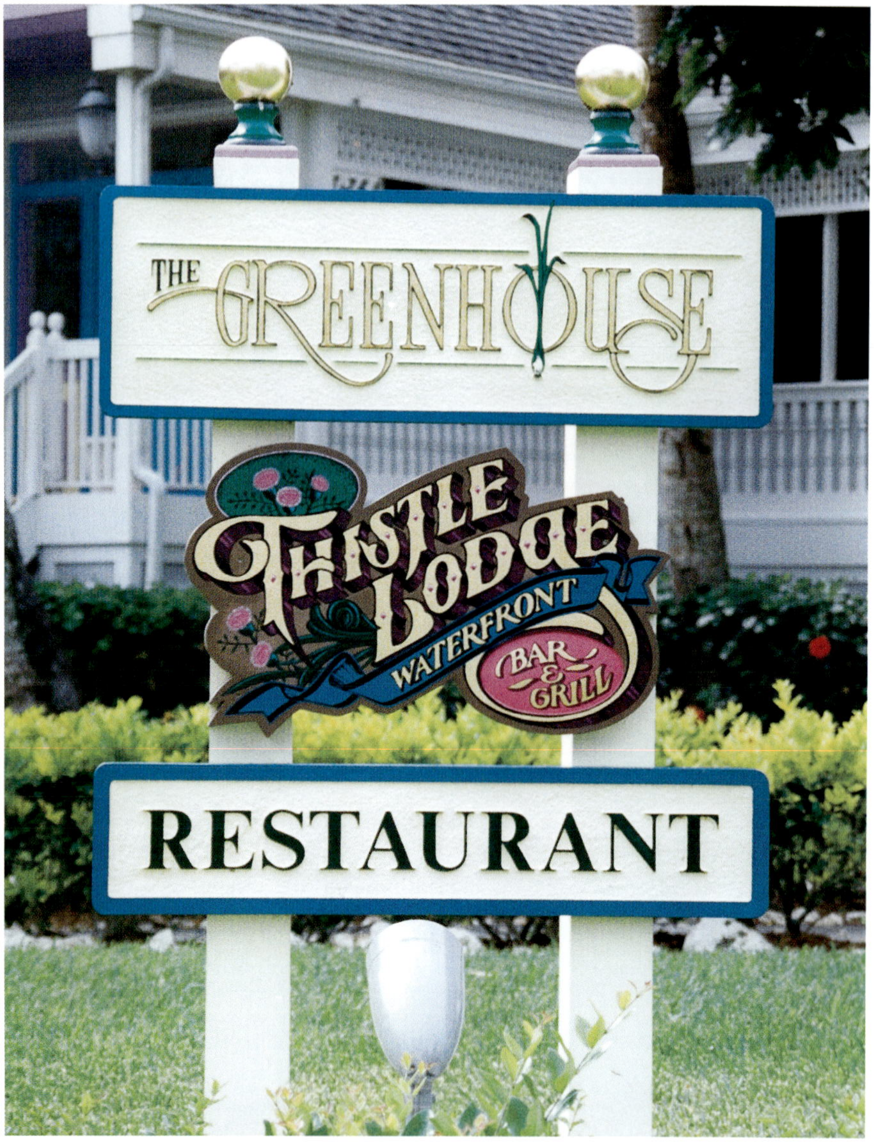

DESIGNERS

Chip Carter
Randy Tuthill
Island Designs
P.O. Box 114
Captiva, FL 33924
(813) 395-2222

FABRICATORS

Chip Carter
Randy Tuthill
Marilyn Carter
Island Designs

Sandblasted and flat urethane are used in these signs that have backgrounds finished in yellow latex. Enamel paints are used on the other parts. The main ID panel is 4 ft. 6 in. x 6 ft. 8 in. and stands 10 ft. tall. The other signs are under 40 sq. ft. as required by code. The logos used were designed for each restaurant, but also to work together as a program to achieve a Victorian look.

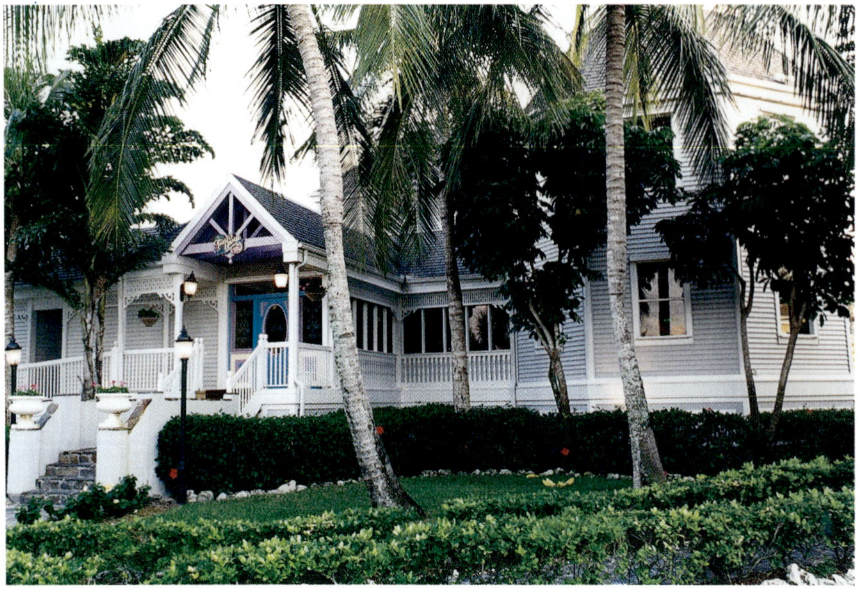

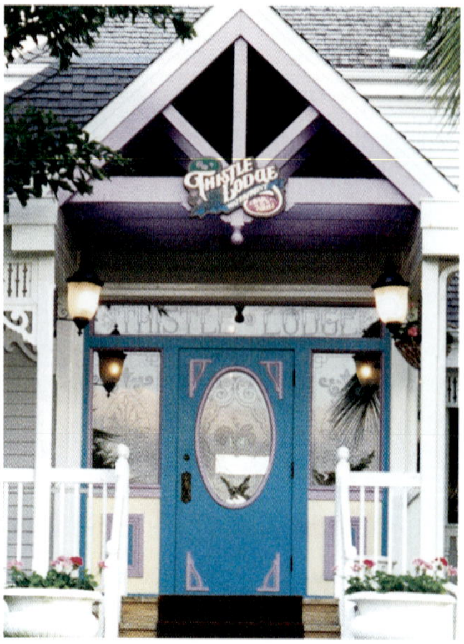

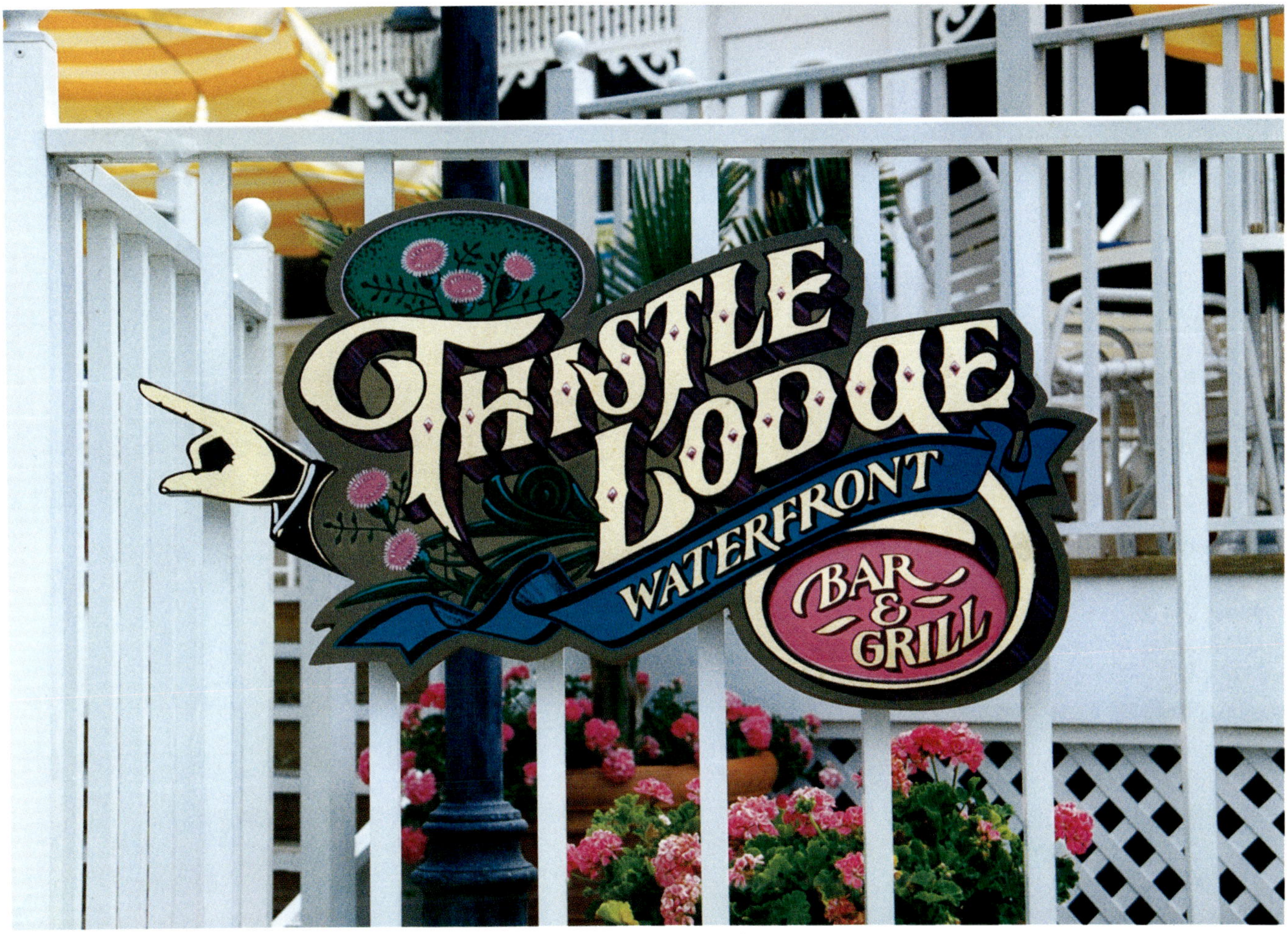
THISTLE LODGE
WATERFRONT
BAR & GRILL

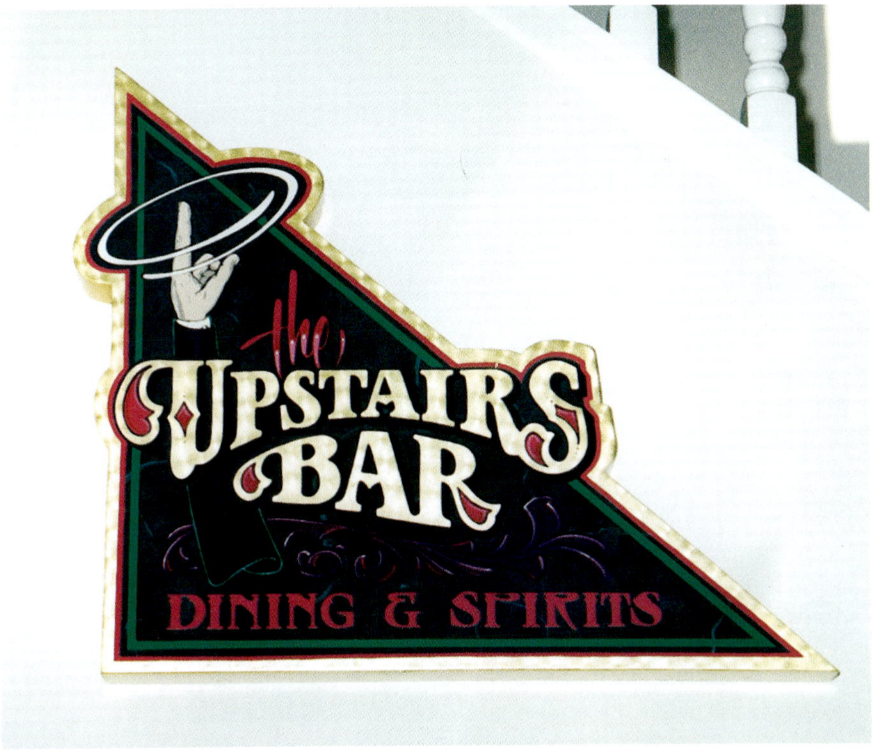
the
UPSTAIRS
BAR
DINING & SPIRITS

DESIGNER

Ben Robinson
Madden Marketing and Design Group, Inc.
12001 N Central Expressway, Ste. 820
Dallas, TX 75243
(214) 960-9696
Fax: (214) 960-9554

FABRICATOR

Murphy Graphics
3008 Skyway Circle South
Irving, TX 75038
(214) 594-6660
Fax: (214) 594-6772

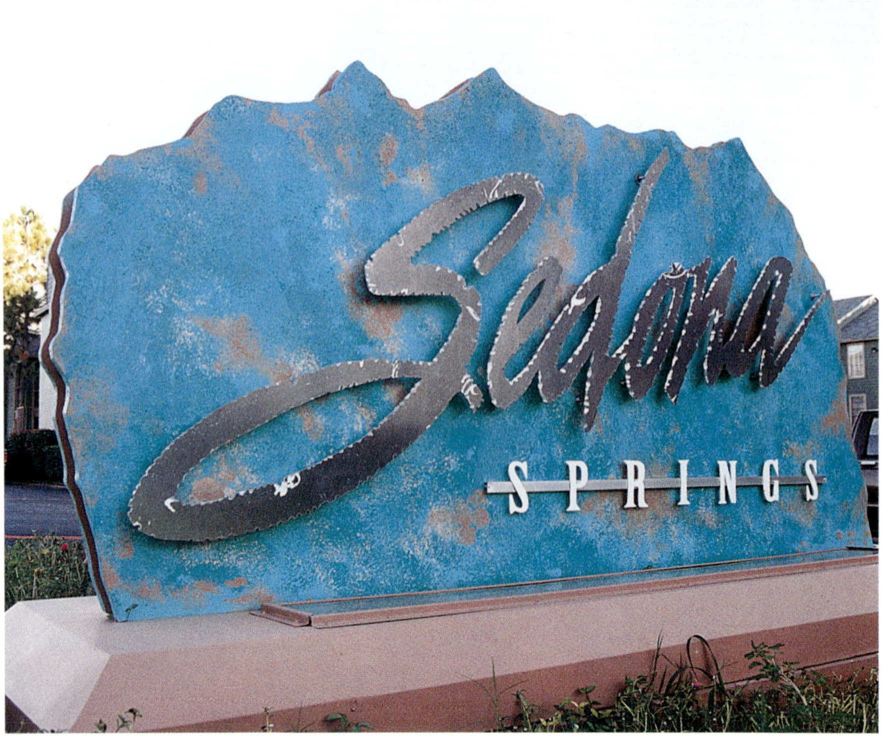

This 5 x 7-ft. identification for an apartment building is double-faced Medex® composite wood panel that is die-cut and sponge-painted. The pin-mounted letters are ½-in.-thick polished aluminum with an aluminum base. Floodlights shine through the 18-in.-high base.

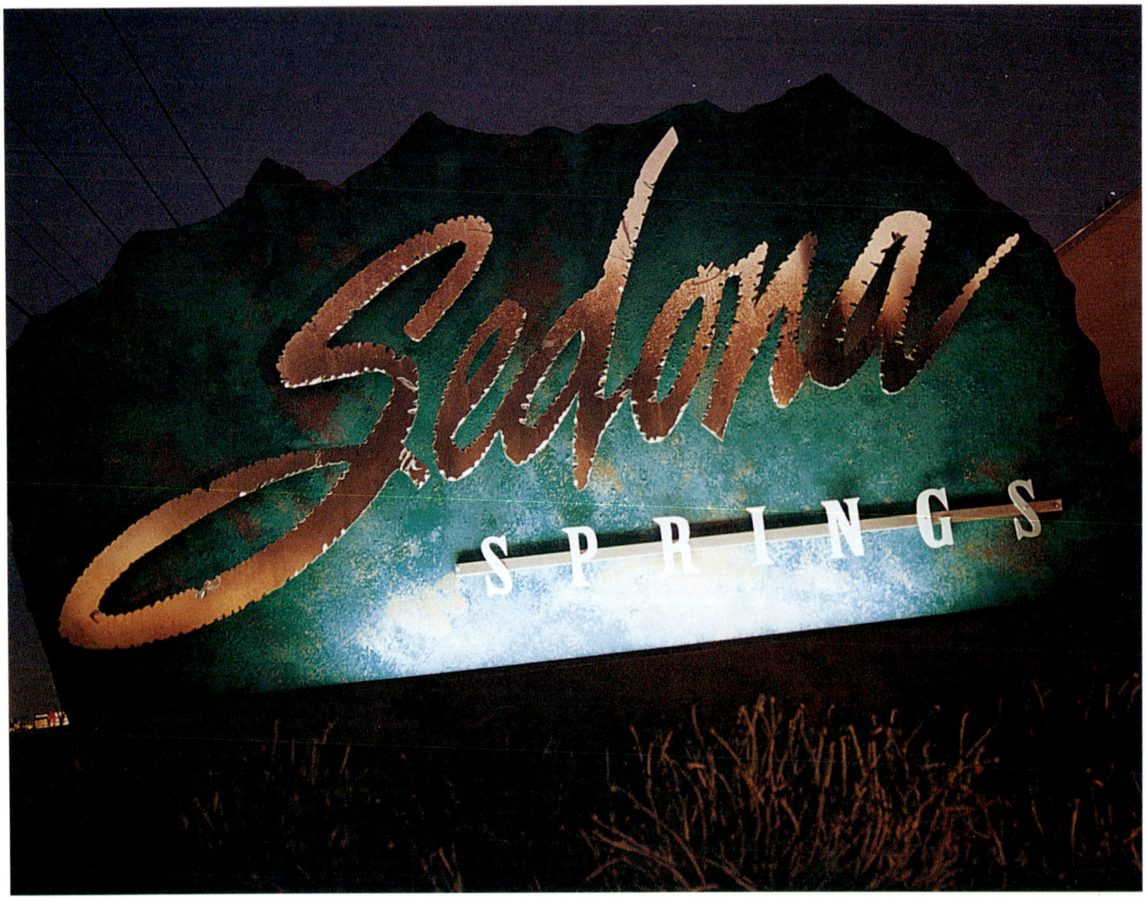

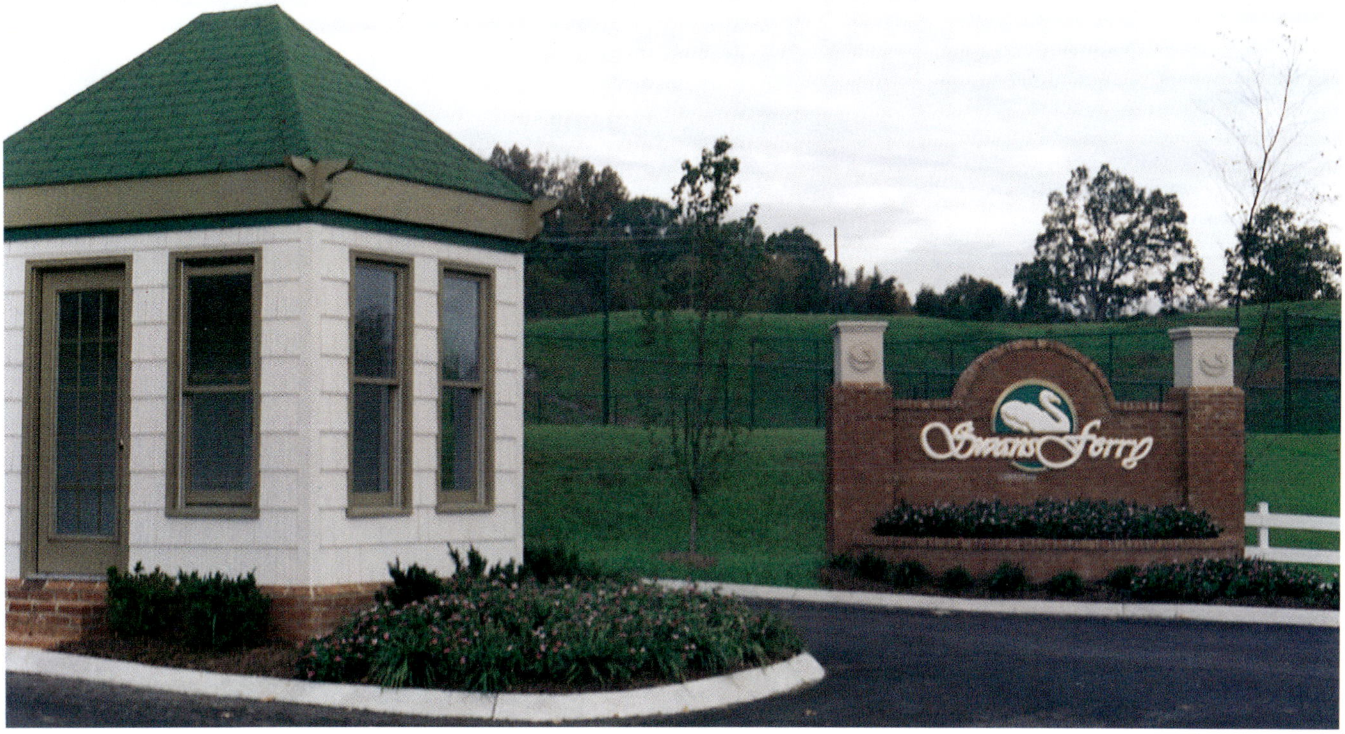

DESIGNERS

Donna Koester (logo)
627 Broadview Dr.
Sevierville, TN 37862
(423) 453-2638

Brother Zank
Custom Craftsman Signs
1767 Wears Valley Rd.
Sevierville, TN 37862
(423) 429-1934
Fax: (423) 429-1935

FABRICATORS

Custom Craftsman Signs

Bob Ownby (brickwork)
3636 Sims Rd.
Sevierville, TN 37862
(423) 453-7467

The signage for this golf-course and subdivision is 100% 15-lb. Sign Foam® high-density urethane. The carved letters are gilded with 23K on the second layer. The circle logo is sandblasted Sign Foam to which the swan and gilded trim are applied.

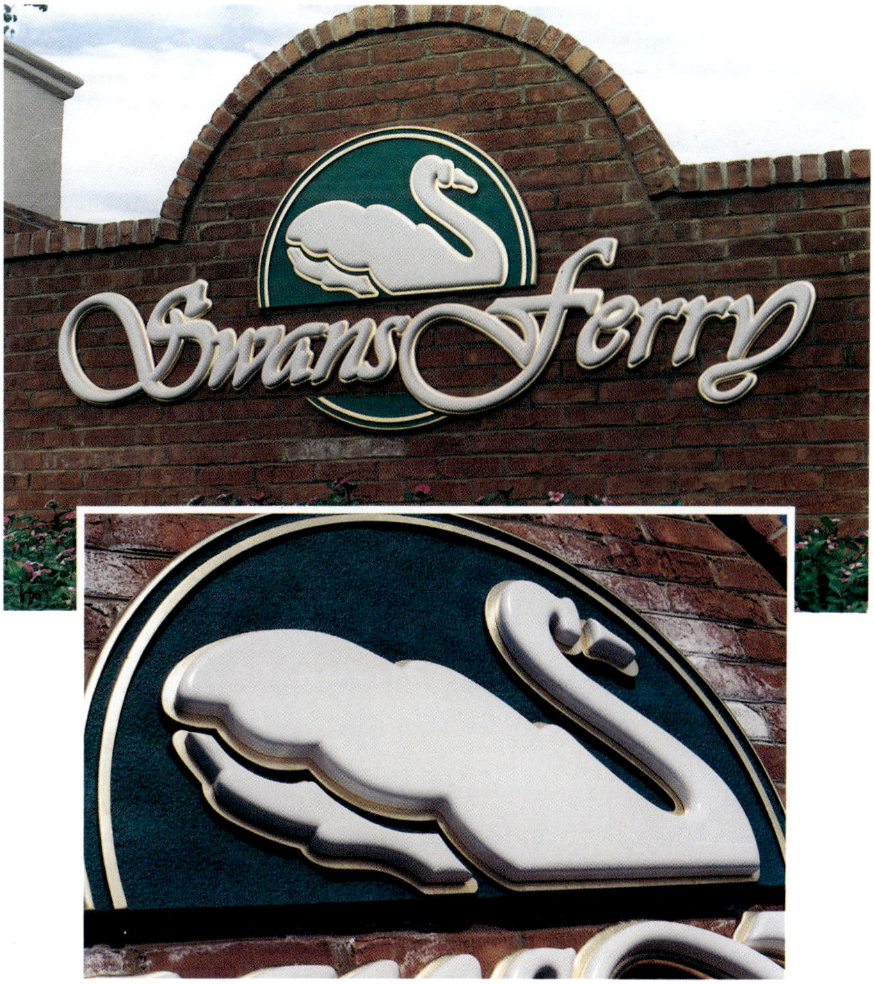

DESIGNER

Ben Robinson
Madden Marketing and Design
Group, Inc.
12001 N Central Expressway, Ste. 820
Dallas, TX 75243
(214) 960-9696
Fax: (214) 960-9554

FABRICATORS

United Sign Adv.
3309 Empire Blvd. SW
Atlanta, GA 30354
(404) 766-4870
Fax: (404) 762-5803

Marble Craftsman
8456 Newman St.
Douglasville, GA 30134
(404) 949-2019
Fax: (404) 949-5198

Bill Breed Architectural Concrete
101 Johnston Circle
Palmetto, GA 30268
(404) 463-1932
Fax: (404) 463-2635

This 6 x 16-ft. identification for an apartment incorporates cast stone, brick, a granite face and tile accents. The emerald-pearl granite is sandblasted with gold lithochrome. The granite is inset into two double-faced, 16-in.-thick, cast-stone panels, which project out above the marble wall and brick columns. The base planter is almost ground level with the base of each column.

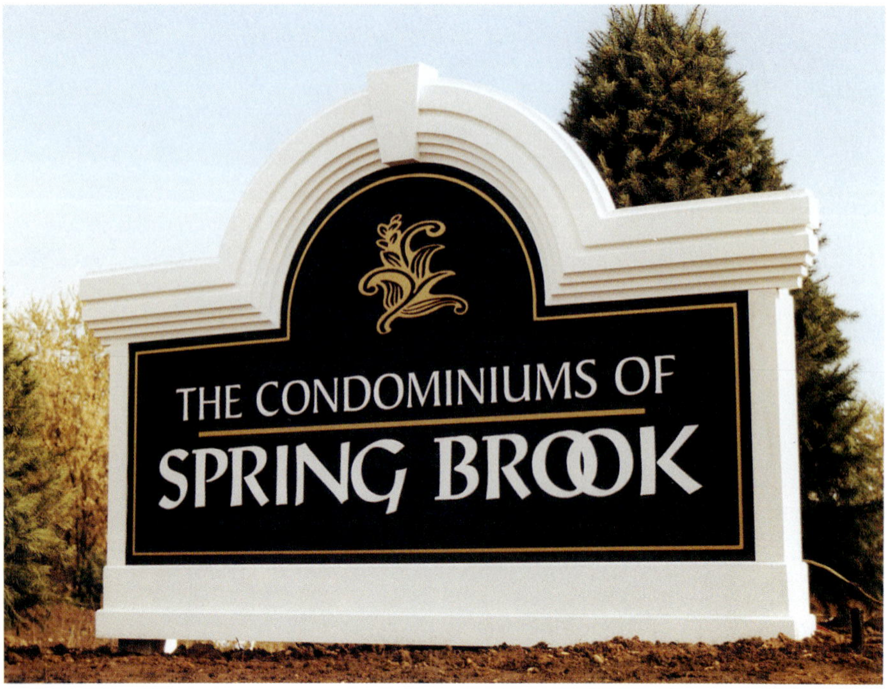

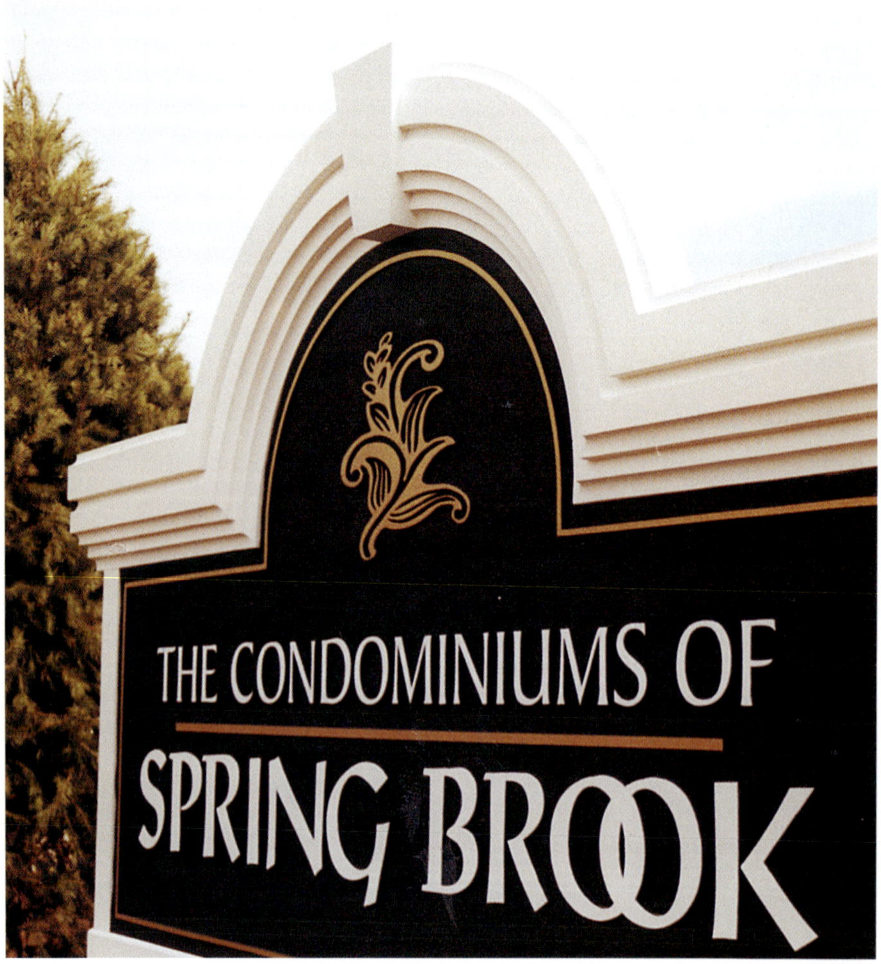

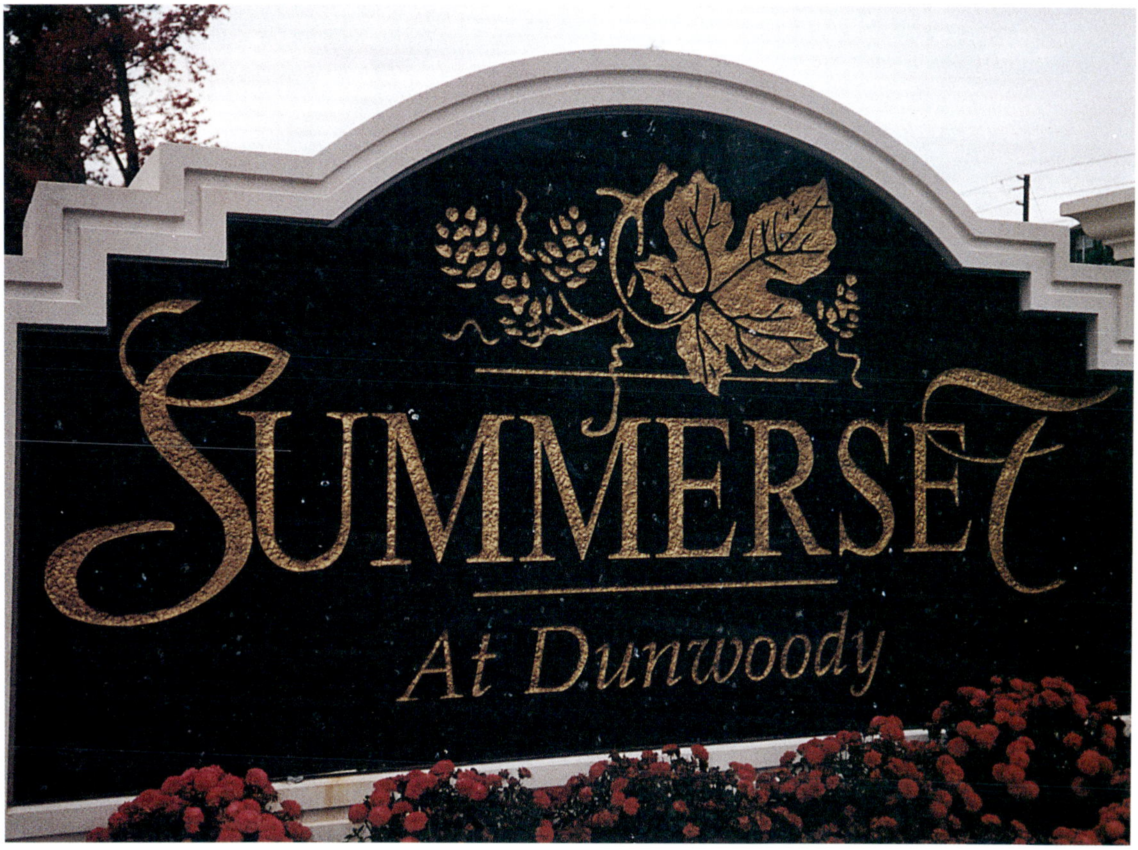

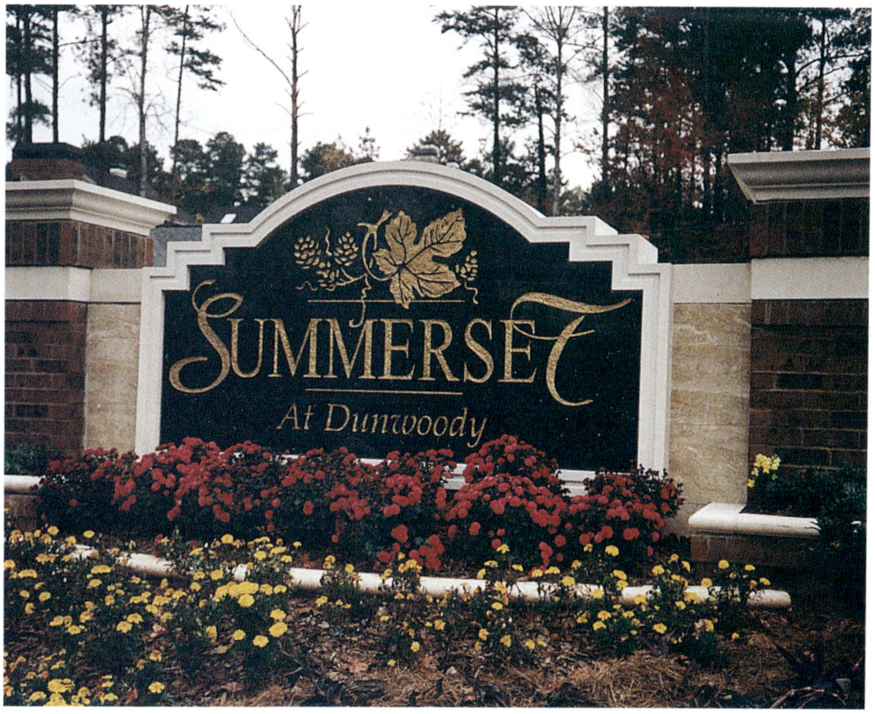

DESIGNER

Jay Allen
Shawcraft Sign Co.
7727 Burden Rd.
Machesney Park, IL 61115
(815) 282-4105
Fax: (815) 282-4147

FABRICATOR

Shawcraft Sign Co.

This entry monument for a subdivision stands 5 ft. high and 7½ ft. wide. The sandblasted, high-density-urethane sign has a redwood base and corner trim. The crown molding is multi-layered urethane. All of the signs are painted with acrylic latex paint, with gold metallic water-based paint on the graphic.

COMMERCIAL

DESIGNER

Gerald J. Mazzara
Architectural Forum
4801 W 81st St., Ste. 101
Minneapolis, MN 55437
(612) 831-5926
Fax: (612) 831-9069

FABRICATORS

Robert C. Kinghorn Assoc.
3835 Tonkawood Rd.
Minnetonka, MN 55345
(612) 930-0947
Fax: (612) 935-9788

Johnson and Peterson (masonry)
P.O. Box 232
Wayzata, MN 55391
(612) 473-3030

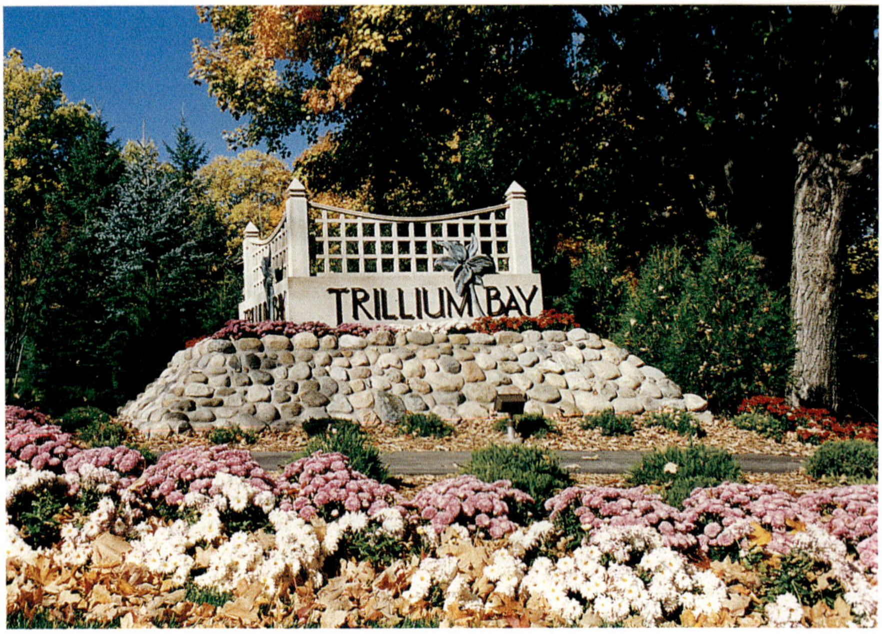

This entry monument for the luxury Lakeside residential development comprises two 18 x 18-ft. L-shaped monuments of two signs each. The sign boards are 2 x 10-ft. laminated cedar with custom-cut ½ x 12-in. anodized aluminum letters. The four Trillium flowers are 22 x 46 in. and 6 in. deep. They are created from cast bronze using the "lost-wax" method.

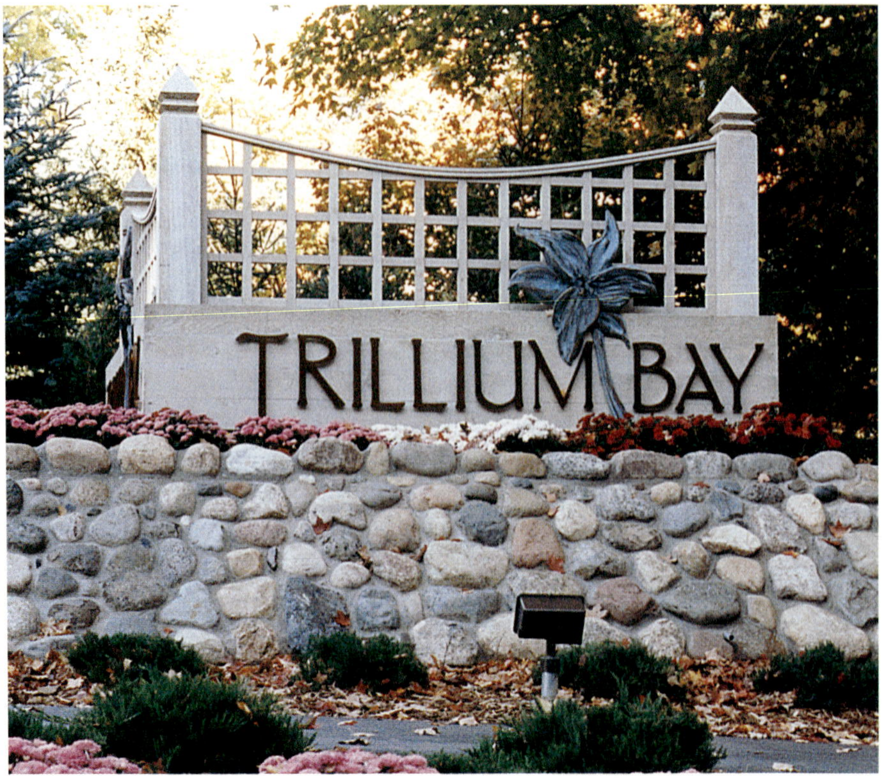

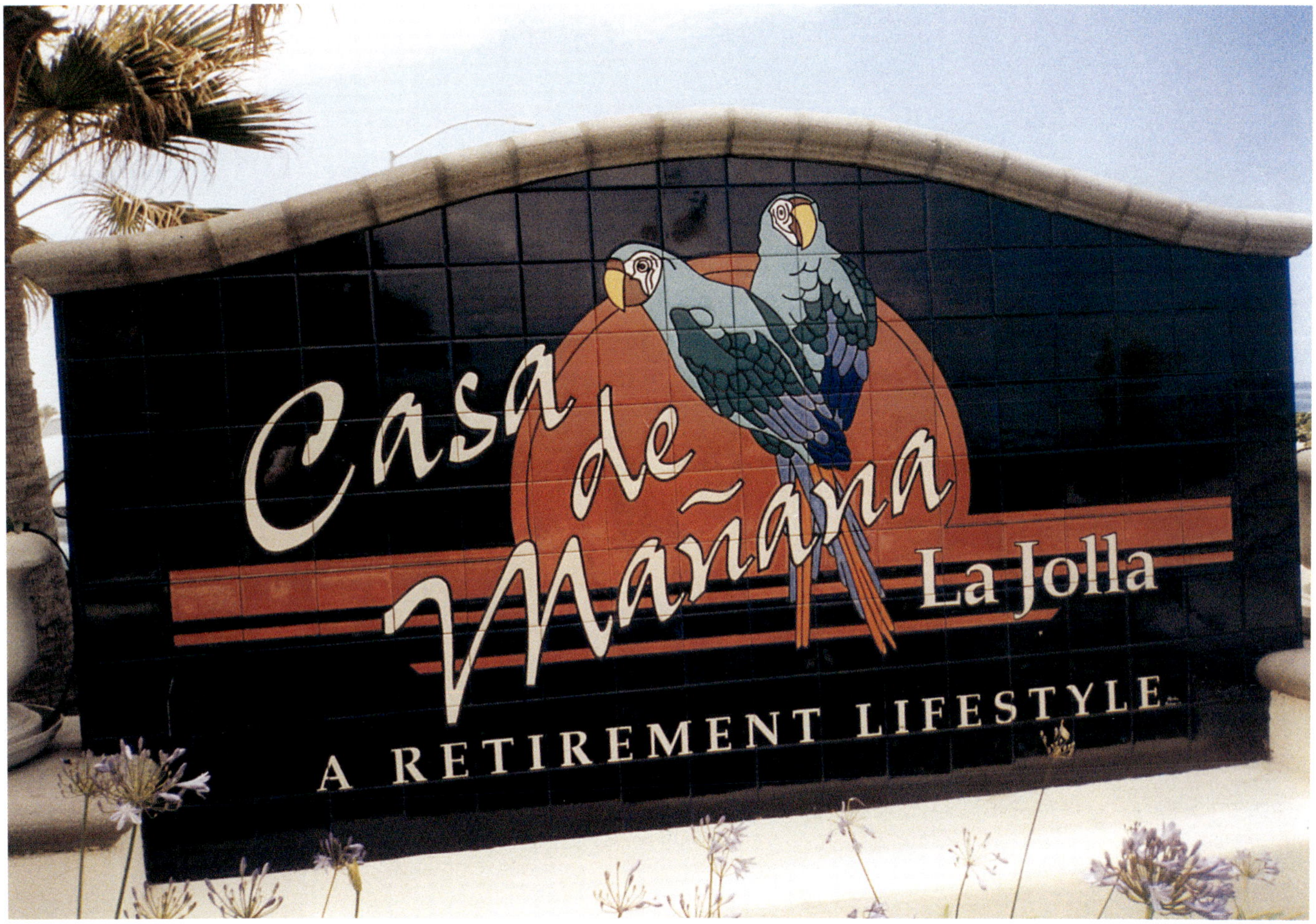

DESIGNER

Chris Bazner
Motivational Systems, Inc.
2200 Cleveland Ave.
National City, CA 91950
(619) 474-8246
Fax: (619) 474-0678

FABRICATOR

Motivational Systems, Inc.

This entry monument for a retirement community features a Spanish motif of soft arches in a stucco finish. The computer-generated logo is hand-glazed on 6 x 6-in. bisque tiles that are modeled after the architecture on Catalina Island off the coast of California. The double-faced sign spans 5 x 7 ft.

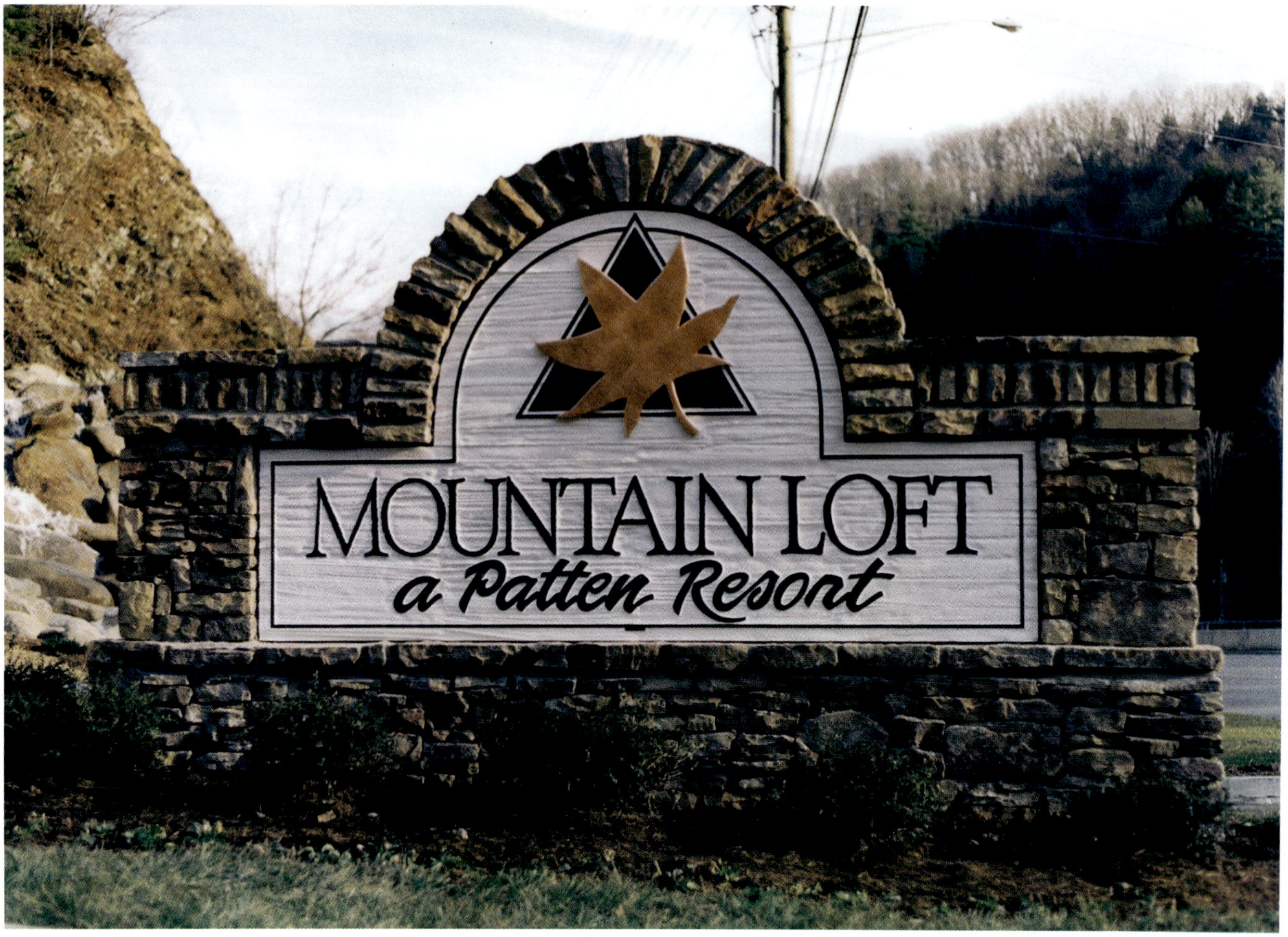

DESIGNERS

Brother Zank
Custom Craftsman Signs
1767 Wears Valley Rd.
Sevierville, TN 37862
(423) 429-1934
Fax (423) 429-1935

Peter Langham
(Landscape Architect)
45 W. Crossville Rd., Ste. 502
Roswell, GA 30075
(404) 642-1255

FABRICATORS

Custom Craftsman Signs

Doug Huffaker
Stonework
625 Lewelling Rd.
Sevierville, TN 37862
(423) 453-9415

The 13-ft. deeply recessed stone monument accepts a blasted GraphiKore® panel on each side with copper gilded Sign Foam® leaf logos.

DESIGNER

Jay Allen
Shawcraft Sign Co.
7727 Burden Rd.
Machesney Park, IL 61115
(815) 282-4105
Fax (815) 282-4147

FABRICATOR

Shawcraft Sign Co.

The entry monument for this residential development is 72-in. high and 108-in. wide. A sandblasted redwood sign panel is painted with gold metallic water-based enamel on the text. The background is acrylic latex paint.

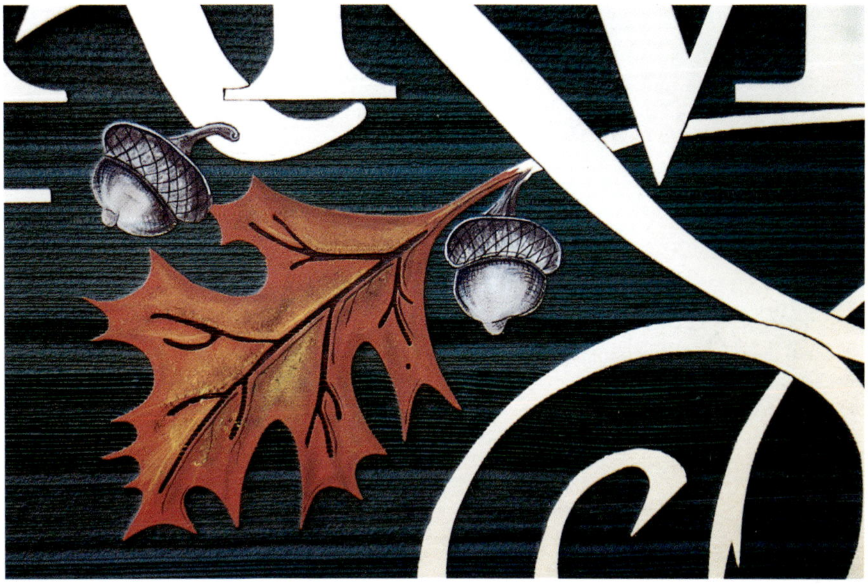

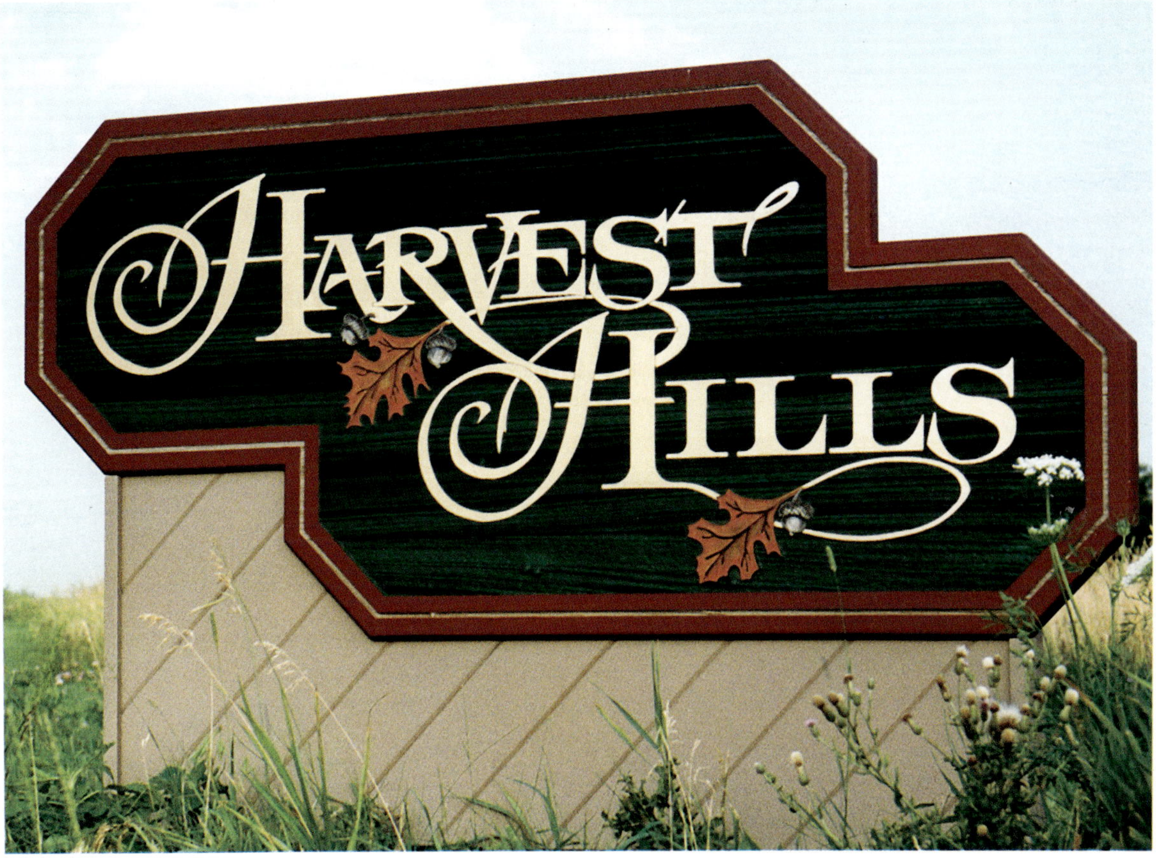

ENTRY MONUMENTS COMMERCIAL

DESIGNER

Randy Johnson
Urban Design Group, Inc.
1621 18th St.
Denver, CO 80202
(303) 292-3388

FABRICATORS

John Wilfong
Mark Schemenauer
Sundance Awning Systems
515 Ferguson Dr.
Orlando, FL 32805
(407) 849-1337
(cover)

M & J Materials, Inc.
9808 International Dr.
Orlando, FL 32819
(407) 345-8316
(frame)

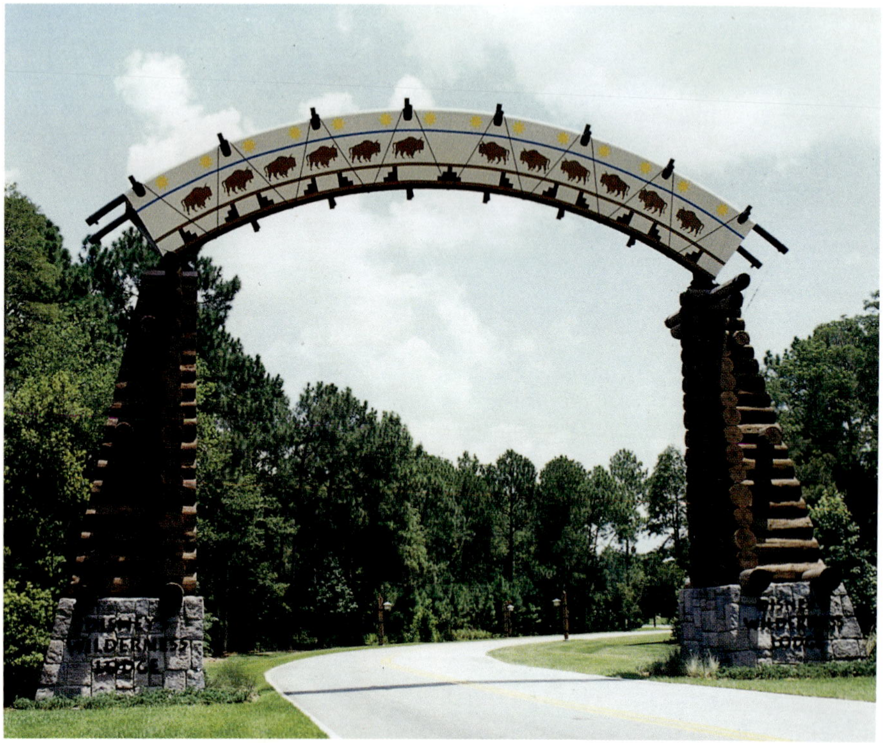

A Western-themed entrance arch was designed and fabricated for Disney. An arched triangular steel truss is covered with fabric on three sides with duplicate graphics applied on two sides. All graphics are handcut by Sundance artists. The graphics involve three unique designs, consisting of 28 twelve-in. sunbursts, 24 two-ft. buffalo and 26 geometric shapes separated by three different colored stripes. The graphics are applied using 3M pressure sensitive vinyl and covered with a GPS protective coating. Brown colored nylon rope is used to simulate leather cord and provide a means to secure the fabric to the frame.

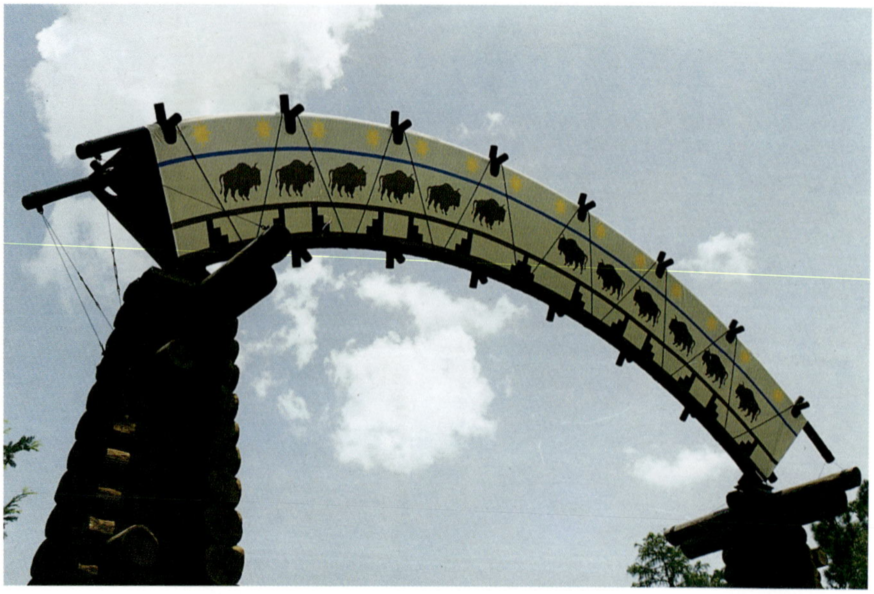

DESIGNER

Brother Zank
Custom Craftsman Signs
1767 Wears Valley Rd.
Sevierville, TN 37862
(423) 429-1934
Fax: (423) 429-1935

FABRICATOR

Custom Craftsman Signs

This freestanding, 15-ft. cedar structure features painted MDO and vinyl identification graphics.

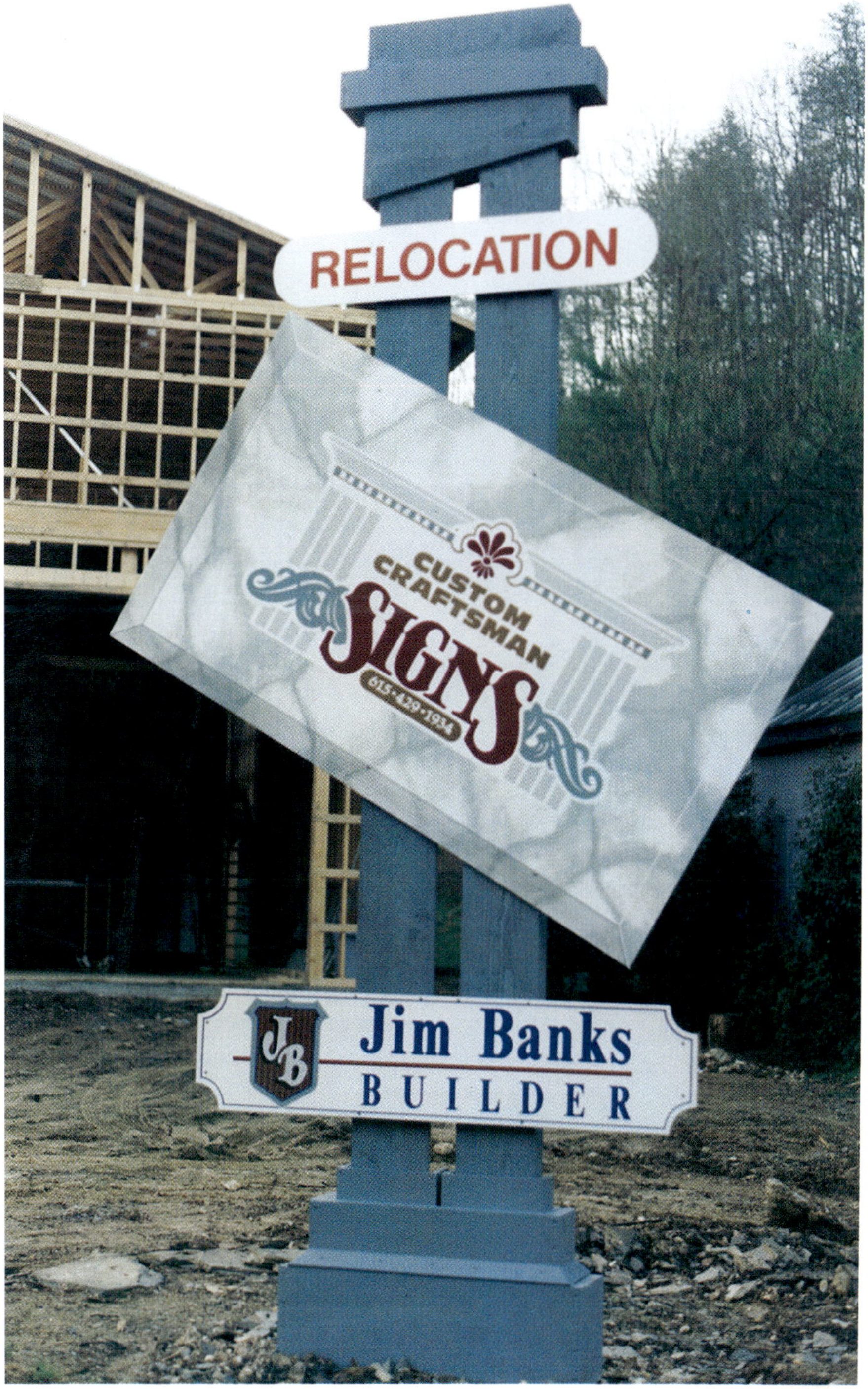

DESIGNERS

Al Lowrie
Kraig Yaseen
Yaseen Design Studio
434 Turner Dr.
Durango, CO 81301
(970) 247-4467

FABRICATOR

Yaseen Design Studio

This double-sided 42 x 60-in. restaurant sign is fabricated from .125-in. aluminum. Decoration includes 23K gold lettering, variegated borders, vinyl secondary copy and striping, and hand-airbrushed shadows on all copy.

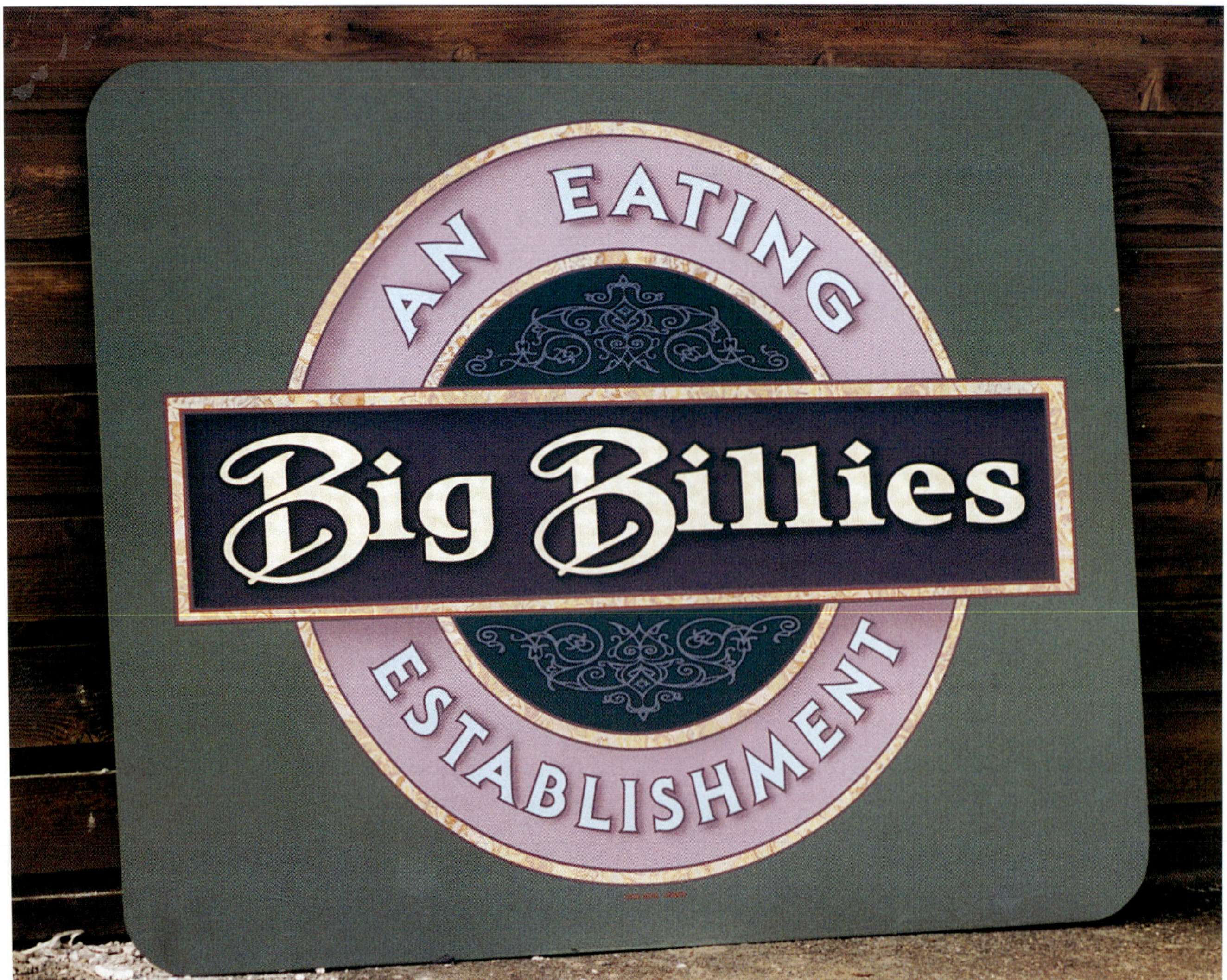

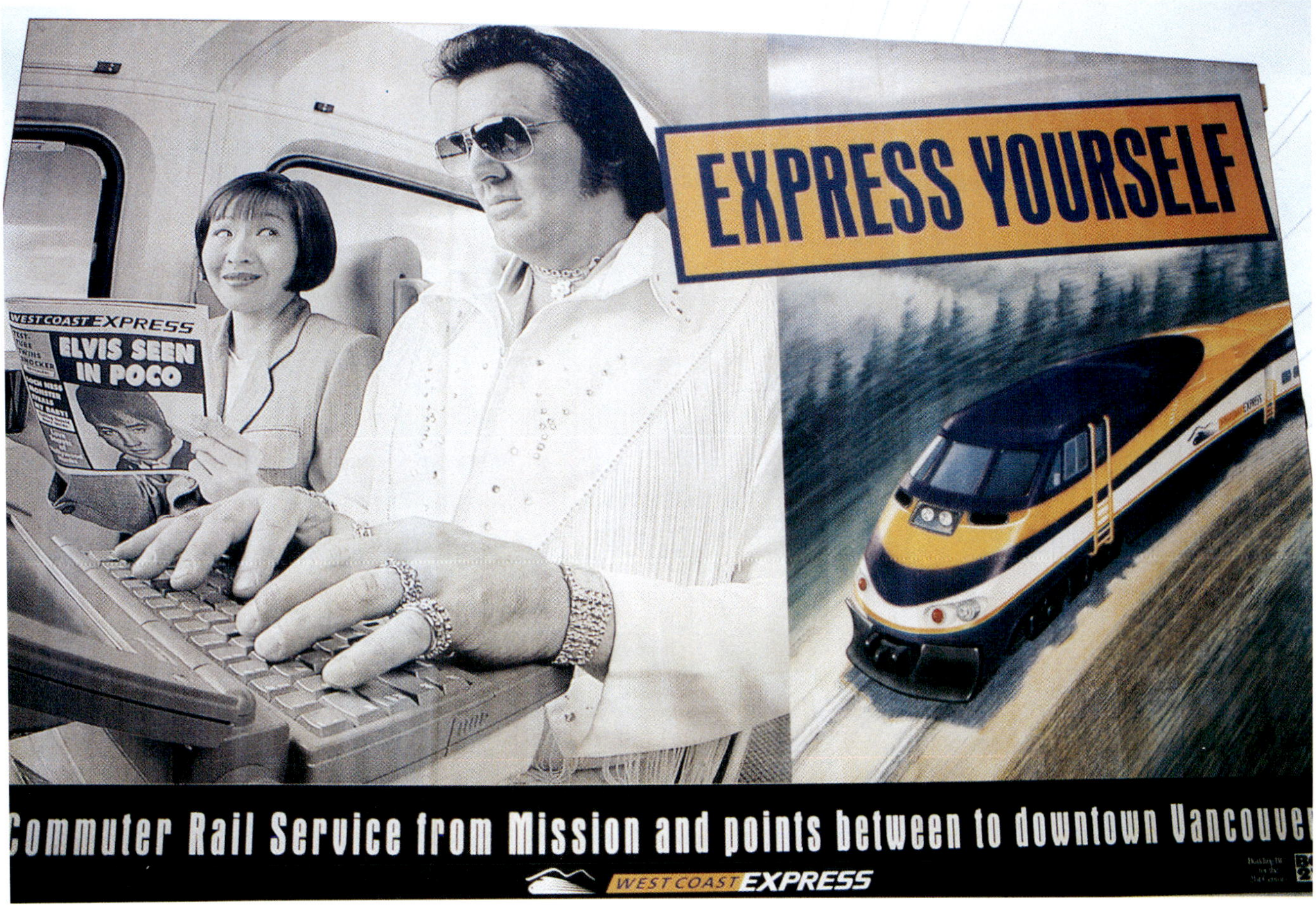

DESIGNERS

Ken Koo Creative
225 W. 8th Ave.
Vancouver, BC, Canada V5Y 1N3
(604) 879-0300
Fax: (604) 879-0399

Alexis Mackintosh
Metaphoric Media
#117 42 Fawcett Rd.
Coquitlam, BC, Canada V3K 6X9
(604) 527-1001
Fax: (604) 527-1002

FABRICATOR

Metaphoric Media

This is one of a series of posters designed to promote new transit routes in various communities. Spanning 8 x 12-ft., these posters utilize proprietary waterproof outdoor inks applied to waterproof paper using inkjet equipment.

INDEX DESIGNERS

INDEX

FABRICATORS

SIGN DESIGN AND FABRICATION BOOKS AVAILABLE FROM ST PUBLICATIONS